D0238574

LIVING ABROAD IN
SPAIN

CANDY LEE LaBALLE

PRIME LIVING LOCATIONS IN SPAIN

THE CANTABRIAN COAST

Cantabrian *Sea*

Avilés

La Coruña

ASTURIAS

Gijón

SANTANDER

GALICIA

OVIEDO

Llanes

Torrelavega

Lugo

Parque Nacional
Picos de Europa

CANTABRIA

SANTIAGO DE
COMPOSTELA

León

Burgos

Pontevedra

Ponferrada

CASTILLA
Y LEÓN

Ourense

Palencia

Vigo

Chaves

VALLADOLID

Zamora

River

Viana do
Castelo

Doero

ATLANTIC

Porto

Segovia

Douro *River*

Salamanca

Ávila

MADRID

OCEAN

Guarda

MADRID

Coimbra

MADRID

PORTUGAL

Plasencia

TOLEDO

Cáceres

Santarém

EXTREMADURA

Ciudad Real

LISBON

Badajoz

MÉRIDA

Évora

La Albuera

Puertollano

Lierena

ANDALUSIA

River

Odemira

Córdoba

Jaén

Guadalquivir

Huelva

Parque
Nacional
de Coto de
Doñana

SEVILLA

ANDALUCÍA

Costa de la Luz

Faro

Utera

Granada

Jerez de
la Frontera

Málaga

Cádiz

San Pedro

Costa *del* *Sol*

Algeciras

UK

Gibraltar

Strait of Gibralter

Tanger

Ceuta

CEUTA

MOROCCO

La Palma

Parque Nacional
de Garajonay

SANTA CRUZ
DE TENERIFE

Lanzarote

La Gomera

Tenerife

LAS PALMAS DE
GRAN CANARIA

El Hierro

Parque Nacional
del Teide

Gran Canaria

Fuerteventua

CANARY ISLANDS

To Canary Islands
1,320 km or 820 mi

Contents

At Home in Spain

Blame it on Hemingway. He sparked the romantic idea of Spain – furrow-browed bullfighters, defiant passion, hearty red wine, long-lingering lunches, endless fiesta – in America's imagination and we've flocked to the Iberian Peninsula ever since. The seductive staccato of flamenco has also caught our attention and Spanish stars like dancer Sara Baras and guitarist Paco de Lucia regularly sell out their American performances. And then there is the food. Long before Spanish super chef Ferran Adrià appeared on the cover of the *The New York Times Magazine*, Americans had adopted paella, and gazpacho and tapas could be found not just in Manhattan dining rooms but also in Boston, Detroit, New Orleans, Des Moines. . .

So how much did these images color my expectations of Spain? A lot. But they were mostly right. Consider my second day in Madrid. I was invited to lunch in Lavapiés, an old working-class barrio of winding cobbled streets. Up three flights of creaking steps a group of friends of friends had gathered to welcome me – three Spaniards, two Americans, and a Canadian who had come to Spain to learn to dance flamenco. We drank *tinto de verano* while Alfonso, an Alicante native, made paella. He assured me that the best *arroces* (rice dishes) hailed from his hometown, not neighboring Valencia. By the time the oversized pan of fragrant rice made it to the table, it was well into late afternoon and we ate with relish until the last bits of crusty *soccarat* on the bottom of the pan were gone. As the sky darkened, someone broke out a Spanish guitar and hand-clapping filled the room. A bottle of whiskey appeared, drinks were poured, the Canadian began to dance, her fingers tracing shadows like lace on the wall.

In the eight years since that afternoon, I've had more versions of that meal

than I can count – fire-roasted fresh sardines on a Málaga beach, tiny lamb chops cooked over smoldering grape twigs in La Rioja, barbecued *calçots* (green onions) overlooking a rocky Costa Brava cove. But Spanish *ambiente* infuses more than just food. In the morning, I join chattering *señoras* in the local market to peruse vats of glistening olives, ropes of Navarra peppers, a hundred types of Spanish cheeses, artisan honeys, and a dazzling display of sea creatures – silvery eels, bins of live snails, milky mounds of squid, prehistoric barnacles, tangles of pink octopus, cigar-sized ruby red shrimp. My afternoon jog is finished with a long sprint along the vast façade of an 18th-century palace. In the evening, I dine on transparent slivers of *jamón* in a trendy wine bar on an old medieval street.

Of course Spanish life has its modern-day drags – metal shutters roaring open and shut several times a day, constant traffic and no place to park, mind-bending bureaucracy for even the simplest tasks, waiters who clean every table in your vicinity before looking at you, office politics – *in Spanish*. But, you get used to all that and the *mil* pleasures of living here far offset the negatives. Spaniards say, *En España se vive muy bien* (In Spain one lives very well) and they are right. Though skyscrapers now outweigh Moorish palaces, mid-day siestas have been abandoned for modern efficiency, and *döner* kebabs shops rival tapas bars, this is still Spain. *Don Quixote* and Gaudí, rhythmic hand-clapping and the art of flicking open a fan, generous people and their immense joy for life are just as relevant today as they were back when Hemingway first set foot in Spain.

▶ WHAT I LOVE ABOUT SPAIN

- A fine glass of Ribera del Duero vino rarely costs more than $2
- No one thinks twice if you have a glass or two of Ribera del Duero during a workday lunch
- When nightclubs play old Spanish pop everyone sings along with frightening enthusiasm
- The more trash—napkins, toothpicks, olive pits, shrimp shells—on the floor of a tapas bar, the better the food
- Bullfights are described in the Arts Section of the daily papers with language approaching poetry
- A *tortilla español* may look simple, but there is an art to making a good one
- Spaniards really do work to live, not live to work: consider 30 days annual paid vacation, over a dozen long weekends per year, four months maternity leave
- Bad wine is easily fixed—add *gaseosa* (sweetened soda water) and you have *tinto de verano*—the wine of summer
- Toast topped with olive oil and salt is a perfectly normal way to start the day

- Greeting everyone as you get on an *ascensor* (elevator) and saying goodbye when you get off
- The legions of house-coated señoras who mop the cobbled sidewalks in front of their houses every morning
- The *fondo*, a communal pot of money that friends contribute to when they go out—the money is used to pay for everyone's drinks
- The number one flavor of potato chips is *jamón* (cured ham)
- Balancing a plate of tapas and a *caña* (small draft beer) while standing back-to-elbow in a crowded bar is not as hard as it seems
- Deep-fried food is healthy as long as it is deep-fried in Spanish *aceite de oliva* (olive oil)
- Companies dole out massive goodie baskets at Christmastime jammed with half-a-dozen pork products and several bottles of Spanish wine
- Listening to Manu Chao and watching the sun set over the Atlantic at a *chiringuito*—a ubiquitous beachside shack serving drinks, food, and beats right on the sand
- The loofah-like quality of towels left to dry on a line in the Spanish sun

WELCOME TO SPAIN

INTRODUCTION

A 1960s Spanish tourism campaign famously promised "Spain is Different." By different, it meant a beachside version of *Carmen* with unlimited sun, sand, and sangria. That image is still partly right—dark-eyed *señoritas* do occasionally tuck flowers behind their ears, bullfighters continue to embody tradition and passion, the tacka-tac of flamenco is very much alive and well and Spaniards instinctively clap along in cadence (it is much, much harder to do than you think). The sixty million or so tourists who visit Spain annually can attest to all of that. But, the country is so much more and a better slogan would be "Spain is Diverse." Beyond beaches, expect soaring mountains, rolling orange hills, vast vineyards, wetlands, and Europe's only desert. Not to be outdone, the weather contrasts all that advertised sun with rain and mist worthy of Ireland and enough snow to sustain over 600 miles of ski trails—including a few famous Andalusian runs just a stone's throw from the Mediterranean Coast. Diversity also has a place at the Spanish table and typical Spanish dishes include sophisticated Catalan sauces, meaty Asturian stews, and of course,

fragrant Valencian paella. Spanish architecture is a feast of variety as well with white-washed villages in Andalucía, thousand year-old Moorish palaces in Sevilla, Córdoba, and Granada, the delirious whimsy of Gaudí's buildings in Barcelona, and majestic medieval castles just about everywhere else.

So what about the people? Spaniards themselves acknowledge their diversity, after all the country has four different official languages—Castilian Spanish, Catalan, Basque, and Galician—and several immigrant communities that make up nearly 12 percent of the population. There are cultural differences too and those are most joyously witnessed in the country's year-round festivals. Consider the mammoth bonfire parties in Valencia, solemn Easter Week processions in Andalucía, mock battles between Christians and Moors in

a narrow, twisting street in Altea, Costa Blanca

© CANDY LEE LABALLE

BESAME MUCHO (KISS ME A LOT)

The first time you meet a Spanish person you'll immediately notice a cultural difference. In Spain, people pucker up just to say hello. Whether two people meet for the very first time or they're old friends, in both social situations and informal professional ones, Spanish people kiss twice – once on each cheek. (For the novices, go for the right cheek first.) This custom is the norm when two women are introduced and when women and men meet. The one exception is a greeting between two men – in those cases a handshake will suffice. In more formal business meetings or those involving international parties, a handshake is the norm.

To many Americans, this custom can seem hilariously time-consuming, especially when large groups of people come together and twenty minutes later, every conceivable pair has exchanged a total of four pecks on the cheek. All practicality aside, the custom is a reflection of the country's warmth and it's for that reason that most foreigners appreciate the two-kiss routine. But whatever your opinion on it, it is considered polite behavior and it's a good idea to adopt it. Every introduction will be an awkward one if you thrust out your hand for a handshake just as someone leans in for a smooch.

THE SPANISH CLOCK

Benjamin Franklin's old adage, "early to bed and early to rise makes a man healthy, wealthy, and wise," is not often repeated in Spain – a country where there's an altogether different approach to time. The Spanish clock may in fact look like the American one, but the hour marks have entirely different meanings.

Unless you have to catch a train or be at the office, morning is leisurely in Spain. People can sleep until noon on a Sunday morning and when they finally rise, the day still stretches out before them. Lunch begins around 2 P.M. and lasts up to two hours during the week, longer on weekends. Afternoon kicks off after lunch and goes until about 8 P.M. when you've officially hit evening; it's perfectly appropriate to greet people with a *buenas tardes* (good afternoon) until then.

Late afternoon, around 7–8 P.M., Spaniards across the country pour into the streets for a *paseo*. This leisurely stroll around the neighborhood has been part of Spanish culture since way back when Cervantes wrote about it in the 16th century. Around 9:30 P.M. you can begin considering your options for dinner. Whether you opt for a tapas bar or a restaurant, if you try to make it any earlier the dining room will be so vacant that you might expect tumbleweeds to blow through. Dinner is typically served until about 11 P.M. and sometimes even later. Should you want to head out after your meal, midnight is a good hour to meet up with friends, and you may find yourself returning home in the *madrugada* (early morning), just before the sun rises.

The siesta was once an occasion for a nap in Spain, but that's no longer the case. However, a form of the siesta is still alive and well. Stores generally close between 2 P.M. and 5 P.M. after which they reopen for another three hours. Offices also give their employees a two-hour break around this time. Though some indulge in a long leisurely lunch, most modern Spaniards are more apt to take a spinning class or catch up on some shopping and there is even a growing movement among workers to eliminate this long daytime break in favor of going home earlier (office workers typically wrap up their day around 7 P.M.).

It's also worth noting that the idea of punctuality is only sometimes taken seriously. For example, if your boss tells you to be at the office by 9 A.M. every morning, it's a good idea to be on time. Planes and trains also leave and arrive according to their schedules. However, if you make a plan to meet a Spanish friend for lunch and she arrives 10 or 15 minutes late, she's still on time by Spanish rules.

The process of adapting to the Spanish clock is a lot like overcoming jetlag – it's a rocky adjustment but once you're acclimated, you'll feel right in sync with the locals.

Alicante, human castle building in Tarragona, dancing fire-breathing dragons in Cataluña, and of course, the infamous running of the bulls in Pamplona. Beyond these biggies, every town in the country, no matter how small, has its own homegrown festival full of tradition, yes, but also unfettered frivolity—dancing, drinking, dunking *churros* (fritters) into hot chocolate—until the wee hours of the morning.

And there, between the thunder of bulls' hooves and the explosion of fireworks, hidden in plain sight of diversity is what binds the Spanish together—a passion for living. From Madrid to the Mediterranean, Asturias to Andalucía, Spaniards—no matter their social, economic, or political background—jump head, heart, and soul first into life. Meals are leisurely, wine-fueled affairs that often end in *sobremesa,* a lively post-meal conversation; vacations are long—four weeks with dozens of holidays thrown in; family bonds and friendships are sacred and time is allotted to nurture both; taking an evening *paseo* (stroll) is an essential marker of daily life; going out for tapas is so much a part of culture that it has its own noun, *el tapeo.* It is these similarities, expressed in friends, food, and frivolity that define Spanish culture, and entice the expat. It may take a bit of work to join the party when you first arrive—settling in, learning the language, making friends—but when you do, you'll find out that while Spain may be different and very diverse, it is also your home.

The Lay of the Land

Spain makes up the bulk of the Iberian Peninsula which it shares with Portugal. It is bordered by France and Andorra in the northeast, the Bay of Biscay in the northwest, the Mediterranean on the East and Southeast and the Atlantic Ocean on the western border not shared with Portugal. At the southern tip of Spain, Gibraltar—which is controlled by Great Britain and has the best fish-n-chips on the Peninsula—soars above the Strait of Gibraltar that separates Spain from Northern Africa by a mere nine miles of usually treacherous water. Two groups of islands—the Islas Baleares (Balearic Islands) located off the eastern coast of Spain in the Mediterranean Sea and the Canarias (Canary Islands) off the coast of Africa in the Atlantic Ocean—as well as the North African cities of Ceuta and Melilla are also part of Spain.

For a country smaller than the state of Texas, Spain's geographic diversity is stunning. For starters, it is the most mountainous country in Europe. The majestic Pyrenees, marking the northern border of the country and separating it from the rest of Europe, are the most famous but the relatively tiny Picos de Europa is the most dramatic, rising to nearly 9,000 feet just a few miles inland from Cantabrian Coast. From Cataluña south to Murcia, the Mediterranean coast harbors an infinity of pristine beaches and nearly inaccessible coves while the inlands are marked by fertile farmlands and grove after grove of sweet-smelling Valencia oranges. Andalucía is home to Spain's wettest region, its only desert, and its highest mainland mountain. Madrid sits on a wind-blown *meseta* surrounded by sienna-colored land patched with olive groves, wheat farms, and vineyards. Galicia, comprising the country's northwestern corner, juts out over the tumultuous waters where the Atlantic Ocean meets the Cantabrian Sea and is rainy, fertile, and chock full of salty coves and inlets.

Spain is ribboned by four mighty rivers—the Ebro runs from the Cantabrian mountains to the Mediterra-

© CANDY LEE LABALLE

Fragrant olives are sold in bulk throughout Spain.

nean; the Duero which cuts through Castilla La Mancha and lends its name to Spain's famed Ribera del Duero wines; the Tajo crosses central Spain and is the longest in Iberia; and the Guadalquivir which courses through Andalucía and helped make Sevilla the port for the New World. With such powerful rivers coursing through Spanish history, it is notable that the country didn't choose to put its capital city alongside any of them. Many people who visit Spain are struck by the fact that unlike most European capital cities, Madrid's river, the Manzanares, trickles alongside the city like a geographical afterthought. The capital was chosen for its strategic location—Madrid marks Spain's exact geographical center—and not for its waterway.

Despite all the water surrounding and zigzagging across it, Spain is prone to drought and 2008 brought the worst drought in decades to the country. Valencia, Cataluña, and other Mediterranean regions were hit the worst, with Barcelona's reservoirs dropping to a very dangerous 19 percent of capacity. Residents in these areas saw fountains and pools drained, public water fonts shut off, and faced strict water restrictions. But this is nothing new. These regions have had water issues for decades, yet in areas like Costa Blanca and Costa del Sol, golf course after green, sprinkler-fed golf course has gone up— not to mention sprawling resorts, hotels, and spas. All of this development is fine and dandy if water supplies can be assured and Spain has often sought to solve the problem by diverting water from its aqua-blessed northern regions to its parched areas. Yet political maneuvering, environmental concerns, agricultural demands, and development deals have all converged and clashed in ways that has put most water-diversion plans six feet under. In the process, regions have waged "water wars" against each other—Aragón vs. Cataluña, Castilla La Mancha vs. Murcia—and against the national government. What the solution will be is unclear, but without doubt, sooner rather than later Spain will have to come together to tackle what many agree is the most pressing problem facing the country today.

COUNTRY DIVISIONS

The 1978 constitution divided Spain into 17 *comunidades autónomas* (autonomous communities). Each of the separate communities has its own local government and the mayors and town councils that oversee matters such as education and the arts are elected by local people. The central government is based in Madrid and it handles issues of foreign policy and national affairs. As is the case in the United States, many issues demand overlap between the regional and national governments.

Spain's regional communities are further broken down into 50 provinces which are usually named for their main city. Smaller units of division emerge from there including townships. Towns also have a say in government affairs via their administrations called *municipios* (town councils).

© ALFONSO MORCUENDE

cow art in the Lavapiés barrio of Madrid

POPULATION DENSITY

In 2008, the Spanish population hovered around 46.2 million people and the gender breakdown was 49.6 percent men and 50.4 percent women. Madrid is the most populous region with over 5.6 million inhabitants. The greater Barcelona area is second with 4.6 million. Spaniards enjoy a life expectancy of 77.2 years for men, 83.7 years for women. Spanish women have one of the highest life expectancies in all of Europe. However, Spain also has one of the lowest birth rates in the world with an average of 1.3 children born per woman in Spain. An average of 2.06 is needed for Spain to replace its population over a generation. This has prompted the government to take measures to encourage families to have children including the so-called *cheque bebé*, a €2,500 check for each baby born to legal residents of Spain. The birthrate has indeed grown over the last five years, but studies reveal that is mainly due to the country's booming immigration population rather than procreation among Spaniards.

WEATHER

Although Spain lies on the same latitude as southern New England, it has a climate that is mainly Mediterranean—warm summers, temperate winters. But extremes are also the norm in Spanish climes and summer produces at least a few days that are so hot you might wonder if the scalding pavement will melt the soles of your flip-flops. Conversely, winter days in some parts of Spain are to-the-bone cold and snow storms are not unheard of. The variety of Spain's weather patterns is due to altitude and proximity to water.

The classic stereotyped Spain of long, sunny days is best enjoyed in the southern reaches of the country—Andalucía, Valencia, Costa Blanca. Winters are mild and summers long, dry, and very hot. Inner Andalucía gets so hot in the dog days of summer that many locals simply pack up and leave for cooler climes and an extended vacation. Then again, Spain's quirky weather patterns has also given Andalucía its rainiest region, Sierra de Grazalema which has an average of 85 inches

© ALFONSO MORCUENDE

A lone fisherman braves the Atlantic.

of rain per year. Another Andalusian mountain range, Sierra Nevada, boasts enough snow to support one of Spain's most popular ski resorts. And just to take the chill out of the region, the eastern part of Andalucía is home to Europe's only desert. If you are a fan of early Clint Eastwood films, you will recognize this region as the sight of many Spaghetti Westerns including *The Good, The Bad, and The Ugly.*

The northern regions lying along the Cantabrian Sea and the Atlantic are mild with warm summers and wet, windy winters. With an average of 35 inches of rain per year, this area has earned the nickname of Wet Spain and locals don't venture far without an umbrella or parka. In fact, the trendier hotels in Bilbao and San Sebastián feature umbrellas as part of their room perks. The north is also more humid than the rest of Spain leading to fog, especially in the mountains. In winter, the mountain regions are prone to snow—often quite a few feet—quite a surprise for those who were sold on the "sun and sand" Spain.

Extreme temperatures reach, well, extremes in the center of Spain—the vast *meseta* (tableland) where Madrid is located. Summers are horrifically hot, winters are cruelly cold and despite centuries and centuries of this, many buildings in the old city centers are neither heated nor air-conditioned. An exception is the vast department dreamland of El Corte Inglés and in summer you'll find an awful lot of relieved looking people soaking up the supersized air-conditioning; in winter, they huddle around the front door where megablowers push hot air out. But all this drama is quickly forgotten come spring or fall—both seasons are fantastic in the *meseta*—balmy and sunny by day, yet just chilly enough for a sweater in the evening.

Social Climate

While people from around the world have long sought out better lives in Europe, immigration is still relatively new to Spain. Undoubtedly, the delay was partly due to Franco's rule, and also a result of Spain's formerly weak economy. Today Spain is both democratic and fiscally strong, and waves of immigrants have made their way to the country—often with the idea of carving out a better life. The majority of Spain's immigrants come from Eastern Europe, Latin America, and North Africa. In 1981, just a few years into Spanish democracy, the number of foreign residents in Spain accounted for barely half of a percent of the population. By 2008, the figure was over 11 percent with some 5.2 million foreigners calling Spain home. The number would be higher if it could include those *sin papeles* (without papers or illegal) whose numbers are suspected to be in the hundreds of thousands.

As a result of massive influx of immigrants, the physical "face" of Spain has changed. Even 10 years ago, it was tough to find non-Spaniards in Madrid. Today, a visit to Plaza Chamberi in an upscale, old-Spanish family kind of neighborhood finds a food store run by a Chinese family, a couple of Malians selling sunglasses from a bench, Peruvians, Cubans, and Ecuadorians waiting on tables in the outdoor cafés, a few Romanian construction workers taking a break, and in the playground, a rainbow of children from Africa, Asia, and Latin America. While some applaud the development pointing out that the new arrivals offer Spain a variety of benefits including a bolstering of both the economy and the low birthrate, others view the changes as a threat to Spain's traditions and a drain on the system. Though a volatile issue, immigration has been a less explosive topic in Spain than it has been in other western European countries, and that bodes well since it's certain that immigration in Spain is not going away.

Spain is also a popular destination among people who are simply looking for a change and northern Europeans in particular have forged their own communities throughout Spain's coastal regions—in some areas on Costa del Sol, you can go days without hearing Spanish spoken at all. Americans have also moved to Spain though in smaller numbers than their northern European counterparts—too small to create distinctly American communities though you will find small circles of American expats in the larger cities.

SPAIN AND FOREIGNERS

On the whole, Spanish people are quite open to foreigners. They'll quickly help you with directions, they'll compliment your Spanish, and they might even pepper you with questions on everything from where you come from to how you're enjoying Spanish culture. Socializing is big fun in Spain, a place where life is lived in the public sphere, not behind closed doors. However, Spanish society is also very polite. People dress just a little more formally than they do in the United States, personal questions are reserved for good friends, and an invitation to someone's home is a breakthrough symbol of friendship—such invitations are not extended casually.

And are Spanish people so open with *everyone,* even Americans? You betcha, but you will find infinite complexities in Spain's relationship with the United States. Spanish marquees are loaded with Hollywood films, *The Simpsons* and *House* are adored, Levis jeans spell cool, McDonalds restaurants mark

© BEA MORA

passing through the majestic 18th-century Plaza Mayor in Salamanca

the streets of every city, and American music blares out of taxis and clothing stores. Given all that, it sure seems as if the Spanish have warm feelings towards the United States—or at least they like American stuff. There are occasional charges of cultural imperialism (yep, the very thing that brought Big Macs overseas), and these exports might cause a few benign misconceptions about what U.S. culture is *really* like, but nothing too serious.

The real anti-Americanism stems from U.S. global policy and its more conservative writers, and the frustration of the Spanish on that point can cause grumbling among the older generations and angry protests by the younger ones. This spilled over into outrage at the start of the Iraq War when then Spanish prime minister Aznar supported the initiative. Hundreds of thousands of Spaniards protested against the war in the streets of Spain and it was the only time in my many years of living here that I witnessed true anti-American sentiment. On the other hand, during the 2008 presidential campaign and the subsequent election of Barack Obama as president, Spaniards rallied around the U.S. The inauguration was covered live on every major television station and parties were held throughout the country. For a week after, Spanish friends sent me dozens of text messages congratulating me for the change. However, on the individual level, ire towards (or adoration for) the American government rarely bleeds into attitudes towards Americans themselves. Most everyone makes a distinction between a country's politics and its citizens, and in Spain anyone who makes an effort to learn the language and enjoy the surrounding culture will likely be warmly regarded.

HISTORY, GOVERNMENT, AND ECONOMY

Though Spaniards pride themselves on the uniqueness of their culture, the truth is that Spain has a tangled family tree with branches belonging to Greeks and Phoenicians, Visigoths and Celts, Romans and Africans, Muslims and Jews. Spanish culture is laced with their legacies—from the Aqueduct in Segovia to the Alhambra in Granada, the stone pressing of olive oil to the cultivation of oranges, almonds, and wine grapes, the wail of flamenco to the Latin roots of Castilian Spanish. Modern Spain is no less extraordinary. Born in the 15th century through the marriage of two ambitious young royals, Spain as we know it has given rise to the Inquisition, the map-altering voyages of Christopher Columbus, and a devastating civil war. Spain's recent past is defined by its emergence as a flourishing democracy and vital member of the European Union while current history is being written by 21st century issues of immigration,

economic crises, and terrorism. But as much as Spain marches forward, it proudly keeps one foot in the past—midnight Semana Santa processions, bulls roaring through narrow streets during fiestas, paper-thin slices of *jamón ibérico* savored with a glass of sherry, a deep siesta after a leisurely Sunday lunch—are all rich proof that history is very much alive in Spain today.

History

ANCIENT SPAIN

In the late 1990s, archaeologists in Atapuerca near Burgos in northern Spain unearthed remnants of a previously undocumented 800,000 year old hominid. In 2007, a jaw from this species now labeled *Homo antecessor,* was dated at 1.2 million years, making a very strong case that Spain was home to the first Europeans. Fast-forward a million years or so to find the Paleolithic Magdalenian people roaming northern Spain. The images they painted on cave walls in Altamira, Cantabria date to 15,000 B.C. and vividly document their hunter-gatherer lifestyle. With the dawning of the New Stone Age and the onset of agriculture, pottery, and textiles, the locals put down roots and sometime around the third millennium B.C., settlements arose along the Ebro River which traverses northern Spain. These people became known as the Iberians (ancient Greek for "dwellers on the Ebro"). When Central European Celts crossed the Pyrenees between the 9th and 7th centuries B.C., they settled in northern Spain and soon merged with the Iberians to become the Celtiberians.

Around 1100 B.C., the Phoenicians arrived on Spain's Atlantic Coast. Cádiz—once a prosperous Phoenician town called Gadir—dates to this period and is thought to be western Europe's oldest city. The Greeks followed and by 600 B.C. had fully settled in, bringing with them writing, currency, the grapevine, and the olive tree. The Carthaginians eventually pushed the Phoenicians and Greeks out of the western Mediterranean and in the 3rd century B.C. built their commercial empire in Spain. During the Second Punic War, Carthage fell to Rome and *Hispania* was added to the Roman Empire.

ROMAN HISPANIA

Though the Iberian tribes fiercely resisted, by 19 B.C. the entire Peninsula (with the notable exception of the País Vasco) had been conquered by the Roman Emperor Augustus. By the 1st century A.D., Hispania had become a highly cosmopolitan extension of the Roman Empire. The Romans built roadways and cities, created an irrigation system and improved agriculture, instituted a

SAINT JAMES OF... SPAIN?

During the Reconquest, the Christian effort to purge the country of the Moors was growing forceful and it became clear that the northern armies had more than military might – they also had God on their side. The Christians widely accepted that Santiago Apóstol (Saint James) aided them in their quest to establish a Christian country. Of course, it helped that the guy was buried in Spain.

But wait... Didn't St. James die in Jerusalem? Okay, perhaps it's best to begin with a little background. The story goes that, after having preached throughout the Mediterranean for most of his life, Santiago, Saint James the Apostle, (or, more precisely, his body) arrived in the Galician town of Padrón after a seven-day voyage in a stone boat that came from Palestine. Exactly how the stone boat became buoyant is unclear. After some heated negotiating with the local tribes (which resulted in their subsequent conversions to Christianity), the bones of the saint were laid to rest some 15 miles to the northeast of Padrón, where they were discovered by a shepherd named Pelayo in the year 813. A cathedral was built on the spot and the city of Santiago de Compostela grew up around it.

By this time Christian Spain had been fighting the Moors for over a hundred years. A hero was needed to help the troops keep up the good fight and soon reports of Santiago appearing at Reconquest battles throughout Castile started appearing. During the battle of Clavijo in 834, lore maintains that a vision of St. James astride a majestic white horse appeared and the apostle slew 70,000 Moors right then and there. The Catholics won the battle and from that pivotal moment came the popular rallying cry, *¡Santiago, Matamoros!* (St. James, Moor slayer!).

Once the Moors had been pushed out of northern Spain, pilgrims started arriving from all over Europe, convinced that the powers of Santiago Matamoros could work wonders for them – thus was born the Camino de Santiago (St. James' Way). For centuries, this 500-mile route has led millions of faithful to the cathedral in Santiago and the grave of the long-dead saint. Though no reliable statistics exist about how many people attempt the Camino, the city's tourism board suggests the number is around 100,000 per year. The route is a UNESCO world heritage site and an integral part of the Spanish culture. In fact, Santiago the saint/slayer, is the patron of Spain and his feast day July 25th is a holiday throughout the country.

legal system, and introduced Latin, which later formed the basis of Spanish. During their rule, large numbers of Jews arrived to Hispania and settled in the Mediterranean area. Around the 3rd century A.D., Christianity took root in Andalucía and conversion quickly followed. By this time, the Roman Empire had begun to falter and its stronghold over Hispania was weakened by Iberian revolts, Germanic invasions, and the imminent arrival of the Visigoths.

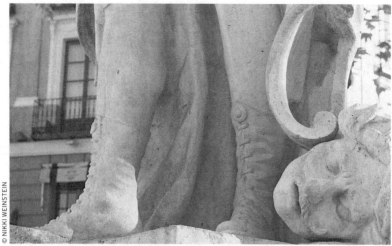

The statues of the royals outside the palace in Madrid reveal both the best and the worst of Spanish history.

THE VISIGOTHS

Around A.D. 410, the Visigoths had conquered most of the Iberian Peninsula and built their capital in present-day Toledo. Life under their rule was not easy and their 300 years are remembered for their brutishness and cruelty. However, this unruly bunch also gave Spain its most enduring spiritual legacy—Christianity. In an effort to quell rebellions by the Hispano-Romans, Visigoth King Reccared converted to Orthodox Christianity, helping spread the faith throughout Iberia.

Despite the unifying influence of Christianity, all was not well in the Visigothic state. They had inherited the legacy of Rome but did not have the political savvy to make it work. Rebellions, assassinations, usurpations, and general treachery chipped away at their power. It wasn't long before others began to intervene in internal disputes and royal elections.

THE MOORS

Following the death of Mohammed in A.D. 632, Islam rapidly spread across the globe, soon reaching North Africa. The decline of the Visigothic kingdom gave the Muslims (also known in Spain as Moors or *moros*) an irresistible opportunity to expand their faith (and rule) into the Iberian Peninsula. In 711, the governor of Tangier, Tariq ibn Ziyad, assembled some 10,000 troops and made the successful invasion across the Strait of Gibraltar. Visigothic Spain fell easily, and in just three years the Moors controlled the entire peninsula.

They renamed it Al-Andalus and for nearly 800 years ruled it in an era of unrivaled prosperity.

The 9th century saw the rise of the golden age of Moorish Spain. While the rest of medieval Europe wallowed in the Dark Ages, Spain was alight with new forms of architecture, mathematics, astronomy, philosophy, and literature. The Moors introduced new agriculture and irrigation methods which allowed a host of new crops—oranges, almonds, dates, rice, saffron, and cotton—to flourish. Marketplaces, public baths, and universities were built as well as some of the world's grandest structures including Granada's Alhambra. Yet, despite their advancements, Moorish Spain destabilized over the centuries. Power struggles among the Moors themselves resulted in the fragmentation of Al-Andalus into 39 separate *taifas,* or petty kingdoms. Meanwhile, Christian monarchies in the north of Iberia began joining forces against their common enemy. As the Moors weakened, the Christians grew—a dramatic shift in power that heralded the birth of modern Spain.

A tower rises above the old city center of Teruel.

© CANDY LEE LABALLE

THE RECONQUEST

Shortly after the Moors arrived on the Iberian Peninsula, the Christians began their *reconquista* efforts. The struggle would last over 700 years. As the kingdoms of Asturias, León, Navarra, Castilla, and Aragón strengthened and merged, they pushed the Moors farther and farther South through near constant battle. By 1469, when Fernando of Aragón married Isabel of Castilla, the days of Moorish rule were numbered. The Spanish kingdom forged by their marriage was a potent force, and in region after region, battle after battle, they beat back the Moors in a fervent push to unite all of Spain under Christian rule. The final battle occurred in 1492 when Christian forces entered Granada and ousted the Moors from their holdout in the Alhambra. This victory gave rise to Spain as we know it today.

THE GOLDEN AGE

King Fernando with his cunning and Queen Isabel with her piety were an indomitable force and their impact on Spain is still felt today. The same year that they won Granada, they financed Columbus's (Colón in Spanish) voyage in search of a new passage to Asia. Though he famously lost his way to Asia, what Columbus did find changed world geography forever. The explorer claimed the Caribbean islands, the West Indies, and the coasts of South and Central America for Spain, setting off a wave of Spanish colonization. Native Incan, Aztec, and Mayan tribes were quickly conquered and converted to Catholicism. In return for the gift of religion, Spanish conquistadores like Hernán Cortés and Vasco Nuñez de Balboa reaped local gold and silver and it wasn't long before Spain had become the world's wealthiest nation. The country's Golden Age was well underway. However, back in Spain, the fanatically religious Isabel ushered in measures that would forever cast a dark cloud over Spain's most prosperous time in history.

The Inquisition as practiced under Queen Isabel is well documented as one of the most horrific examples of religious piety gone wrong in history. It's purpose was to root out religious heresy and purify the land from "infidels"—namely Jews and Muslims. The Inquisition used atrocious methods of torture to determine one's religious loyalties. Soon political interests intervened and essentially anyone living under Spanish rule could be called upon by the Inquisition. Those under suspect almost always died in the course of their trials and their possessions were seized for the state—a very effective way to gain financial profits and control political dissidents. During the 300 years in which the Spanish Inquisition was in full effect, it was responsible for the deaths of thousands and the expulsion of hundreds of thousands.

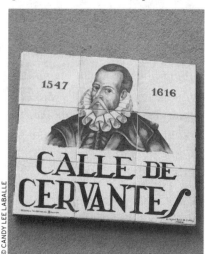

The streets of Madrid's Barrio de las Letras bear the names of Spain's Golden Age writers.

When not killing in the name of Catholicism, Isabel and Fernando occupied themselves with securing Spain's place in Europe by intermarrying their children with European royalty. Their daughter, Juana La Loca (Joan the Mad) and her Hapsburg husband Felipe el Hermoso

(Philip the Handsome) inherited the Spanish throne upon the death of Isabel in 1504. However, Juana was deemed unfit to rule and Fernando resumed control until his own death in 1516. At this point, Juana's son Carlos I (Charles I) took over the throne, launching the Hapsburg rule of Spain. During his 40-year rule, Spain expanded well beyond Spanish borders, eventually encompassing much of Central Europe and the Americas. Carlos I was crowned Holy Roman Emperor Carlos V in 1630 by the Pope, making Spain the seat of the Holy Roman Empire and further solidifying its world power.

THE FALL

Though the 16th and 17th centuries were without doubt Spain's Golden Age—the immense wealth pouring in from the New World, the expansion of the Spanish empire across the globe, and the rise of an artistic heritage forged by names such as El Greco, Velázquez, and Cervantes—it also marked the beginning of Spain's decay. The empire's seemingly limitless funds were redirected into financing incessant warfare. Political chaos rose as Spanish riches fell and in 1556, Carlos V abdicated the throne and entered the monastery of Yuste in La Rioja. By the time his son, Felipe II (Philip II), took over in 1558, Spain was hopelessly in debt.

Though he moved Spain's capital to Madrid and had the massive monastery–palace El Escorial built, Felipe II did Spain much more harm than good. While the home front was riddled with widespread insurgency and revolt, the fanatically Catholic monarch was busy spending Spanish fortunes on Counter-Reformation efforts. In 1588, he sent his invincible Spanish Armada to conquer England and its "heretics," the Protestants. Spain's 125 ships were soundly defeated by Sir Francis Drake and his men. This marked the beginning of the rise of English power and the end of Spanish glory.

The Hapsburg dynasty ended in 1700 and shortly thereafter, the War of the Spanish Succession broke out between Spain, France, England, and Austria. When it ended 14 years later, Spain had lost Belgium, Luxemburg, Milan, Naples, Sardinia, and Menorca. France declared Philip of Anjou (Felipe V) king and Spain fell under foreign dominion. Portugal, which had been united with Spain for 60 years under Felipe II, was returned to the Portuguese, the British gained control of Gibraltar, and the French occupied the rest of the Peninsula. Spain had now lost almost all its territories, a good portion of its population, and most of its wealth.

Felipe V's acension to the throne marked the beginnings of Borbón rule in Spain. Throughout the 18th and 19th century, they would gain and lose power several times. The current royal family of Spain are Borbóns. Felipe

V who ruled Spain from abroad for over 40 years contributed significantly to the development of the country. He built the Palacio Real in Madrid and La Granja in Segovia and he also ushered in the Enlightenment, a period of national reform—political, intellectual, and governmental. Carlos III, who took the throne in 1759, is synonymous with this era. He reorganized the nation's infrastructure, reformed its agriculture, and advanced modern urban planning. Madrid was a particular beneficiary of his rule and he is known for transforming Spain's capital from a dusty, chaotic town into the elegant capital that it is today.

THE 19TH CENTURY

Despite the advances of the Enlightenment, Spain continued to weaken throughout the 19th century. Napoleon Bonaparte, in his stampede to overtake Europe, took advantage of the chinks in Spain's armor to name his brother Joseph king of Spain in 1808. Few Spaniards were willing to accept the new French monarchy, and on May 2, 1808 they rose up in revolt, helping to spark the brutal, six-year Peninsular War—known in Spain as the *Guerra de Independencia*. It was a landmark event for Spain in that it solidified the concept of Spanish nationality. With the creation of Spain's first constitution in the city of Cádiz on March 12, 1812, Spain entered a new phase in its long history, one that has endured into the present day: constitutionalism. The most recent constitution was drawn up in 1978.

Almost on the heels of the Penisular War, Spain endured a series of succession clashes known as the Carlist Wars—battles between the royal descendents of Carlos V to retake control of Spain. This near constant warfare took a devastating toll not only on Spanish soil, but on its holdings as Spanish colonies in the Caribbean, Africa, and the Americas took advantage of Spain's weakened state to seek independence. By 1833, only Cuba, Puerto Rico, and the Philippines remained under Spanish dominion. However, these were soon wrested from Spain during the Spanish-American War.

By the end of the 19th century, Spain was a fledgling constitutional monarchy, yet that milestone meant anything but a happy ending. The country was in the midst of chaos so virulent that it undermined every political step forward. Labor disputes were constant, the countryside's working class angrily objected to the rich landowners who controlled them, and Basque and Catalan separatists were becoming increasingly unruly. Everyone had an opinion, no one could agree, and the country was ripe for a revolution.

This era was marked by a series of turnovers in power, vastly divergent governments, and violently opposed political parties. The First Republic, established in 1873, was built on the principle of internally self-governing provinces bound to the federal government by voluntary agreement. This government, which is similar to the one in place in modern Spain, was plagued with problems, both international and internal, and folded in less than two years. It was replaced by the restoration of the Borbón monarchy, first led by Alfonso XII and then his son Alfonso XIII. The rise of the Second Republic ousted the monarchs in 1931 forcing the royal family into exile, and ushered in one of Spain's most liberal rules. The left-wing Republicans drafted a new constitution which gave women the right to vote, legalized divorce, created a separation between religion and state, and granted autonomy to Spain's many regions. This was all too much for conservatives factions, who supported both the monarchy and the Catholic Church. General elections in 1933 brought a radical swing back to the right with a church-backed group gaining power.

CIVIL WAR

In protest to the rule of the right, mini-revolutions swept over the country and the state of general chaos across the country increased. The left's choice of political weapon was labor strikes, but the volatile environment often turned these into violent armed uprisings. This happened in October of 1934 when Asturian miners violently occupied the city of Oviedo, killing right-wing politicians and priests alike. Up-and-coming military leader Francisco Franco intervened on behalf of the ruling government and mercilessly crushed the rebellion. This incident definitively divided the nation into *los dos Españas,* the left and the right.

It was obvious to everyone that the country was dangerously fractured and an election was called in 1936 with the idea of appeasing the people. The Popular Front represented the political left, and it beat the conservative Falange Española party (a party similar to the fascist parties then popular in Germany and Italy) by a hair. Supporters of the losing party immediately flew into a violent uprising. In July 1936, the military joined the fray, holding a coup d'etat against the government. Chaos ensued and the country rapidly descended into Civil War. Franco was chosen as the leader on the Nationalist (conservative) side with the full support of the Spanish military, while the Popular Front (liberals, also known as Republicans) fought back with a contingent of forces made up of labor unions, international socialist groups, and autonomous regions of Spain including País Vasco and Cataluña.

It is impossible to exaggerate the horrors of the war. The fighting was ruthlessly brutal, pitting neighbor against neighbor and both sides massacred civilians—more than 350,000 people died in just three years of fighting. The battle for Spain caught the world's attention and in many ways acted as a precursor for the issues that would embroil Europe in World War II. Nazi Germany and Fascist Italy stood firmly behind Franco and the Nationalists, providing troops and supplies, while the Communist Soviet Union assisted the Republicans. International groups from around the world also rushed to the Republicans' aid, including the American Lincoln Brigade. The Republicans also won the support of notable figures including Ernest Hemingway and George Orwell, both of whom rushed to Spain to join the fight against fascism. The Republicans fought with as much vigor as the Nationalists, but they were hopelessly out-manned and out-skilled. After Franco's troops took Madrid on March 28, 1939, the Republicans surrendered and Franco proclaimed victory on April 1.

DICTATORSHIP

General Francisco Franco became dictator of Spain and his party, the *Movimiento Nacional* (National Movement) became the country's sole political party. Franco ruled with an iron fist. With the unqualified support of the Catholic Church, he reformed the country into a unified dictatorship that lasted four decades. He began by meting out vengeance against Republicans and an estimated 100,000 liberals (or suspected liberals) were executed during his reign. Labor unions were outlawed. Regionalism became a crime and independently-minded Catalans, Basques, and Galicians were regularly targeted by the government. Spanish was declared the one and only language of Spain and all regional languages were banned under severe penalty. Catholicism was instituted as the official religion and nonbelievers were persecuted.

On the social front, Franco was no less oppressive. All of the progressive rights granted under the Second Republic—civil union, divorce, female suffrage—were revoked. Women were no longer allowed to hold jobs once they married and could not open their own bank account. Thousands of intellectuals, scientists, writers, educators, and artists were forced to take refuge in neighboring countries or risk imprisonment or death. Their absence rendered Spain devoid of cultural life.

Just a few months after Franco rose to power, World War II began. The general avoided direct involvement in the war although he was ideologically aligned with Axis forces. His stance during the war alienated him from the world community and most countries broke off diplomatic relations with Spain; until 1955 Spain was not invited to join the United Nations. The forced isolation hurt the country's economy and exacerbated the *años de hambre* (years of hunger), the desperate era of poverty and hunger following the war that led thousands of Spaniards to emigrate abroad for work.

By the 1960s, the Spanish economy had started to recover and Franco had begun to relax his rule and Spaniards were subjected to far less cultural censorship. However, military presence—Franco's main means of controlling the people—was ever noticeable, with Guardia Civil (military police force) officers on nearly every street corner. Despite this show of might, the Basque separatist terrorist group called Euskadi Ta Azkatasuna (ETA, Basque Homeland and Liberty) rose to prominence in this era, launching many terrorist attacks during the seventies.

Although Franco had restored the Spanish monarchy in 1947, he waited until 1969 to invest Juan Carlos de Borbón, a grandson of King Alfonso XIII, with the title of Crown Prince. The young monarch was groomed to take the general's place as Spain's leader. And when Franco died on November 20, 1975 the Spanish people fully expected Juan Carlos to pick up right where Franco had left off—but Spain was in for a surprise.

DEMOCRACY

Two days after the death of Spain's dictator, 37 year-old King Juan Carlos I took the throne. He promptly shocked the nation when he appointed Adolfo Suárez—a man know to favor democracy—as prime minister. In quick succession, political parties, trade unions and strikes were all legalized, and the first general national election in 41 years was called for June of 1977. Suárez's democratic party won most of the seats. In December of the following year, Spain's newly formed *cortes* (congress) ratified a new constitution and Spain was on its way to becoming a stable democracy.

During Suárez's rule, Cataluña, País Vasco, Galicia, and Andalucía were all approved for statutes for self-government, something that would have been unheard of just five years earlier. By 1983, Spain had been divided into its present-day 17 autonomous communities with individual regional governments and elected parliament representatives.

However, not everyone was pleased with the new direction of the government. Some Franco supporters wanted a return to his form of government. In 1981, a lieutenant colonel of the Guardia Civil led a coup d'etat, storming congress with troops and taking the prime minister and several parliamentary leaders hostage. Within hours, Juan Carlos, dressed in full military regalia, appeared on television, commanded the Spanish military to support him, and promised the people that democracy would proceed. The military complied and the coup ended without bloodshed. Democracy was assured and for that, to this day Juan Carlos is highly revered in Spain.

MODERN SPAIN

In the elections of 1982, the Socialist Workers' Party (PSOE) won the vote and Felipe Gonzaléz became prime minister. The party won three more consecutive elections and during that time, Spain flourished. The middle class grew exponentially, women moved out of the home and into the universities and work force, a national health system was created, and state education was drastically improved. Spain also began to make a mark on the world stage—joining NATO in 1982 and the European Community (precursor to the European Union) in 1986. Membership brought on an economic upswing that carried the country into the 1990s. In 1992—the 500th anniversary of the most important year in Spanish history—Spain did what it does best, celebrate. The World Fair's was held in Sevilla and the summer Olympics took place in Barcelona.

Though they had held power for 14 years, the PSOE was increasingly embroiled in scandal and few were surprised when the Popular Party (PP), a conservative party with roots in Francoism, won the 1996 elections making José María Aznar president. During his period in office, with the help of European Union aid, Spain progressed rapidly—by 2000 the country's economy was the fastest growing in Europe and unemployment had dropped dramatically (factors which contributed greatly to his reelection that year). However, Aznar's popularity fell towards the end of his second term, especially regarding his mishandling of the 2002 *Prestige* oil spill off the coast of Galicia and his support of the U.S. invasion of Iraq. In 2004, he decided to not seek reelection and Mariano Rajoy ran as the PP candidate. Throughout the campaign, polls and pundits all agreed that Rajoy would easily win. Tragic events deemed otherwise.

On March 11, 2004, bombs exploded on four Madrid trains packed with morning commuters. One hundred ninety-one people died and nearly 1,800 were wounded. In the hours after the bombings, Aznar publicly blamed ETA, the Basque separatist group, despite strong evidence to the contrary. When the news broke that Islamic fundamentalists and not ETA were responsible for the bombing, the Spanish people were outraged. They felt that Aznar had lied about the bombers' identity in order to protect his own party's reputation. (During his time in office, Aznar had maintained rigid policies regarding ETA; he also supported the war in Iraq despite the fact that an estimated 90 percent of the Spanish people opposed it.) The ensuing political scandal also stirred up old antiwar sentiment. Just two days after the bombing, the Spanish people went to the polls in record numbers and elected José Luis Rodriguez Zapatero of the PSOE.

The newly elected PSOE government implemented a series of progressive changes—the legalization of gay marriage, easing of restrictions on divorce and abortion, reform of the educational system—that raised the ire of both conservatives and the Catholic Church. The PSOE also approved legislature giving the region of Cataluña more autonomy and expressed a willingness to talk with ETA (rescinded after the terrorists broke a truce by bombing a parking garage at Barajas airport in Madrid in December 2006). These two initiatives in particular were seized on by the opposition PP and much of Zapatero's time in office has been spent in a vicious war of words and public attacks between the PSOE and the PP. In the elections of 2008, Zapatero won by a very fine margin. However, the ensuing economic crisis that gripped Spain as well as the rest of the world, once again plunged his government into controversy as the PP as well as other organizations sharply criticized PSOE economic policies. Opposing viewpoints and political mudslinging once again consumed the nation's attention. In other words, it was Spanish politics as usual.

Government

Spain is a constitutional monarchy with a democratically elected government that handles the daily affairs of Spain and a king who holds the title

of Head of State. The leader of the political party that wins the majority of seats in the Cortes Generales (Parliament) becomes Presidente del Gobierno (regularly called Prime Minister in English) and appoints a cabinet of ministers. The Cortes Generales consists of two houses—the 350-member Congreso de los Diputados (Congress) and the 208-member Senado (Senate).

Though a multiparty system, the right-of-center Partido Popular (Popular Party), or PP, and the left-of-center Partido Socialista Obrero Español (Socialist Party), or PSOE, dominate Spanish politics.

© CANDY LEE LABALLE

Spain's Congress is located in Madrid.

Izquierda Unida, the United Left, is the third most-powerful party. It has little hope of winning the majority in Parliament, but its presence is significant enough to draw votes from the two dominant parties.

The country is divided into 17 autonomous regions with corresponding governments. Their relationship to Spain is much like the state–federal relationship in the United States, but more politically divisive. As a result, regional political parties hold sway in those regions. The most significant are Convergence and Union (CIU) in Cataluña and the Basque Nationalist Party (PNV) in the País Vasco. Their self-serving presence in parliament is a constant headache for both the PP and the PSOE.

And then there is the king. The royal family has been a pillar of Spanish society for centuries and the current king, Juan Carlos I, is a descendant of the Borbón family. However his current role is nothing like what it was back in the good old medieval days. His duties today are mainly diplomatic and he is highly visible in both national and international affairs (though diplomacy took a medieval backtrack when Juan Carlos asked Hugo Chávez of Venezuela *¿Por qué no te callas?*—Why don't you shut up?—at the 2007 Ibero-American Summit).

Many Spaniards applaud the monarchy simply due to tradition of the royal institution, while others want to abolish it, arguing that as such it plays an inconsequential role in today's society. The *prensa rosa* (gossip press) which follows the royals with glee, would disagree. However, there is still much reverence for Juan Carlos who oversaw the peaceful transition of Spain from dictatorship to democracy. During his lifetime, it is very unlikely any action will be made to dethrone the royal family.

Economy

From the devastating "years of hunger" following the Spanish Civil War to the 9th largest economy in the developed world by 2007—Spain has had quite an economic ride. In the 1950s, early aid came from the U.S. when Franco allowed Dwight D. Eisenhower to build four military bases on Spanish soil. In addition to a huge wad of money, the relationship helped redeem Spain in the eyes of the world and in 1955 the country was admitted to the United Nations. The military-base-for-money deal also helped spark *el milagro Español* (the Spanish miracle), the amazing financial rebound of Spain. Fueled by industrial development, deregulation policies, infrastructure investment, and a significant remittance of currency from

MODERN DAY FAIRY TALE

Letizia Ortiz Rocasolano was born in 1972 in the industrious little town of Oviedo in the northwest of Spain. Her grandfather was a taxi driver, her mother was a nurse, and her father was a journalist. Like all girls of that era, Letizia grew up with the vast possibilities offered to women after Franco's death. She decided to follow in her father's footsteps and studied journalism. After a brief marriage to one of her literature professors, she focused on her career and by 2002 had become a news anchor at a national television station. She was a model of the modern Spanish woman – hard-working, dedicated, smart, independent. Then she met the prince.

For over a decade, the love life of **Prince Felipe de Borbón y Grecia,** heir to the Spanish throne, had fueled heated debate in the popular press. Impossibly tall, dark, and handsome, the prince was widely considered Europe's most eligible bachelor. He had been romantically linked to statuesque blondes for years including a lingerie model from Norway and a socialite from New York. Those relationships had riled a Spanish public who longed to see the future king married to a Spanish woman. As he approached

35, the press was relentless in pursuing leads into the prince's love life. In response, he publicly stated several times that he would marry only for love.

In November of 2002, Letizia traveled to Galicia to cover the sinking of the *Prestige* oil tanker off the coast of Spain. Prince Felipe was there too, assessing the damage. They met, and in a coup worthy of a spy novel, managed to begin dating without the press nor the public catching on. Letizia's father later said that even her family had no idea. In September of 2003, Letizia gave some college friends a tour of the television station where she worked. When one asked about her love life, Letizia confessed that was dating someone she might marry. Her friend said "Well, if you get married and I don't find out about it I hope you're very happy." Letizia replied, "Don't worry. You'll find out."

On October 31, 2003, Letizia gave her last on-air report. She then went to her Madrid apartment, packed up her bags, and moved into the guest wing of the royal residence. The next day the royal family sent out a press release announcing the engagement of Felipe and Letizia. Spain went

Spaniards living and working abroad, Spain's economy grew 7 percent per year from 1961 to 1973.

Tourism in particular contributed to Spain's revival as the world discovered that the country's endless beaches and *siesta y fiesta* culture made for the ideal vacation. Sprawling resorts sprang up along the Costa del Sol in Andalucía and the Costa Brava in Cataluña and the number of foreign visitors skyrocketed from three million in 1959 to more than 34 million in 1979. Today, tourism is

wild. The press couldn't believe they had been duped and scoured photographs for evidence of the relationship. All they could find was a single photo of the prince greeting a line of reporters, including Letizia, at an awards ceremony the month before. Though there was some rumbling over Letizia's divorce and her commoner background, the public overwhelmingly accepted her. She was a face they knew and trusted, and a homegrown girl to boot. Felipe's official title is Prince of Asturias, and the public liked that Letizia was from Asturias. Even the segment of the population that opposes the monarchy system, couldn't help being moved by the romance of it all. The Catholic church, so powerful in this country, also gave their consent as Letizia's first wedding had not occurred in a church.

The couple chose Madrid's La Almudena Cathedral as the sight of their royal nuptials, marking the first time a royal wedding would be held in the city in a century. At the 1906 wedding of King Alfonso XIII and Scottish Princess Victoria Eugenie, an anarchist rebel threw a bomb at the royal procession as it wound through Madrid. The royals survived, but 20 bystanders were killed. Terrorism was not far from the minds of Felipe and Letizia as they planned their May 2004 wedding. On March of that year, terrorists had bombed four commuter trains in Madrid, resulting in 192 deaths and the worst crime of terrorism ever committed on Spanish soil. Security for the wedding was tight, airspace was cleared overhead, and thousands of troops were stationed in the city. The couple cancelled bachelor and bachelorette parties and a city-planned fireworks show out of respect for the victims, instead directing the money into a fund for the victims. They also dedicated their wedding ceremony to the victims.

Despite torrential rain on the day of the wedding, Madrid glowed with joy. Thousands of flowers, colorful banners, and lights decorated the city. Tens of thousands of well-wishers lined the streets. Over 1,000 dignitaries, from Prince Charles of England to Nelson Mandela of South Africa, attended the wedding. In a bow to Spanish royal tradition, just before Prince Felipe said "I do," he looked over to his father for approval. The King nodded his consent and Letizia, a career-minded commoner, became the Princess of Asturias and the future Queen of Spain.

still Spain's most important economic generator. In 2007, the industry added $57 billion to Spain's coffers.

The good times only came to an end when the oil crisis of 1973 put the brakes on economies worldwide. It wasn't until the mid-1980s that Spain began to recover, boosted considerably by European funding as a result of Spain's entrance into the European Community (later the European Union or EU). In the late 1990s, Spain aggressively pursued a free-market economy, deregulating

© CANDY LEE LABALLE

Spain's economy ticks at the Stock Exchange in Madrid.

Spanish industries through liberalization and privatization. In 1999, Spain was among the first group of European countries to adopt the single currency euro. In subsequent years, the high unemployment rate fell steadily and Spain emerged as one of the most dynamic economies in Europe.

However, by 2008 cracks in Spain's robust economy were evident. The country's trade deficit had reached critical levels and it was losing competitiveness. Inflation and unemployment were climbing once again. The situation was fueled by the explosion of the Spanish property bubble which had seen housing prices rise dramatically in the early 2000s. Meanwhile, soaring oil prices hit industries from fishing to agriculture and put a big dent in tourism as frugal travelers worldwide stayed close to home. The worldwide economic crisis added fuel to the fire and in January of 2009, Spain had entered recession.

PEOPLE AND CULTURE

Spaniards are quick to declare that they work to live rather than live to work and it does truly seem that careers, though important, take second place to personal lives. Americans often say that while the general standard of living is lower in Spain than it is in the United States, the quality of life is much higher (though by a "lower standard of living" many mean that there are no 24-hour super Wal-Marts, no cooking channel, and no half-off wings during happy hour). Of course, the Spanish are as varied a group as any and the serene days of a tiny Galician town are nothing like the frenzied activity that defines daily life in Madrid. Still, even in the Spanish capital people obey the infamous, Spanish concept of *mañana*—or "why do today what you can do tomorrow"—and the afternoon siesta still dominates business hours. Spaniards also have more vacation days than people in the United States and they make time in their daily schedule to take an evening *paseo* (walk), linger over dinner, and participate in the ubiquitous fiestas that draw locals and visitors alike into bacchanalian, all-night revelries. This is unquestionably a country that knows how to have a good time.

A NIGHTLIFE SURVIVAL GUIDE

Going out is a ritual practiced throughout Spain. Even the tiniest village will have a few bars and at least one late-night place. Going out is so common it even has its own verb, *ir de marchar*, which roughly translates as "bar-hopping." Once you arrive in Spain, it won't be long before you'll want to tap into this late-night side of the culture. Here are a few tips on how.

What is a nightlife spot? The line separating a tapas bar from a bar from a café is very flexible, and it is quite possible that the same place where you have your 9 A.M. coffee will be where you end up dancing until dawn. In general, a café is more known for eating than for drinking. For a bar, it's the reverse. However, many bars begin as tapas bars and morph into club mode once the clock swings into single digits. Throughout Spain, cafés, bars, and tapas bars will be the first to close down, usually by 2 A.M..

Clubs, discos, and *discoclubs* are up next. The variety is astounding – from heavy metal dives to trendy VIP clubs to anything-goes gay discos. However, there are a few things they have in common. Most will charge an *entrada* (cover charge) of anywhere from €5-20. In exchange you'll receive a slip of paper. Don't toss it out! It is valid for your first drink, whether you choose a cheap beer or a pricey cocktail.

What does it cost? After your first drink, you'll have to pay for your drinks. Prices depend on the club, what you drink, the town, and the time of year, but expect to pay anywhere between €4 and €18, with €8 being the average. Unlike in tapas bars or cafés, in clubs you have to pay as you order. Tipping is not required; in fact, bartenders in clubs are notorious for being inefficient and rude. Tipping them will not much improve things, in fact, it will probably just earn you a "pathetic sucker" look. Also, remember to bring cash. Few clubs will accept credit cards.

What to drink? As with dining, the Spanish follow some social norms about drinking. Beer and wine is drunk until about midnight or until you hit the first club. *Copas* (cocktails or mixed drinks) are usually only consumed at clubs. *Shots* (chupitos) are not usually ordered and there is no concept of "a beer and a shot." One exception is at a *chupitería*, a shot bar that specializes in sweet, low-alcohol shots. Fancy cocktails – Cosmopolitans, White Russians, Manhattans – are not readily available. One exception is *mojito*, a Cuban concoction with rum and mint that is wildly popular all over Spain. Most cocktails are of the single mix variety – *ron y coca-cola* (rum and Coke), *gin-tonic* (gin and tonic), *vodka y zumo de naranja* (vodka with orange juice). Note that in Spain, *whisky* is always scotch-whisky. If you want bourbon, it is best to ask for a brand name such as Jack Daniels. Be aware that Spanish pours are heavy. Three to four shots of alcohol are poured into a tall glass and the mixer (juice, soda, etc.) is served in a bottle on the side. If you are not used to such heavy pours, pace yourself.

Are there fire codes in Spain? Technically, bars and clubs are limited as to the number of people they can allow in. In practice, few follow the rules. If you are out on a Friday or Saturday night, expect to be jam-packed in a bar or club to sometimes scary proportions. Wear lots of deodorant and be ready to be jostled about. Definitely keep your personal belongings to a minimum and take advantage of the coat check if available. If you don't do well in crowds, go early or stay as close to the door as possible. Spaniards are more than accustomed to these types of crowds and generally show respect, allowing people to pass through to the bar and not getting angry when pushed by the crowd. In fact, if you go out regularly in the states, you'll be delighted to learn that the concept of bar brawl just doesn't exist here. At night, the general attitude is we are all out to have a good time, why fight? Go with the flow, relax, and you too will soon be a *la marcha* expert.

What about the smoke? Spain has been slow to ban smoking in public places. Though sweeping public smoking laws were recently enacted, enforcement is sporadic at best. Smaller bars are allowed to choose to be smoking or non and most go with the former. Larger bars must provide for smoking and nonsmoking sections, however the smoking section is often just a part of the bar that has been roped off. Suffice it to say, if you are allergic to smoke, you won't enjoy going out in Spain very much. Try to choose an open-air bar or stay close to the door. Your clothes will reek of smoke once the night is done. If you can't wash them (typically the case with coats or jackets), hang your items on the clothesline overnight. The cool air will have the smoke smell gone by morning.

© CANDY LEE LABALLE

a bottle of wine chilling in a fountain in an ancient bar in Madrid

BULLFIGHTING IN SPAIN

Along with flamenco and tapas, few things say Spain as much as bullfighting. But is that image an archetype of authentic Spain or a shameful stereotype? Depends on who you're asking. *La corrida* (the bullfight) has been a part of Spanish culture since the early 1700s and is known as the *fiesta nacional*. Hemingway lauded it in his 1932 tome *Death in the Afternoon*. Ava Gardner brought it glamour in the 1950s when she was a regular at the bullfights in Madrid. Today, it is a multimillion-euro business and employs some 200,000 people from bull handlers to matadors. Top bullfighting fairs such as those in Madrid and Sevilla sell out to well-dressed crowds of adoring *aficionados* (fans) who claim that bullfighting is an integral cultural tradition of Spain.

But, as Hemingway noted, "Anything capable of arousing passion in its favor will surely raise as much passion against it." And that is increasingly the case today, especially among animal rights activists who denounce bullfighting as animal torture, pure and sinful. Wherever a bullfight is scheduled, you'll find protestors collecting signatures, chanting, and even lying seminaked in pools of fake blood, *banderillas* (a dart used in the bullfight) attached to their backs. Though many of the protest groups are Spanish, they have the backing and marketing pull of international groups like PETA as well.

A 2006 Gallup poll found that 72 percent of Spaniards were not interested in bullfighting and just 7 percent identified themselves as fans. That apathy has fueled hopes of the *antitaurinos*, as those who oppose bullfighting are called. So did the Minister of Environment, Cristina Narbona, who in 2006 called for a ban on killing bulls in the ring saying, "I am deeply ashamed of living in a country with such a tradition." This was notable as the minister's father was one of Spain's foremost bullfighting experts. Another blow to bullfighting came in 2008 when the national television station of Spain, TVE, announced it would no longer show bullfights during prime time.

So does this mean there will be no more death in the afternoon? Not likely. At the same time that movement against bullfighting has heated up, so has the popularity of the event and modern matadors are superstars. Known

Regionalism and Nationalism

The fact that Spain is home to four separate languages is just one indication of the country's cultural diversity. More often than not the differences take the form of local pride. People from Andalucía maintain ties to their agrarian roots and to flamenco while those from Asturias might brag about their Cabrales cheese. Madrileños swear their city is the best, while Barcelonans are equally convinced of the same. How in some cases, regional pride has morphed into calls for increased autonomy.

© NIKKI WEINSTEIN

a *picador* poised in the bullring

as *toreros*, their lives are detailed in the press, they marry royalty, and in the case of Cayetano Rivera, they also walk the catwalk in Milan. Names like El Cid, El Fandi, El Fundi, Sebastián Castella, and Morante de la Puebla can sell out bullrings and command top salaries. But the man who is credited with breathing new life into bullfighting is José Tómas, who came out of retirement in 2007 to capture the country's imagination as the most spectacular bullfighter in generations. Fans have waited all night in line to get a chance to see him perform, shelling out up to €1,000 for a ticket. One commentator said that Tómas demonstrates "the beauty of death" inherent in bullfighting. Which brings us back to the protestors, who ask, can the deliberate death of an animal ever be anything less than cruel?

Who is right? Is it artistry or slaughter? Each person has to decide that for themselves, but one thing is for sure, it is doubtful that bullfighting is going away anytime soon.

Though it is easy to chalk regional sentiment up to cultural and even geographic differences, in the case of Spain, national politics are also to blame. It started with the 1978 Constitution which promises both "the indissoluble unity of the Spanish nation" and "the right to autonomy of the nationalities and regions integrated in it." This noble sentiment has led to quite a bit of political strife.

In Cataluña, the move for greater autonomy has been mainly political and in 2006, Catalans approved the Catalan Statute of Autonomy, a law that greatly increased their self-rule and received backing from the national

WELCOME TO SPAIN

© CANDY LEE LABALLE

Regardless of region, plenty of Spaniards love a good glass of wine.

Socialist government. País Vasco, which actually enjoys more autonomy than the rest of Spain, harbors a separatist movement calling for full independence from the Spanish state. The terrorist group Euskadi Ta Askatasuna (ETA) endorses the movement through bombs, blackmail, kidnappings, and assassinations which has resulted in over 800 deaths since the group's founding. While ETA's violence is executed against the wishes of the majority of Basques, many also support increased autonomy from Spain. For evidence of that, consider the success the nonviolent but independently minded Basque Nationalist Party (PNV in Spanish, EAJ in Basque) enjoys in local elections.

Ethnicity and Class

Although modern Spaniards came from a mix of people including Celts, Romans, Moors, and Jews, the population has remained remarkably homogeneous since the Reconquest in the Middle Ages. Yet there is one ethnic minority that has lived in Spain for centuries—the Romas (*gitanos* in Spanish, gypsies in English), nomadic peoples with ancient origins in India. The first record of Romas in Iberia dates back to the 15th century—though they weren't recognized as citizens until the 1970s. Today, approximately 700,000 call Spain home. Originally they settled in Andalucía and were instrumental in the creation of flamenco—Spain's most famous cultural export. Flamenco music and dance is still a very vital part of *gitano* culture. Though many individual Romas are well integrated into the greater Spanish society, the vast majority are not. A 2007 study by the Spanish government found that modern-day Romas have much higher levels of poverty and illiteracy compared to the rest of Spanish society and are subject to high levels of racism. Nearly 50 percent reported being discriminated against when applying for jobs or renting apartments. Several Roma-rights organizations are trying to reverse the racism, but it is exacerbated by the fact that many Romas tend to be insular, living in very tight-knit communities—often in *chabolas* (shantytowns) on the edges of larger cities—and they tend to stay out of mainstream society. Many Spaniards view them as lazy, untrustworthy, and criminal. Yet, this view is not always considered racist. Shortly after moving here, a new Spanish acquaintance commented that the U.S. was a racist country. In responding, I pointed out the racism against *gitanos* in Spain. He looked at me like I was *loco* and said, "That's different."

IMMIGRATION

In 1998, 637,000 foreigners resided in Spain. Thanks to Spain's economic boom, that number had exploded to over 5 million—11 percent of the population—by 2008. The majority of foreigners in Spain come from Romania, Morocco, and Latin America—mainly driven by economic factors rather than lifestyle choices. There has also been a recent influx of Sub-Saharan Africans arriving to Spanish shores in *pateras,* rickety boats that set sail from Africa and face dangerous seas to make it to Spain as a gateway to Europe. Official figures show Sub-Saharan Africans currently make up about 4 percent of the population.

The Spanish, in general, have accepted this with much less xenophobia than in other European countries. Attitudes towards immigrants are generally sympathetic, something which is partly attributed to the fact that rather recently Spaniards themselves fled as economic immigrants to other countries in the difficult years following the Spanish civil war. In addition, immigration in Spain has helped boost Spain's low birth rate, contributed to population growth, and added fuel to the Spanish economy.

Nevertheless, immigration is a tempestuous topic. There have been several high profile cases of violence against immigrants including a 2007 attack on a 16-year-old

© BEA MORA

Moorish arches are a common architectural feature throughout Andalucía.

Ecuadorian girl on the Barcelona metro and a November 2008 clash between Senegalese immigrants and residents of Almería. As the Spanish economy began faltering and unemployment reached record levels, some turned blame towards immigrants. The center-right Partido Popular (PP) party were key among them and in 2007 campaigned on a platform that included strong anti-immigrant sentiment. Yet, it was the ruling Socialist party in 2008 that created the Plan of Voluntary Return—a program designed to encourage legal immigrants who are unemployed in Spain to repatriate to their home country in exchange for the payment of their unemployment benefits in a lump sum.

A completely different case involves Europeans and North Americans who have relocated to Spain, mainly to larger expat communities on the warm Mediterranean coasts. Rather than considered immigrants—which they of course are—these mainly white, mainly economically self-sufficient foreigners are considered *guiris,* slang for foreigner that can be positive or negative depending on the context in which it is used. Part of this attitude stems from the fact that these immigrants are not seen as a drain on the economy. Rather than seeking economic stability in Spain, they are attracted to the sunny weather and relatively inexpensive lifestyle (compared to their home countries). Chief among them are the British (over 300,000 officially, but a million are estimated to call Spain home) and Germans (133,000 officially). Other large populations come from Denmark, Sweden, Norway, and Ireland. But, what about the Americans you're thinking. The Spanish census of 2008 counted 34,057 North Americans legally resident in Spain. Of course, that does not take into account the many thousands that are estimated to be here *sin papeles* (without papers or illegal). By their very nature, they are a tough group to count. But if you are thinking of joining them, you can find plenty of information on Spain expat forums where the topic of "illegal American" is *muy popular.*

Customs and Etiquette

The Spanish are extremely social and love to be out and about. Workers gather in cafés several times a day, entire families take to the streets in the evenings for a *paseo* (stroll). Parties, group dinners, and of course, fiestas, fiestas, fiestas are a way of life. They also love to talk, freely giving advice and opinions on everything. After a dinner party, this tendency is expressed in the tradition of *sobremesa* (literally, table covering), an animated, drawn-out post-meal conversation. Yet, despite the gregarious warmth of Spanish society, the culture is also ruled by a distinct formality. In the United States, everyday exchanges

© MEGAN CYTRON

a young boy dressed for fiesta

might begin with a casual "hello," the Spanish begin conversations with more traditional greetings like *buenos días* (good day) or *buenas tardes* (good afternoon).

Spaniards also monitor their public behavior, taking care to not be socially unacceptable. The famous Spanish *sentido de vergüenza* (feeling of shame) is one of the key differences that you'll notice among your new neighbors. You may have no problem sending a dish back to the kitchen because it is too salty; a Spaniard would rather eat it than suffer the embarrassment of complaining. If you are sharing a plate of *croquetas* or *calamares* with Spaniards, you'll find them hesitant to take the last one. It is often not until the waiter is ready to take the plate away that someone will say "okay, okay, I'll eat *la vergüenza*," literally "the shameful one."

You might also detect a sense of tradition in the natural evolution of friendships. You'll likely know a Spanish person for much longer than you would someone in the United States before exchanging the personal details of your lives. Questions that an American might ask easily of a new friend can come off as pushy or probing in Spain. Of course it's possible to form close and lasting relationships with Spanish people but it's not done quickly. Although patience is required, the payoff is that the notion of friendship in Spain runs deep and is usually something that lasts for years or even a lifetime.

DINING CUSTOMS

While dining at a table, keep both hands on the tabletop, a hand in the lap is considered bad manners. You should not eat foods with your hands, except those specifically meant to be eaten that way (olives, chicken wings, canapés). For almost everything else, a fork and knife is used. Breakfast croissants, grilled sandwiches, even fruit, are eaten with cutlery. Of course, on the other extreme, it is perfectly acceptable to throw napkins, sugar packets, and olive pits on the floor of tapas bars. If you dine with Spaniards, particularly for tapas or dinner, you'll find that they often eat directly out of one big serving

WELCOME TO SPAIN

© CANDY LEE LABALLE

Having tapas is a Spanish dinner alternative.

platter. If a first course, including a salad, is ordered, side serving plates are rarely used—everyone just sticks their fork in. Another big surprise for North Americans comes with the arrival of the check. It is always divided evenly, regardless of what each person consumed. Protesting that you "only had a bite" is considered not only rude, but cheap.

Desayuno (breakfast) is a light meal typically consisting of coffee, fresh-squeezed orange juice, and a pastry or toast. *Churros* (fried strips of dough) are a common choice as is the decadent, *croissant a la plancha,* a buttery croissant, sliced lengthwise, buttered and grilled, then served with still more butter and marmalade. Most working Spaniards have a brief breakfast at home and follow that with a second breakfast with workmates. Cafés generally fill up around 10 A.M. as workers stave off hunger with a piece of *tortilla* (potato omelet) or a pastry.

La comida (lunch) is eaten between 2 and 4 P.M. and is the main meal of the day consisting of a starter, entrée, and dessert. During the week, Spanish restaurants offer a *menú del día* which includes these three courses plus a drink (soft drink, beer, or wine) for an average of €10. Sunday lunch is a big tradition with Spanish families and if you marry into a Spanish family, it will be your tradition too. The meal, typically prepared by the Spanish mother or grandmother, will be hearty—paella or *cocido* (Spanish stew). After lunch, the family may disperse for a *siesta* and regroup around 5 P.M. for a coffee or *la merienda,* another essential part of the Spanish meal cycle. Children are huge fans of this early evening snack and, why not, lunch is long gone and dinner won't be for a few more hours. *La merienda* can be any light snack, but my Spanish husband swears the best *merienda* is a bar of chocolate between sliced bread.

La cena (dinner) is often lighter than lunch, though it really depends on the occasion and the diners. It is often consumed around 10 P.M. and if eaten at home, can often seem like an American breakfast. Fried eggs are popular and a Spanish ad for a low-fat cereal suggests replacing breakfast and dinner with their flakes. When dining out, it is not unusual for a dinner party to end way past midnight. And often, a sit-down meal is forgone for an evening of tapas-hopping.

The last dining time worth mentioning is not really about food. *El aperitivo* (apertif) refers to a light drink you have (usually with friends) around 1 P.M., particularly on Sundays. Drinks of choice include vermouth on tap, a glass of sherry, or a *caña* (a small draft beer). They are usually accompanied by complimentary tapas and you need to be careful to not fill up on them because your big Sunday lunch awaits!

Gender Roles

In the early 1980s, Pedro Almodóvar began releasing his movies into a society still testing out its new democracy. At that time, the films' depictions of sexually liberated women and daringly gay characters assaulted Spain's still-tender sensitivities rather than reflecting its cultural norms. Twenty years later, those once invisible subcultures now mirror very real aspects of modern Spanish society. A women is in charge of the Ministry of Defense, another serves as Vice President, and gays and lesbians enjoy rights that few other nations endow, including the right to marry. Of course, the country is still no utopia and the shocked dismay that some viewers had toward Almodóvar's early films is still felt, particularly in conservative political and Catholic circles.

WOMEN IN SPAIN

Mainstream feminism reached Spain late compared to the United States thanks to Franco and his 40 years of ultraconservative dictatorship. Under his brand of Spanish nationalism, women were—well, this quote from a Franco-era educational pamphlet sums it up: "God's first idea was 'man.' He thought of woman afterwards, as a necessary complement, as something useful." Married women belonged to their husbands who could legally beat them, they couldn't open a bank account on their own, and working outside of the home was all but officially restricted. And of course, divorce and contraception were illegal. Though his regime did ease social policies by the 1960s, women remained oppressed due to the archconservative morality that permeated society.

After the "ding-dong the dictator's dead" revelry died down, women made up lost ground fast. Of course, sexuality was one of the first taboos to go and that was reflected in the *destape,* a genre of comedic Spanish films notable for nude women traipsing through the scenes—often for no reason at all. Today, contraception is both legal and widely available, restrictions on abortion have been loosened, divorce is also legal (though not as common as in the United States), and the single, liberated Spanish woman is as ubiquitous as Starbucks in Madrid.

Women also make up nearly 50 percent of the workforce, they're entitled to generous maternity leave, and female politicians are hardly an anomaly. In fact, in 2008, the Socialist prime minister Zapatero—who once famously declared "I am a feminist"—appointed more women than men to his cabinet including a female vice president and a female Minster of Defense (who was seven months pregnant when she made her first official troop inspection). If anyone doubted his government's commitment to equality, Zapatero also created the Ministry for Equality, and yes, its minister is a woman.

Yet, despite these advances, conservative attitudes persist. After the appointments, one prominent conservative commentator called the ministers, a "battalion of inexperienced seamstresses." That attitude is less vocal, but more relevant, in the workforce, which despite the high numbers of female workers, metes out larger salaries to their male counterparts—by some estimates up to 30 percent more. And those generous maternity leaves? It has resulted in married women of child-bearing age having a tougher time getting a job. "Are you planning on having a baby?" is a common question in the interview. If the potential employee says no and gets the job but also gets pregnant soon thereafter, the company will often find a creative way to fire her.

On the homefront, *machismo* also seems alive and well as studies show that women still shoulder the bulk of household duties, though plenty of Spanish men, including both my husband and my father-in-law, take on their share of the diaper changing, dish washing, and dinner preparing. More troubling, statistics show an alarmingly high rate of domestic abuse with reported cases on the rise. The nightly news is filled with reports of women murdered at the hands of their male partners and the yearly numbers are tracked like homicides are. However, it is not clear if the rise is due to an actual increase in abuse or an increase in reports. As part of the equality campaign, the government has raised public awareness of domestic violence and pumped funds into hotline numbers, safe houses, and rehabilitation programs for abusers.

GAY AND LESBIAN CULTURE

When Spain legalized gay marriage in 2005, it gave gay and lesbian couples the same legal footing as heterosexual couples, including the right to adopt children. Spain is currently one of just six countries that afford their citizens this right. A survey showed 66 percent of Spaniards supported the measure and in the first year after its passage, over 4,500 gay and lesbian couples were married in Spain. Yet, conservative opinion backed by the Catholic Church has opposed the measure. Some conservative politicians have refused to perform wedding services for gay couples. And in December of 2008, the Church sponsored a Christian Family Day rally in Madrid; one of the day's strongest subtexts was the dangers of gay marriage to Spanish family life. Still, it is very doubtful, even if the government switches back to the conservative Partido Popular party in the 2010 elections, that the law will ever be reversed.

This high-profile issues has brought gay and lesbian issues directly into the living rooms of every family in Spain and it is quite safe to say that the country's gay and lesbian population is definitely out of the closet of oppression created by Franco's dictatorship when being gay was a crime. In large cities, it is not uncommon to see gay and lesbian couples holding hands or walking arm-in-arm. And there are many areas of Spain that have a very visible gay vibe including the barrio of Chueca in Madrid, "Gayxample" in Barcelona, Sitges on the Costa Brava, and Ibiza. In these enclaves of tolerance—and, yes, impeccable style—gay and lesbian couples are free to be as affectionate and overt as they want. Gay pride is also on very flamboyant display during Día de Orgullo Gay (Gay Pride Day). Parties are held around the country, but few match the weekend-long festival held in Madrid's Chueca. The event attracts an estimated one million visitors and pumps several times that amount in euros into the local economy.

Religion

For over a thousand years, Catholicism has been an integral element of Spain's national identity. The Reconquest, the forced conversion and expulsion of Muslims and Jews, the Inquisition, the triumph of Christianity throughout the New World, and the enforcement of the faith as state religion under Franco's dictatorship have made the terms "Spaniard" and "Catholic" nearly inseparable. You'll still see crosses hanging on the walls in bakeries and shrines to the Virgin set up in cobbled alleyways, but the truth is, Catholicism today is less a spiritual guide for living than a cultural marker of modern Spanish life.

JEWS IN SPAIN

Since the Catholic monarchs Isabel and Fernando expelled the Jews from Spain in the 14th and 15th centuries, Spain has upheld a tradition of exclusion to such an extent that even today, more than 500 years later, many Spaniards have never even met a Jew. The absence of Jews becomes obvious if you look at the menu at any Spanish restaurant: heavy on the ham, light on the bagels and lox.

Spain wasn't always so unfriendly towards Jews. Once upon a medieval time, Jews were prominent and prosperous on the Iberian peninsula. They held official posts, served in the military, and worked as artisans, doctors, and philosophers. All that remains today of their great legacy are a few old Jewish neighborhoods known as *juderías* (Sevilla, Toledo, Girona, and Barcelona are home to some of the most atmospheric of these) as well as a few synagogues which have long been transformed into Catholic churches.

Jewish history in Spain began long ago, some sources tracing it to before the birth of Christ. The most significant period of time for *Sefarad* (Spanish Jews) was under Moorish rule during the Golden Age (711-1100s). In 711, Jews aided Moorish invaders in wresting control of Spain from the oppressive Christian Visigoths who had been ruling the country for several hundred years. The change in rulers ushered in an era of relative peace for the Sefarad. Jews from other areas such as the Middle East joined those in Iberia, which had become somewhat of a promised land. For the next few centuries, Jews, Moors, and Christians lived together in harmony. The three diverse cultures flourished side-by-side and members of each faith rose through the ranks of society. Toledo was one of the most notable examples of a town enriched by this Middle Ages multiculturalism.

As the Christian forces began to assume power throughout Spain, a wave of anti-Jewish sentiment took root. In towns where Jews and Christians had once lived peaceably together intoler-

Baptisms, first communions, and weddings are traditionally held in the Catholic Church, but the ceremonial aspect pales beside the boisterous after-parties. Even at baptisms, Spaniards are apt to eat, drink, and dance into the wee hours. And almost every fiesta is a celebration of a religious event: the bonfires and fireworks of Las Fallas in Valencia honor Saint Joseph; the daring and debauchery of Pamplona's bull runs are dedicated to Saint Fermín; the solemn, drum-beating processions of Semana Santa (Easter Week) act both as a social event and a public demonstration of faith; and local festivities—every town in Spain has its own official fiesta marked by fun fair attractions, costuming, music, drinking, bullfights, and dancing in the streets—are normally celebrated on the feast day of the local patron saint. Spain enjoys

ance arose. Things came to a very bloody head in 1391 when a series of pogroms were carried out on Jewish communities in Sevilla, Barcelona, Valencia, and Córdoba. Thousands of Jews were killed and synagogues were destroyed. One reaction to this violent intolerance was the massive conversion of Jews to Christianity. From the 15th century on, a new social group of *conversos*, or newly converted Christians, began to rise through the ranks of Spanish society, obtaining powerful positions – often by becoming very vocal, and very severe, detractors of Judaism.

In 1478, Isabel and Fernando instituted the infamous Spanish Inquisition with the goal of spreading and maintaining Catholic orthodoxy throughout their kingdoms. Jews, Muslims, and *conversos* were frequent targets of Inquisition courts and were often killed during the course of their trials. With the 1492 fall of La Alhambra, the last Moorish stronghold on the peninsula, the Christians rose to absolute power with a vengeance. That same year, Jews were given an ultimatum – convert or get out. They were allowed to take their personal possessions, but land, houses, gold, and silver were to remain with the Spanish state. An estimated 200,000 Jews were driven out of the country by this edict. Those who remained attempted to integrate into Catholic Spanish society but it was difficult. They suffered discrimination and were continually under threat of the Inquisition's tribunals.

The Inquisition was not abolished until 1834 and the edict of expulsion wasn't officially repealed until 1968, however by the mid-1800s, Jews had begun to trickle back into Spain. Today, Jews are still a very small fraction of the population – an estimated 40,000 Spaniards identify as Jewish. However, Sefarad culture is being revived. Many of the old *juderías* and synagogues throughout Spain have been reopened and serve as cultural centers, museums, and once again, houses of worship. In December of 2008, Madrid held a public Festival of Lights in celebration of Hanukkah for the first time.

several national holidays thanks to Catholic events, Epiphany (January 6), Holy Thursday and Good Friday, the Assumption of the Virgin (August 15), All Saints' Day (November 1), and the Immaculate Conception (December 8), as well as Christmas day. Rather than run off to church, Spaniards are more apt to run off for a minivacation for the *puente* (long weekend) created by these holidays.

It may not come as a surprise then that the Catholic faith in Spain is experiencing a steady decline. A December 2008 survey by the Spanish Center for Sociological Research (CIS) found that 76 percent of people polled identified themselves as Catholic, but over 50 percent admitted they never went to church. Just 14 percent said they attended most Sundays. In addition, 11 percent identified themselves as agnostics, 6 percent as atheists, and approximately 2 percent were of other faiths. The Church is also losing ground in the Spanish school system, where religious classes are offered throughout primary and secondary school. Over the past decade, the number of students enrolled in these optional Catholic classes has slowly declined, especially among older students with less than half of secondary and upper high school students enrolling in religion classes.

In addition to Catholicism, many other faiths are also practiced on Spanish soil, thanks in part to the

© BEA MORA

a Catholic nook on a street in Andalucía

upswing in immigration in recent years. Christian faiths number an estimated 400,000 practitioners, including evangelical Christians, many of them of African and Latin American origin, and Protestants, chiefly the British and Northern European communities. The Muslim community is estimated at more than a million and the Jewish population is near 40,000. There are also communities of Buddhists, Mormons, and Jehovah's Witnesses—don't be surprised if a bright-faced *hermano* (brother) comes knocking at your door.

The Arts

Spain has one of the richest artistic legacies in the world. Consider the melting candle wax towers of Gaudí, the thousand-year-old red-and-white marble arches of Córdoba's Mezquita, the crazy cubed faces of Picasso, the world famous wanderings of *Don Quixote*. The country is awash in jaw-dropping cathedrals and rambling Roman aqueducts, thousands of museums house paintings from the medieval to the ultramodern, and celebrated odes of love and heroics line the country's *bibliotecas* (libraries). For as long as Iberia has existed, its people have been writing, painting, sculpting, and building—an abundance of artistic expression that has earned Spain 29 UNESCO World Heritage designations for cultural heritage.

LITERATURE

Spanish literature tells the intricate story of Spain from ancient, bloody wars fought over land and power to modern-day satires of popular, urban culture. Academics have long squabbled over a starting point to Spain's literary timeline. In order to find common ground, they have often looked to the beginning of Spanish—the very language itself. It's largely thanks to the efforts of Alfonso X, "the Wise," the king of Castile and León (1252–1284), that Castilian emerged as the dominant tongue of Spain. He advocated the use of Castilian Spanish as a written language for fiction, philosophy, and history. Among the important works that emerged during and in the wake of Alfonso X's reign, *El Cantar del Mío Cid* is the most famous. The poem tells the story of Rodrigo Díaz de Vivar, a national Spanish hero and soldier-for-hire. El Cid, as he is known, went on to capture Valencia for the Christians. While the epic poem first appeared in 1140, it is a version from 1307 written in troubadour verse that remains best known.

Of all the periods in Spanish arts, the Siglo de Oro has won the most acclaim—and justly so. From the 15th to 17th centuries, this Golden Age saw the flowering of drama, the picaresque novel, and Catholic mystic poetry. The era's most popular poets were considerably less than spiritual. Francisco de Quevedo (1580–1645) is known for his use of *conceptismo,* a writing style of sharp, pointed language, witty metaphors, and double meanings. It is rhythmic and amusing, and made Quevedo quite the man about Madrid. He produced a vast body of poetry that criticized the hypocrisy and greed rife in Spanish society including powerful entities like the Inquisition. However, his most venomous work was often aimed at his arch-rival Luis de Góngora (1561–1627). Góngora was Quevedo's greatest rival and made his name in a style of poetry known as *culteranismo,* a complex style laden with convoluted metaphors, ornate language, and obscure vocabulary. Where Quevedo's verse was terse, Góngora's was dense. Though he died in poverty, he was so well-regarded that his style came to be known as *gongorismo.* Both men remain among the most important figures in Spanish letters today.

During the 17th century, several theaters opened, inciting a flurry of playwrights eager to fill the freshly built stages with their works. Many plays of the age earned lasting critical praise—especially those by Lope de Vega, Lope de Rueda, and Tirso de Molina, whose play *El Burlador de Sevilla* is the origin of Don Juan, literature's most notorious playboy. However, the Golden Age's undisputed poster boy is Miguel de Cervantes (1547–1616). His name is practically synonymous with Spain itself and his opus *Don Quixote,* is one of

PARTY THROUGH THE YEAR

If you think people are exaggerating when they say that Spaniards really know how to party, just check out the country's calendar – it's more loaded with events than the king's PalmPilot. Whichever month you choose to visit Spain, you'll be able to catch some sort of festival and you should take advantage of those occasions – to see Spain in the midst of fiesta is to see the country in its prime. Whether the festivities are religious, centered on the arts, or just an excuse to eat, drink, and dance in the streets, you'll find a riotous good time. Here's one kick-up for every month of the year.

January: Stately San Sebastián gets loud and crazy the third week of January when the annual **Tamborrada** rolls around. At midnight on the 19th, thousands of uniformed drummers take to the streets of the Parte Vieja and begin beating their drums as they parade around. They keep it up for 24 hours, with only a short break around dawn for a brandy breakfast. It is said the tradition started centuries ago when a chef went to draw water from the town well. He began to sing and soon, others in line to draw water began to accompany him by beating their pots. Today, the different drumming groups are made up from various gastronomic societies which accounts for the various chefs you'll see in the processions.

February: New Orleans, Rio de Janeiro, and Trinidad are world famous for their Carnivals. True hedonists know to add Cádiz to the list. This tiny 3,000-year-old town puts on a carnival party to rival any in the world and was the only Spanish city that blatantly ignored Franco's ban on Carnival. The 10-day **Carnaval** rocks Cádiz with equal amounts of pageantry and debauchery. Music is a big focus of the festivities, and various *chirigotas* (costumed choruses) show off their singing with hilarious tunes that poke fun at the government, famous personalities, and current events. However, you'd be forgiven if you mistook the festival for a drinking competition.

March: There's just one place to be between March 15-19 – Valencia for **Las Fallas.** Although the towering papier-mâché puppets that were artfully created over the course of the year take center stage, the crowds are equally enamored with firecrackers, giant pans of paella, costumed parades, and flowing *agua de Valencia* (mimosas made with Valencian orange juice). If you can make it for just one day, make it the last one – that's when the puppets are set on fire in a monumental display that attracts thousands of revelers.

April: After Sevilla finishes with Semana Santa, the holy week processions, it's time let loose in festivity. **Feria de Abril** is a weeklong celebration that takes in a mock village of massive *casetas* (tents). Expect prancing horses, *señoritas* in flouncy dresses, free-flowing sherry, and dancing until daybreak.

May: A meander through the maze of cobbled streets in any Andalusian town allows brief glimpses of lush gardens hidden behind locked doors. The citizens of Córdoba swing open the wrought-iron gates for the annual **Patio Festival,** revealing tiny whitewashed patios in spectacular full bloom. Bougainvillea, jasmine, lemon and orange trees, rosemary, honeysuckle – the smells are as heady as the colors are intense. General appreciation is welcome, but the real goal for the patio owners is winning a prize in the **Concurso de Patios Cordobéses.**

June: Alicante may be a small city, but there's nothing petite about the bash it throws every summer. Much like Valencia's Las Fallas, Alicante's **Hogueras de San Juan** is centered around a ritual burning of gigantic, papier-mâché puppets. There are also fireworks, open-air bars, music, and partying on the beach every night until dawn.

July: Every July, the world converges upon Pamplona for the festival of **San Fermín.** Although similar events take place all over Spain throughout the year, thanks to Ernest Hemingway, the festival has been immortalized and "running with the bulls in Pamplona" has become a "rite of passage" for young men the world over (women are not allowed to run). It is seven days of nonstop fiesta as locals and visitors alike drink, dance, and drink some more. Bands wake the townspeople up before dawn, people begin tippling at breakfast, and the truly fearless (or arguably moronic) run with the bulls to the bullring.

August: For most of the year, Buñol doesn't have much going on, but come late August, about 30,000 visitors descend on the tiny town for **La Tomatina,** the world's largest food fight. The gala gets going early when truckloads of ripe, juicy tomatoes arrive, and everyone begins lobbing the pulpy fruit at each other (goggles are suggested – tomato juice in the eye stings!) About an hour later, the fire department drenches everyone with hoses, the city cleans itself up, and before long it is back to its sleepy little self.

September: Barcelona explodes during its four-day **La Mercè** "festival of festivals." In addition to the usual roster of Spanish fun – food

booths, dancing in the streets, parades, and fireworks, expect *correfocs,* fire-breathing dragons who wind their way through the very crowded streets armed with firecrackers, and *castellers,* human towers created by several layers of men standing on each others' shoulders. Once built, a boy – as young as five years old – clambers to the top.

October: Seafood lovers head to the small town of O Grove in Galicia for a seafood fest to end all fests. The 10-day **Festa do Marisco** celebrates the bounties of Galicia's *rías* (estuaries) with nonstop gorging on oysters, shrimp, prawns, scallops, crabs, octopus, and lots of spiny, prehistoric looking creatures you never knew tasted so good. It is all washed down by flowing rivers of Galician wine.

November: Madrid is the cultural center of Spain during the **Festival de Otoño** (Fall Festival) which runs mid-October to mid-November. This performing arts festival sponsors hundreds of performances in dance, music, theater, and circus, highlighting both Spanish and international performers.

December: The last month of the year means **Navidades** (Christmastime) throughout Spain. The Christmas season is celebrated with massive bazaars (Madrid's Plaza Mayor and Barcelona's Santa Llúcia markets are among the best), elaborate light displays, life-sized Nativity scenes (Spaniards form very long lines to see the best ones), the Christmas lottery (televised all day on the 22nd), and practical jokes (the 28th is Spain's version of April's Fools). Christmas Eve is spent with family enjoying a long, lavish meal, but after the last drop of *cava* is downed, younger family members pile out into the streets for all-night partying – the next day is a holiday after all!

the most important works in the history of fiction and has spawned a cultural legacy that has reached across centuries, cultures, and genres. Beyond *Quixote,* Cervantes was markedly prolific and wrote both novels and plays up until his death on April 23, 1616—the same day that Shakespeare died.

The literary movement known as the Generación del 1898 (Generation of 1898) emerged as Spain was in a period of decline—it lost all of its colonies following the disastrous Spanish-American War of 1898, the economy slumped, and political instability and societal unrest grew. This group of writers is exalted not just for the inherent value of its work but also for its determination to define Spanish identity in the midst of this chaos. Their work criticized Spanish politics and society of the time, advocated intellectualism, encouraged radicalism, and evoked imagery from a romanticized Spain of centuries past. The writers of this generation broke new ground in literature—Antonio Machado is oft referred to as the father of contemporary Spanish poetry and Miguel de Unamuno is regarded as the best of the Spanish existentialists.

Some thirty years later, the Generación del 27 made their contribution to Spain's literary legacy. This group of writers—including famed poet Federico García Lorca—created a new genre of Spanish letters that imbued traditional Spanish themes with an avant-garde sensibility. They were most prolific during the Second Republic, a time of great liberty and creative freedom in Spain. Beyond writing, other artists linked to the Generation of 27 include painter Pablo Picasso and filmmaker Luis Buñuel. However, the Spanish Civil War put a damper on their creative output. Lorca was executed early in the war and following the Nationalist's victory, Franco censored the arts harshly—many of the Generation of 27 artists went into exile. A notable exception is Vicente Aleixandre who remained in Spain and won the Nobel Prize for Literature in 1977.

It's impossible to emphasize how drastically literature changed after Franco's death in 1975. Suddenly, insufferable restraints were lifted and Spanish writers were free to express themselves however they chose. Contemporary authors—some critically acclaimed, others popularly adored—include Josefina Aldecoa, Juan Goytisolo, Elvira Lindo, Javier Marías, Rosa Montero, Arturo Pérez-Reverte, José Luis Sampedro, and Carlos Ruiz Zafón.

ART

Spain's artistic tradition began when prehistoric people rendered wild bison and boar on cave walls and the Altimara Caves in Cantabria are considered the "Sistine Chapel of Pre-Historic Art" for their wealth of 20,000 year old paintings. Fast forward several millennia and Spaniards were still painting on walls, this time in the Middle Ages. Spanish artists created beautiful frescoes on church walls. The Monastery of Pedralbes in Barcelona is home to some fine examples by Ferrer Bassá (1285–1348), a painter in King Alfonso IV of Aragón's court.

Spain's most applauded Renaissance artist, El Greco (1541–1614) (The Greek), was born in Crete but spent most of his life in Toledo, Spain. His majestic painting *El entierro del Conde de Orgaz* (The Burial of the Count of Orgaz) which hangs in the Iglesia de Santo Tomé in Toledo, is considered a Renaissance masterpiece.

Spain's Golden Era brought Diego de Velázquez (1599–1660)—one of the world's true masters—to fame in the royal court. He was just 24 when he became Felipe IV's court painter, a position he held until his death. His realistic portraits of kings and queens, servants and jesters, were enhanced by presenting their subjects seemingly distracted by some unseen influence. *Las Meninas* is a brilliant example and considered by many to be the most important painting in the world. It is the biggest draw at Madrid's Prado Museum.

A century later, it was Francisco Goya (1746–1828) who took the royal court by storm. He began his career as a cartoonist in the royal tapestry factory but the superiority of his work led him to the Spanish court where he eventually became the court painter for Carlos IV. However, his works ranged far beyond royal subject matter. His *La Maja Vestida* and *La Maja Desnuda*— nearly

© NIKKI WEINSTEIN

Modern architecture appears throughout the country, even at small seaside museums like this one in Galicia.

identical paintings, one of a woman dressed, another of her undressed—are among his most famous. He also depicted what he called the "foibles and follies" of Spanish society in a series of scathing etchings. As Spain descended into warfare, Goya chronicled history with *El dos de mayo* (second of May) and *El tres de mayo* (third of May) both depicting the 1808 invasion of Madrid by French troops. Late in life, his subject matter took a very dark turn and he produced the so-called Black Paintings, the most famous of which *Saturn devorando a su hijo* (Saturn Devouring His Son) hangs in the Prado.

A man from Málaga would take up Goya's role as Spain's most important painter. Pablo Picasso (1881–1973) began painting at a very early age, churning out semimasterpieces in his teens. He then went on to change art forever through the introduction of cubism. While his most famous work *Guernica*— a black-and-white masterpiece depicting the horrific bombing of a Basque village by Nazi fighter planes—stands in Madrid's Reina Sofía, the Museu Picasso in Barcelona and the Museo de Picasso in Málaga house the most extensive collections of his work in the world.

Picasso's contemporary, Joan Miró (1893–1983) is typically classified as a surrealist, but he loathed labels and instead produced art that was uniquely his own—part surrealist, part expressionist, part free drawing. Born in Barcelona, he lived and worked for most of his life in Palma de Mallorca. He produced paintings, sculptures, ceramic pieces, mosaics, and tapestries that combine bright colors and deceptively simple shapes to great effect.

The other great artist of this period was Salvador Dalí (1904–1989). The *maestro* of the surrealist movement, Dalí's vivid images warped the line between reality and dream. His 1931 work *La persistencia de la memoria* (The Persistence of Memory)—of the notorious melting clocks—is his most famous example. Dalí eventually split with the surrealists over politics but continued with his unique art style, expanding into sculpture, furniture, photography, and film.

Few contemporary Spanish artists can measure up to the standard set during the earlier part of the 20th century, but Antoni Tàpies (1923–present) comes very, very close. A prolific painter, sculptor, and mixed-media artist, Tàpies work evokes elements of surrealism, Dadaism, and expressionism, though he is generally considered a European abstract expressionist. Whatever the label, there is no question that he is the most important Spanish artist living today.

ARCHITECTURE

The dominant architectural styles throughout the country are Moorish (hailing from North Africa), Romanesque and Gothic (French imports), and Renaissance and Baroque (thank you, Italy) and over the centuries, several architectural hybrids have evolved that are distinctly Spanish. Exactly where you'll find each style hints at Spain's history. For example, Romanesque churches (8–13th century)—compact stone structures with minimalist angular lines and rounded apses—are mainly spread around Cataluña and along the Camino de Santiago and other early Christian enclaves such as Asturias and Zamora. Moorish structures (dating from the 8–15th century) characterized by their geometric designs, vividly colored tiles, rounded archways, and fine calligraphy etched in stucco walls are spread throughout Spain, but are most concentrated—and most spectacular—in

© CANDY LEE LABALLE

Frank Gehry's Guggenheim is one of Spain's most renowned buildings.

Andalucía. The Alhambra, Córdoba's Mezquita, and Sevilla's Alcazar are all masterpieces of the genre.

The Gothic (13–15th century) style took over Spanish church design with a spectacular vengeance. At once ornate and imposing, Gothic architecture utilized technical innovations that allowed Spanish churches to become bigger and better. With peaked arches, ribbed ceilings, and flying buttresses, these churches were built to last. The cathedrals of Burgos, León, and Toledo, all hailing from the 13th century, are prime examples.

One very distinctive result of cultural blending is *mudejár* (12–17th century), a Spanish architectural style that blended Gothic and Moorish aesthetics. At the time that many of Spain's most monumental works were being built, many of the country's best builders were Muslims. They added their distinctive Moorish flourishes—geometric designs, carved brickwork—to buildings commissioned by Christians. Aragón has an exemplary collection of such structures, of particular note the Cathedral of Teruel.

The Renaissance (15–16th century) hit with a chisel. Buildings were still constructed in heavy stone as in the Romanesque and Gothic periods, but they were ornamented with delicate detail and sculpture, most often around doorways and windows. The elaborate facades echoed the intricately detailed work of *plateros* (silversmiths) giving this new style the name Plateresque. The University of Salamanca is a spectacular example.

The Baroque style (17–18th century) with its dramatic use of light, opulent ornamentation, ceiling frescoes, and spacious circular naves arrived in Spain and took on the influence of the Churriguera family of architects. The resultant Churrigueresque style utilized elaborately carved facades full of over-the-top ornamentation. The Western facade of the Cathedral of Santiago and most of the old center of Salamanca are prime examples of this style.

Neoclassical (18–19th century) architecture provided restrained contrast to the exuberance of the Plateresque and Churrigueresque movements. Full of simple geometric shapes, blank walls, and tall columns, it was a favorite of Carlos III who gave Madrid a makeover with neoclassical structures including the Museo del Prado, the Plaza de Cibeles, and the monumental Palacio Real.

Modernisme (late 19–early 20th century) burst forth from Cataluña and caused the world to rethink all its assumptions about architecture. It was inspired by art nouveau—the eclectic, florid, nature-based architectural style that emanated from Paris. In Cataluña, it was adopted and morphed into surrealist reinterpretations of Gothic architecture. Important architects of this movement included Lluís Domènech i Montaner and Josep Puig i Cadafalch. However, it was Antoni Gaudí who became world famous for his radical, visionary works. Over the course of four decades, he erected ethereal buildings all over Cataluña and Spain. Of note are Barcelona's La Sagrada Família church and the hilltop hideaway of Parc Güell.

In the 21st century, Spain has continued to be an architectural hot spot, drawing top architects from around the world. Frank Gehry is at the top of this list and the titanium whimsy of his Guggenheim Museum in Bilbao and Marques de Riscal Winery in La Rioja have helped turn these two regions into international destinations. Frenchman Jean Nouvel built the Torre Agbar, a phallic-looking skyscraper covered in colorful LCD filaments

© CANDY LEE LABALLE

Gaudí's curve-crazy architecture is a common sight in Barcelona.

in Barcelona and the Museo Reina Sofía extension in Madrid, an imposing glass and steel structure topped by a colossal shiny red overhang. Also in Madrid, Barajas airport got a much-needed expansion when British architect Richard Rogers built Terminal 4, a massive structure made light with an undulating bamboo roof, natural lighting, and rows of canary yellow supports.

Not to be outdone, contemporary Spanish architects are very active too. Catalan Enric Ruiz Geli, Barcelona's EMBT Studio, and Mansilla+Tuñón Arquitectos are all destined to become architectural legends. Valencia native Santiago Calatrava already is. The award-winning architect has built impressive structures worldwide from the Milwaukee Art Museum to a train station in Zurich. However, the collection of his works standing in Valencia, including the La Ciutat, an arts and science complex, are some of the best examples of his dazzling, white, almost mechanical forms.

PLANNING YOUR FACT-FINDING TRIP

Before you make the trans-Atlantic leap to living in Spain, you'd best consider a visit so you can learn a little more about the country. A vacation certainly won't be like living in Spain but it's the closest you can get. The trick is to try and see beyond the *fiesta y siesta* culture and get a glimpse of day-to-day Spain. The itineraries below will give you the basics of some of the most interesting areas to live in Spain, but use them as a guide, not a path. Rather than rushing around with a "must-see" checklist gripped tightly in hand, slow down and follow the scent of garlic sizzling in olive oil to a tapas off the beaten path, seek out the source of the clackety-clack of flamenco you hear somewhere down the street, stay up later than you normally would wandering a maze of centuries-old streets by moonlight. Go, explore, and hopefully along the way, you'll find the Spain that will eventually become your home.

Preparing to Leave

Spain is an awfully big country and chances are you won't be able to cover all 194,607 square miles of it on your trip. Consider the time you do have and the areas you are most interested in to work out an itinerary. Madrid and Barcelona are natural starting points, but be sure to do some research to help plan your visit from there. Start looking through guidebooks, such as *Moon Handbooks Spain,* check the travel pages of major newspapers, and of course do online research. If you want to make it to a major festival such as Las Fallas in Valencia or the San Fermín (the running of the bulls) in Pamplona, plan your trip around those dates.

WHAT TO TAKE
Passports and Credit Cards
U.S. citizens do not need a visa to enter Spain for stays of up to 90 days. You will need your passport, a copy of your passport in case yours gets stolen or lost, and your state driver's license if you will be renting a car. An international driving permit will also be required by the rental agency. Get one cheaply and quickly at any stateside AAA office.

Of course, don't forget any credit cards/debit cards that you will use during your trip. Just be sure and call your bank to let them know that you will be making purchases in Spain—fraud prevention services often kick in when a card is suddenly used abroad. Also, be aware that Spanish law requires merchants, restaurants, and hotels to request I.D. when a credit card is used; your stateside driver's license is sufficient. You will not need to carry your passport, however, you should have a copy of it in your wallet just in case.

Medical Insurance and Prescriptions
Many U.S. medical policies cover emergencies in another country, call to confirm that yours does. You also might receive limited coverage if you pay for your airline ticket with a credit card. Even if you have some coverage from either your insurance policy or your credit card, travel insurance can be a big help, not only with health issues but also with lost luggage, delayed or canceled flights, and theft or loss. Numerous companies offer policies, and a travel agent can make a specific recommendation, however, be sure to read the fine print. Some companies leave you on your own when it comes to "dangerous activities," such as hiking and scuba diving. Others require you to pay upfront for medical services and then apply for a reimbursement once

you return home. At a minimum, be sure your policy covers ambulance service and emergency flights home.

If you take prescription drugs, be sure to bring enough to last the length of your trip. Have a copy of the prescription or a photocopy of the drug's label in case you need a refill; Spanish pharmacies will fill most prescriptions with the exception of narcotics. Also, you might check with a pharmacy about the cost of a refill whether you need it or not. Spain's drug costs are much lower than those in the United States, often even lower than your regular co-pay. Also note that travel to Spain does not require any special immunizations.

Clothing

When packing, try to stick to light, mix-and-match clothing that doesn't need ironing. Larger hotels will be able to offer you an iron, but smaller, cheaper places may not. Though Spaniards tend to be both more fashionable and formal than Americans, almost anything goes in terms of dress. In spring and fall, be prepared to layer with a few light sweaters and maybe a jacket. In summer, keep in mind that you will sweat a lot so you should have enough light shirts so that you can change a couple of times per day. Many religious monuments forbid sleeveless clothing, so be sure to carry a light sweater or shawl if you plan on visiting such places. And, do bring your own swimsuit; bathing wear is ridiculously overpriced in Spain. In winter, bring gloves, hat, and coat if you are going anywhere but the Mediterranean coast. If you will be going out to a nightclub, the same kind of club-wear you'd don in the U.S. is fine here. For upscale restaurants, bring upscale clothing—nice slacks and a collared shirt for men, a dressy outfit for women. Very few places will require men to wear a jacket and tie.

You will be walking a lot, so comfortable shoes are a must. However, you will need dressier footwear for nightclubs, high-end restaurants, and upscale cultural events. Keep in mind that Spain is a major producer of footwear, so you might want to have a little extra cash worked into your budget for a new pair or three. Items such as accessories, sunglasses, and jewelry are completely up to you and what you want to carry, though expensive items are best left at home.

Personal items should be kept to a minimum if you will be moving around a lot. The weight is not worth it. For women, you'll want your makeup and beauty items and any specific products for skin conditions. Anything else can be bought here, including shampoos, toothpaste, and other hygiene items, though nicer hotels will provide such toiletries. Sunscreens tend to be a bit more expensive in Spain, but they are readily available. If you really must bring a hair dryer, make sure it is small and adaptable to Spain's 220 voltage. Bigger hotels usually have a hairdryer in the bathroom. At smaller hotels, check with the front desk, they often have a *secador de pelo* on hand.

Electronics

If you bring rechargeable items such as digital cameras, video recorders, laptops, or cell phones, double-check to make sure the charger can handle 220 voltage and pick up a European plug converter. Spanish outlets feature two round holes about an inch apart. If you can't find one, don't worry, they cost less than €1 at any hardware or department store in Spain.

Currency

Spain is part of the European Union and adopted the euro in 2002. Euro bills come in 5, 10, 20, 50, 100, 200, and 500 euros; coins in 1, 2, 5, 10, 20 and 50 *céntimo,* as well in 1 and 2 euros. Be careful, a one euro coin may look like a quarter but it is worth six times as much!

You can buy euros from your bank in the states before leaving or at an exchange office, in the international terminal of most airports. However, the best rates for exchange are found at *cajero automáticos* (ATMs) which are plentiful throughout Spain. You'll pay a fee, of course, but it is often less than the commission charged at exchange offices and banks. Spanish ATMs will detect that your card is foreign and offer you the option of English for your transaction. If not, the two phrases you need to know are *sacar* (withdraw) and *cuenta corriente* (checking account). Practice the same precautions at Spanish ATMs as you would at home—try not to use the ATM while alone, cover the keypad as you punch in your PIN, and be very aware of anyone near you. If you have memorized your PIN by letters, learn the corresponding numbers before you leave home—ATMs in Spain almost never have the letters printed on them. Also before leaving, be sure to inform your bank's fraud department of your intention to use your card in Spain and while you are at it, check on your maximum withdrawal amount. Finally, have a backup card, traveler's checks, or U.S. dollars, in case your card is damaged, lost, or stolen.

Traveler's checks are on the verge of extinction, but are still accepted at banks and currency exchange offices (most restaurants, hotels, and shops will refuse them). To exchange traveler's checks for cash, you will need a valid passport. A commission fee is usually charged for the transaction and you often won't get the best exchange rates. However, traveler's checks do offer some security if they are lost or stolen. The most commonly accepted are those from American Express.

When traveling through Spain, you should always carry small bills and coins with you. Taxis are not obliged to accept anything over a 20 euro bill and often do not have change. Tip: At the airport, take out an amount of money not divisible by 50, for example, €120. That way you are sure to have a few 20 euro bills to get into town with. Metros and buses are easier to board using change, rather than bills and things such as luggage storage or soda machines often only take coins. Finally, smaller cafés, restaurants, and shops often only take *efectivo* (cash) and generally refuse to break large bills.

Security

Once you get your hands on euros, guard them closely. Petty theft is common throughout Spain and there is an entire class of thieves that makes its living off hapless tourists. Always keep in mind that thieves are waiting for the moment when you are distracted. At cafés, sitting on park benches, wandering museums, make sure that you are aware of your surroundings. Thieves often dress like tourists to get close to their victims—keep an eye on anyone nearby and a hand on your goods. And never, ever leave anything unattended, even for a second.

In general, women shouldn't toss their wallets into bags without zipped closures, and men shouldn't keep their wallets in their back pockets. If you carry a backpack, turn it around to your front when moving through crowds or on public transport. Bags with straps should be slung diagonally across your body. Money belts are a safe solution for carrying large bills and credit cards—just be sure to keep some smaller bills in your pocket for easy payments and always remove cash from your money belt in a private location such as a bathroom stall.

The best step for self-protection is to leave most of your valuables in your hotel room, so even if you do fall victim to a pickpocket you won't lose everything. However, the lower down on the price chain your hotel, the more chance for robbery by a hotel worker, and shamefully, hotel management almost never offers more than an apology. Use the room safe if available and if you have a laptop bag, put a lock on it.

If you are robbed, seek out the closest police officer or call tel. 90/210-2112 to make a report in English. It is unlikely that you will ever regain your belongings, but the police report can help if you have travel insurance. If your passport was among the items stolen, you'll have to report to your nearest embassy, and they will also ask for a police report. The American embassy in Spain is located in Madrid (C/Serrano, 75, tel. 91/587-2240, http://madrid. usembassy.gov). If credit cards were among your losses, contact the credit card company and/or your bank immediately.

Tipping

Tipping is not expected nor required in Spain. In restaurants and bars, a small service fee is usually including in the prices. Wait and bar staff are paid regular competitive wages and not reliant on tips—leaving a little extra is truly just a way to thank someone for good service. Tips are almost never left when you are served at a bar in a café. In restaurants, when you are served a seated meal, a tip up to 5 percent is common, though again, not required. Never tip in nightclubs or discos as it is not encouraged and will not lead to faster service nor bigger drinks. Rounding up to the nearest euro is recommended for taxi drivers, while hotel porters should get a euro for helping with luggage.

WHEN TO GO
Spring and Fall

Spring and fall are ideal times for almost every region of Spain. Temperatures are moderate throughout the country and on the Mediterranean coasts the waters are warm enough for swimming. Spring is particularly wonderful in both Madrid and Barcelona. After the gray days of winter, both cities burst into bloom. The cities get giddy as cafés put out their sidewalk tables, street musicians emerge with their accordions, and couples (young and old) take to kissing on sidewalk benches. In Galicia and along the Cantabrian coast into País Vasco, spring and fall will still be chilly and wet—have a jacket and umbrella on hand. While in Valencia and Andalucía, both seasons are still warm enough for seaside fun, without the heavy crush of summer heat and tourists.

Except in summer havens like the Islas Baleares, most everything in Spain will also be open in spring and fall, and prices will be down from their summertime highs. Of the two seasons, fall tends to be less busy as so many people are starting school and getting back to their daily post-summer lives. And fall has fewer festivals, while spring teems with them including Semana Santa throughout Andalucía, the Feria de Abril in Sevilla, Moros y Cristianos in Alicante and Valencia, and San Isidro in Madrid.

Winter

Winter offers cold temperatures, especially in the *meseta,* central plateau, where Madrid sits. In the mountainous regions, snow and ice are common while rain pummels the northern coasts. Meanwhile, the Mediterranean coasts and the Islas Baleares remain sunny, though the waters are too chilly for swimming and you'll need a sweater for the evenings. However, the cities make up for what the weather withholds. With fewer tourists, long lines are gone at museums and monuments, restaurants aren't crowded, hotels have more availability, and prices drop. Hotel rates can reduce by as much as third. The downside of this is that hours are often reduced in winter—check the opening and closing times before planning your day. In the Islas Baleares, many places shut down altogether in winter. Several of Spain's liveliest festivals are held in Winter—Carnival reaches riotous proportions in both Sitges and Cádiz and Las Fallas, the world famous papier-mâché torch takes place in Valencia.

Summer

Summer is a victim of its own beautiful excess. The Mediterranean and Atlantic beaches are simply sizzling and not just because of the temperatures. This is peak tourist season—prices are at their highest, rooms are at their scarcest, and sights, restaurants, bars, and clubs are packed every night of the week. If you want to visit the coasts during this time, book ahead and consider having your vacation in June or July. August is the traditional Spanish vacation month and entire inland villages seem to pack up and plop themselves at the beach. The Pyrenees and Picos de Europa are green and warm in summer, while the northern coasts are at their most inviting.

The least attractive of sights in summer are the cities. Madrid and Barcelona are positively seething with tourists, temperatures are viciously hot, and hotels are scarce (when you do book, make sure your room has air-conditioning). Andalusian cities are even worse. Come August, when the Spaniards head for vacations, these vibrant cities slow way down as stores, restaurants, and bars close up for the month. Of course, there are still places to shop, eat, and dance—just a lot fewer of them than usual. Still, summer brings with it Spain's best, or at least most notorious, festivals including San Fermín in Pamplona, Tomatina in Buñol, Valencia, La Merce in Barcelona, and the *verbenas* (street parties) of Madrid.

Arriving in Spain

The majority of flights to Spain from North America land at Madrid's Barajas airport while a few land in Barcelona. In either city, your first step will be to clear customs which, in most cases, simply means that an official flips through your passport and stamps it. Once you've collected your bags and entered the main terminal, you are just a subway, bus, train, or cab ride away from your Spain fact-finding mission.

CUSTOMS AND IMMIGRATION

Chances are you won't have to open your suitcases when you go through customs but the Spanish *aduana* do have the right to stop anyone and they seem to choose at random. Limitations on what you can bring into Spain are on par with U.S. restrictions: duty-free goods such as liquor, wine, tobacco, and perfume are restricted and other goods such as meat and dairy products are banned. If you are a smoker, save your cigarette purchases until you arrive in Spain—tobacco is considerably cheaper than in the U.S. You can bring new merchandise into Spain for personal use or for gifts—but keep your limits down. Customs can label bulk items as intended for commercial use and levy a hefty fine.

PUBLIC TRANSPORTATION

Most of the country's airports are connected to a metro (subway) system, bus lines or trains that run to the city center. If there's a metro station connected to the airport as is the case with Madrid, just follow the signs and once you reach the station you can buy a ticket from the booth and get a free *mapa de Metro*. Barcelona has a commuter train, run by the national train service, RENFE, departing the airport every half-hour, but it is a very long walk from the terminal. A better bet is the Aero Bus which leaves the airport every 12 minutes heading towards the city center.

Taxis to and from the airport tend to ratchet up the highest fares but after a long international flight, you might prefer comfort over cost. Outside every airport you'll see a clearly marked taxi stand. Don't expect your driver to speak English, so if you don't speak Spanish, have your address written down so the driver can read it. Prices are clearly labeled in Spanish and English inside every taxi and fares must be kept on the meter. Again, be sure to have bills of €20 or smaller as *taxistas* are not obliged to break anything bigger.

Accommodations

Hostales are small, locally owned and operated, motel-style accommodations and can be anything from dingy to delightful. *Fondas* are similar properties, but tend to have less frills. *Pensiones* are a step up from both and typically have a restaurant or small dining room. All three cost considerably less than conventional hotels (€25–80, depending on the location and type of room).

© CANDY LEE LABALLE

A *hostal* is Spain's version of the motel.

Backpackers can unfurl their sleeping sacks at *albergues juveniles* (youth/backpacker hostels) throughout Spain. Though aimed at the under-26 crowd, most do not have an age policy. Expect bunk beds, shared baths, a common kitchen/living space, no privacy, and prices less than €20 per person. Tip: If you are a couple traveling together, it may cost the same or even less to rent a double room in a *hostal*.

Properties with hotel in the title always feature private rooms with bath and are rated 1–5 stars, with corresponding increases in prices and amenities. Upscale Spanish hotel chains include **Abba** (www.abbahoteles.com), **AC** (www.ac-hotels.com), **Husa** (www.husa.es), **NH** (www.nh-hotels.com), and **Sol Meliá** (www.solmelia.com). Spain has very recently undergone a boom in boutique hotels; find good listings at www.notodohotels.com (Spanish only) and www.rusticae.es.

For a truly only-in-Spain experience, book a night or two at a **parador** (www.parador.es). These state-run luxury hotels are built inside medieval castles, monasteries, and other centuries-old buildings (there is one located in the Alhambra in Granada!). A double runs around €130. Finally, a *casa rural* is a family-operated country home. They range from free-standing houses with no amenities to small B&B-type properties with home-cooked meals. Found in smaller Spanish towns and throughout the countryside, they start at about €45 for a double and can be booked through websites such as www.toprural.com.

During the off-season, it is not necessary to book ahead. However, when tourism picks up, it can be extremely difficult to find last-minute lodging.

In general, high season is July, August, and Easter week; off-season is everything else, however many towns have festivals and events that qualify as high-season sprinkled throughout the year, so be sure and do your research ahead of time to ensure that you have a room. When booking, note that a *habitación sencilla* is a single room and a *habitación doble* is a double, and be sure to ask for *cama matrimonia* (a double bed) if you want one large bed as opposed to two singles.

Food

Tapas

Tapas are Spain's most famous culinary creation and the sooner you learn a few "tapas tips," the sooner you'll be *tapeando* like a local. In Madrid and much of the center of the country, a small tapa is served with your drink for free. It can simply be a bowl of potato chips or maybe a small portion of a pork stew the chef prepared that day. In Andalucía, free tapas are larger in size, but slightly higher drink prices reflect that. In most other places in the country, tapas cost €1–5.

Tapas are often advertised on menus by size. A *ración* is big enough to share between two or three people. If you are dining alone, ask for a *media-ración* which is half-sized. A *pincho* is bite-sized, often served with a toothpick. In the País Vasco, they are called *pintxos* and have been elevated to an art form with bar after bar specializing in these tiny treats. *Montaditos* are small rolls stuffed with anything from chorizo to tortilla. *Tostas* are tapas served on top a thick slice of rustic bread.

Tapas readily available throughout the country include *tortilla española* (potato and egg omelet), *croquetas* (croquettes made with béchamel and bits of ham), *patatas bravas* (fried potatoes with a spicy tomato sauce), *patatas ali-oli* (cold potato salad with garlicky mayonnaise), *pimientos de Padrón* (bite-sized green peppers fried in olive oil and salted—some very hot), *gambas al ajillo* (shrimp sizzling in olive oil and garlic), and *boquerones* (fresh, white anchovies marinated with garlic). And of course, don't forget Spain's beloved *jamón*—cured ham made from Iberian black pigs. Almost every tapas bar in the country will have at least one leg of *jamón*, hoof and all, hanging over the bar.

Regional Specialities

On the heartier side, Spain's cuisine is well-defined by the saying *la geografía manda* (geography dictates), as each region offers up dishes based on local ingredients. Valencia and Murcia are known for their vast rice paddies, produce, game, and seafood—all of which come together deliciously in Spain's most famous dish—paella. Cataluña, wedged between the Mediterranean, the Pyrenees, and France, brings each of these regions to the table in unique combinations of land and sea such as *andonguilles amb sepia* (meatballs with squid) or *conill amb cargol* (rabbit with snails). País Vasco with its ample coastline does wonders with fish, especially the classic *bacalao al pil-pil* (cod cooked in olive oil and garlic over a low fire); the name comes from the popping sound the fish makes as it cooks. Andalucía responds with *pescaíto frito* (a mixed platter of seafood dusted with flour and fried lightly in olive oil).

The central plateau area of Spain, where Madrid is located, specializes in oven-roasted meats and stews—*cochinillo asado* (roasted suckling pig), so tender it can be cut with the blunt edge of a plate, is nearly mythical. And of course, even non-foodies know that Spain is home to culinary madman Ferran Adrià of the world-famous El Bulli. Madrid, Barcelona, and above all, San Sebastian, are home to Michelin-starred eateries and award-winning *pintxo* bars.

Spanish Dining Times

You'll never fit in at the table if you don't set your hunger clock to Spanish dining times. Breakfast is a light meal consisting of coffee, juice, and a

Legs of *jamón* (ham), Spain's most revered delicacy, are sold throughout the country.

pastry and can be readily had up until noon. If you really must have your eggs and bacon, look for an Irish bar or the restaurant chain Vips. Lunch is a lingering three-course meal consumed between 2 and 4 P.M. It is offered at most restaurants as a *menú del día,* a value-priced meal consisting of first, main, and dessert courses with drink. This is a great way to sample the fare of a restaurant that might normally be out of your budget. Dinner starts no sooner than 9 P.M. and could be a sit-down meal or a selection of shared tapas. In both cases, don't expect to finish up before midnight if dining with friends. It is tough to get fed outside of these hours, though most cafés will have *tortilla* on offer throughout the day. However, if you are planning on living here, you should get used to the dining hours early on—unless you choose to share your meals with lonely waiters and misinformed early-dining tourists.

Sample Itineraries

If you have a good idea of where you want to settle in Spain, head straight there on your fact-finding trip. If not, start with the cities of Madrid, Barcelona, Sevilla, San Sebastian and/or Valencia to get a feel for the country's diverse urban offerings and to serve as a base for side trips.

ONE WEEK

If you have just one week, it's best to enjoy your time in a few places rather than wasting it in transit. After landing in **Madrid,** spend two days taking in the sights including the "Golden Triangle" of art museums: the Museo del Prado, the Thyssen-Bornemisza, and the Reina Sofía. Don't miss the regal 15th century Plaza Mayor where bullfights, coronations, and executions used to occur, the opulent Palacio Real, Europe's largest palace, and the Gran Vía, one of Spain's most bustling streets. Get a feel for the buzz of the city, away from the monuments, by taking Bus 27 from the Prado, up the lovely Castellana boulevard. The bus cuts through the heart of the city, giving you a glimpse most tourists never see. In the evening, take a tapas-tour through the twisting medieval streets of La Latina or head out in search of *la marcha* (partying) in the bars lining the 16th century Barrio de las Letras.

On the third day take the 35-minute train ride to **Toledo,** one of Spain's true gems. At its medieval height, Toledo was home to three cultures—Christian, Muslim, and Jewish—who lived side by side, imprinting the town with their individual art and architecture. Two thousand years later, their remains, including churches, synagogues, and medieval buildings, have turned Toledo into a living museum.

The next morning take the high-speed AVE train to **Barcelona,** one of the world's most mythical cities. Spend the first day wandering the medieval streets of El Born and Barri Gòtic—don't miss the Museu Picasso, a mesmerizing collection of the artist's work, and the Museu d'Història de la Ciutat, chronicling the city's 2,000-year-old history starting from the Roman ruins upon which the museum is built. Have lunch at a lively stall in the bustling La Boqueria food market and book dinner at one of the city's temples of haute Catalan cuisine. The next day, think Gaudí and head for La Pedrera, La Sagrada Família, and Parc Güell. Definitely plan a detour to the neighborhood of Gràcia, a traditional working-class barrio that draws many expat residents. Plan your evening along the beachfront in the funky Barceloneta or in the upscale Port Olímpic. The day before you leave, consider a day trip to the lively beach town of **Sitges** or the dramatic mountain refuge of **Montserrat.**

TWO WEEKS

With two weeks, you can add **Andalucía** and **Valencia** to your itinerary. Fly into Madrid and spend three days as above. On the fourth day, take the early morning high-speed AVE train to **Sevilla** where you can spend two days visiting the

Real Alcázar, the Cathedral, and La Giralda (if you are feeling feisty, climb the steps of this 12th century tower for a spectacular view over the city). At nightfall, head for dinner or tapas in the Barrio Santa Cruz, a magical maze of whitewashed walls draped in colorful bougainvillea. Don't miss an evening of flamenco in Triana, a barrio nicknamed "the cradle of flamenco."

Day six, take the AVE train to **Córdoba** to visit La Mezquita, an 8th century hallmark of Moorish culture. In Córdoba, tapas are a religion and you definitely want to spend the evening tapas-hopping with the locals. Day seven, catch

an ancient alleyway in Granada's Albaicín

the early morning train to **Granada** and your pre-booked reservation at the magical Moorish palace of Alhambra, one of the loveliest buildings in the world. At night, see a flamenco show at a cave in Sacromonte. The next day, get lost in the tangled streets of the ancient Albaicín. Unwind that afternoon with an Arabic bath at the atmospheric Gran Hamman before catching the overnight train to **Valencia.**

Start day nine in Valencia's Ciutat Vella, or "old city." Don't miss the Baroque Palacio del Marqués de Dos Aguas, the bustling food market El Mercat, the 15th century Lonja de la Seda, and the imposing Cathedral. By evening, head to the winding streets of El Carme, Valencia's medieval mecca of arty boutiques, creative cuisine, and bars, bars, bars. The next day, visit the Ciudad de las Artes y las Ciencias, an ultramodern, all-white clutch of cultural centers including a science center, a planetarium, an opera house, and Europe's largest aquarium. For lunch, try Valencia's most famous dish, paella, at a restaurant along the seashore. Be sure to save time for some relaxing on the beach. On day eleven, take the train to Barcelona and follow the one-week itinerary, before heading back via the high-speed AVE train to Madrid and your flight home.

ONE MONTH

Now this is the way to see Spain! With a month, you can enjoy the best of this diverse land while having plenty of time for side trips to places off-the-beaten path. Follow the two-week itinerary, adding a day or two to Madrid to see the nearby town of **Segovia** with its Roman aqueduct, medieval fairy-tale castle, and clutch of 12th century Romanesque stone churches. Also add a couple of days to Barcelona to explore barrios such as bohemian El Raval or the elegant Montjuïc, home to the Fundació Joan Miró and some amazing views over the city.

In Andalucía, consider adding a few side trips. **Ronda,** a picturesque white-washed town, sits high above a dramatic gorge and offers spectacular views, an atmospheric Moorish quarter, and the oldest bullring in Spain. **Mojácar** wraps itself around a hilltop high above the Mediterranean, offering a labyrinth of flower-filled streets, tiny tapas bars, and art galleries while the nearby beaches of Cabo de Gata offer some of Spain's most pristine landscapes. From Valencia, it is a quick flight over to the **Islas Baleares,** a quartet of glistening Mediterranean islands.

A month also allows you time to explore the culture and cuisine of País Vasco—the Basque Country. Start with the overnight train or a plane from

© CANDY LEE LABALLE

the boardwalk along La Concha beach in San Sebastián

Barcelona to San Sebastián. With its belle epoque mansions, crescent-shaped La Concha beach, elegant seafront boardwalk, and historic medieval quarter, San Sebastián is a delight for the senses. Add the gastronomic pleasures of its *pintxo* bars and multiple Michelin-starred restaurants and you might not want to leave. Be sure to take a detour to nearby Hondarribia, tucked above a colorful fishing port close to the French border. In this charming medieval town, you can dine on exquisite sea-fresh fish and spend the night in a 10th century palace that once hosted the Columbus-sponsoring royals, Isabel and Fernando. Your final destination is **Bilbao,** home to the titanium delirium that is the Frank Gehry–designed Museo Guggenheim. Don't miss the bustling Mercado de la Ribera, a stroll along the River Nervión, and a visit to the *pintxo* bars in the medieval quarter of the Siete Calles.

With a few days left, consider taking an inexpensive national flight to **Santiago de Compostela,** the capital of the rugged region of Galicia. While not the largest nor most dramatic of Spain's many cathedrals, Santiago's cathedral—the destination of millions of pilgrims for thousands of years—is surely the most mythical. By evening dine on Galician delights like *pulpo* (boiled octopus with paprika), *empanada gallega* (a seafood and tomato pie), and *tarta de Santiago* (almond cake).

Practicalities

Here are some tried-and-true choices for sleeping and eating well throughout Spain. It's a good idea to book ahead year-round as local fiestas and international conferences keep hotels throughout Spain pretty busy. If you are traveling in summer, be sure the hotel you choose has air-conditioning. And if you are not fond of climbing stairs, confirm that there is an elevator. Finally, if you are driving, check to see if the hotel has parking. If not, inquire about the nearest *aparcamiento,* and expect to pay between €10 and €25 per day. Accommodations prices listed are for doubles in mid-season. Restaurant prices are per person for a meal plus drink. Expect prices to fluctuate based on season.

MADRID

Madrid's native cuisine doesn't extend much beyond *cocido madrileño* (a meaty broth thick with chick peas), however as the melting pot of Spain, the city teams with regional Spanish restaurants serving everything from Valencian paella to Asturian *fabada* (a bean and sausage stew). And, to the delight of the country's growing legion of hard-core foodies, Madrid chef's are getting bolder and brasher in the kitchen. The result is a reservations-required roster of Michelin-starred dining rooms and upscale eateries. Hotels in Madrid run the gamut from absolute dive to absolute luxury, but one thing they all share in common is the requirement to book ahead. Festivals, holidays, and year-round conferences means the more than 78,000 rooms in the capital fill up fast!

Accommodations

Proving that cheap can be chic, **Hostal Santa Isabel** (C/Santa Isabel, 15, tel. 91/528-0063, www.hostalsantaisabel.com, €50) is a budget traveler's dream; located very close to Atocha train station. A stone's throw from Madrid's most emblematic plaza, **Hotel Plaza Mayor** (C/Atocha, 2, tel. 91/360-0606, www.h-plazamayor.com, €80) offers cozy little rooms with free Wi-Fi, some with views over the ancient terra-cotta roofs of old Madrid. Sophisticated and serene, **Hotel Meninas** (C/Campomanes, 7, tel. 91/541-2805, www.hotelmeninas.es, €140) is a retreat of modern decor and boutique amenities around the corner from the Palacio Real. High tech meets old world in the five-star **Palacio del Retiro** (C/Alfonso XII, 14, tel. 91/523-7460, www.ac-hotels.com, €230), a gilded mansion turned glamorous hotel overlooking the Retiro Park.

Food

The boisterous **Taberna Maceira** (C/Jesús, 7, tel. 91/429-1584, €25) offers inexpensive Galician fare—steamed shellfish is recommended—on rough-hewn tables under verdant green walls. Galician white wines are served in traditional ceramic bowls. A second location is around the corner at C/Huertas, 66. Very popular with locals, **El Lacón** (C/Manuel Fernández y González, 8, tel. 91/429-6042, €18) offers tapas in the lively downstairs bar (your first one is free with your drink) and hearty Spanish fare in the dining rooms upstairs— try a *tabla,* a wooden platter piled high with grilled vegetables, steamed seafood, or savory sausages. Opened in 1725, **Sobrino del Botín** (C/Cuchilleros, 17, tel. 91/366-4217, www.botin.es, €40) is the world's oldest restaurant and a Madrid institution. The original stone oven has served *cochinillo* (roast suckling pigs) to everyone from Hapsburgs to Hemingway—the dish is featured as the last supper in *The Sun Also Rises.* **La Viridiana** (C/Juan de Mena, 14, tel. 91/531-1039, €100) figures high on the list of Madrid-bound foodies. Self-taught chef, owner, and gregarious guy Abraham García is nothing short of a genius, creating magical fusions of traditional Spanish cooking. And unlike in many haute houses, portions are big enough to satisfy. Wash it down with a *vino* from the list 23,000 bottles strong.

BARCELONA

Barcelona's chefs are known for both their commitment to Catalan traditions and their willingness to shatter them (Ferran Adrià hails from Cataluña). On the traditional side, expect *butifarra blanc* (a mild, white sausage), *escalivada* (grilled and marinated vegetables), *pa am tomàquet* (bread rubbed with tomato and garlic), *fideuà* (Catalan paella made with noodles), and *suquet* (fish and potato soup). On the cutting-edge side of the menu, Michelin-stars abound and truly anything goes—do some research on www.egullet.com to get the latest on the city's ever-evolving restaurant scene. Regarding hotels, try to keep

The ongoing construction site of La Sagrada Família is a must-see in Barcelona.

© CANDY LEE LABALLE

as close to the old center as possible if you plan on going out past midnight during the week, it can be impossible to catch a taxi after the metro closes.

Accommodations

For years, **El Jardí** (Pl. Sant Josep Oriol, 1, tel. 93/301-5900, www.hoteljardi-barcelona.com, €79) has consistently provided cheap but charming sleeps in the center of Barri Gòtic. If you can afford it, upgrade to a room with a terrace overlooking the gothic Santa María del Pi church. Just off Las Ramblas, **Barcelona Apartments** (Rambla Canaletes, 125, tel. 93/317-8356, www.bcn-accommodation.com, €90) offers a selection of simply furnished, but fully-equipped apartments for rent by the day. **Banys Oriental** (C/Argenteria, 37, tel. 93/268-8460, www.hotelbanysorientals.com, €100) offers a sophisticated retreat—modern decor, rustic wood floors, hushed service—in the heart of the buzzing El Born barrio. Located in Raval, **Casa Camper** (C/Elisabets, 11, tel. 93/342-6280, www.camper.es, €220) offers an ambience somewhere between Polynesian den and urban loft. The result is a very comfortable, very cool hotel. Perks include lush Camper-brand robes and slippers (no, you can't keep them!), Wi-Fi, and a commitment to environmental friendliness (shower water is recycled to run the sewage system and water the vertical garden).

Food

Located in Raval, **Mam i Teca** (C/Lluna, 4, tel. 93/441-3335, €20) is a haven of exquisite Catalan fare, including fresh tapas, hearty stews, grilled meats (the lamb chops with fresh mint are divine), and delicate sauces, excellent artisan cheeses and charcuterie are house specialties. The only drawback is its tiny size—the six tables go fast. **Bar Pintxo** (Mercat de la Boquería, €15), located in the midst of the market, has made culinary waves round the world. There is no menu and the waiter—often owner Joan Bayan himself—will ask you *"pescado o carne,"* "fish or meat." Either way, you can't go wrong. **Ateneu** (Plaça de Sant Miquel, 2, tel. 93/318-5238, €20), located in Barri Gòtic, offers creative takes on traditional Catalan cuisine—including lovely seafood dishes—at excellent prices. The austere dining room has long attracted Barcelona intellectuals. **Cinc Sentits** (C/Aribau, 58, tel. 93/323-9490, www.cincsentits.com, €90) lives up to its name in stimulating the five senses with imaginative, intriguing fare. Indulge yours with the tasting menu, and, do reserve ahead.

ANDALUCÍA

Andalucía is known for simple rustic food culled from both land and sea. Don't miss the local *jamón ibérico de bellota,* a silky cured ham that melts on the tongue, *mojama,* a chewy, flavorful air-dried tuna, or *pescaito frito,* a mixed plate of fish fried in olive oil. Especially in Córdoba, expect large, free tapas offered alongside your drink (this is one place in Spain, where a little tip at the bar is a good idea!). Wash it all down with a glass of world famous *jerez* (sherry). For accommodations, keep in mind that Andalucía is one of the most popular stops for tourists to Spain, so book early. Also, if you plan on staying in one of the old city centers, expect to lug your luggage a few blocks as there is rarely drive-up access for taxis.

© CANDY LEE LABALLE

A palm tree shades a street corner in Andalucía.

Accommodations

In Sevilla, the **Hotel Amadeus** (C/Farnesio, 6, tel. 95/450-1443, www.hotela-madeussevilla.com, €90) is a tiny gem located in the Barrio Santa Cruz. Located in an 18th century manor, it features colorful tiled walls and a rooftop terrace with great views over the old city. **La Casa del Maestro** (C/Niño Ricardo, 5, tel. 95/450-0007, www.lacasadelmaestro.com, €140) is located in the home of legendary flamenco guitarist and teacher, Niño Ricardo, and Andalucian themes dominate this boutique property—lots of blue and yellow tiles, guitar motifs, and bullfighting suits in niches along the stairs.

In Córdoba, **Hotel Mezquita** (Pl. Santa Catalina, 1, tel. 95/747-5585, www.hotelmezquita.com, €49) is a lovely family-run hotel in a pair of converted 16th century houses. Expect an atmospheric tiled courtyard, public spaces crammed with local art and antiques, and simple, comfortable rooms, some with a view over the Mezquita. **Hotel Maimónides** (C/Torrijos, 4, tel. 95/748-3803, www.hotelmaimonides.com, €125) takes its design cues from La Mezquita with a carved wood ceiling in the lobby and tiled arches throughout. The real deal is directly across the street, making this hotel's location one of the best in the city.

In Granada, the whimsical **Hostal La Ninfa** (Plaza Campo del Príncipe, s/n, tel. 95/822-7985, www.hostallaninfa.net, €65) offers simple but sweet rooms and a food lovers location on a plaza lined with tapas bars. In El Albaicín, **Casa Morisca** (C/Cuesta de la Victoria, 9, tel. 95/822-1100, www.hotelcasamorisca. com, €150) is a boutique hotel tucked into a spectacular Moorish building dating from the 15th century. You'll feel like you've landed back in medieval Granada—only with extra fine linens, air-conditioning, and Wi-Fi.

Food

In Sevilla, you can tapas-hop throughout Barrio Santa Cruz, but only in **Bar Giralda** (C/Mateos Gago, 1) can you do it on the grounds of a 10th century Arabic bath house. Also in Santa Cruz, **Corral del Agua** (Callejón del Agua, 6, tel. 95/442-0714, €35) offers classic Andalucian fare in an ancient building amid flickering candles, lush flowering plants, and trickling fountains.

Tapas bars abound in Córdoba, just follow the locals! For more substantial fare, **Casa Pepe de la Judería** (C/Romero, 1, tel. 95/720-0744, €35) located in a traditional Cordovan home, has offered delicious Sephardic (Spanish-Jewish) dishes—try *berenjena con miel* (eggplant with honey)—since 1928. **Bodegas Campos** (C/Los Lineros, 32, tel. 95/749-7500, www.bodegascampos. com, €40) occupies a clutch of old houses including an ancient bodega, and features a menu that offers updated Andalusian cuisine.

In Granada, **Mesón El Yunque** (Pl. San Miguel Bajo, 3, tel. 95/880-0090, €16) features inexpensive Andalusian food and a lively terrace on one of El Albaicín's most popular plazas. **Cunini** (Pl. Pescadería, 14, tel. 95/825-0777, €35) offers the most exquisite fish in town—appropriate as it is located on a square that translates to "fishmonger." Have a full meal in the dining room or graze on tasty tapas from the sea at the bar.

VALENCIA

Valencia is the home of Spain's most famous export—no, not Penelope Cruz—paella! And it would be shame if you didn't try this most Spanish of dishes here in its hometown. Your best bets are the many *arrocerías* (rice restaurants) along the beach. For dining variety, head to El Carme—especially Calle Roteros—and browse the menus in the windows. Regarding accommodations, you need to decide between city center or beachfront. Easily traversed by tram, bus, and inexpensive taxis, the distance between the two areas is not feasibly walkable. Both areas boast wonderful restaurants, but for shopping, tapas-hopping, and lively plazas, choose the city center. If your plan is sun, sand, and siesta, stick with the beach. If you want to attend Valencia's March madness, the Las Fallas festival, book at least six months ahead.

© CANDY LEE LABALLE

In Valencia, you must eat the paella.

Accommodations

Proving that cheap doesn't have to be, well, cheap, **Hostal Antigua Morel-lana** (C/En Bou, 2, tel. 96/391-5773, www.hostalam.com, €55) offers cozy, well-kept rooms very close to the central market. **Hotel Ingles** (C/Marqués de Dos Aguas, 6, tel. 96/351-6426, www.solmelia.com, €125), located next to the stunning Palacio de Marqués de Dos Aguas, has long been a Valencia favorite for classic style and attentive service. The award-winning **Palau de la Mar** (C/Navarro Reverter, 14, tel. 96/316-2884, www.hospes.es, €160) is a lush cosmopolitan refuge located within a stately 19th century mansion.

There are several midpriced lodgings on the beach, but the **Hostal El Globo** (Po. Neptuno, 42, tel. 96/372-7777, www.hostalelglobo.com, €80) consistently offers good value for money. Simple rooms are elevated to spectacular when you splurge on a sea view. **Las Arenas** (C/Eugenia Viñes, 22, tel. 96/312-0600, www.hotel-balneariolasarenas.com, €190) offers a resort-style hotel with panoramic sea views and all the amenities you'd expect from a five-star hotel.

Food

Casa Chimo (Po. Neptuno, 40, tel. 96/371-2048, closed Wed., €20) is a blue-and-white tiled paella house fronting Las Arenas beach. It is always packed with locals clamoring for its amazing rice dishes. In the city center, **Restaurante San Nicolas** (Pl. Horno de San Nicolas, 8, tel. 96/391-5984, €35) is a cozy family-run dining room known for its excellent paellas and fish dishes. **Ca Sento** (C/Méndez Núñez, 17, tel. 96/330-1775, €80) is an award-winning, family-owned establishment that takes fine fish and seafood dining seriously. Son Raul handles the creative dishes while mother Mari focuses on traditional rice dishes. Father Sento adds personality and charm to the classy dining room. Reservations are required. Tiled to the hilt, **Horchateria Santa Catalina** (Pl. Santa Catalina, 6, tel. 96/391-2379, www.horchateriasantacatalina.com, €5) has been serving *horchatas* (a milky drink made from tiger nuts) and pastries to Valencianos for nearly two centuries—truly a classic.

PAÍS VASCO

The refined flavors of Basque dishes—impeccable seafood, fresh vegetables, carefully rendered sauces—are as easy to come by in a corner dive as they are in a fine dining room. Both San Sebastián and Bilbao have plenty of both. You could easily spend all your time filling up on delectable bite-sized morsels at endless *pintxo* bars but if you have the cash, consider splashing out at a world-famous restaurant. Sleeping arrangements are easy to come by year-round, but you'll need reservations in summer, particularly in San Sebastián which converts into a resort town during the warm months.

Accommodations

In San Sebastián, **Pensión Itxasoa** (C/San Juan, 14, tel. 94/342-0132, www.pensionesconencanto.com, €63) offers five cozy rooms overlooking the bay. **Hotel Niza** (C/Zubieta, 56, tel. 94/342-6663, www.hotelniza.com, €120) offers lovely service, modern rooms, and a spectacular location right on the La Concha boardwalk. For a room facing the bay, book early. In Bilbao, **Bilbao Jardines** (C/Jardines, 9, tel. 94/479-4210, www.hotelbilbaojardines.com, €70) is two-star hotel with upscale aspirations. Rooms are minimal and spacious and the location, in the heart of the old center, can't be beat. Inspired by the Guggenheim, a spate of ultralux modern hotels have opened in the past few years. One of the best is the extravagant **Gran Domine** (C/Alameda Mazarredo, 61, tel. 94/425-3300, www.granhoteldominebilbao.com, €180) which features a 75-foot stone and glass sculpture towering in the atrium, spacious stone bathrooms in the ultramodern rooms, and spectacular views from the rooftop terrace where breakfast is served.

Food

In San Sebastián, the best *pintxo* bars are located in Parte Vieja and Gros. Always ask for the specialty of the house, and of course, do like the locals and keep moving—one bar, one pinxto, one drink, and go. Places not to miss include **La Cuchara de San Telmo** (C/31 de Agosto, 28), **Bar Txeptxa** (C/Pescadería, 5), and **Aloña Berri** (C/Bermingham, 24). For insight into how one of the world's top chefs, Martín Berasategui, got his start, try **Bodegón Alejandro** (C/Fermín Cabeltón, 4, tel. 94/342-7158, €45, reservations required), the traditional Basque restaurant owned by his family. The menu is always set for the day and may include scrambled eggs with cod and raisins, grilled turbot with spicy garlic sauce, or roasted pork in wine. There are several Michelin-starred restaurants in and around town, but **Arzak** (Alto de Miracruz, 21, tel. 94/327-8465, www.arzak.es, €120) has held their three stars the longest. Juan Mari Arzak and his daughter Elena oversee a research kitchen where their exquisite New Basque cuisine is constantly evolving. Reservations are essential and the tasting menu is recommended.

© CANDY LEE LABALLE

Pintxos are an art form in San Sebastián.

Bilbao's *pintxo* bars are concentrated in the Casco Viejo and in Abando especially along Calle Licenciado Poza. Don't miss **Zuga** (Pl. Nueva, 4), **Café Bar Bilbao** (Pl. Nueva, 6), and **El Globo** (C/Diputación, 8). **Café Iruña** (Jardines de Albia, s/n, tel. 94/423-7021) is a century-old restaurant decorated in Andalusian tiles and offering excellent Basque cuisine including a great value *menú del día* (three-course lunch). País Vasco is also famous for its cider houses and you can have an inexpensive, atmospheric cider-fueled meal at **Arriaga Asador** (C/Santa María, 13, tel. 94/416-5670, €25). Meanwhile, **Aizian** (Av. Lehendakari Leizaola, 29, tel. 94/428-0039, www.restaurante-aizian.com, €75) draws foodies from around the world to its striking wood-striped dining room for Michelin-starred, cutting-edge cuisine.

DAILY LIFE

MAKING THE MOVE

So you've visited Spain and fallen head over *pies* (feet) for the place. You've done your homework and know where you want live, boned up on your Spanish, maybe even made some Spanish contacts via the Internet. You are ready to go. Just one question nags—How? How do you move to Spain? Is it legal? What about visas—do you need one? If so, how do you get one? And what about all your stuff? What should you ship over? And how?

For a major move to another country, it is normal to have endless questions. Your first step is to do some research. This book is a great start, but don't neglect online resources, especially forums and blogs dedicated to living in Spain. With planning and patience, your move to Spain shouldn't be too difficult.

© CANDY LEE LABALLE

Visas

Your first step to getting permission to live, work, and/or study in Spain will be applying for a *visado* (visa). With the rare exception, you will have to do this in the United States, in person, at least a few months before you intend to arrive in Spain. You have to apply at the Spanish consulate with jurisdiction over your legal home address in the United States. There are Spanish consulates in Boston, Chicago, Houston, Los Angeles, Miami, New Orleans, New York, San Francisco, Puerto Rico, and Washington DC.

For most visas, you'll need to request an appointment at your local consulate, and bring the following with you: Two completed Application for Schengen Visa forms which can be downloaded from the website of Ministry of the Exterior (www.maec.es); a passport valid for the length of the visa you are seeking; proof of your U.S. address; four passport-sized photos; a medical certificate stating that you are in good health; and a clean police record from your home state for the last five years—this document must be sealed with the Apostille of Hague. You must also bring at least three photocopies of all of these documents. Show up without the copies and you may well be rescheduled for another appointment. Do not take the this information as the bottom line; confirm with your local consulate all the documents you will need as some consulates have slightly differing requirements.

TOURIST VISAS

U.S. citizens holding a passport valid for the next six months need not concern themselves with tourist visas at all—the stamp you receive in your passport upon entering the country *is* your tourist visa. Technically, upon entry you should also be in possession of a return ticket home—though that requirement is rarely enforced.

As Spain is a party to the Schengen Agreement, your tourist visa (and any visa, actually) is valid for all Schengen countries: Austria, Belgium, Bulgaria, Cyprus, Czech Republic, Denmark, Estonia, Finland, France, Germany, Greece, Hungary, Iceland, Italy, Latvia, Lithuania, Luxembourg, Malta, Netherlands, Norway, Poland, Portugal, Slovakia, Slovenia, Spain, and Sweden. This means you can travel freely among these nations for the duration of your tourist visa. But do not think that you can automatically renew your tourist visa by popping out of the Schengen countries, to say Morocco or England, and then popping back in with a new stamp. Your tourist visa is good for only 90 days in any Schengen country during a 180-day period. That means, three months in, three months out.

DOCUMENTS, SEALS, AND TRANSLATIONS – OH MY!

Oh the paperwork! Apostile, *empadronamiento, jurado* – what does it all mean? Here is an alphabetic rundown of some of the more common things you'll need for dealing with Spanish bureaucracy. You may not need all of them; you may need more than is listed here. Just remember the law of Spanish bureaucracy – whatever you don't have, you will need! Also, keep in mind that most of these documents will take time and money to receive, so start the process early. Then again, in many cases, the Spanish government will only accept documents that are less than 90 days old – so don't start the process *too* early.

Apostile of Hague: *The what of who?* Despite its lofty name, this is basically a stamp verifying that a document is legal and authentic. All countries that are party to the Hague Convention can use this process to verify the legality of documents that are shared between countries. Documents such as your birth certificate or police record may require the Apostile so that Spain will accept them as authentic. You cannot get this seal from the U.S. Embassy. It can only be issued by the Secretary of State of your home state and you must contact them for the correct procedures as it varies from state to state. And, yes, you will have to pay a fee; more for rush jobs.

Empadronamiento: One of the first Spanish words you should learn, this refers to being registered on the *padrón*

(city registrar) of your community. To *empadronarse,* visit the *ayuntamiento* (city or town hall) or a *junta de distrito* (neighborhood administrative office) to fill out the application and present your passport and proof of your address in Spain – deed to your home, rental lease, or other documents. If you are living with someone who is *empadronado* at that address, they may have to go with you. You do not need a visa or even be legal in Spain to *empadronarse.* You cannot be kicked out or penalized in any way as the *empadronamiento* is confidential. If you are legal in Spain, you need to be *empadronado* for everything from residency extensions to enrolling your children in school.

Medical Certificate: The *certificado médico* that you need for a visa is basically a letter from your doctor stating that you do not have any contagious diseases, drug addictions, or mental problems. The easiest way to get this is to write up the letter yourself – using the exact wording that the consulate requests – and then make an appointment with a clinic and ask them to do whatever tests they feel are necessary to rewrite and sign such a letter on their letterhead. Usually this consists of a blood test, a urine test, a physical exam, and a series of questions.

Photocopies: Okay, this is not exactly a document, but it bears repeating – bring triple copies of everything. You may end up throwing them out, but that is better than waiting two months for an appointment with the consulate, driving five hours, standing in line 45 minutes, and then being told that without copies they can't take your application. And no, you can't use their machine. And no, they don't know a nearby copy shop.

Police Record: The *certificado de antecedentes penales* is document showing you have a clean police record from the state police of your home state for the last five years. If you moved around in that time, you'll have to get a police record from each state where you lived. You'll have to contact your state police department directly to request it and it will normally come with a fee.

Translations: Wait, you weren't thinking that just getting the documents is enough, were you? *Jajaja* (That is hahaha in Spanish). Not only must they all be translated into Spanish, but they must be translated by a *traductor jurado*, an officially licensed translator, similar to a sworn translation. Of course not all documents will need translations but it is a good idea to determine which do at the beginning of the process. You can find a few licensed translators in the U.S., but their prices will be exorbitant. If you must get some documents translated before you leave the U.S., look for a *jurado* on the official list maintained at www. maec.es – you'll have to search to find it – and see what you can work out.

Living in Spain means *mucho* paperwork.

If you want to exceed your three-month limit, you must apply for a *próroga de estancia* (extension) prior to the expiration of your current tourist visa at the local *comisaría* (police station). But don't get too excited. This extension is generally limited to extraordinary cases which may include: emergency medical treatment, engagement (with actual wedding plans in Spain) to a legal resident of Spain, extension of research or studies, or humanitarian reasons. Each reason requires a specific application called a *modelo* and may require submission of any or all of the following: your passport, passport photos, proof of finances, and proof of medical insurance. While the application is being reviewed, you can legally stay in Spain—and as this could take months, you in essence get an extension while you are waiting for one. If approved, you can stay for the additional time granted (either 90 or 180 days). If denied, you'll be ordered to leave upon the expiration of your current visa, or within 72 hours if your visa is already expired.

STUDENT VISAS

Whether you are interested in a semester abroad, graduate study at a Spanish university, or a formal Spanish language course, if you want to study in Spain for longer than three months, you'll need a student visa. Be sure to start the process early. Because Spain is such a popular study-abroad locale, the processing time for the applications can take up to six weeks. There is no rush service, so don't ask. Spanish consular personnel are not known for their willingness to help and pushing them to hurry is likely to backfire. In addition to the above documents, you'll also need the official letter of acceptance from your place of study and proof of health insurance to cover you during your stay. You may also be required to show proof of financial means for the duration of your studies. The New York website lists this at $1,000 per month, but the amount could vary depending on the consulate. This can be waived if you have a letter from the school stating that all expenses and tuition have been previously paid.

Residency Visas and Work Permits

Many expats have compared the futility of applying for a residency visa for work to trying to bicycle to the moon. Sure, the process is rife with red tape, conflicting information, and a good dose of illogic, but the bottom line is, if you want to live here for the long-term, you'll have to confront the visa demon and find a way to make it work.

Before you begin, there's one important thing to know: you don't need a work visa exactly—permission to earn money in Spain is built into specific visas. That means that independent business owners must apply for one kind of residence visa that grants *permiso de trabajo* (permission to work), while those who will be employed by a company should apply for a different visa. Depending on your job offer (for example, permanent or temporary), your visa might have any number of time and geographical restrictions. And some jobs don't require a work permit at all—this type of residency is good for civil and military personnel employed by the Spanish government, accredited members of the foreign press, foreign teachers who have been offered positions at Spanish universities, and some missionaries are all free from the visa process. Your local consulate can evaluate if you qualify for this, as can the organization that is offering you work in Spain.

RESIDENCE VISA TO WORK AS AN EMPLOYEE

The first hurdle is getting a Spanish firm to hire you. The easiest route is to get hired by a multinational in the United States and then finagle a transfer to their Spanish offices. You can, of course, apply directly to Spanish firms in Spain, but remember by law they must first post the job with the *Instituto Nacional de Empleo* (National Employment Institute) or INEM, offering it to qualified Spaniards and EU nationals. This means you can forget about using your English ability as a way into a position as a bilingual sales person; Brits not only speak English too, but they have the legal EU rights to work in Spain.

A way around this is if the job has very specific requirements tailored to your skills. But, how do you find such specialized jobs? First, you need to find a firm that wants to hire you (or a friend with a business). They need to then ensure that the job description is tailored as much as possible to your background and to eliminate the possibility of any other applicants. Once the job has been posted for a few weeks with no qualified applicants, the business can request permission to hire someone from outside of the EU—ie, you. Marcus, a chef from New Orleans, was offered a job in Madrid as a Cajun chef—he

VISA SUCCESS STORIES

No doubt about it, it is tough for an American to get a working visa in Spain. A tight job market, mountains of paperwork, conflicting consulate directives, all lobbed on top of linguistic and cultural differences means that many earnest, job-seeking Americans end up never getting a visa at all. But, there are success stories too and they are as varied as the people who tell them. There is no one way to get a Spanish work visa but in the stories below you'll see some themes – a lot of pluck, a bit of luck, and the ability to build and work contacts.

Alana, from California, was working under the table as an English teacher at an academy in Salamanca. She built up a good relationship with them and when they had an opening for an international marketer for their Spanish language division, they offered her the job. They sponsored her work visa and she got her residency card. When she left that job, she hired a lawyer who helped her change her visa to self-employment, and now she works for herself as an *autónomo* English teacher.

Amanda was also working under the table as an English teacher and she also built up a good relationship with one of her employers. They eventually agreed to sponsor her for the visa – as long as she

handled all the legal fees and other expenses.

Christine, a talented investment banker from Florida, used her extensive contacts to find an opening with a top international bank in Spain. Her visa went through smoothly as her company used its own powerful contacts to make sure it did.

Jerry works for a major information technology firm in the U.S. When an opening for a long-term project in Spain came up, he jumped at it. The company sponsored his visa. His wife Sal joined him and lived here for years without papers. Eventually, she was able to apply for a visa through the *arraigo* program which allows residency if you can prove that you have roots in the country.

Jill had a student visa and began working part-time as an English teacher for a Madrid company. As the firm expanded, they wanted to retain her services and hired her as a full-time in-house English translator, sponsoring her visa.

Lorna arrived in Spain to do a masters in Spanish. She made many connections at her university and when her degree was finished, the director of the program offered her a full-time position with the school. That was 15 years ago and now she has Spanish citizenship.

Marcus, a chef from New Orleans, was looking for a way to stay

had no competition at INEM. Chris, a bass player from D.C., was hired at a local music school after the owner created a job for an English-speaking bass teacher with performance experience in the American jazz scene. One note, the job description should not require a degree. If it does, then you will have to present your degree validated by the Spanish authorities in a process called *homologación* (recognition). This is a very long, complex process with

in Spain legally. He contacted some top restaurants, built up a network, and finally found a restaurant willing to sponsor him as a Cajun chef in Spain – bam! – there was no competition among Spaniards or EU citizens for that position.

Maria was working for a major multinational computer manufacturer based in the U.S. When her husband got a job offer in Madrid, she contacted her HR department for a transfer. Fortunately, they had an office in Madrid and due to her high-performance with the company, they allowed her to transfer and also sponsored her visa. The company's international legal department handled all the details.

Michelle had made an impression on her Spanish host family when she did a summer abroad in Sevilla. Later when she wanted to return to Spain permanently, the father of her family, a prominent attorney, hired her as a bilingual intern in his firm, sponsoring her visa.

Peter, a former financial correspondent in Spain, used his contacts to land a PR position with a top Spanish bank. The bank handled all the paperwork.

Rebecca, a marine biologist from Miami, wanted to work in sea conservation and also live in Spain. Fluent in Spanish, she did her homework and found a European conservation group with offices in Madrid. She contacted them and after flying over for an interview, she landed a job as the shark specialist in Spain. The group hired a lawyer with major *enchufes* (contacts) in the Ministry of Exterior and her visa was approved in record time.

Scott had been working under the table as an English teacher for years with no chances of getting sponsored. One of his friends had a small company and agreed to "hire" him as a consultant, filing all the paperwork for his visa. Scott had to pay the legal fees.

Victoria was working in telecommunications in the U.S. and desperately wanted to return to Spain where she had spent time as an exchange student. Fluent in Spanish, she researched the top firms and spent a year faxing CVs and calling HR departments. Finally it paid off when one of the companies had an opening that required fluent English. It took over six months, but she eventually got her visa and her wish to return to Spain.

Wendy from New York took advantage of a layoff to follow a longtime dream of living in Madrid. On the way, she stopped off in Paris to visit a friend. The friend's husband liked her chutzpah and asked her to open a division of his small, but profitable company in Spain. She accepted, the firm hired a very posh lawyer, and within the year she had her visa and business cards identifying her as Director for Spain.

no guarantee of success and could result in your not being perfect for the job description created perfectly for you.

Another insider's move is to find someone to hire you for a job that is hard to fill. Each quarter, the Ministry of Labor publishes a list of such jobs by region, the *catálogo de ocupaciones de difícil cobertura* (find the most recent link with an online search engine). The 4th quarter list of 2008 was heavy on

You'll have to face a little bureaucracy in order to unlock the door to Spain.

sea-faring jobs, medical positions, and barbers, but it is worth taking a look at because the jobs on this list do not have to be posted with INEM; the employer can apply to hire you directly. Jeff, who had been teaching illegally for an academy in Valencia, was finally hired as a mechanic for the academy's small fleet of vans under this loophole.

No matter how you get your offer of work, the next step is for your would-be employer to apply for permission to hire you with the Ministerio de Trabajo (Ministry of Labor). They will be given an appointment in one to three months at which time they will have to submit a variety of documents including official job application and job offer forms, tax information on the company, certified copies of your passport valid for the duration of your job, and more. You do not need to be present at this appointment. Major multinationals will usually handle all of this with their in-house legal team. If the duty falls to you and you really want your best shot at approval (and avoid waiting hours and hours in various lines), then hire a lawyer or *gestor* (administrator) specialized in immigration, visas, and/or labor. However, some things are completely out of your hands, no matter how good your counsel. For example, the company offering you the work contract must be completely up-to-date on all their tax obligations. One Washington expat had everything in perfect order and was assured by her lawyer the visa would go through; unfortunately they didn't know that her would-be employer owed some overdue social security payments. Visa denied!

If all goes well, the processing time can take several months, possibly up to a year; you can either return home to the states to wait it out or remain in Spain if you still have time on your tourist visa. Use your wait time wisely to start gathering your visa documents—police record, medical certificate, etc. If the request is approved, a certified letter will be sent to your employer. This letter goes by many names depending on which consulate you ask, but in general it is a *certificado de resolución favorable* (certification of favorable resolution).

Once you have that letter, you have 30 days to apply for the visa. This means traveling to the Spanish consulate with jurisdiction for your home state and submitting all the documents listed above under *Visas* plus the original and copies of the approval letter. Once this is done, you wait. How long is up in the air. Some Americans have reported that with the certified letter, the visa has taken just a few days. Others report waits of several weeks, even months. As part of the process, some of the consulates will take your passport, therefore you cannot travel to Spain during this time. Patience young Spain-hopper; it will happen soon.

RESIDENCE VISA FOR INVESTORS OR SELF-EMPLOYMENT

Definitely one of the more complex visas, this is best reserved for those with a clear business vision and the expendable cash to pursue it. In addition to all the documents required under *Visas,* you'll also have to present a variety of additional documents from business plans to investment records. If your business proposal requires it, you'll also have to submit your degrees or certificates, translated into Spanish and validated by the Spanish authorities. You may also be required to have full international health coverage and a bank balance of at least $100,000.

If you are willing to make such a huge investment for this visa, hire an expert to do it right. You can check with your current legal counsel for advice on international lawyers dealing with Spain. Just be sure you hire a Spanish insider; the *enchufe* (contact) culture so prevalent in Spain means that if you have a lawyer who is local, you may have some advantages. But note, some Spanish consulates will not allow your lawyer to actually participate in meetings. Once your visa is approved, you can apply for your residency card and begin the process of setting up your business in Spain.

DAILY LIFE

NON-LUCRATIVE VISA

This is the visa for the rich and mobile. The *no lucrativo* visa allows you to live in Spain, but not earn money. Why would you want to? A basic requirement for this visa is proof of $75,000 for each year you plan to stay in Spain plus an additional $15,000 for each dependent (consulates vary on the exact amount). In addition, you'll need to have full health insurance coverage. You may also need to show proof of your own housing in Spain. Sounds straightforward right? Think again. Despite meeting all the requirements, Americans are turned down for this visa at a fairly high rate. Why? Who knows? Some suspect the Spaniards of playing a little tit-for-tat since it is so difficult for their citizens to acquire visas in the U.S. The real reason is probably a lot more complex and no doubt has to do with bureaucracy, politics, immigration policies, and even crime. An American couple looking to move to Barcelona on their very substantial funds were turned down without reason. A few weeks later, the same woman who had denied their visas was arrested for taking bribes. The moral of the story? When in Spain, expect even the simplest tasks to be complicated.

RETIREE VISA

The *visado de jubilados* is exactly what it is named for—retirement. It does not give you permission to work in Spain, just to kick back and relax in the land of sun, sand, and sangria. You'll need the documents mentioned above, plus proof of income for life—a retirement or pension plan indicating total annual payments of at least $10,000 plus an additional $1,700 for each dependent who comes with you. You will also have to show proof of a health insurance plan to cover you while you are in Spain. In some cases, you'll be asked to prove a relationship to someone already resident in Spain, but this does not seem to be enforced in all cases. A check of the online Spanish forums seems to indicate that this is a pretty tough visa to get and can take up to six months to process. Like the non-lucrative visa, this one seems to have a high rejection rate for U.S. citizens.

RESIDENCE VISA TO REUNITE A FAMILY

If you are married to a Spaniard or a legal resident of Spain, you can apply for this visa. You'll need to submit the usual documents as listed under *Visas* above, as well as proof of your relationship to the legal resident (a marriage certificate and/or the *libro de familia,* the Spanish family book documenting legal relationships) and proof of your spouse's legal residence in Spain (passport or residency) as well as their *empadronamiento* (registration in the local city hall). If your spouse is not accompanying you to the consulate, a notarized photocopy of their passport or residency certificate will do just fine. In addition, your family member in Spain should have already filed a formal petition with the local police department in Spain requesting the *visado de reagrupacion familiar* and you must include a notarized copy of that.

Residency

Getting the visa is just the first step in gaining your residency in Spain. As you are probably starting to figure out, bureaucracy in Spain is one big pain. But chin up, with visa in hand, you are almost done. Your visa is only valid for 90 days and it offers you just one entry into Spain. When you arrive to your Spanish destination you'll have to hustle over to your nearest *oficina de estranjeros* (foreigner's office) to request your *tarjeta de residencia* (residence card). To find the office nearest you, do a search on the Ministry of the Interior's website (www.mir.es). You may need to make a *cita previa* (appointment) depending on the requirements of that office. And, if you live in a big city like Madrid or Barcelona, you will more than likely have to wait in long lines, regardless of your appointment. If you've contracted a lawyer, they will usually arrange for someone to wait in line for you.

You'll have to bring several things in addition to your passport with visa including a filled out *solicitud de certificado de registro como residente comunitario o tarjeta de familiar de ciudadano de la unión,* also known as the EX16. This is the form to request the card. You'll also need four passport photos (these will be used for your card, so put on your best smile). Depending on the type of residency card, you may also need a medical certificate, your work contract or business plan, proof of a Spanish family member's citizenship and your relationship to them (their ID card, your Family Book), your *empadronamiento* (registry in town hall), proof of health insurance, proof of financial means, acceptance in an accredited school—in short, pretty much the same documents you presented at the consulate, only now they should be all translated into Spanish by a *traductor jurado,* a translator certified in Spain.

You'll also need at least two copies—oh, go ahead and bring three! They may not take the copies, but go without and I promise you the Murphy's Law of Spanish Bureaucracy will deem the copies necessary and you'll have to go scrambling to find a copy shop. Finally, you'll have to pay a small fee, less than €10. However, even this is not a simple procedure. You will need to take Modelo 790, a form for *tasas administrativas* (administrative fees) to a bank and pay the fee there (download the form at www.mjusticia.es); turn in your stamped copy with the rest of your documents. If all goes well in a couple of months you'll receive a letter stating the time, date, and location of the office where you can pick up your card.

Your residency visa will be valid for a variable amount of time. Most work visas begin with a one year validation; family reunification visas have five years; student visas may last only as long as the course you are taking. Eventually, you'll have to renew your visa. Once a dreadful undertaking that involved hours of standing in chaotic lines, the renewal process has now been put online. Search for the *Renovaciones de Autorizaciones de Extranjería* on the website of the Ministry of Public Administration (www.map.es). Student visas and expired visas are excluded from the online system.

If your residency is for employment, your employer should apply for your Social Security and set up your tax payments to *hacienda* (the Spanish version of the IRS). If you are self-employed or an entrepreneur then you'll have to do both of these things on your own. And if you will be paying into the social security system, you can also sign up for the health care system by visiting the *centro de salud* (health center) that corresponds to your home address.

NIE: YOUR SPANISH IDENTIFICATION NUMBER

Your residency card will include your *número de identificación de extranjero,* your foreign resident identification number. This is as important as a social security number in the U.S. and you should probably memorize it as you will have to use it for everything from getting a cell phone contract to buying property to filing taxes. In fact, pretty much anytime you fill out any form in Spain, you will need your NIE. It is not to be confused with the DNI, the *documento nacional de identidad* (national identity document/number) that all Spanish citizens have. Though, in day-to-day life, people will ask for your DNI, and what they mean is your NIE.

Another number you'll hear a lot about is the NIF, the *número de identificación fiscal* (tax ID number). If you have an NIE, you will not receive a separate NIF, the NIE will be used for all taxation purposes. However, if you do not have a NIE, but are operating a business, own property, or are involved in other taxable activities in Spain, you will have to apply for an NIF with your local police station. The NIF does not mean you have the right to reside legally in Spain. And, as long as we are talking tongue-twisted acronyms, know that there is also a CIF, which is a tax ID number for businesses.

SPANISH CITIZENSHIP

So can you skip all this residency run-around and go right for the gold—citizenship? Sure you can—as long as one of your parents is Spanish or if you were born in Spain and at least one of your parents was born in Spain too (diplomats excluded!), or if you were born in Spain and your parents for whatever reason are unable to share their own nationality with you. Everyone else has to first establish legal residency as indicated above and then wait.

The normal time to qualify for *nacionalidad por residencia* (citizenship through residency) is 10 years. However there are several exceptions. You may be eligible in 2–5 years if one of your grandparents was Spanish. Latin Americans, Sephardic Jews, and a handful of other nationalities need only wait two years. Spouses of Spaniards are eligible after being married one year (and still married at the time of application). The website of the Ministry of Justice has a long list of exceptions. Click on *nacionalidad* at www.mjusticia.es.

The advantages of citizenship over permanent residency include never having to worry about renewing your residency again, eligibility for a Spanish passport, and voting rights. To apply for citizenship, go to your local *Registro Civil* (Civil Registry) with the following: a completed *solicitud de nacionalidad española por residencia* (form requesting citizenship), passport, current residency, your birth certificate translated and with the Apostille of Hague seal, em*padronamiento* (registry in town hall), a police record from your home country, and a police record from Spain. Other documents may be requested from job records to marriage certificates. The application can take up to a year to process. And, if you do not have two last names (all Spaniards do), you'll have to choose a second one. The best legal option is your mother's maiden name.

During the Spanish citizenship process, you will have to sign a document renouncing your U.S. citizenship, the *Acta de Adquisición de la Nacionalidad*. Though U.S. law states that this is enough to revoke your citizenship, another law provides a sort of loophole. Basically, it comes down to intent. If your *intention* in signing that document was specifically to renounce your U.S. citizenship, then yes, your citizenship could be revoked (of course, not only does the State Department not have access to the Spanish document you will sign, but intention is notoriously prickly to prove). If your intention was solely to facilitate your Spanish citizenship application, then you can indeed retain your U.S. citizenship. All the legalese can be found on the State Department's website, which you should consult. However, in practice, you will not lose your U.S. citizenship when you take on Spanish citizenship. In fact, the U.S. will even help you to change your U.S. passport to include your new second last name. Finally, keep in mind that even if you hold a Spanish passport, U.S. law requires that you enter the U.S. using your American passport.

ILLEGAL RESIDENCY

If after reading all of the above, your head is swimming, you are not alone. The visa process for non-EU citizens is daunting and even if you do wade your way patiently through it, there is no guarantee that you'll get the visa you applied for. You can be completely qualified, do everything right, have the best *enchufe* in town, and still end up rejected. Even if you assume that your application will be granted and the visa issued, it could take up to a year and require at least one, maybe two, flights back to the states. Collecting all the required documents costs money and time and lots of running around. And this is exactly why so many Americans, and other non-EU citizens, don't bother with the process at all. Many people find it easier to stay in Spain *sin papeles* than go through all the red tape, time, and money it takes to become legal. This is particularly true for people who are planning on living in Spain for only a year or two.

Of course, staying in Spain beyond your 90-day visa is illegal. You can be detained, fined, and/or even deported. The rules governing your detention/deportation are actually set by the European Union and new regulations state that detention time can be a maximum of six months, 18 months for exceptional cases. However, fair or not, most of the action taken against illegal immigrants is on Africans, Latin Americans, and other nationalities. While an American citizen running afoul of the immigration rules can be prosecuted, it rarely happens. But never say never! Ask around in any expat circle and you'll hear of an American deported or denied entry to Spain.

If you are considering this option, do your research—Spain blogs and forums are full of advice on this issue. And be prepared to live with a certain level of anxiety. Any encounter with the police could lead to a request for your papers. In the south of Spain and areas where there is a high concentration of foreigners, police often make spot checks for papers. Every time you fly out of Spain, you'll have to worry about being caught. If you work illegally, you will have no rights—no rights to holidays, sick days, workers' compensation for injuries, no health insurance, no assurance of fair and equal treatment, not even a guarantee that you'll be paid. Many an illegal English teacher has lost a paycheck because the academy knew that the teacher had no recourses for getting it.

However, for those that are determined to live *la vida española* at all costs, moving to Spain without a legal visa is often the only route. Those who wish to stay longer will use their initial time here illegally to make contacts, find a job, enroll in a university, and/or meet a *media naranja* (soul mate) to marry. Many are successful, but even more, frustrated and dejected, pack it in and head home after several years of living illegally in Spain. It is just not a long-term option.

ARRAIGO: ROOTS RESIDENCY

The word *arraigar* means "to take root," and illegal immigrants who have become rooted in Spanish society for over two years may be able to get legal residency through a process called *arraigo* which was put into place in 2005.

An *arraigo laboral* is a work exception, requiring proof of having lived in Spain continuously for two years and having worked for a company for at least one year. Filing for this exception requires that you denounce your employer for hiring you illegally. This will result in a fine of some sort for your employer including the possible collection of back taxes and social security payments they should have paid on your behalf. Depending on your relationship with your employer, you may or may not want to pursue this route.

The *arraigo social* is a social exception, requiring proof that you have lived in the country for at least three years and have roots in your community. These roots could be a relationship with a legal resident of Spain or proof of your connection to your community, including social networks, language fluency, and more. You will also need to have a work contract—that has not been put into effect yet—for a minimum of one year. Your would-be employer must also be up-to-date on their tax and social security obligations.

In addition to the above documents, you must present your valid passport, a police record from your home state with the Apostille of Hague seal (translated into Spanish), a clean police record from Spain, proof of your continuous presence in Spain—preferably your *empadronamiento* (registry in town hall),—two passport-sized photos, and a completed Form EX-00, *solicitud de autorización de residencia* (request for residence authorization). Of course, don't forget your photocopies!

All documents must be turned into your local Oficina de Extranjeros (Foreigners' Office)—you will have to call ahead for a *cita previa* (appointment). You may be required to have an interview—bring all your documents in copy and be ready to show off your stellar Spanish (Catalan or Basque) speaking skills! If you are approved, you will be given one year of legal residency—you have to sign up for Social Security for your residence to take effect—and you will have 30 days to apply for your residency card. If you are denied, you are typically given 90 days to leave the country.

Though the *arraigo* seems pretty straightforward, you'd be wise to get some legal input to be sure that you qualify for this exception to residency requirements. You would hate to go through it all only to be denied. There are

several informative sites detailing the process (all in Spanish); try www.arraigo
.es, http://arraigo.com.es, and www.parainmigrantes.info.

Spanish Consulates

Whether your first visit is virtual, by phone, or in person, the Spanish Consulate will be your first headbutt with the worst of Spanish bureaucracy. Scan
forum after forum, talk to expats, read Spanish blogs and you'll encounter
hundreds of horror stories of everything from blatant misinformation from
a consulate employee to a random change of rules between the time you call
the consulate and the time you show up. And then there is the, um, let's call
it consular demeanor. Americans have reported being yelled at, having papers
flung back at them, and being made to wait hours for a set appointment.

Number one in dealing with the Spanish consulate? Expect the worst. You
may get lucky as Phil from Ohio did, who recalled no problems at all with the
"cute Spanish *chica* in a sundress" who attended him in the Chicago consulate. Or, like Wendy, a Harvard grad who was hired as an executive in Spain,
you may have your application tossed back at you because you printed the visa
application out single-sided, not double-sided. When Wendy protested that
there was no mention of that requirement on the website or when she called,
she was told, "it is always this way."

Sometimes you show up with every document, correctly filled out and cop-
ied to their specification, only to be told that you suddenly need something
else. Jen, applying for her student visa, showed up at the Washington consulate with all requested documents and was told that she couldn't apply as they
wanted a new document from her—mainly a notarized letter from the owner
of the home she'd be living at in Spain. Rob, also applying for a student visa,
was told he had to change his private health insurance plan which he paid for
in monthly payments to a plan paid for up front by a year. If something like
this happens to you, you will have no choice but to comply with the request—
the consulate will not accept a partial application under any circumstances.
And finally, some consulates are just plain unhelpful. When I called the
New Orleans consulate inquiring about the visa process for my marriage to
a Spaniard, I was told to check the web and then hung up on before I could
ask a follow-up question.

About the only way to defend yourself when dealing with the consulate is
to be as polite as possible, keep records of everything, especially the names of
anyone you speak with on the phone and printouts of all requirements listed
on their website. Finally, learn to practice your very own form of the "ohm"

chant to not lose your temper. Arguing, yelling, crying—none of it will work in the face of consular opinion. Consider the experience an initiation ritual—believe me, your future life in Spain will be full of moments of illogical, inept, and even rude brushes with bureaucracy.

Your first step before approaching the consulates is to do some homework. Most of the consulates have their webs attached to the greater website of the Ministry of Foreign Affairs (www.maec.es). Once inside the site, search for "Embajadas y Consulados." When you find the embassy for your state, you'll have to dig around to find the visa requirements—some sites have a "Visa" button to click, others have the info tucked under "Consular Services." And, as of the publication of this book, the Chicago consulate still maintained its own, very informative site (www.consulate-spain-chicago.com). The main thing you want to know, in addition to the specific requirements for your visa are: does the consulate have jurisdiction over your home address and do you need to make an appointment or can you just show up. Some consulates don't take appointments, but do take only a set number of applicants per day. If that is the case—get there early! Finally, you'll have to pay a nonrefundable fee when you turn in your visa application. As of the end of 2008, it was $100.00. Don't rely on your good old plastic Visa for this, some Spanish consulates take cash, but others require money order only.

Moving with Children

Believe it or not, moving your pet to Spain requires more work than moving your children does—at least when it comes to paperwork. As long as you include your children's individual applications, medical certificates of good health, and their birth certificates in your visa application, they'll also get their visas when you do. However, once you arrive in Spain things get a little trickier.

Young children adapt to new cultures with mind-boggling ease and pick up new languages at breakneck speed. Yet adolescents and teenagers struggle a little bit. Not only is

babies taking a break in Madrid's Plaza de Colón

© ALFONSO MORCUENDE

language-learning harder for them, but they tend to suffer more from homesickness. They miss their old friends (not to mention MTV reality shows, Taco Bell, hockey games, and Ranch dressing on everything). All of this can lead to them having a tough time adapting in Spain. This can affect their performance in school and their overall attitude, lead to depression, and cause many a scene ending with a teary-eyed plea to "go home."

A lot of this can be resolved as they settle into their new school. If you move to a community with a very large expat population, the local public schools will not only have other native English-speaking children, but also special Spanish language tutoring for new arrivals. If you are in place without such an environment, you should seriously consider a private international school for your older children. Not only will the language of instruction be English, but the curriculum and afterschool activities will be more in line with what your child had at home. Spanish public schools rarely offer extracurriculars and even though a child of any age can usually survive being thrown into a school where they don't know the language nor the culture, it really isn't very fair to them. If you cannot afford an international school, you may want to reevaluate if your move abroad is really the best thing for your older child.

For kids of all ages, it is a good idea to keep a few things in mind. Before even leaving home, enroll your children in a local Spanish class. Even the basics of the language will give them a leg up when they arrive—and may even

children playing soccer in an Asturian plaza

© CANDY LEE LABALLE

add to their enthusiasm when they can realize they can read signs and communicate a little with the neighbors. Also, rather than trying to amp up your children's enthusiasm for Spain by asking them to build shoe-box dioramas of the country's great historical moments and dragging them through one museum after another, pursue things that they'll actually enjoy. Even the smallest towns will have a roster of children's activities available. Check into the expat community to find events in English or with other expat children. Big cities like Madrid, Barcelona, and Valencia will have ongoing children's events from puppet shows to theater. A good resource is the online version of the weekly leisure magazine, Guía del Ocio (www.guiadelocio.com); just choose your city and click "niños." Larger cities will also most likely have an expat forum dedicated to children. In Madrid, try www.kidsinmadrid.com, in Barcelona, www.kidsinbarcelona.com. Also based out of Barcelona, cul-TOURa (www.cultourabcn.com) specializes in Catalan culture classes for kids—a great way to introduce your child to the culture if you move to Barcelona or Cataluña.

Kids are creatures of habit and feel better when they are in familiar surroundings. Bring as many of their personal belongings over as you can, furniture included, and try to re-create their stateside bedroom in their new Spanish casa. Make the effort to take regular walks with your kids through your new neighborhood. Take them on the metro and the busses and learn together how to get around town. Bring along a map and explore the area together. Consider giving your child a guidebook and letting them plan the day's activities. They will feel more excited about visiting a place if they selected it.

As much as you may want to immerse yourself in the local Spanish culture, for your kids' sake, seek out a local expat organization—American Women's Club, International Newcomer's Club—anywhere that you could meet other parents who are raising kids in Spain. Not only will they be an invaluable source of information for you, but you might be able to arrange play dates for your younger kids, or other events for older kids. Find some local contacts through Mum Abroad Spain (http://mumabroad.com).

Finally, rest assured that you are bringing your kids to a wonderful place. The temperate weather means more sun time for playing outdoors. And Spaniards adore children; they are welcome at almost any event—weddings, late dinners, evening strolls, museums, shops, even bars. It is not unusual during the summer and on weekends to see kids playing in the squares at midnight while their parents enjoy tapas with their friends at a nearby sidewalk café. Pull up a chair and let your child play under the night sky.

DAILY LIFE

Moving with Pets

© CANDY LEE LABALLE

Be a good neighbor and let your pooch go in the canine area.

If you can't live without your *mascota* (pet)—don't fret. Most standard household animals are allowed in the country without quarantine—so long as their vaccinations and papers are in order. Pets must be microchipped (have an identifying microchip inserted in their neck) or tattooed and be vaccinated against rabies. Pets under three months are not allowed in country and certain dogs considered "potentially dangerous" by the Spanish government (pit bulls, some terriers, Rottweilers) are strictly controlled. Get your paws on all the details at the comprehensive site run by the Spanish Ministry of Environment and Rural and Marine Affairs in the United States (www.mapausa.org).

Before traveling, your pet must also have a *certificado veterinario* filled out by an accredited veterinarian. This form must then be certified by a Veterinary Services Official from the USDA. There are usually only a few of these officials in each state, so go to www.aphis.usda.gov and search for your local Veterinary Services Office early in the game. The certificate can be downloaded from www.mapausa.org.

Be sure and let your vet know that your pet is moving with you to Spain so that he/she can give your furry friend any additional vaccinations. These may include, for dogs, distemper, hepatitis, leptospirosis, and parvovirus; for cats, feline gastro-enteritis and typhus.

Upon arrival in Spain, find a local *veterinario* to issue your pet its Spanish health certificate. You'll need to take this booklet to all vet appointments while in Spain. And before an emergency strikes, locate the nearest *clínica veterinaria* with 24-hour *urgencias* (emergency) service. You'll also have to register your dog with your local town hall. And, even though your pet has an identifying chip or tattoo, an old-fashioned collar with your name and number is a really good idea in case your *mascota* goes missing.

If you've been to Spain before, then you've undoubtedly dodged piles of poop on public streets. You'll be shocked to discover that Spain does in fact have pooper-scooper laws but they are broadly ignored. Spaniards are so blasé about it that instead of complaining the way an American might, they have convinced themselves that stepping in dog *caca* is really good luck. (Despite what your neighbors do, you should buck the system and pick up after your dog.) Each municipality has its own rules regarding where dogs are permitted to run free, but all dogs must be leashed in public areas.

On the whole, life is good for Spanish pets. Animals are adored and dog owners out on walks with their pooch will discover that their dog is a great conversation starter. However, take particular caution if you live in a rural area. Spanish hunters and some farmers are known to leave pieces of poisoned meat strewn about in an effort to kill foxes and other animals viewed as pests. If your dog were to eat it instead, it could be fatal. Additionally, you should speak to your Spanish vet about any health hazards that might be endemic to your area of Spain.

DAILY LIFE

What to Take

Relocating to Spain has little in common with packing up your stuff and carting it to a new house on the other side of town; in this case you'll have an ocean to cross. It's generally agreed upon by expats that the best approach is to first figure out what you can leave behind; an assessment that is more often personal than practical. Keep in mind the bottom-line: Anything that you need and most of what you want can be found in Spain.

Of course, money will play a part in what you bring over. Students and young expats with no job lined up and no family to house, should bring only what will fit in the baggage allowed by your airline. Executives being sent to Spain, families, and others with money to spend can consider taking over more. Still, unless you are really attached to your furniture, you may want to consider selling it or putting it in storage. Spain offers a wealth of opportunities to buy beautiful home furnishings spanning the spectrum of budget and design—from Swedish furniture megamart IKEA to designer-owned boutiques in Barcelona to the antique shops of Madrid's Rastro flea market.

If like me, you collect, uh, stuff—salt shakers, antique picture frames, ugly lamps—and don't have the funds (or a clear enough vision of your future) to ship it over in one fell swoop, consider storing it. Of course, renting a storage facility will probably defeat the purpose of saving money on shipping, so ask around for a relative with ample attic space. My parents' attic holds my ever-dwindling collection of stuff. Dwindling because each time I go home for a visit, I bring an empty suitcase that I fill up with whatever I decide I can no longer live without. This year it was my amazing collection of disco ball Christmas tree ornaments and several antique hats.

ELECTRONICS

You're probably wondering if you should take your electronics and the answer to that is a resounding maybe. Spain uses a 220-volt electrical system, like the rest of continental Europe. You don't have to know what that means, you just have to know that the North American system is different (it uses 110 volts) and the bottom line is that you can't plug your American hair dryer into a Spanish outlet—the plug itself won't even fit. For this and other small electronics—toasters, clock-radios, shavers—you can use a power transformer which transforms the 220 volts into 110. Transformers work best on small, low-draw items with no significant motors in them. But, there is the catch— these small, inexpensive items are easily bought in Spain. Again, unless you are desperately attached to such a small item, sell it in a garage sale and save the space in your shipping. For large ticket items—refrigerator, washing machines—don't even bother bringing them over. Not only will it cost a fortune to get a transformer big enough to run these monsters, but Spanish houses are much smaller than those in the U.S. and it is doubtful your supersized American appliance will fit.

Feel free however, to bring over any lamps you love. The wiring has nothing to do with electricity. Just buy a Spanish bulb once you arrive, stick on a plug adapter (a small plug that transforms your items electrical prongs into the round prongs common to Spain), and you've got *luz* (light).

COMPUTERS

Computers are more expensive in Spain than they are in the United States so you might want to hang on to the one you have if you can. Some U.S. desktops have a switch that transfers the rate of power and allows the computer to function in Europe with a plug adapter. All laptops automatically make the switch (as do digital cameras, most video cameras, cell phones, and many devices meant for a mobile world).

However, there are a couple of drawbacks to bringing over your computer. As soon as you leave U.S. soil, the warranty that came with your computer is meaningless—you can't make good on it in a Spanish store that sells the same item and most companies won't ship replacement pieces abroad. Of course there are ways around this. Ordering parts through eBay, having family members ship them to you, and finding a local repair person if needed. If you truly have a problem that requires warranty service, you can always hold off on the repair until you head home for a visit or pay for it out of pocket. Finally, if you have to make a call to your computer manufacturer's service center, do so through Skype—800 calls are free.

The last note on electronics is only for people with Macs. You will be a rare (but growing) breed in Spain. Until recently, Spain priced Macs far higher than PCs and the discrepancy resulted in fewer Mac users. The prices have begun to drop down but most people still use PCs and you'll have to look a little harder to find software that is Mac compatible. When I had a DSL line installed on my MacBook, the technician spent three hours struggling with a job that usually takes about 20 minutes. Halfway through the ordeal he confessed that he had never even touched a Mac before. For service and parts, check the Spanish site www.apple.es.

SHIPPING OPTIONS

You don't absolutely have to see the contents of your house sold off in a tag sale or on eBay—you can ship just about anything to Spain, but the cost for that service adds up fast. One couple on the verge of relocating hoped to ship 1,500 pounds of beloved possessions from Los Angeles to Barcelona. When an international moving company gave them a quote of $2,700 for the service, they shopped around for a better price but they couldn't find much improvement. Ultimately, the couple arrived in Spain with a lighter load. Many people take one look at the quadruple-digit price tag that's typically attached to shipping the entire contents of a home and quickly come to the conclusion that sentimental value is overrated.

But for some people, especially for families with young children, sending some items separately is unavoidable. The Internet is full of listings for international shipping companies that will be able to pack up your home for you, deliver your cargo to your Spanish doorstep, and take care of every detail in between. Check expat forums for recommendations. As is usually the case, the better the service the higher the price. You can knock down the cost by boxing your things yourself and collecting them from the port or drop-off center in Spain. There are several regulations you will have to adhere to in order to ship your household goods to Spain. A reputable shipping company will take you through these steps and it is worth the extra money to pay for this service. The *aduana* (customs) regulations can be quite daunting and expensive if you make a mistake. In theory, used household goods that will be

DAILY LIFE

in your possession in Spain for at least a year are not subject to duty taxes; in practice, Spanish customs seems to apply taxes at will. An experienced shipper can help you avoid this.

You can handle mini-shipments through USPS priority mail (airmail) for international packages. (If you once mailed items to Spain on the slow boat, sorry, that cheapie option was discontinued in 2007.) For small items, the price of shipping is not too bad, though it can add up for bigger packages. In addition, the value of the items must be listed on the shipping package and if it exceeds $100, *aduana* (Spanish customs) may very well slap you with a customs tax. It will have to be paid at the time the package is delivered or you will have to go down to the post office and pay it. There is often a lot of discontent regarding the tax as it seems that Spanish customs has a tendency to overvalue the goods in your box. Be sure that whoever ships them for you, marks the items as "used household goods" or "used clothing" and lists a price of less than $100.

HOUSING CONSIDERATIONS

Finding housing is the issue that people sweat out the most before arriving in Spain and there's no wondering why. House-hunting is stressful enough in your own country. When you toss a foreign language and a new set of laws into the mix, the prospect can seem downright overwhelming. Your list of initial questions might seem endless now but rest assured that every query you have has an accessible answer.

The Spanish Housing Market

The Spanish real estate market went through a period of dramatic inflation from the late 1990s through the mid-2000s. Housing prices rose annually 15 percent from 1999 to 2005. This was fueled by a near mania among both Spaniards and

© CANDY LEE LABALLE

foreigners to acquire property. Spanish banks scrambled to attend the buying frenzy and started doling out mortgages with then–unheard of 40- and 50-year repayment plans. By 2006, Spanish homes were overvalued by some 30 percent. At the same time, Spanish and foreign constructors built new housing at an unprecedented rate. When this real estate market burst in 2007–2008, housing prices plummeted, sales ground to a near halt, construction was paralyzed, and buyers were left with overvalued homes, many that they could no longer afford due to rising interest rates and the economic crisis that gripped Spain in 2008.

This has a few main impacts on foreigners seeking to live in Spain. It is now a buyer's market. Prices are falling and many people are desperate to get rid of their properties. You better have some good financing though, as banks have tightened their lending practices sharply. For renters, it is not so good. The real estate crash has locked the door on home ownership and caused a rush to rent. You can guess the results—increased rents, particularly in the big cities. A one-bedroom apartment in Madrid that cost €500 in 2003, was renting for €1,000 in 2008. However, rental prices in Spain's world-class cities still pale in comparison to prices in U.S. cities like New York, Boston, and San Francisco. And, if you are willing to live in the suburbs or in a smaller town, just a few hundred euros a month can secure a fantastic apartment.

Renting or Buying

The decision to rent or buy is a highly personal one. A lot depends on your finances—very few newly arrived teachers will have the funds necessary to even consider buying. Retirees, on the other hand, may want to invest in a property soon after arriving. For most expats, however, starting out as a renter is the best bet. You can try out different neighborhoods and even cities with no long-term commitment. Even more, renting gives you time to decide if Spain really is for you. In either case, I strongly recommend that you do not sign a contract or make a deposit of any sort before arriving in country (unless you are dealing with a very trusted friend). You need to be on the ground, walk the neighborhoods, smell the bread baking at the local *panadería*, browse the colorful, chaotic stalls at the local market.

When you do begin to look at homes, take your time, get a feel for what's out there, and don't jump at the very first place that you see. Consider issues such as noise pollution and proximity to public transport. Being in the center of town has advantages but will the street noise drive you *loco*? Does the apartment have a good amount of natural light? Would you feel safe walking home late at night?

CRACKING THE CLASSIFIEDS

Here are a few terms you should know when renting or buying your casa in Spain:

aire acondicionado – air-conditioning

agencia – rental agent

amueblado – *furnished*

antigüedad – older

armario empotrado – built-in closet

ascensor – elevator

aseo – half-bath

ático – top floor

bajo – ground level

baño completo – complete bath

bien comunicado – located near public transport

buhardilla – attic

calefacción – heat

casero/a – landlord/landlady

chalet – detached house, villa

cocina – kitchen

comedor – dining room

como nuevo – like new

communidad – a monthly fee to the building association

dormitorios – bedrooms

ducha – shower

embaldosado – tiled

escritura – notarized deed of sale

fachada – facade

finca – farmhouse, usually large

jardín – garden

gastos – fees or expenses, also utilities

gastos incluidos – utilities included

hipoteca – mortgage

impuesto – tax

inmobiliaria – real estate agency

interior – an interior apartment, not facing the street

inquilino/a – tenant

lavadora – washing machine

lujo – luxury

luminoso – plenty of light

moqueta – wall-to-wall carpet

nomina – pay slip or proof of salary

nuevo – new

parcela – building plot

parking – parking space

particular – rented by an individual, not an agency

piscina – pool

piso – floor, as in "the building has five floors"; also flat or apartment

pozo – water well

reformado – renovated

rústica – rural or agricultural

salón – living room

se alquila – for rent

se vende – for sale

suelo de madera – wood floor

terraza – terrace

trastero – storage room

urbanización – community development

ventana – window

a "for rent" sign at a seafront apartment complex in Andalucía

Check out your future barrio at different times of the day and on weekends. Dawn, a Canadian writer in Madrid, signed a rental contract on a lovely apartment overlooking a peaceful plaza. She didn't find out until a few nights after moving in that the plaza hosts weekend *botellóns*. Literally meaning "the big bottle," these open-air gatherings draw hundreds of teens and their big bottles of whiskey and wine and have made her weekends anything but peaceful.

RENTING

The rental process is Spain is pretty similar to what you may be used to back home—find a place you like, pay a deposit, sign a contract, move in. However, one major surprise for Americans is the concept of "furnishings." Most apartments are rented *amueblado* (furnished)—and that means everything from the shower curtain to the sheets. You may not like your landlord's taste in mock medieval wall-hangings, but unless you want to lose your deposit—don't toss them out. On the other extreme, some apartments and most houses will be unfurnished, which means, practically unfinished. You may open the door to find just walls, a floor, and doors. Basics such as refrigerators, light fixtures, and towel racks are considered furnishings. If you are looking at an unfurnished rental, you'll need some cash set aside to make the place livable. You may be able to work out a deal with the landlord for reimbursement at the end of your lease; if not, there is a very active resale market among expats. In fact, before you buy your big ticket items, check with your local English-language publications to see what's for sale.

Finding the Right Place

Rentals are found through the same avenues you would use anywhere—word-of-mouth, classified ads, and agents. One of the best avenues is through the *enchufe* (contact). Ask everyone you know what they know. As rental law tends to be skewed in favor of the tenant, many landlords prefer to rent to someone who comes recommended. Another way to find a great unlisted gem is to look up. Walk through the barrio you want to live in and watch the upper balconies for a *se alquila* (for rent) sign and call from the street. You may be able to go up and see the place right then and there. You can also try asking porters in any building that you like if apartments are available—it's a long shot but you might get lucky.

Why so much concern with finding an unlisted place? Well, particularly in big cities, good places go fast. A well-located, well-priced rental listed in online or print classifieds will often be rented the very same day the ad appears. You can spend hours reviewing ads only to make the calls and find out, sorry, *ya*

Wherever you live in Spain, you'll have a market nearby.

está alquilado (it's already rented). Don't let that stop you—people find rentals through the classifieds all the time; just make sure you check online sources several times daily and scour the classifieds the moment they come out.

Searching for a rental online has pretty much become the norm in Spain thanks to the wildly popular classified housing site Idealista (www.idealista .com). You can search in Spanish or English by neighborhood anywhere in Spain. Of course, you can search by price range, number of bedrooms, and furnishings, but you can also look for places with elevators, swimming pools, or terraces. Create a profile to receive emails whenever a new listing meeting your requirements pops up. When you find a place you like, take a look at the *anuncio visto* (ad seen) tracker. If it is in the single digits—call ASAP. If it is in the tens of thousands (and many are), the rental is probably long gone. Also check Craigslist Spain (http://geo.craigslist.org/iso/es) and Loquo (www .loquo.com), but beware, both of these sites have a fair share of fake ads. If anyone demands you pay up front to see a place—it is a scam!

The king of the classifieds is *Segundamano* (www.segundamano.com). They do have an online version, but the printed paper seems to have better prices. One theory is that the people publishing in the paper tend to be older and not comfortable with the new-fangled Internet thing and may not be aware of the higher rents they can ask for their properties. So, put your mouse down, get out your pen, and start circling. *Segundamano* is printed twice a week, Wednesday and Saturday. Buy your copy in the early morning and start calling by breakfast. English-language publications, both print and online, are also great sources of rental properties.

If you'd rather soak up the sun and sangria instead of slog through ads, you might want to contact an agent. *Agencias de inmobiliaria* (real estate agents) usually have a long list of rentals in addition to for-sale properties. They can help find an apartment to meet your needs and facilitate the rental process. They will charge at least one month's rent for their services. *Do not* pay a fee prior to finding your apartment; any agent requesting a fee up front is out to scam you. In larger cities and areas with large expat populations, you'll also find many "relocation agents" or "room finders." They function much like Spanish real estate agents, though all your dealings will be in English. Fees should be about the same, however some offer increased services—from legal assistance to language school options—and of course, these services will be extra.

Rental Prices

If you are from small-town Iowa, you may be shocked at the price of rent in Spain. Come from New York or Boston, and you'll be convinced you've hit the rental jackpot. That said, prices for rentals vary wildly. In general, prices are higher in the big cities and lower everywhere else. Regional capitals offer good value for your euro, making city living affordable, while small towns and rural areas provide the cheapest living options. As everyone knows, rental prices are dictated by location, location, location and that is especially true within Spanish cities. Rentals within a city's *casco viejo* (historic center) tend to be higher than prices in newer neighborhoods. In coastal towns, rentals near the beach will be pricier than those further inland. You'll have to do specific research in your future Spanish hometown to get an idea of prices, but expect a one-bedroom to run anywhere from €300 to €1,000; properties with three or more bedrooms can start as low as €700 and zoom up to quadruple digits, again all depending on location.

Other factors that result in increased prices include: elevator, a fourth floor walk-up will be a bit cheaper than a fourth floor with *ascensor;* terrace, the dream of all

A working-class barrio in Madrid attracts younger expats.

urban dwellers in Spain is to have a *terraza* overlooking the neighborhood, and apartments that have one will rent for higher than those without; *calefacción* (central heating), many older apartments do not have central heating which makes for either very cold winters or very expensive ones if you decide to use electric heaters; *exterior* apartments which feature sun-filled windows facing the street tend to be higher-priced than *interior* ones which overlook the dark inner courtyard (though interiors tend to be quieter).

Leases

Contratos de arrendamiento (rental contracts) are generally for five years, but many landlords offer foreigners one-year leases to start. The contract is an official document that must be notarized and recorded with the Spanish Property Registry (the landlord takes care of both of these things). If you are nervous about signing a contract in Spanish, have a Spanish friend accompany you when it is time to sign or hire a lawyer or a *gestor* (administrator) to assist you. The contract must include property details, monthly rent, payment options, and contract length. During the first five years, rent can only be increased according to inflation—which means increases are minimal. Despite this contract, it is fairly easy to break a lease. In general, you should give at least one month's notice if you want to move out early. Though the landlord may not like it, there is little he/she can do about it other than keep your deposit. On the other hand, landlords cannot force you out before your five-year contract is up.

Before putting pen to paper, be sure to check for damages to the property so you won't be held accountable for them later on. If something is broken when you sign the lease make sure that it's either fixed or, if it's a problem that you can live with such as a crack in the ceiling or a loose floorboard, detail it in the contract. If the property needs repairs during the course of the lease, the law states that the landlord is responsible for repairs to maintain the rental property—this includes plumbing, electrical, and structural problems. In an emergency, the tenant can order repairs and pay for them out of pocket; the landlord must later refund the tenant. If you have a furnished property, the landlord must also maintain the furnishings—repairing the refrigerator, replacing the sofa—as needed. However, the tenant is responsible for any damages they may cause, whether from an accident or daily wear and tear. As you can imagine, this leads to some major confrontations. I once rented an ancient apartment in the center of Madrid. The closet door was creaky from day one, but when it fell off two months later, the landlord said it was my fault. Not only did I not repair it, but his bad attitude sent me looking for another place and I broke my lease within the year. If a landlord values your tenancy, he/she will work with you. And, if you get a good landlord, be thankful, and willing to work also with them.

If your landlord decides to sell the place, by law you must receive the first offer on the home. You may or may not be interested in buying at all, but it's worth knowing that you do have priority over everyone else including the landlord's family. You'll be given 30 days to reply to the offer and if you discover that the place was sold without an offer having been made, you have a month to annul the sale of the home. Likewise, if the property was sold at a lower price than the one your landlord offered you, you can cancel the sale.

You do not have to be a legal resident to sign a lease for a rental property in Spain. However, many landlords do require a *nómina* (salary/pay stub) showing that you have a regular salary that will cover the cost of the rent. If you don't have one, it doesn't mean you'll be turned down as a renter, but it may be a lot harder for you. Finding a landlord who doesn't require a pay stub can be a bit of luck or a good contact. Many will forego the request for a pay stub in exchange for a multimonth bank guarantee called an *aval bancario*.

For details more on rental law and your rights as a tenant, as well as assistance with rental leases, visit an *oficina de información de vivienda* (housing information office) in your neighborhood. These centers offer free support and advice to both renters and landlords, and can be very useful in avoiding problems. When her landlord tried to up her rent by more than €100, Megan from DC visited her local office and got a copy of the Spanish law saying that the rent could only be increased by that year's cost-of-living increase. Her landlord backed off.

Moving In and Other Expenses

Upon signing a contract, tenants will be required to pay a *fianza* (deposit). Rental law sets this at one month, but in practice landlords charge up to six months. As in the United States, the deposit is to ensure that the apartment is returned in good condition and that the lease is adhered too. However, also as in the states, your behavior regarding the deposit will depend on your relationship with your landlord. Michael from California, has dealt with enough shady landlords in Cataluña that he now regularly refuses to pay the last month's rent, telling the landlord to use the deposit.

Many landlords also request an *aval bancario* (bank guarantee) which can range 3–12 months rent. The tenant must deposit this money in a bank where it will be held for the duration of the rental contract—the bank where you have your Spanish account should facilitate this. When you leave the apartment, you must get a letter from the landlord stating that you are no longer rent-ing the flat so that the *aval* can be cancelled by the bank and returned to you (minus administrative fees). Of course, if there is time left on your contract, there could be some difficulties in recuperating your money. Clarify all the details of the *aval* with your bank, and if you can, with a lawyer.

What all of this means is that moving into a rental apartment in Spain can be very expensive. Imagine you use an agent and find a great studio for €500. Now, the agent wants a one-month fee and the landlord wants two months' deposit, plus a six-month *aval*. You are looking at €4,500 just to move in! So, how can you reduce the costs? Look for a place that does not ask for an *aval*. You are less likely to have to provide one if you: can present a *nómina* (salary/ pay stub); have citizenship in Spain or are married to a Spaniard (yes, there is some xenophobia among landlords); rent in an area with high vacancies— outlying or less desirable neighborhoods; or, find your apartment through an *enchufe* (the old friend of a friend concept so relevant in Spain).

Once you and the landlord have settled on the rent and decided to *aval* or not to *aval*, you can pay the initial fees in cash or bank transfer (a direct trans-fer from your bank account to the landlord's account). If in cash, be sure to get a *recibo* (receipt). For your regular monthly transfers, a copy of your bank account is sufficient as a receipt.

Tenants must pay for *gastos* (utilities including gas, electricity, water, phone, and Internet) and they may be billed directly to you or be billed to your land-lord who will in turn charge you. Another important cost to be aware of is the monthly *comunidad* (community fee to maintain the communal facilities). Though the landlord is responsible for this fee, it is often passed onto the ten-ant. So, you may find a great place for €900 but then after speaking with the owner learn you have to also pay €100 per month in community fees.

Sharing an Apartment

If your funds (or patience for paperwork) are just not up for renting on your own, consider sharing a place. This is probably one of the best options for young, single people moving to Spain. If this sounds like you, see the 2002 French film *L'Auberge Espagnole* which documents the adventures of a French student sharing a Barcelona apartment with a Spaniard, an Italian, a Dane, a Belgian, and an German. This could be you! How? Easy, consult the same exact resources mentioned above but tailor your search to *piso compartido* (shared piso).

Price depends greatly on the city and neighborhood where the apartment is located as well as the amenities included. Even in a major metropolis like

Barcelona or Madrid, you will very rarely see shared apartments for more than €500 per month—often much cheaper. Your rent may include *gastos* or you may have to pay them separately. Some roommates may also have a policy for sharing food and other household costs. Clarify this before moving in.

BUYING

So you've gotten to know the market and you're ready to make a piece of Spain your very own. Many of your initial steps will be similar to what you'd expect back home. First, you need to know where you want to live—on the sunny Mediterranean or in buzzing Madrid, in misty Galicia or way off the path in a tiny *pueblo blanco* (whitewashed village) in Andalucía. Once you've solved that geographic glitch, think about the type of home you want—an apartment, a detached house, a rural property such as a farmhouse or old barn, or even a cave. (*¿No me crees?* Check out www.livinginacave.com!)

Next, think about price. A lot depends on your personal finances, but be aware, if you must have a two-bedroom apartment with terrace in the heart of Barcelona, you will be paying a lot more than if you wanted a three-bedroom place in the suburbs of Granada. Once all of that is settled, you'll need to get a mortgage (unless you've got the cash to pay in full), you'll have to sign some contracts, transfer over the deed, pay a few taxes, and move in! Of course, nothing is Spain is that simple, so read on.

The most notable difference between home sales in the United States and Spain is in the unwritten part of the transaction. Don't be surprised if the seller or agent talks openly about avoiding taxes. One document that might look wildly off is the *escritura* (deed)—perhaps you'll see that the home's dimensions on paper appear to be much smaller than the actual house is. That's a deliberate discrepancy made to save money. A seller might also request a portion of the sale in *dinero negro* (black money) in order to avoid taxes. Though the government has become stricter in these matters, fudged numbers and cash exchanges are still quite common. If a seller or agent suggests such a deal, you don't have to comply—again, consult your lawyer for options.

Get Informed

Before you start to buy a property, you'll probably have a few (dozen) questions on your mind—from how much does a home cost in Spain to how do I go about buying one to how can I keep from being ripped off. Reading this book is a decent start, but just that. Do your homework. Buying a home is a huge financial commitment—add Spanish property law, tax issues, and a whole new culture of buying and selling, and you've got quite an undertaking

© ALFONSO MORCUENDE

If you want to buy, look out for the *se vende* (for sale) sign.

DAILY LIFE

on your *manos*. Almost anything you need to know about purchasing a home in Spain, you can find on the Internet—however, don't just peruse sites dedicated to housing, check out Spanish news sources like Expatica (www.expatica.com/es) and international papers such as *Financial Times Europe* (www.ft.com/home/Europe) for information on the Spanish housing market. Check online expat forums such as Spain Expat (www.spainexpat.com), Expat Forum (www.expatforum.com, search for the Spain link), Euroresidentes (www.euroresidentes.com), and expat blogs for insider's tips on the housing situation. And if you have any contacts of your own in Spain, don't hesitate to ask for information. Knowing what to expect when buying a Spanish home will make the process a lot less *estresante* (stressful).

Get a basic grip on prices by browsing the Spain section of the international housing portal, Kyero.com (www.kyero.com), one of the most complete sites offering information on buying a property in Spain. Search for their free downloadable Spanish House Price Index, which compares price listings throughout Spain quarterly. Another fantastic resource is www.spanishrealestateforum.com which includes listings, advice, FAQs, and great opportunities to seek out information through their forum. Though it is tough to price a place by the square meter as one meter of property in a swanky neighborhood or an attractive, older building costs far more than the same in a working-class area or building in need of renovation, without an elevator or air-conditioning, the Sociedad de Tasación (www.st-tasacion.es) makes a good effort. Search their site for *precios de la vivienda* to see biannually updated estimates on the average cost per square meter of properties throughout Spain.

Get Help

Though you can go DIY, my advice is DGT ("don't go there"). Unless you have an in-depth understanding of Spanish property law, an excellent command of the language, and are buying from someone you trust, don't buy on your own. An *abogado* (lawyer) will not only help you through the legal details of buying in Spain, but can check out the property for back taxes or liens, file the correct papers with the government, and apply for any permits needed for post-purchase upgrades. Look for a lawyer who is knowledgeable in Spanish property and be sure to discuss fees before contracting their services. Do not use a lawyer suggested by the sales agent of the property; your best interests may well be overlooked in the process.

Which brings us to the agent. There are two types of agents—those that have complied with governmental requirements and registered as an official real estate agent (they can show you their certificate and registration number) and those that have not. This is not illegal, but rather a result of very fuzzy real estate sale laws. You'd be wise to work with licensed agents simply because they tend to be more informed. The most complete licensing is offered through the Agentes de la Propiedad Inmobiliaria (API); an agent with API certification has been accredited by the Ministry of Development and must follow strict guidelines and charge standard set fees. Other independent, and reputable, licensing agents include Gestor Intermediario en Promociones de Edificaciones (GIPE), and Leading Property Agents of Spain (LPA) which is based in Andalucía. A good agent should also offer you a wide selection of properties to view but even so, speak to more than one in order to broaden your search. On the other hand, it is possible that you will find the perfect house and have to deal with the agent that is brokering it. Either way, your lawyer should make sure that the agent plays by the rules.

Finding the Right Place

Once you've narrowed down your geographic region, you'll have to find a property for sale there. The same methods mentioned above under renting are valid for finding a home to purchase. Instead of looking for a For Rent sign, keep your eyes pealed for *se vende* (for sale). Find extensive listings at sites like Kyero (www.kyero.com) and Idealista (www.idealista.com), by visiting an *inmobiliaria* (agent), and by checking the classified of both Spanish and English publications.

Regardless of whether you decide on an apartment, a detached house, a rural home, or any other type of dwelling, you should know that there are generally three options for purchasing: a new home that is ready to move in to; a used home; or a *sobre plano* (off plan). This last option was quite popular during the height of the building boom. Developers sold apartments that were not yet built, using the income to then fund the building. By law, the developer should turn over the apartment within six months of the agreed-upon delivery

© CANDY LEE LABALLE

If you move to the Costa Blanca, you could live on a corner like this.

date. In practice, this rarely happened. Local news abounds with stories of hapless buyers left paying mortgages on dwellings that were never finished or finished shoddily. And, with the market in flux following the 2008 real estate crash, dozens of Spanish developers were declaring bankruptcy. As a result, buying off plan is a risk you'd be better off avoiding.

You should also consider the *tierra* beneath your feet. Land in Spain has three basic classifications. *Urbano* (built-up) land is thoroughly developed. It may be within a town or city limits or may consist of an *urbanización* (development) of homes grouped together. *Rústico* (rustic or rural) land is undeveloped and lacks basic infrastructures such as multilane roads, water, and electricity. It is basically any land that is not urban and includes the vast majority of Spanish land. *Urbanisable* (developable) land is more or less the gray area between rustic and urban. It means the land has not been developed but is in the process of being so.

Rustic land can be rezoned as developable at any time. This means, if you own property in such an area, you will become liable to contribute to the cost of new infrastructure to make the area urban. Of course, on the other hand, a change such as this will make the value of your property soar. Therefore, be sure you know exactly how your future property is zoned. And if it is *rústico*. find out if there are any development plans in the works. A lawyer is indispensable in this process.

If you are considering property in Valencia, know that in 1994 the regional government passed the Ley Reguladora de la Actividad Urbanistica (Law on Urban Development Activities) to promote urbanization. It has come to be known as the Valencia Land Grab law which sums up its insidious use. It states that rural land can be rezoned for development at the whim of the government. Thousands of expats and Spanish homeowners were basically left helpless as corrupt Valencian officials working in tandem with private developers stripped rightful owners of their property, forcing them to sell at a deep discount and in some cases demolishing their homes outright. The law is such a grave violation against Valencia residents that the Spanish government has been brought up on charges in the European Human Rights Court. Though the law was modified in 2004, it is still best to be careful when buying in this region. One way to avoid the problem all together is to not buy property located on or land designated as *rústico* (rustic or rural); if your property is labeled urban, then you will have no problem.

Another land issue to keep in mind is the Ley de Costas (Law of the Coast) which was designed to reduce the overdevelopment of Spain's coasts. By law, all Spanish coasts are public, and to preserve them, the government is halting coastal development. It sounds like a really good idea until you realize that part of the process involves evicting people who have lived on the coasts for generations. Owners of property near the waterfront have to make a special appeal to the government for the right to remain in their home. This right can be rescinded at any moment, therefore these homes are basically worthless—they can't be sold due to this law. So, if someone tries to sell you a waterfront home for a steal, it is most likely you who is getting robbed.

Paperwork

Once you've found a place to buy, you (or your lawyer) will have to launch the paper trail. First, you'll need an NIF, a *número de identificación fiscal* (tax ID number). If you have legal residence in Spain, then your NIE, *número de identificación de extranjero* (foreign residents identification number) functions as your NIF. If you do not have legal residency, you can request an NIF from your local police station. As this process could take a while, do it well before you begin your house hunt.

Next, you need to know the property is up to legal snuff. Visit the local Registro de Propiedad (Property Registrar) for a copy of the *nota simple,* a certificate that indicates: the legal owner of the property (should be the same as the seller); any outstanding debts on the property; a description of the property; the type of land it is built on; and any information about rights that others may have over the property (governmental rights to build pathways, pipes, or other infrastructure). You'll also need to visit the local office of the *catastro* (land registry) for a certificate detailing the land, including its boundaries, size, and layout. You'll need to ensure that the *impuesto de bienes inmuebles* (real estate tax) are paid. This annual tax is tied to the property; if you purchase a property with back taxes, you'll assume liability for paying them. If you are buying in a development, then you'll also want to consult the *plan parcial.* This document indicates the plan of current and future building planned for your development and should be registered at the local town hall.

Mortgages

If everything is in order, you can make an offer on the home. Once a price is agreed upon, you'll sign a private contract with the seller, paying a small amount to have the property taken off the market. Later, you'll sign a public contract in front of the *notario,* but before you can get to that all-important event, you'll have to apply to a Spanish bank for an *hipoteca* (mortgage). The mortgage will be based on the assessed value of the property, not the actual sales price. To determine this, the bank will direct you to hire an *empresa de tasación* (assessor) to make an evaluation of the home. The maximum mortgage for nonresident foreigners is 60 percent of the total assessed value of the property, 80 percent for residents.

Bear in mind, as of the writing of this book, the housing market in Spain was virtually frozen and mortgages nearly impossible to obtain. As a result, the government of Spain was investigating modifications to the sector. Again, do your homework to know the status of the market and banking regulations before you start looking for a Spanish home to buy.

The Contract

Your lawyer, banker, and seller (or seller's agent) will work together to get to the highlight of this buying blitz—the *contrato compra-venta* (sales contract). It will have to be done in the notary's office, according to his schedule. Don't worry, everyone involved recognizes the notary as the god of the entire process and will adjust their schedules to comply. After all, if you don't sign the contract with the notary, then you don't get a mortgage, the house doesn't get sold, and no one makes any money. At a minimum the contract must include: the amount, rate, and terms of the mortgage; a description of the home; and a declaration that the property is free of outstanding charges. Once you add your *firma* (signature), you are literally almost home!

Taxes and Fees

In addition to the portion of the mortgage that the bank will not finance, you will have to pay your lawyer, the notary, the assessor, any *gestor* services that

DAILY LIFE

you employ, and taxes. The buyer must pay the *impuesto de transmisiones patrimoniales* (property transfer tax) upon signing the contract—that's 7 percent of the purchase price. By law, the *impuesto sobre el incremento del valor* (capital gains tax) is the responsibility of the seller but the common practice in Spain is for the buyer to agree to pay it. You'll also have to pay a fee to the Property Registry in order to file the deed in your name. And that is it. With everything paid and filed, you are now the owner of your very own piece of España!

Building

Maybe you are more of a DIY kinda person and dream of building your own *casa* in the Spanish sun. You won't be the first foreigner to do so. So many have written books based on their experiences that you'd expect the local *librería* (bookstore) to have a genre entitled "expat building adventures in Spain." One word of caution: Do not undertake a building project if you cannot snap into a Zen-like calm in the face of red tape and inexplicable delays. You will inevitably face your fair share of hold-ups, back-ups, and plain old screw-ups. Chalk it up to the Spanish philosophy of *mañana* (tomorrow), a dose of corruption, or just plain bureaucracy, but there's no getting around it—hence all those books!

After scouting out the land, you'll have to confirm that you can legally build there. For this, you'll have to consult the local town hall on the zoning of the land. Is it *urbano* (built-up), *rústico* (rustic or rural), or *urbansible* (developable)? Further, all *parcelas* (plots) available for development are further restricted—a building must be a certain size in relation to the land itself. There might be other zoning regulations from limits on the height of the structure to its distance from the road. You'll also want to know about any public rights to the land. For example, perhaps the land can be developed but if a public bike path crosses the property, you'll have to make sure that the path remains unobstructed. Finally, you will want to ensure that no major roads or other obtrusive construction are planned nearby. Get this information at the local town hall by viewing the Plan General de Ordenacion Urbana (building plan). You'll also need a *nota simple* (simple note or certificate) from the Property Registry confirming the details of the seller and confirming that the land has no outstanding taxes. Once this is all checked out, you'll need to hire an architect to draw up the plans in accordance with these legal restrictions.

Once you have that information, you're ready to move onto the mortgage, which works exactly like it would if you were buying a house. Again, it goes

Historic buildings are often adorned with gorgeous old doors.

hand-in-hand with the sales contract, and the entire process will be overseen and endorsed by a notary. Once the contract is signed and taxes are paid, you can apply for the building permit. With the detailed plans from your architect, you can request this *permiso* at the local town hall. You'll also have to hire a builder—be sure to work only with a licensed builder so you have legal recourse should anything go wrong. Be aware that illegal and corrupt builders are rampant in Spain. Get references, talk to others who have used builders, and when you find a builder, check out their qualifications and license. Have your lawyer check out the builder's contract. It must state the cost of the project, the payment terms, the date of completion, a description of the job, and the financial penalty should the home be finished late. The home should be insured while it's under construction, and the builder usually takes out the policy. For future reference, you should know that you'll have six months from the signing of the deed to have the builder make corrections to faulty work.

Flash forward to the time when your new home has been built. Before you pack your bags and prepare for the move, you'll have to register your property now that it exists. In general, the steps are as follows. The architect should issue you a Certificado Final de la Dirección de la Obra, certifying that the building is complete. Take that to town hall where you can get a Licencia de Primera Ocupacion, licensing you as the first occupant. Now, you can make an appointment with your *notario* for the issuance of an *escritura* (deed). Finally, you can register the property with the Registro de la Propiedad. Connect the utilities and move in!

RESTORING

If you want to make alterations to your property—even something as minor as adding a terrace or garage—you'll need permission. For a small fee, your local *ayuntamiento* (town hall) can provide you with the necessary license. However

© NIKKI WEINSTEIN

DAILY LIFE

take note: Many people ignore the fact that they need to get permission, especially for small, interior jobs. If you do this, you will get caught. How do I know? One of the less pleasant facts about *vecinos* (neighbors) is that they are famous for the very unneighborly practice of calling the police whenever they hear construction going on. If you have your license, the police will confirm that and ignore your neighbor. If you do not, at a minimum, you will be ordered to stop construction; at a maximum, you'll be fined and obligated to dismantle whatever you've started to build.

THE RAIN IN SPAIN DOES *NOT* FALL ON THE PLAIN

If you're used to hosing off your driveway, scrubbing down your car, and taking long, leisurely showers, you'll want to amend your ways once you reach Spain. Water is a resource in this mostly parched land. And while there is rain, it does not fall much on the plain nor in many other areas of the country. Northern Spain has ample rainfall and the Ebro River regularly overflows its banks but areas like Murcia, Valencia, Barcelona, and other regions along the Mediterranean coast face annual droughts and water shortages. On the famous sunny *costas*, wastewater is recycled and used to irrigate crops and keep the golf courses green. But when the local population increases tenfold during the high season, the region's water resources are stretched to their brink; some farmers' very livelihoods are on the line when supplies dip too low.

In the past Spain sought to rectify this problem by diverting water from regions swimming in it to those dying of thirst. The first such plan was put into place in the 1960s, linking the Tajo River (Tagus in English) which runs through the central west of the country to the Segura River which flows through the southeast. Though the Segura is mostly in a state of semidrought, this diversion resulted in the influx of some 600 million cubic meters of water per year, allowing farmers in Murcia—often called the "garden of Europe" for its vast farmland—to water their crops. But, there was a backlash too. The guarantee of all this new water led many farmers to switch from low-water crops such as figs, dates, and lemons to high-water crops such as maize and lettuce. This has exacerbated the drought situation in Murcia and led to much regional controversy pitting farmers against developers and regions against each other.

A more recent scheme to divert water from the Ebro to parched areas in the Mediterranean was met with great public protest in regions through which the river flowed. There were widespread concerns that the diverted water would go to fill swimming pools and water golf courses. Though some of the claims were exaggerated, political maneuvering and legal loopholes in the most parched regions of the country have indeed led to just these sorts

Household Expenses

The cost of living in a house includes upkeep—you'll have to fix things from broken pipes to wiring problems. Though such services in Spain tend to be lower than in the United States, they can still add up on a poorly maintained property. Another major cost is your homeowner's insurance. The premium is based on the size and value of the house as well as of your belongings. While Spanish law does not require that you have such a policy, if you have a mortgage the bank demands one.

of situations. In some areas, golf courses have had their greens labeled "farmland" and therefore eligible for inexpensive water meant for irrigation. In a further twist, the Ebro diversion plan led many developers to count on the future influx of water and even more resorts and golf courses were built in anticipation. Farmers were not immune to the water frenzy and many expanded even further into high-water crops. When the plan was all but scrapped in the early 2000s, all of these parties were left literally high and dry.

In addition to water diversion, Spain relies on underground water wells and desalination plants. The former are susceptible to pollution, salting, and literally running dry. Many look to the latter as the solution to the country's water problem. Spain was the first European country to build a desalination plant and has become a world leader in desalination technology with over 700 plants currently in operation and several dozen more in construction as this book when to print. However, desalination operations have been decried by environmentalists in part due to the high amount of energy needed to run them.

Regardless of how Spain reacts to its water woes, Mother Nature soldiers on. Climate change and reduced rainfall are leading to the desertification of areas of southern Spain. 2008 saw some of the most severe droughts ever in the country with water reservoirs dipping to nearly empty in many regions. Barcelona was one of the hardest hit areas and the local government began levying stiff fines on the misuse of drinking water to fill swimming pools, wash cars, or water gardens. Summer rationing of water and increased water costs are a given along the southern Mediterranean region.

What all this means to you is this—learn to conserve water. If you are building in Spain, consider foregoing the pool and let the kids join the community pool instead. In your home, rented or bought, replace old taps and faucets with those that consume less water. If you garden, get to know cacti and other succulents that don't require heavy watering. Think shower, not bath. Turn off the tap while you brush your teeth. Doing these things will make you part of the solution to the water problem in your new homeland.

Facturas (bills) will comprise a chunk of your household expenses.

If you live in a building or a community of homes, you'll also have to pay a monthly *comunidad* (community fee) which covers the expense of shared amenities such as a pool, doorkeeper, or parking garage. Costs vary depending on the total number of properties and the size of your unit, but the range usually starts at about 0.075 percent of the shared community cost and can go as high as 0.1 percent.

UTILITIES

Your utility costs will vary depending on where you live and the size of your household. If you're settled in the south where winters are mild, then you're heating costs will be minimal. Of course, you'll want air-conditioning running straight through the infernal heat of summer, and that will increase your overall payments. If you're in the mountains you'll have colder winters but more temperate summers, so the costs will ultimately remain about the same. However, if you're living in Madrid or on the Spanish tableland in the center of the country, you'll have cold winters, hot summers, and your utility bills will be a good portion more than they would be elsewhere. In 2008, my three-bedroom apartment in Madrid generated bimonthly electricity costs of €40 for electricity, €25 for gas. In the coldest months of winter, those prices doubled.

Of course before you worry about paying utilities, you'll have to make sure they're hooked up. Electricity is an easy one. Just call or stop by the local company's office to sign a contract (Iberdrola and Endesa are two of the largest providers). You'll need to bring along your ID and the previous owner's contract. If you will need gas for heat or hot water, contact the local gas company (Gas Natural is the largest provider) to set up a contract. Parts of Spain are dangerously parched and thus water is heavily regulated. Your local municipality will manage your water supply and can set up your account.

LANGUAGE AND EDUCATION

A brief trip to Spain requires no more Spanish than that found in a pocket-sized phrasebook. But if you're interested in anything more than a train ticket or a cup of *café con leche* (coffee with milk), you'd better break out the Spanish books. You'll need to speak the language to negotiate a work contract, buy a home, visit the doctor, and just about any other activity you can think of. But beyond basic survival, you'll need the language to make friends, to build a social circle, to fit in. From popular television shows to political discussions to the lingering after dinner conversations called *sobremesa,* almost every utterance you'll hear will be in *castellano* (Castilian Spanish). If you can't join in, the mere sound of discourse can feel like an unintentional affront. You'll be forced to remain silent, stuck on the fringes of your new community. There is just no getting around it—speaking Spanish is *imprescindible* (indispensable) if you want live here for the long-term.

SPEAKING IN TONGUES

You've downloaded hours of Spanish podcasts into your iPod, dog-eared your old Spanish textbook, and memorized a few key phrases like where is the bathroom and how much are the clams. Then you arrive in Spain and immediately notice the signs are posted with words you don't recognize and people are speaking in a tongue that sounds nothing like what you heard in the last Almodóvar film. No, you are not crazy. As locals will eagerly point out, you are no longer in Spain, you are in Cataluña. Or Galicia. Or País Vasco.

Though Spanish – or, more correctly, Castellano (Castilian Spanish) – is the official language of the nation and constitutes the mother tongue of the vast majority of Spain's 45 million inhabitants, there are several regions where the local language holds co-official status. These include Català (Catalan), Gallego (Galician), and Euskara (Basque).

Use of the regional languages – especially Català and Euskara – has deep political and social underpinnings. The dictator Franco maintained his iron grip on Spain in part by squashing any expression of regionalism. He enforced Castilian Spanish as the sole official language of the nation and the

regional tongues were banned from public use in all forms including the media, schools, street signs, and art. Even those who chose to speak the languages at home had to be careful lest a nosy neighbor report them to the authorities. Speaking a regional language was enough to warrant suspicion and even arrest.

All that changed when the dictator died in 1975. Democracy was promptly restored in Spain and great efforts were made to reestablish the use of the other *lenguas españolas*. Daily press, radio, television, books, and websites in these languages now flourish and the numbers of native speakers are growing. In the regions where they hold co-official status, they have often supplanted Castilian Spanish as the language of instruction in public schools and in governmental proceedings. These regional tongues are also commonly used in shops, bars, and street signs. Though you will be able to get along quite fine with Spanish if you move to Cataluña, Galicia, or País Vasco, you will need to learn the local lingo if you ever want to truly fit in.

CATALAN

Català is a Romance language that sounds and looks to the uninitiated

But wait, there's more! Castilian Spanish is not the only *idioma* in Spain. If you move to Cataluña, País Vasco, Valencia, the Islas Baleares, or Galicia—you're in for a linguistic bonus—these regions speak one of three co-official languages of Spain, Catalan, Basque, and Galician (see the sidebar *Speaking in Tongues* for details). Though Castilian Spanish is also spoken in these regions, again, if you want to fit in over the long-term, you'll have no choice but to do double-duty on your language learning.

© CANDY LEE LABALLE

the typical lettering used in Basque language signs

like a blend of Spanish and French. However, it is its own language, at least as old as the other Romance languages and is spoken by an estimated nine million people. In addition to Cataluña, it is the co-official language in the Islas Baleares and the language of choice in the tiny country of Andorra. A very similar version of Catalan is also spoken in Valencia, though there it is called Valenciano.

BASQUE

Unlike all other languages in western Europe, Euskara is not part of the Indo-European language family and cannot be linked to any other known language. It stands alone as the sole relic of an ancient tongue used by pre-Roman tribes. As such, it is considered one of the oldest documented languages in use in the world today. Today it is the co-official regional language spoken by more than half a million people in northern Spain.

GALICIAN

Gallego sounds like a mix between Spanish and Portuguese and, in fact, both Portuguese and Gallego derive from the same ancient language. There are an estimated three million speakers of Gallego, mainly in Galicia, though great numbers of Galician immigrants in Argentina also speak the language. In fact, the Argentinean word for a Spaniard is "gallego."

Of course, the more entrenched you become in Spanish culture, the more you'll come in contact with Spain's educational system beyond language learning. Maybe you'll choose to earn a master's in a Spanish university or have your American degree officially recognized in Spain. Even if you're not planning on enrolling in classes yourself, you'll still want to know a little bit about Spain's education system, especially if you're a parent looking to place your child in a school.

Learning the Language

Can you even manage in Spain if you don't speak Spanish? It's difficult but, yes, you can get by. If you live here awhile, you are sure to run into expats who've managed just fine for decades with only minimal Spanish (though this really only functions well in large expat communities such as those on the Mediterranean coasts and the Balearic Islands). With the help of a decent phrasebook, you'll likely be able to handle everyday tasks such as shopping for groceries or asking for directions. Inevitably you'll hit a few situations that demand verbal communication and for some of them, pointing and pantomime can get the job done. When the squeaking of the bedroom door began to make me crazy, I went to the nearest *ferretería* (hardware store) and pointing at their own front door began making my own squeaking noise. After a lot of laughter at my expense, I finally got a can of lubricant and vowed to take my Spanish beyond *principiante* (beginner) and get to the juicy stuff such as *chirriar* (to squeak).

Everyone approaches learning differently, but you should figure out a tactic—the idea that adults can soak up an entirely new language from merely being around it is a myth. Talking with Spanish friends of course helps immensely, but typically your friends won't stop midconversation to correct your every error. Most people will let you slide by with mistakes because they won't want to make you feel bad when they know that you're making such an effort. In a way, their self-control is a good thing—the strain of constant instruction in social situations wears on both the teacher and the student. So while immersion alone works enviably well with young children who manage to become bilingual in what seems like the course of just one school recess, adults who want to learn Spanish should seek out formal instruction.

SPANISH INSTRUCTION IN THE UNITED STATES

As part of your *gran plan* to move to Spain, you would be wise to add Spanish lessons to your to-do list well before leaving the United States. If there is a community college or adult education center in your area, more than likely they will offer Spanish classes. If you live in an area with a large Hispanic population, you may even be able to find a private instructor. Larger cities will also offer private language academies. Of course, prices vary extensively from nearly free to several hundred dollars for a course. Do your research to find the best course for you, but keep in mind a few things. Teachers might be native speakers or Americans fluent in Spanish.

If you're intent on studying with someone who grew up speaking Spanish, call and ask about the teacher before enrolling. Also, be aware that there is a difference between the Spanish spoken in Spain and the Spanish spoken in Latin America and other parts of the world. Some of it comes down to humorous vocabulary. For example, if your teacher is from Latin America, you'll learn to *tomar el autobús* (catch the bus), but in Spain, locals *coger el autobús* (catch the bus). Why the difference? In many Latin American countries, *coger* is slang for "have sex with," so unless your teacher is pretty kinky, you'll learn to *tomar*. Other differences will be more profound once you move to Spain. Consider pronunciation. In Spain, the letter "z" and the letter "c" before "i" or "e" are pronounced like the "th" in "thin," while many Latin Americans pronounce them like an "s." So a beer in Mexico may be a "sir-vay-sa" but in Spain it is a "ther-vay-tha." Another key difference is grammatical. In Spain, the plural form of you is *vosotros,* while in Latin America it is almost always *ustedes.* In addition, if you find a teacher from Spain, they will also be able to give you some insight into the culture and lifestyle of the country, and maybe even a few contacts for when you arrive. However, whether your teacher is from Barcelona or the Bronx, the basics of grammar and bulk of vocabulary is *lo mismo* (the same).

If you want to learn the Queen's Spanish, get ye to New York City and the **Queen Sofía Spanish Institute** (www.spanishinstitute.org). This Spanish culture and language organization requires students to pay a membership fee before signing up for a class—a chunk of change buys a year's access to a host of lectures, conversation groups, films, and other cultural activities. Similarly, the Spain-based **Instituto Cervantes** (www.cervantes.es) has centers throughout the world including schools in New York City, Chicago, Seattle, and Albuquerque; each location offers an array of programs, many of which are intensive. If you don't live near one of the four locations or if you can't fit a class into your schedule, Instituto Cervantes also has online options.

SPANISH ONLINE

Probably the most convenient and certainly the most inexpensive way to get to grips with *español* is through online study. Type "learn Spanish" into your Internet search engine and you'll get millions of hits from podcasts to videos to downloadable booklets. You'll have to spend some time perusing the sites to find one that works for you. Some are totally free, some require a membership fee, and still others you pay per downloadable lesson. Some of my favorites are **Coffee Break Spanish** (www.coffeebreakspanish.com), an award-winning series of weekly Spanish lesson podcasts taught by a pair of friendly Scots. You can sign up for free weekly downloads into iTunes or download individual mp3s. There is also a series of membership fees that offer access to past lessons, worksheets, quizzes, and more. **Notes in Spanish** (www.notesinspanish.com) is a series of beginner, intermediate, and advanced Spanish lessons based on conversations about life in Spain and focusing on the language and phrases that are used in everyday conversation in Spain. Podcasts are free to download; transcripts, lessons, and vocabulary logs require a fee. Ben and Marina, the English–Spanish couple who created the series also run the very informative blog and podcast **Notes From Spain** (www.notesfromspain.com) which they produce from their home in Madrid.

SPANISH INSTRUCTION IN SPAIN

Español para extranjeros (Spanish for foreigners) is big business in Spain. All the major cities have a long list of academies from which to choose and many smaller towns have quite a few too. You will also find courses for business Spanish, Spanish for children, and combination Spanish language/culture courses.

Academias offering intensive classes, options to live and eat meals with a Spanish family, and excursions to local sights are a popular choice for those nervous about settling into Spain on their own. Convenience does not come cheap and fees can reach as high as €800 per week depending on the school, number of classes, type of housing, and number of meals per day. If you do decide to go this route, I highly suggest you do your homework including re-searching the academy; some very well-known academies with fancy websites and glossy brochures, do not live up to their promises. To avoid getting stuck, enroll in the shortest program possible. If you love it, you can always extend; if not, there are dozens of other academies in town who will be happy to take you on. And when booking your program, check the average age. One of the most popular schools in Madrid offers dozens of classes per day to hundreds of students. What they don't advertise is that average student age is between 16 and 22; the 10-minute break between classes sounds akin to a Friday night tailgate party after a homecoming win. The handful of gray-haired students can be found cowering in the corners. Rather than pre-booking a program with an academy before you arrive, I'd suggest you first get to Spain, get a little settled, and then seek out a local school. You can choose based on lo-cation, class size, price, types of classes, and variety of extracurriculars. You may find that the inexpensive little academy around the corner from you of-fers exactly what you need.

If you have a *tarjeta de residencia* (residence card) or a student visa, you can enroll in the Escuela Oficial de Idiomas (Official Language School). This government-run institution offers two hours of study per day for less than €90 per semester, however not all of the 160+ schools in the system offer Spanish. The website, www.eeooiinet.com, offers lists of schools, instructions for enrolling, and more. Unfortunately, like many government websites in Spain, it is very poorly organized and full of dead-end links. Get a Spanish person to help you or search the web to see if there is a school near your home. To register, you will need to present a copy of your high school or university transcripts, translated into Spanish, and sealed with an Apostille de Hague and apply for a seat in the class on the day specified by the school.

If you want to know what's on the menu, you'll have to learn a bit of Spanish.

Yes, it is a lot of hassle, but you are guaranteed very good Spanish lessons taught by highly qualified instructors for less than a euro per day.

You can choose to learn Spanish solely for your own survival in Spain, or you can set yourself a higher goal. The Instituto Cervantes offers an exam leading to the Diploma de Español como Lengua Extranjera, better known as the DELE. This certificate, recognized by the Spanish Ministry of Education, Culture, and Sports, awards competence in Spanish as a foreign language at three levels: *inicial* (beginner), *intermedio* (intermediate), and *superior.* You can learn more from your language academy—most offer a specific course geared towards passing the exam—or through the Instituto Cervantes (http://diplomas.cervantes.es).

If your schedule is too *loco* (crazy) for a regular course or you prefer to learn privately, a tutor will be easy to find. Check the *anuncios por palabras* (classified ads) of the Spanish papers, online sites such as Loquo (www.loquo.com) and Segundamano (www.segundamano.es), and the classifieds of the local English-language publications. Prices run €8–€20 per hour depending on the teacher's experience and location. If you do attend a Spanish-language academy, you can also subtly inquire among the instructors for private lessons. The sad fact is that Spanish academies pay peanuts and many of the teachers are happy to take on additional work.

Education

Spain's educational system is not considered among the best in Europe. There are continuous problems with underfunding, overcrowding, and outdated teaching methods based on passive memorization. And extracurricular activities are nonexistent—no football team, no debate team, no prom committee; there's not even a prom! That said, the standards of education within the classroom are quite demanding compared to the United States and students are expected to learn a higher degree of information including mandatory foreign language instruction. The educational system underwent a total reform in 1990 and is still being tweaked by the government.

As this book went to print, the country's public schools were fitfully implementing a new government-mandated course on Civic Education, which focuses on ethics and good behavior as well as touching on thorny subjects such as gay marriage. The university system too was undergoing a massive overhaul to conform to European standards called the Bologna Accords. Major changes in curricula, majors, and degrees were expected.

EDUCATING YOUR CHILDREN

In Spain, schooling for children between the ages of six and 16 is mandatory and there are three options to meet this requirement. *Escuelas públicas* are free state-run schools. *Escuelas concentadas* are semiprivate schools that receive state subsidies. Tuition is free to minimal, though there are many additional costs for parents. *Escuelas privadas* are private schools, often prestigious, and almost always quite costly. British and American schools in Spain fall under this category. The Catholic Church is rarely too separate from the school system in Spain. Many semiprivate and private schools are Catholic and most public schools offer a Catholic religion course, though parents may have their children opt out of it. Homeschooling is still quite rare. For a very in-depth overview into how the schooling system in Spain works visit the website Schools in Spain (www.schools-in-spain.com) which is in the process of listing details on over 30,000 schools throughout the country.

Public schooling is completely free to all children in the country, even those of illegal immigrants. However, parents are expected to pay for books and materials, an expense which can exceed a few hundred euros annually. Students must attend a school close to their home, so if you want your child to attend a specific school, make sure you purchase or rent a home nearby. Lists of public

PUBLIC OR PRIVATE?

Deciding how to educate your child is entirely personal, but making your choice might be a little easier if you have a few facts first. If you opt to enroll your children in a Spanish public school, you won't be alone—plenty of other American parents have done the same and often with good results. Children younger than 10 years old pick up language skills much faster than adults and, not surprisingly, young children adapt best to Spain's public education system. Another perk to public education is that your child will have school friends in the neighborhood, whereas the kids in private schools usually live in homes scattered throughout the area. Expatriate parents often choose public primary schools for their child and later switch to private secondary schools—mainly with an eye on preparing them for college in the states.

In 2006, the Spanish government made a commitment to ensure that all students in Spanish public schools would could become fluent in English by the age of 16 and many public schools have also chosen to offer a bilingual Spanish-English education. Though slots are limited in these very popular schools, it is worth looking into. A complete listing of all schools authorized by the Ministry of Education can be found at www .mepsyd.es/centros.

If you prefer that your children be taught completely in English in an English or American environment, then consider private schooling. In addition to the exclusive use of English, these schools will better prepare your child for that American college application process. Unlike public schools, private schools offer extracurricular activities from sports to internships. The quality of the education is excellent and they almost always have diverse student bodies with children from around the world. Still, it's good to note that Spanish kids also attend international schools; in fact, they usually make up a large portion of the student body so your child would not be isolated from Spanish culture during the school day. Also, older students tend to do better in international schools where they can speak the language and understand the culture. There is no shortage of international schools in Spain and you can find listings at the Ministry link above as well as at www.schools in spain.com and http://spain.english schools.org.

schools can be picked up at your local *ayuntamiento* (town hall). There is normally a two-month registration period early in the year when you can apply for your child's position in the class. You'll need to bring his/her identification (national identity card, birth certificate, passport); proof of immunization; proof of *empadronamiento* (enrollment in the local city hall); and other documents as required by the specific school. If your child is over 12, you'll also need his/her education records from his previous school to be *homologado* (validated) by the Ministry of Education, a process that can take several months. Be sure to do

DAILY LIFE

the door to a high school in Madrid

this before arriving to Spain if you want your child to attend a public school. (See below under *Universities* for more details.)

But it is not quite that easy. The Spanish school system offers places in each school based on points. Points are obtained if the parents live and work near the school, if siblings already attend the school, if the family income level falls below a certain point, and for other various reasons. What this means is that you may not be able to get into the school of your choice. The best schools—including the handful of *colegios públicos bilingües* (bilingual schools)—in any area tend to be tough to get into as Spanish parents are notorious for manipulating the system. If you are not lucky, your child may be sent to another, less desirable school. However, persistence pays off. One American couple were determined that their son Oscar attend the public school in front of their Madrid home. The school also happened to be one of the best in the city. They were told no, Oscar had to go elsewhere. Mom and Dad weren't willing to do that so they proceeded to visit the principle every day for a month and finally out of sheer exasperation he bumped Oscar up on the list and gave him a spot at the school. Semiprivate schools also have their own points system, which can be a bit more selective depending on the school.

Private Spanish schools follow the same format as the public schools, but it is quite common that a student will remain in the same school from age three until they leave for university. Many expats, and Spaniards who want their child to have a bilingual education, choose private British or American schools in Spain. A listing of British schools can be found at the National Association of British Schools in Spain (www.nabss.org). Schools accredited by the American system are listed on the website of the U.S. embassy (http://madrid.usembassy.gov/edu/listen.html). These schools are particularly attractive if you will be returning to the U.S. before your child graduates as there will be no problem transferring credit. However, be ready to pay up. Private schools can cost anywhere from a few hundred euros per month to a couple thousand. The American schools in particular are quite expensive—over €20,000 per year for high school level courses.

School Levels

Educación infantil or *guaderia* is preschool for children aged 3–5. It is not obligatory, but most parents take advantage of it as an educational boost for their children and a free alternative to a babysitter. From six on, education is compulsory and up to the age of 11, children attend *educación primaria* (primary school), also called *colegio.* From 12 to 16 years of age, they attend *educación secundaria obligatoria* (secondary education), also called ESO or *instituto.* It is the Spanish version of high school. The last two years of schooling, *bachillerato,* are optional, but if the student wants to go on to a Spanish university, they become required. Upon completion of this phase of education, a student can take the *pruebas de acceso a la universidad,* Spanish university entrance exams, also called *selectividad.* Students may also opt to attend a technical or vocational school instead.

UNIVERSITIES

Spain has a long tradition of university education. The Moors began a system of higher learning long before anything like it appeared in the rest of Europe, and Spain's oldest university, the University of Salamanca, was founded in 1218 and is still in operation today. The country currently has over 50 public universities and over 20 private institutions and some of them rank among the best in the world. However, for the most part, they suffer from some of the same problems as in the lower schools—overcrowding in the classroom and a dependence on rote learning. American students regularly complain about the lack of interaction in the classroom; students

taking a modern study break on the steps of the 800-year-old University of Salamanca

© BEA MORA

are expected to listen and take notes, and that is pretty much what they do. If you want a more American experience in Spain, there are a handful of American universities with campuses here including Suffolk University, Saint Louis University, Middlebury, and Schiller International. And, of course, dozens of American universities offer study abroad programs. The website of the U.S. embassy offers an extensive listing (http://madrid.usembassy.gov/edu/univer.html). Again, the university system was in flux as this book went to print due to implementation of the Bologna Accords which were expected to address some of these concerns as well as overhaul the degree-granting policies.

If you want to study at a public university in Spain you'll have to have your American education credentials validated through the Ministerio de Educación, Política Social, y Deporte (www.mepsyd.es/educacion/titulos/convalidaciones.html) in a process called *homologación* (recognition) for degree, studies, or certificates with no equivalent in Spain or *convalidación* (validation) for those that do have a Spanish equivalent. To start the process, you'll need to get your official transcripts sealed with an Apostille de Hague translated by an *jurado* (official) translator, and submit these materials along with the application to the Ministry. Do not expect justice or logic in this process. Kristin, an American with a biology degree and a teaching certificate wanted to teach science at a local bilingual Spanish school. After nearly a year of wrangling, the Ministry decided that her U.S. education had no equivalent in Spain and like it or not, she is now earning a new degree in the Spanish system. Another American, Vicky, finished all but two courses of her master's in Spanish literature at a top Spanish university when the Ministry let her know that her validation was invalid, and subsequently, so was her nearly-there master's.

Undergrads may also be required to take the *selectividad* Spanish university entrance exam which is offered online by the National University for Distance Leaning (UNED) (www.uned.edu/selectividad). Of course, excellent Spanish will be required. For graduate programs, you may or may not need the validation process and you may or may not need to take an entrance exam. Spanish may even be optional. Each school will have different requirements depending on the program. Contact the school for details.

Spain is also home to three of the world's top-ranked business schools. IESE Business School (www.iese.edu) and Esade (www.esade.edu) both based in Barcelona and Instituto de Empresa (www.ie.edu) in Madrid attract thousands of MBA students from around the world annually. The application process is quite similar to what you'd expect from a top American MBA program.

HEALTH

The World Health Organization (WHO) ranked Spain 7th in performance of its health service system out of 190 countries (the United States ranked 37th). Therefore, any worries about getting good health care in Spain should be dismissed. And, when you finally make your move to the country, you'll join some mighty healthy ranks. Spaniards have a life expectancy of 79.78 years—higher than the European Union average, and lower than average rates of heart disease, stress, and infant mortality. Health care in Spain is either free, or next to free, for all citizens and residents. However, even if your status is less than legal in the country, you will be treated in emergency situations. And, if you end up having to pay out-of-pocket, you'll be happy to learn that Spanish medical services and pharmaceutical products cost a fraction of what they do in the United States. About the only drawback to Spain's health care service is language—doctors, nurses, and hospital personnel have about the same level of English as the rest of the population, that is next to none.

© CANDY LEE LABALLE

Types of Insurance

In Spain people talk about *publico* or *privado* health care, that is the free state-run health care service or the private system of doctors and hospitals funded by private insurers. All Spaniards, their dependents, and legal residents of Spain who contribute to the Social Security system are entitled to use the free system. Nationals of other European Union countries and some non–E.U. nations, particularly in Latin America, may also qualify for coverage depending on any applicable treaties between Spain and the foreign country. Many residents in Spain, both nationals and foreigners, also enroll in a private system to amplify their medical options. Those with no legal rights to use the public system, have no choice but to go private—but if that is you, don't worry, private policy prices are considerably cheaper than in the U.S.

PUBLIC CARE

The public health care system is governed by the Ministry of Health (www.msc.es) and not only is it highly rated, it is also free. Anyone contributing to the Social Security system—Spaniard or not—is entitled to a national health card and use of the system. It covers anything from a sprained ankle to pregnancy to cancer treatment. Of course, "free" can be defined as "supported by taxes," but the bottom line is that when you see a doctor or take an ambulance ride, you will not have to pay anything out of your own pocket and you will never go without treatment. If you are not the dependent of a Spaniard, for example, through marriage, you'll have to get into the Social Security system before you can join the system. This means you enter as either a self-employed *autónomo* or as a business owner or your employer must be making monthly *social seguridad* payments on your behalf.

To register for the health system, you must visit the *centro de salud* (health center) that corresponds to your home address. In urban areas, expect to find one within 15 minutes' walk of your home. The Ministry of Health has a center locater on its website, but like many Spanish websites, it is difficult to navigate; you'd be better off asking a neighbor. Bring your proof of social security (social security card, work contract or other documents as pertains to your particular case), NIE (Spanish identification card), and a copy of your *certificado de empadronamiento* (local registration certificate). This document certifies that you live in a particular neighborhood and can be acquired with a visit to your local town hall. The chapter *Making the Move* has more on the *empadronamiento* process and how to acquire your NIE.

© CANDY LEE LABALLE

Many expats choose to have both public and private insurance.

Within three months, you will receive your *tarjeta sanitaria* (health card) in the mail. You will also be assigned a *médico cabecera* (general practitioner). To see your doctor, all you need to do is call your health center and request a *cita previa* (appointment). Usually, you will get one within a few days. And when you arrive for your appointment, you'll be happy to find that the medical staff sticks very closely to the appointment schedules—very rarely will you have to wait more than half an hour. In addition to seeing doctors, participation in the health care system entitles you to have lab tests, buy discounted drugs (you'll pay about 40 percent of the cost), and receive basic dental care. Ambulance rides, operations, and hospital stays are also covered.

If you need to see a specialist, your general practitioner will give you the referral. But here is where it gets a little sticky. If you are dealing with an emergency situation, you most likely will get a very prompt appointment. If your problem is deemed nonemergency, the wait to see a specialist or schedule an operation can be insufferably long. Many gripe about the length of the waiting list for hospital beds, too. Depending on the area and the hospital, the wait can be as long as six months. The last common complaint voiced is about the extras. Alternative medicine, thorough postoperative care, geriatric assistance, and psychiatric treatment are not as readily available as they are on private plans. For these reasons, private health care is often used as a backup service by those who can afford it.

PRIVATE CARE

Most Americans living in Spain choose private health coverage. Some go that route because paid plans offer more perks and shorter waits than the national health service. Others pay for coverage because as nonresidents they have no other choice. And for some visas, for example student visas, the Spanish government requires that you have a private plan covering you in Spain before they issue the visa.

The most popular of the private insurers is **Sanitas** (www.sanitas.es), the Spanish branch of the British health care giant BUPA. It offers a variety of plans, from bare bones to upscale coverage including hospitalization and worldwide care. There is also a dental coverage supplement. Other popular private insurers include **Adeslas** (www.adeslas.es) and **Cigna** (www.cigna.es). **Asisa** (www.asisa.es), **DKV** (www.dkvseguros.com), and **Mapfre** (www.mapfre.com) are all Spanish-owned companies and have fewer resources in English. For an overview of several plans available in Spain and beyond, contact English agent David Harris (www.mainlyhealthplans.com, tel. 60/952-2300) who works with several insurers, Sanitas and BUPA International among others. Brokering insurance plans to expats in Spain since 1992, he is expert in finding the plan best suited to your needs and is more than willing to help you wade through the paperwork, all in English.

Prices for private coverage start from about €50 per month for the most basic services. There are also co-payment charges of up to €20 per doctor visit. To determine your exact costs, speak with an agent or contact the company directly. But, in general, private coverage in Spain is a fraction of what a similar policy would cost in the U.S. For example, at the end of 2008, the cost of a comprehensive Sanitas policy for my family of three (two adults in their late 30s and a baby under one), was just €124 per month. Of course, private plans do not cover prescription drugs, but again, those costs are just a fraction of what they are in the U.S. Finally, many Spanish companies offer private health insurance to their employees as part of their benefits. If yours does, definitely take advantage of it.

Sanitas, as well as other plans in Spain, generally have an upper age limit of between 60 and 70, depending on the policy. In other plans, there will be a surcharge for older policyholders. Though a medical exam is generally not required to obtain coverage, you will have to complete a medical questionnaire and those with preexisting conditions or a history of heart attack or cancer will more than likely be refused coverage. Again, contacting a knowledgeable Spain-based agent will help you find the policy best-suited for your needs. Agents do not charge the clients for their services as they are paid by the insurance company. See the *Resources* chapter of this book for a listing.

Most private health insurance policies do not require you to choose specific primary care doctor. You can just call up anyone listed in the *guía de médicos* (doctor guide) provided by your plan. If you need specialized service, diagnostic tests, or surgery, the doctor will then give you a *volante* (referral) which you will have to get authorized by calling your insurer. Some of the providers run their own one-stop health centers such as the Centro Médicos from Sanitas which combine a variety of doctors and diagnostic labs in one place.

Your U.S. Plan

If you already have a U.S. insurance policy, don't assume that your plan will give you the same coverage in Spain. Once you step off U.S. soil, you'll face a whole new set of rules with your insurance company.

Granted, not all plans are the same, but most companies do provide coverage abroad in the case of emergencies. In other words, if you have the flu, you have to pay for your doctor's appointment, related tests, and medicine, but if you end up in the emergency room, your bills will be covered. However, you'll likely have to pay your Spanish medical bill upfront and file the forms for a reimbursement that will come to you sometime down the road. It's imperative that you speak with your U.S. insurance agency about coverage abroad to learn exactly what sending in a fat check every month will actually buy you when you're out of the United States.

So should you leave your U.S. plan for a Spanish one? Probably. That is, unless you're moving to a Spanish branch of your U.S. company. If that's the case, your employer presumably sees to your health care, and you might be able to remain on the same plan while abroad. To find out how your corporate plan measures up in Spain, speak to both your boss and your insurance company before accepting your Spain transfer.

Health Clinics and Hospitals

Even the smallest *pueblo* will have at least one publicly-run walk-in medical center—either a *centro de salud* (health clinic), an *ambulatorio* (outpatient clinic), or a *casa de socorro* (first-aid center). Each will be staffed by doctors, nurses, and possibly other medical personnel, and will be equipped to take care of most medical situations and emergencies. If you don't have a *cita previa* (appointment), you can usually walk in for sudden illnesses or emergencies, and if there is space in the schedule, you'll be seen. If there is no doctor available, you may be sent to the *urgencías* (emergency room) of the nearest public hospital.

Hospitales de la seguridad social are entirely public, while *hospitales privados* serve patients with private insurance. For the most part, the public and private sectors work more or less together. For example, an American professor

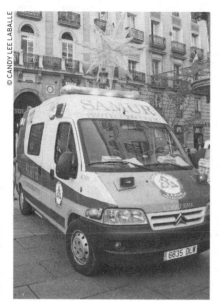

© CANDY LEE LABALLE

an ambulance on crowd duty in central Madrid

at a Madrid-based university went to his public doctor who found a tumor on one of his kidneys. The public system did a scan and biopsy and recommended him to have the tumor removed. But, because it was not an immediate health danger, the surgery was scheduled in several months. The professor's public doctor confessed to him that there actually was a slight danger in waiting and suggested he go to a private doctor if he could afford it. The professor did have private insurance, so he was able to get an operation scheduled within a few weeks. In another case, an American student with private insurance only had a fall and damaged her teeth and jaw. As it was an emergency, she went to the closest hospital, which was public. They gave her first aid and then sent her to another public hospital where a maxillofacial surgeon treated her immediately. She then did all of her follow-up visits with her private insurer.

If you are admitted to a hospital, you'll find more differences between public and private care. In the public hospital, you will share a room with one other person at a minimum, and may even be assigned to a ward with eight or more beds. Anyone accompanying you, will get a chair at most. In private hospitals, you are guaranteed a private room and usually an extra bed for your companion. The similarities unfortunately reflect the worst side of Spanish health care. Forget bedside manner—it is absent in both environments and nurses in particular have a well-earned reputation for rudeness. And, all the old stereotypes about hospital food are true in Spain. It is a shame that a country with such exquisite cuisine serves such rot in their hospitals. In a public hospital, there is not much you can do about it. In a private hospital, you can bring in your own food (with your doctor's permission of course).

So which hospital should you choose if you have both public and private insurance? Depends on the situation. Most Spaniards agree that for life-threatening surgeries and cutting-edge treatments, they prefer the public system. Because the government has more economic ability, they sponsor a lot of the medical research in the country and the public hospitals benefit from the best, newest and most sophisticated diagnostic equipment. However, if time is a concern, things move much faster in the private system. For routine procedures such as labor and delivery, private is often preferred due to the better service in the hospital including private, more comfortable rooms. For this reason, many women who know they want to give birth, will contract private insurance before getting pregnant. Regarding everyday concerns, if you have an illness or injury that requires you to miss work, you will need a *baja* (doctor's note) to give to your employee to ensure your continued payment. Your public *médico de cabecera* (GP) is the only one authorized to submit that sort of bureaucratic paperwork.

A final thing to know, public *urgencías* (emergency) rooms tend to have very long wait times. If you are not in a life-or-death emergency situation, you will definitely have to wait several hours before being seen. The reason is that many people commonly try to jump the waiting list for care by seeking it at the ER. If you do have private insurance, it is worth it to seek out a private hospital for fast ER service for nonemergency situations. If you are in an emergency, do not hesitate to go to the closest hospital available, public or private.

Doctors

The Spanish medical training system is much easier and less expensive than in the United States and therefore you will find many young doctors in practice. This does not mean they are not qualified—in fact, Spanish doctors rate among the best-qualified in Europe. Nonetheless, pay is quite low for the amount of work involved and Spain has increasingly been importing foreign doctors, mainly Latin Americans, to help shore up the shortage. There are also a good many German and British doctors practicing, but they are mainly on coastal areas where there are very large German and British expat communities. Unless you happen to land one of these doctors, it will be tough to find an English-speaking doctor. In both the public and private systems (as in most of Spain in general), few medical professionals speak English. And those that do are pretty well hidden; they will not be listed in the *Guia de Médicos* issued by your private insurer. At your local health center, it doesn't hurt to ask if any of the doctors speak English, just don't count on it. Ask around among other expats and check online resources such as the website of the U.S. embassy in Spain (http://madrid.usembassy.gov) and through forums like www.spainex-pat.com. Some health centers in areas with high expat populations (such as the Mediterranean coasts) will have an in-house translator. If you must see a doctor and can't speak the language, bring a friend along to translate. There are some English-speaking private clinics such as Unidad Médica in Madrid, but be aware, these types of private clinics usually operate on a cash-only basis, no insurance accepted.

Dental Care

There are many good *dentistas* (dentists) throughout Spain and you should have no trouble finding one. If you are working solely off of public insurance, it will be tough to get dental care covered unless it falls under the heading of medically necessary (and no, cavities and cleanings do not qualify). If you have private insurance with a dental supplement, you can see any dentist in your provider's network. If you do not, don't worry you can still open wide and say "aaah" at a number of private dental clinics. After years of pretty much ignoring their dental health, Spaniards are suddenly very conscious of their teeth. As a result, several dental chains have popped up offering everything from fillings and cleanings to root canals and braces. These include Vital Dent, Unidental, and Santa Lucia. The pain they inflict on your mouth will be pretty much equal to what you get in the States, but it will be more than compensated for by the pain you won't get in your wallet. Dental care in Spain costs a fraction of what it does in the United States. One American living here, brings her family for dental work every time they come to visit—root canals, crowns, braces, and sightseeing! The one exception is teeth-whitening procedures. As they are still quite new here, they are more expensive than in the U.S. The lack of English among dentists is as dire as it is among doctors. If you really need to speak in English with your dentist, ask around among other expats, inquire at your neighborhood dental clinics, and check the English-language periodicals as English-speaking dentists will often advertise there.

Eye Care

The best bet for *gafas* (glasses) or *lentillas* (contact lenses) is to go directly to an *óptico* (optician) for free evaluation. They will prepare a prescription for you if needed and sell you the final product. They can also refill your eyeglass prescription so be sure to bring it with you when you move. However, before stepping in, shop around. The optical business is Spain is very lucrative and

HEALTH **151**

that makes pricing competitive. In general, expect prices on par with American prices. San Gabino, Alain Afflelou, Visión Camarillo, and the British company SpecSavers are just a few of the more popular optician chains.

If you have an eye problem, illness, or injury, for social security holders, make an appointment with your *médico cabecera* (general practitioner) at your local health center and if needed, he/she will give you a referral to an *oftalmólogo* (ophthalmologist). If you have private insurance, just call up one of the ophthalmologists listed under your plan.

As in the United States, laser eye surgery is quite common in Spain and there are several clinics that specialize in this elective procedure including Clínica Baviera and Cimo. The concerns, risks, and costs are the same that you'd encounter in the United States.

DAILY LIFE

Pharmacies

Most minor health concerns can be taken care of at the *farmacia*. Pharmacists are able to help with many issues that would require a doctor's visits in the states—from strep throat to a twisted ankle. Pharmacies are listed in every phone book, but it is easier to just find one on the street—just look for the flashing green cross. Pharmacies keep regular Spanish store hours. (9 A.M.–2 P.M. and 5–8 P.M.). Big cities usually have a few 24-hour pharmacies and in each neighborhood and small town, pharmacies take turns as the *farmacia de guardia,* that is, at least one will stay open 24 hours. A sign posted outside each pharmacy will direct you to the nearest *farmacia de guardia* or you can call tel. 098.

Go equipped with your Spanish dictionary to explain what ails you. Unfortunately, many Spanish pharmacists, especially in smaller towns, don't speak English. You will also want to bring a measure of true grit as you will have to shrug off the embarrassment that comes from describing exactly where that rash is or how long it's been since your last lengthy trip to the bathroom. Take consolation in the fact that such conversations are the norm in Spanish pharmacies and the upshot is that the person in the lab coat will almost certainly be able to help you out.

Pharmacies also sell nondrug products such as beauty items and baby products, but expect elevated prices. *Parafarmacias* sell pretty much anything that doesn't require a prescription, while *perfumerías* (perfume shops) or *droguerías* (drug shops) sell everything you'd expect at an American-style drug store—shampoos, hygiene products, makeup—minus the drugs. Alternative medicines and natural treatments can be found at *herbolarios* (herbalist shops) but expect much higher prices for these types of products than in the U.S.

PRESCRIPTIONS

Medicinas may be purchased from any pharmacy and many drugs that would require a prescription in the U.S., are easily bought over-the-counter in Spain. If you have a *receta* (prescription) from your public doctor, you'll pay less than 40 percent of the actual cost of the drug; retirees and the disabled pay nothing. If you have private insurance, you'll have no choice but to pay for the medications up front and seek reimbursement (if that is an option) from your insurer later. However, even if you're paying part or all of the cost on your medications, it won't be a lot—Spain has some of the cheapest prescription drug prices in the EU. In fact, many Americans are stunned to learn that the full cost of a medication they have been taking for years is even cheaper than what they used to fork over as a co-pay.

Be sure and have the pharmacist explain clearly your dosage amounts. *Pastillas* (pills) come in packages of set amounts—they are not broken down into amounts as set by a doctor—therefore, you want to be sure that you buy enough packages to cover the length of your illness.

Disabled Access

Since the 1980s, laws have been passed assuring access to people with disabilities—*discapacitado* or *minusválido* in Spanish. All newer constructions must include accessibility in their blueprints including ramps, elevators, handrails, wide hallways, and Braille signage. Public facilities, from police stations to hospitals, cultural monuments to beaches, are also mostly in compliance with accessibility regulations. Public transport throughout the country has been made accessible or is in the process of becoming accessible, this includes buses, subways, and trains. However, you will definitely want to check the local subway map to see which stations have elevators and/or ramps. In the larger cities—Madrid, Barcelona, Valencia—travelers with mobility assistance will find few barriers to movement.

Despite these advances in accessibility, don't be fooled. Spain is pretty tough on those with physical challenges. Construction is rampant, roads and sidewalks are poorly maintained, and everything from seats at the bullring to parking spots are extra small—barely any room to move on two feet, much less on two wheels. You'll also encounter difficulties in smaller shops, restaurants, and bars as laws to enforce accessibility in privately-owned businesses are weak at best. Bathrooms in particular are difficult to access as they are often located down long, narrow stairs. Many of the *casco viejos* (historic centers) of Spain's cities are very unfriendly to those with mobility limitations. Built way back in medieval times, these atmospheric old quarters feature uneven cobbled roads and next to no sidewalk space. Your *silla de ruedas* (wheelchair) will be in for a bumpy ride.

Once you have your residency in Spain established, you can apply for a *tarjeta de minusválido* at your local *ayuntamiento* (town hall). You'll need to bring proof of your disability as well as your DNI (Spanish identity card). Benefits range from parking passes to subsidized housing and job placement. There are also dozens of organizations throughout Spain that offer support and legal advice to the physically challenged. One of the most powerful is ONCE (www .once.es), the Spanish organization for the blind, which also owns the country's most popular lottery games. National organizations include the Spanish Red Cross (www.cruzroja.es) and the Confederación Española de Personas con Discapacidad Física y Orgánica (www.cocemfe.es), which promotes the living conditions of the disabled and their family members. For local organizations, check with your town hall or search the Internet.

Most towns will have a shop selling and renting wheelchairs, walkers, scooters, and other orthopedic equipment. All of the cost of your equipment will be covered by Social Security (check with your private insurer for their coverage policies). And, if you bring over an electric wheelchair, make sure your battery charger can handle Spain's 220-volt electric system.

Preventive Measures

VACCINATIONS AND DISEASE

As long as you are up-to-date on your routine vaccinations, you won't need to worry about getting any shots prior to your trip to Spain. However, the Centers for Disease Control (CDC) recommends an immunization for hepatitis B if you do not already have one. A tetanus booster is recommended if you will be in contact with nature while in Spain and an influenza vaccine is suggested for children or elderly people who will arrive during flu season (November–April).

Children born to you while in Spain will be recommended for the usual variety of childhood immunization shots. Your doctor will give you the schedule for the vaccinations which begin when the baby is two months old. Under the Spanish health care system, there is no charge for these vaccinations.

You should be as careful in Spain as you would be in the United States when it comes to preventing disease—wash your hands, don't or drink eat anything suspect—but rest assured that you won't be any more at risk for any new diseases than you would encounter at home. The CDC addresses key medical concerns for Americans traveling to Spain at www.cdc.gov/travel.

Sexually Transmitted Diseases

Use the same precautions in Spain that you would in the U.S.—for example, always use a *preservativo* (condom) during any sexual contact. They are readily available throughout Spain at pharmacies and grocers and the prices are comparable to those in the United States. Look for the European CE logo, which means that they have been thoroughly tested. Condoms aren't a 100 percent blocker of sexually transmitted diseases or pregnancy, but they do help immensely.

According to the CDC, AIDS in Spain (called SIDA in Spanish) peaked in 1994 when the number of new cases reported was 7,428. In 2006, that number had dropped to 1,519. By 2007, some 140,000 people were living with HIV/AIDS in Spain, however the number of those with HIV is not clear due to lack of regular testing. As in the U.S., the source of transmission of the disease has slowly tipped from sexual activity to intravenous drug use. And a study in 2008, found that 35 percent of the new cases reported in Spain were coming from the country's growing immigrant community. The bottom line is that HIV/AIDS is still a concern, in the U.S. and in Spain. You know the drill by now, so do it—safe sex, safe sex, safe sex. If you are suspect that you may be infected by HIV or any other sexually transmitted disease, you can receive free testing at your regular health center, through many pharmacies, and by visiting one of the centers listed on www.infosida.es—search for *"pruebas."*

SUNBURN, HEAT EXHAUSTION, AND HEATSTROKE

Don't let those lovely, sunny days in Spain lull you into complacency. The sun can be brutal, especially during the warmer months and on the coast. You should always wear a high-level sunscreen every day. Wearing it at the beach seems obvious, but you can get just as burnt job-hunting in Barcelona as you can laying on the sand in Costa Blanca. Sunscreens are widely available in Spain and the best brands are ISDEN and Eucerin, both available at any pharmacy. Unfortunately, the biggest concern with sunburn isn't a bad burn.

© BEA MORA

Be sure to pack plenty of water for a day on a hot, sunny beach.

A serious scalding is painful in the short term but can lead to skin cancer in the future. Have regular checkups with a *dermatólogo* (dermatologist) if you are fair-skinned or notice any strange looking moles on your skin.

The Spanish sun can also cause other serious conditions from dehydration to heat stroke. In summer, it is vitally important to keep hydrated. Do not wait until you are thirsty to drink water. Thirst is one of the first signs of dehydration. If you fail to stay hydrated then you will be at risk for heat exhaustion, or even worse, heatstroke. Make sure your body remains cool. If you feel yourself overheating, seek out some shade and cool off. The main symptoms of heat exhaustion are headache, dizziness, and tiredness. Heatstroke is much more serious and occurs when the body has been exposed to extreme heat for an extended amount of time without proper hydration. In these conditions, your internal temperature can rise dangerously leading to a loss of consciousness or even death. Avoid this problem by taking a hint from the Spaniards who often retreat behind doors for a break at the height of the day's heat. Particularly, in Andalucía, you'll find the streets virtually deserted between 2 and 6 P.M. as the masses avoid the heat with indoor activities. Join them.

Environmental Factors

WATER AND AIR QUALITY

The drinking water is perfectly healthy in Spain and in many cities, such as Madrid, it tastes good too. That is not so true in rural communities which may rely on well water or in towns such as Valencia, where even the smell of the tap water is unpleasant. A lot of expats, especially those with children, prefer bottled water. Lastly, water from any dubious source—even a seemingly fresh stream—should not be drunk unless it has been treated. Before sipping from public fountains and other sources of water, look for a sign proclaiming *agua potable* (drinkable water).

Spain is very much a part of the industrial age, and that means that the country's environment is less than pristine. However, it is not much worse than what you'd find in the U.S. and in fact, if you go out into the more rural areas of the country, you'll find spectacularly clean air. Back in the city, it is another matter and it is not unusual to see bikers wearing paper masks to reduce the amount of pollution they inhale. Since the early 2000s, the Spanish government has taken various steps to reduce the emission of pollutants into the atmosphere. In 2003, Spain's emissions decreased by 1 percent compared with its figures for 2000. That improvement came as a result of more hydropower and less burning of fossil fuels. In 2008, the government created a new car taxation scheme that will result in reduced prices for cars that emit little to no carbon dioxide. If you live in a city like Madrid, Valencia, Granada, or Bilbao which are known to have particularly dirty air, you may find yourself visiting the doctor more often for respiratory problems. Definitely think about investing in a humidifier or ionizer for your home.

SMOKING

In January of 2006, Spain did the unthinkable. It all but banned smoking in all public spaces throughout the country. This was a remarkable turnaround for a country famously in love with *tabaco*. Prior to the ban, it was common to see people lighting up everywhere—in offices during work, banks, airports, groceries, public transport, and of course, bars and restaurants. Well, being Spain, that last point didn't come off too well, but since the law went into effect, it is now illegal to smoke in public places. The reasoning behind the law was twofold; to protect the health and rights of nonsmokers and to cut down on smoke-related illnesses among smokers.

Since the law, sales of cigarettes have decreased by over 5 percent and more and more people are claiming to have kicked the habit. Of course, you won't believe this if you go out on a Saturday night. The reason for that is a particular quirk of the law as applied to restaurants and bars. If an establishment has more than 100 square meters, it must provide a nonsmoking area. *How* it is provided is up to the owner which means a very big Madrid disco has a small balcony overlooking a dance floor as its smoke-free zone. Guess what smoke does? That is right, it rises and the smoke-free zone ends up being smoke-filled.

Establishments smaller than 100 square meters can choose to be a smoking or nonsmoking business and most, for reasons of pure economics, have chosen to side with the *fumadores* (smokers). This means pretty much any tapas bar you enter will be smoky.

So what's a nonsmoker to do? Deal with it. While the smoke is unappealing to many people, tolerance towards the habit is part of Spanish culture and you won't make any friends by loudly coughing and dramatically waving the smoke away from your face. If you want to be part of the culture here, then you will just have to learn how to tolerate the smoke. A good idea if you are particularly sensitive is to stick near the door or an open window and always opt for a terrace seat in warmer weather. You may find your clothes reeking of smoke when you leave. Air them out overnight by hanging them on your outdoors laundry line. I actually keep an old coat around just for going out at night; I don't care how smoky it gets as long as my new Adolfo Dominguez *abrigo* stays clean. And if you really can't hack it, look for bars or restaurants with signs saying *no se permite fumar* (smoking not allowed).

Safety

Generally speaking Spain is very safe. Violent crimes have not reached the epidemic proportions they have in the United States, and due to stiff gun laws, shootings are almost unheard of. However, petty crime and theft are rampant and, especially for those living in big cities, it will be hard not to meet an expat who hasn't been a victim at least once.

Common sense is your number one preventative measure against the two biggest crimes against expats—pick-pocketing and purse-snatching. Keep your belongings closely attached to your body at all times. In crowds, men should keep their wallets in their front pockets and women should swing their purses around to the front of their bodies and hold it tight. Try to avoid vacant streets and parks at night. If you live in an apartment building, never hold the vestibule door open to allow a stranger into the lobby. It might feel rude to close a door in someone's face, but being safe is preferable to being polite. Robberies often happen in the hallways of buildings after the door was left open. If you are confronted by a criminal with a demand for your belongings, don't argue—simply hand your wallet and jewelry over. Yes, you'll be outraged, but dealing with the hassle beats a face-off with someone who might have a knife.

If you are the victim of a crime, seek out the closest police officer or call tel. 012, the nationwide emergency hotline. To make a *denuncia* (complaint), call

DAILY LIFE

DON'T BE A VICTIM

Living in Spain is very safe. Street crime and random violence is at a minimum compared to the United States. However, Spain is rife with petty criminals and theft and robbery are all too common. Most expats, no matter how entrenched they've become, can count a few times they were victimized. As you assimilate into Spanish culture, learn how to keep yourself safe and what to look for to keep from getting robbed. Make the following habits part of your lifestyle routine.

Stay Connected
The simplest way to not be robbed is to stay connected to your belongings at all times. Backpacks should be zippered at all times and worn around the front when you are in crowds. Any valuables should be kept deeply within the bag, far from the opening. However, be aware that thieves do not only stick their hands in bags and backpacks but have been known to slit them open, particularly in crowded places.

When you are in a restaurant, bar, or Internet café, do not let go of your bag. Keep your bag on your lap, with your arm through the strap. Be sure and stay connected to your goods at places like nightclubs and beaches as well. Do not leave your bag or valuables unattended while you dance or swim.

When taking photos or videos, always have the strap wrapped firmly around your wrist – several times if possible. If you use a shoulder or neck strap, again, keep the item in front of you and your hand

on it when moving through the crowds. Thieves who see a valuable item hanging from a string will sometimes make a run at it whether it is on your body or not.

Finally, be wary when walking and talking on your cell phone. Thieves have been known to run up and rip the phone right from your hand midconversation.

Back to the Wall
You will have to stop and check maps, subway guides, and directions on occasion. While you are checking the above, assume that a thief is checking you out, hoping to take advantage of your distraction to pickpocket or bag-snatch you. Make it that much harder by backing up to a wall before looking at your maps and guides.

Divide Your Assets
Keep small bills and loose change in one pocket in order to easily pay for subway tickets, coffees, and daily necessities. Keep your larger bills and credit cards elsewhere. By Spanish law, you must carry identification with you, so be sure and keep it in a safe place as well.

Cultivate a Crowd Mentality
Whenever you are in a crowd – on the subway, watching a street performer, on busy sidewalk – keep a crowd mentality. That is, be aware that thieves use the jostle and bustle of the crowd to pick pockets, often looking you right in the face while they do it. When you are in a crowd, pull your bag to your chest, put your hand in your pocket over your money, and keep a close grip on your valuables.

Beware of the Bird Poop

This is an oldie but still icky. You are walking along and suddenly something wet and mucky lands on your shoulders. Immediately some kind soul – speaking English no less – appears, claiming a bird pooped on you. They have water and Kleenex and begin trying to clean you up. They are robbing you. Put your hand on your valuables and get way, even if you have to run. Do not talk or engage with the "helper." It takes less than 20 seconds to slip your wallet away – don't give them even a second.

Another common scam is opening a map in your face to ask for directions. While you are poring over the map, their hands are beneath it entering your bag or their friend is behind you doing the same. Other distractions include trying to sell you a flower or a sprig of rosemary. Again, your first step always is to put your hand on your goods, say no, and walk away. Do not worry about seeming rude; someone who is not a thief, will not take offense; only a thief will feign indignity.

Don't Get Angry, Get Away

If you catch a thief mid-action, you will naturally be angry. Don't let that feeling translate into action. Do not, under any circumstances, attempt to retaliate physically. These thieves work in teams. You only see the one with his (or her) hand in your bag, but guaranteed there are four or five nearby and if you confront one physically, the others will descend upon you faster than you can think. It is not worth it. If you do catch a thief at work, look them in the eye, and they will slink away. If a police offi-cer is nearby, you can try pointing the thief out, but the sad reality is they probably won't care and by the time you even get to the officer, the thief will be long gone.

Be Wary at Night

If you are walking alone at night, exercise the same precautions you would have back home. If you live in a particularly desolate area, even if you are on a budget, it is worthwhile to take a cab at night simply for safety's sake. When you enter your building, be sure and pull the door closed tightly behind you. Many thieves will pop in the building before the door closes and rob you in the hallway. If you feel uncomfortable at any time or ac-costed on an empty road, turn, run, and scream "*Socorro!*" (Help!).

What If They Get You?

If you are in an emergency situation or witness a emergency, call 112. This is the national emergency hotline number in Spain. If the crime is done and the criminal long gone, you'll have to report the crime to the police by making a *denuncia* (complaint). Do this by visiting the Comisaría de Policía (police station) closest to you; just be prepared for a long wait. Save time by making the complaint by calling tel. 90/210-2112. You will be given a case number and you can then go pick up your complaint at the police office later. If your passport was stolen, you'll need the police report at the U.S. Embassy to get a new one. If you lost your Spanish identification cards, the police report will also be useful in applying for replacements.

DAILY LIFE

tel. 90/210-2112 which has English-speaking attendants available or visit a *comisaría* (police station) in person. You can also contact Citizens Services at the U.S. embassy for limited advice on what to do next.

Drugs

Marijuana and hashish are the only legal drugs in Spain and they are only legal in very small amounts intended for personal consumption. The catch-22 is that it is illegal to sell them, so in essence, if you are buying either drug, you are risking illegal behavior. You will see people on the street and even in bars rolling hash (called *costo* on the street) cigarettes. Other drugs such as

The municipal police in Madrid patrol the capital city.

ecstasy and cocaine are very easy to come by. Again, they are illegal, unregulated, and dangerous.

Harassment

Verbal and sexual harassment is minimal in Spain. However, it is not unknown and if you end up in a situation where you feel uncomfortable, you should leave immediately. If you are alone and someone begins to follow you and attempts to touch you, pick up your pace and move towards the closest open bar or shop. Or, if you see a couple or group of people nearby, head towards them. Rape and violent attacks are rare, but not unknown. Exercise the same kind of caution you would back home. If you truly feel threatened at any moment, run and call out *"Socorro!"* ("Help!").

EMPLOYMENT

Plenty of Americans assume that if they pound the pavement and flash their ultrawhite smiles, they'll land at best the job of their dreams or at least a job teaching English. However, securing employment is a little trickier than that. For one thing, if you're assuming that your English skills will open doors, think again. People from the United States are runners-up for jobs that require English—those who speak the Queen's English take the prize. That's not discrimination; it's good sense. Because of European Union laws, the English don't require working papers but Americans do. It's simply easier for an employer to hire an EU citizen.

High unemployment adds another complication. As of the end of 2008, Spain had Europe's highest rate of unemployed workers and that number was expected to rise. This means a lot of Spanish people are looking for work too. Naturally, they're in a better position to find jobs than foreigners are. After all, they have connections, better known as *enchufes,* from friends, family, and school that most Americans lack.

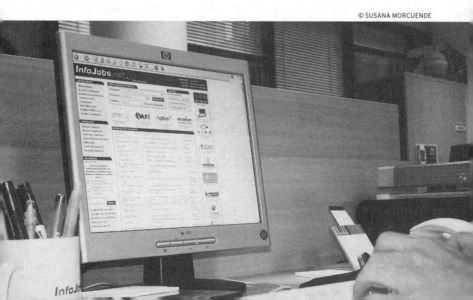

But don't let this gloom and doom dampen your fiesta. While finding work isn't easy, it's far from impossible and there are many ways to do it. Being hired by a U.S. firm to work in Spain, being transferred by your multinational to a Spanish location, or being hired outright by a Spanish firm are all possibilities. The other option is working for yourself, by either freelancing for U.S.-based clients or setting up a business in Spain where being foreign is an asset. Language, restaurant and tourist industries are particularly good bets. However, you'll be facing economic ruin (and probably ridicule) if you open a restaurant with the promise of serving up the best tapas in town. (Telling Spanish people that you can cook better than their mothers is more than a bad idea—it's close to a cardinal sin.) Know your strengths within the Spanish market and use them to the fullest.

Finally, a few words about working "under the table" in Spain. Depending on the political leanings of the group giving the number, estimates on *sin papeles* (immigrants without legal rights to be in Spain) range from a few hundred thousand to over a million. The very fact that these people do not have legal papers, means calculating accurate numbers is impossible, but you don't have to be here long to meet Americans in this situation. Especially among those who plan on spending a short amount of time in the country, working illegally can be attractive. No paperwork, no taxes, no hassle. And it is easier than you think. Language academies, construction firms, and private households regularly hire people without papers. But, even though it can be done, it is illegal and there are serious risks involved. These include at a minimum, fines, and at a maximum, temporary detention and permanent expulsion from the country. An internet search will bring up all sorts of stories of Americans living and working in Spain *sin papeles*. Do your research before even considering this choice. Though it might be a good way to get your foot in the *puerta,* if you want to live in Spain long-term, you'll have to eventually get your papers.

Self-Employment

FREELANCE IN THE UNITED STATES

Modern technology has made borders irrelevant. If you have a laptop and an Internet connection, you can telecommute. If you are an established freelancer in the United States, you can easily work from Spain and continue billing your U.S. clients. Ideal telecommuting jobs include writing, web design, translating, and just about anything where you don't have to show up to an office.

Of course, you will need to maintain a U.S. bank account, and your clients will pay you in dollars which means your salary fluctuates with euro exchange rates. And then there are taxes. The IRS will not be ignored and regardless of where you live, you will have to pay your U.S. taxes on those hard-earned U.S. dollars. And regardless of your resident status in Spain, if you have lived in the country over 183 days in one year, you are liable to file and pay Spanish taxes on your worldwide income. That said, many Americans, especially those who plan to stay in Spain temporarily, choose to stay under the radar, avoiding any and all involvement with Spanish authorities. Pop into any expat frequented bar or run an Internet search and you can hear their stories. If you choose to follow suit, be sure you are willing to accept the risks involved, including fines and back taxes if you are caught. And of course, if you plan on staying in Spain long-term, you'll need to get right with *hacienda* (the Spanish tax office). See the *Finance* chapter for more on both your American and Spanish tax obligations.

FREELANCE IN SPAIN

If you want to work for yourself in Spain, the first word you need to learn is *autónomo*. This is the title given to people who work for themselves. By being legally registered as *autónomo* you can bill clients in Spain, pay income taxes, and contribute to social security, entitling you to use the Spanish health system and to receive a pension upon retirement. However, before you can apply to become *autónomo* you must first have your residency in order, this means you need a residence card with a visa for *cuenta propia* (self-employment) and you need your *número de identificación de extranjero* or NIE (your foreigner identification number). Refer to the chapter *Making the Move* for details on visas, residency in Spain, and NIE cards.

There are two basic steps for becoming an *autónomo*. First, with your NIE in hand, sign up (*darse alta*) to pay taxes with *hacienda*. The form you have to fill out is a *declaración censal* also known as Modulo 036. Second, go to Seguridad Social (the social security office) and sign up for monthly social security payments, *cotización,* using Modulo TA 0521. The minimum you can pay is around €220 though you can choose to pay more. Payments will be deducted directly from your bank account, so have your account number in hand (See *Finance* for more on banking in Spain). In addition, if your work will be carried out in an office or shop where the public is allowed to enter, you will need to also get a *licencia municipal de apertura* (opening license) from your local town hall. And that is it! But, as you have probably started realizing, nothing in Spain is that easy.

Once you are set up as a self-employed worker in Spain, you will have to keep on top of paperwork just as you would if you were working for yourself in the states—only this time it is Spanish. You will have to keep track of all expenses related to your job—office supplies, Internet connection, advertising—as well as maintain all of your billing. For example, you will have to charge *impuestos sobre el valor añadido* or IVA, sales tax on your services provided. The percent charged depends on the type of services rendered and some fields, such as education, are not subject to IVA at all. Depending on the amount of your income, the IVA you charge will have to be filed quarterly (most *autónomos* fall in this category) or monthly. You will also have to file a yearly income tax return, an *impuesto de la renta sobre las personas físicas,* or IRFP. The amount you owe will depend on your income (which is calculated as earnings minus expenses) and can range 0–48 percent.

Jobs for American *autónomos* include teaching English, editorial work, web design and maintenance, playing music, massage therapy, yoga instruction, and just about any type of job you could imagine that can be done as an independent contractor. If you want to set yourself up in a field that requires a special license or professional certification, you'll have to register with the appropriate college. You most likely will have to have your qualifications confirmed by the Spanish government. For example, a medical degree granted in a foreign country does not automatically allow you to practice medicine in Spain. The Ministerio de Educación, Política Social y Deporte oversees the regulation of various professions including the long and often grueling process of *homologación*—the official recognition of your degree or certification obtained outside of Spain.

STARTING A BUSINESS

The next step up from *autónomo* is to set up your own business. And you do want to think of it as a step. Unless you are a major multinational or a franchising giant, you will probably want to start small, and there is nothing smaller than *autónomo*. This is the best way to determine if your business idea will fly. In fact, remember the 0–48 percent tax rates mentioned above? The rate depends on the income you are taking in. If you reach a steady income where your tax rate is over 25 percent, it is time to think about setting up a Sociedad Limitada, an SL or limited company that is commensurate with a small business in the states. Taxes on an SL are set at an initial rate of 25 percent, later rising to 30 percent. Therefore, if you are raking in the euros as an *autónomo,* it is time to move on up to SL. Again, you cannot begin this process if your residency is not established with the correct work authorization. But before you even consider the red tape involved, you need to consider three basic things.

First, and most important, money. How much can you put into your business and how long can you subsist without a profit? In addition to the €3,006 needed to set up an SL, you'll need legal fees, supplies, equipment, office space, and so on and so on. Of course, a traveling massage therapist will need a lot less up-front capital than a restaurant owner, so it is important that you make a budget appropriate for your business. You will also need living expenses while you get your business up and running. A wise approach is to store away the minimum you will need for your first 12 months. Again, this will vary greatly from person to person. Make a budget that will include your housing expenses, food, health insurance, and other costs. Be sure to include the monthly social security payment that you must make regardless of if your business is earning money or not. If you arrive near the end of that first 12 months and you are still dipping into this fund, you might want to reconsider the feasibility of your business.

Second, location, location, location! Where you set up shop will effect both your bottom-line and your type of business. Madrid and Barcelona will have much higher overhead costs than Murcia or Badajóz, but your possibilities will be greater. If you intend to open a sushi restaurant, don't take it to a small town with an aging population that will be stunned by the idea of raw fish and traumatized by the fire in wasabi. Big cities are about as unlimited in their business possibilities as are big cities in the states. Smaller towns will limit your scope, but there are always certain needs including English academies and English day care. If you are planning on an e-commerce venture, you could live in a hut in the Pyrenees as long as you have a good Internet connection. For all other ventures, your type of business and where you will settle down in Spain should be decided on together.

Finally, think about employees. Figure out how many people you'll need to hire and calculate that cost—it's usually a substantial one. The minimum wage for a worker in 2008 was just over €8,000 per year. Employers are also responsible for making the social security payments and providing benefits for employees. However, there are several different types of contracts you can offer, from seasonal to outsourcing, and each will affect your costs. Your best bet if you are starting a business that will require employees is to contract a lawyer.

DAILY LIFE

Establishing Your Business

The steps to establish an SL in Spain are very straightforward. First, request your company name from Registro Mercantil (the trade registry), to obtain a certificate stating that the name you want to use is not already taken. Second, you need to establish capital for the SL. The minimum is €3,006 which you can deposit into an account under your new business name. However, the capital does not have to be in cash; it can be in equipment such as computers. Third, establish the company's *estatutes sociales* (bylaws). It is best to have a lawyer or notary do this. Fourth, take all of the above to a notary who will give you a *escritura pública* (deed) for your business. A Spanish *notario* is quite different from a U.S. notary. A *notario* is a sort of liaison between the public (you) and the government. He/she is responsible for assuring that all your paperwork is correct and legal and his/her signature is as good as law. As you might guess, their services do not come cheap, expect to pay from €300 and up for the SL process. Fifth, return to the Registro Mercantil to pay 1 percent tax on your capital, about €30, and get a stamp on your deed. Sixth, in the same office, register your company in the list of Spanish SLs. This will take about 15 days.

Once the company is registered and the SL established, you can register to pay taxes with *hacienda* by applying for a *codigo identificación fiscal* or CIF, your corporate tax identification number. Finally, you have to register the director of the company as *autónomo* with the Social Security office, to ensure that payments are made for this person. If you will need to open an office or other public space or build a workplace, more steps and licenses are required. In addition, there are various legal requirements regarding shareholders meetings and accounting that you must meet. Add employees into the mix, and you've got even more requirements.

Closely related to an SL, is an Sociedad Anónima, or SA, similar to a corporation in the U.S. This structure requires a lot more capital up front and a host of additional legal regulations. If you are considering this option, you shouldn't be reading this book, you should be consulting with your international lawyers instead.

Paperwork and Administration

If your Spanish is excellent and your patience worthy of a saint, you can register as *autónomo* or set up your SL business on your own. If your bookkeeping is simple enough, you can probably also handle your quarterly tax reports and your yearly personal taxes. If you are ready to go this route, there are many resources to help you. The *Ventanilla Única Empresarial* (www.vue.es, tel.

90/218-1191) is a one-stop office where you can file all the paperwork needed to set up a business, including taxes and social security. There are also advisors on hand to help you with all the various steps and you can usually file for *autónomo* in one morning. The only problem is that offices are few and far between. For example, in Madrid, there is only one office for the entire city and it can take a while to get an appointment. The Spanish Institute for Foreign Trade (ICEX) has a lot of useful information at www.us.spainbusiness.com including the downloadable booklet *A Guide to Business in Spain.* It is well hidden in the website, so run an Internet search on the title to find it. Interes (www.interes.org) is an initiative by the Ministry of Industry, Tourism and Trade to promote business in Spain and includes many how-to guides online. However, be aware that in the 2009 ranking of "ease of starting a business" conducted by the World Bank (www.doingbusiness.com), Spain ranked 140 out of 181 countries evaluated. So, even if you are ready and willing to take on the task alone, you are up against some serious bureaucratic hassles.

With this in mind, you'd be *tonto* not to retain the services of a local professional to help with setup and maintenance of your business or self-employment. Help comes in two main forms: *abogados* (lawyers) and *gestors* (a combination accountant, bookkeeper, administrator). Both can maintain your monthly paperwork, including filing your taxes and filling out bureaucratic paperwork, however, only lawyers can offer you legal advice. Think of a lawyer as an advisor and a *gestor* as an administrator. Many people retain a lawyer to set up their business and then contract a *gestor* on a monthly basis to maintain paperwork and file taxes. However, your particular case will depend on the complexity of your business. Depending on location and the nature of your business monthly fees for a *gestor* start around €40 per month, lawyers around €100. To find a good *gestor* or lawyer, ask around among the expats in the area where you will live and check the classifieds of the local English-language papers. Finally, consult the *Resources* of this book for a list of tried-and-trusted firms.

Types of Businesses

Of course, why bother with all the above red tape if you have a bad business idea. Many foreigners who have started their own businesses have met with great success, but you should move forward cautiously. While Spain is cosmopolitan in many ways, it's also a traditional country. This means people are open to new ideas, but only once they're really, *really* convinced that a different way is worth trying.

The easiest in for American business owners in Spain is to target the expat

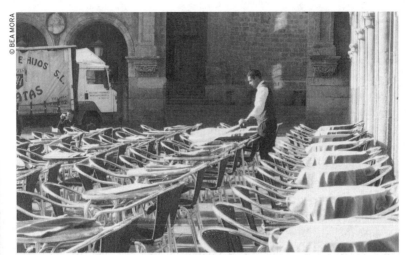

A waiter gets ready for the crowds at an outdoor terrace.

and tourist market with services where speaking English is a plus—inns, tour companies, exercise classes, real estate agents, counselors, wedding planners, midwives, and hairdressers are some of the more successful ventures in this category. Another option is targeting the Spanish market with something only an American can offer. The obvious choice is English language classes, and the demand is as great as ever. During the long, dark days of dictatorship, languages other than Spanish were banned and all films and television shows were dubbed in Spanish. That practice is still in common today, and combined with the generally very poor English instruction in public schools, you have a modern economic power with a workforce woefully deficient in the international language of business—English. Before setting up an English academy, it is a good idea to start out working as a teacher first, either on your own or in another academy. Other successful businesses in this category include nanny and babysitting services, educational consulting for Spanish students interested in studying overseas, translating, and language services for specific sectors, such as English for doctors, engineers, or lawyers.

Finally, you can open a business directed at the general public—expats and Spaniards. These include restaurants, bars, shops and just about any type of business you can imagine. A New Yorker who recently arrived in Spain, set up a successful corporate intelligence business, offering in-depth analysis of corporations to their competitors. This business existed in other parts of Europe, but she was the first to bring it to Spain. A Texan, after a stint in Thailand, noticed a lack of Thai restaurants in Madrid. So he opened not one, but two—both are very popular with expats and locals. Of course, it is a big bonus to have the skills needed for such a business before arriving to Spain. If you've never carried a tray of dinner plates nor managed a crowded bar full of sports fans, you will have a doubly-high learning curve pulling it off in Spanish.

The bottom-line? Know your business and choose your location wisely. With these things settled, you have as good a chance as any to make your venture work. But it is no guarantee. Expat-owned businesses fail all the time. Great location, great know-how, great prospects, great person in charge (you!), and then failure. Why? Consider a group of U.S. architects who had set up shop in Madrid but ended up cashing out and moving back to the U.S. after a couple years of floundering. What they failed to recognize is that in Spain, people will *always* give business to their friends and family before they hand it over to a stranger. I've mentioned the concept of *enchufe* (a contact) a few times and it works both ways. Knowing the right person can open all sorts of doors for you. On the other hand, not knowing anyone can lead to your being locked out of the party. Despite their expertise, the architects couldn't secure enough clients—they had no relatives and too few friends in the country, and because they were relying on a Spanish market for business, their social deficits made all the difference.

Business Practices

The Spanish way of doing business is not the same as the American way. You'll experience some frustrating moments when you approach certain situations in your usual way, only to discover that your get-the-job-done American mind-set gets you nowhere in Spanish business. Many Americans doing business here point to *la reunión* (the business meeting) as a perfect example. Where an American business meeting will follow an agenda and have an objective of solving a problem as quickly and efficiently as possible, Spanish meetings, which regularly last several hours, seem designed to do nothing more than discuss issues to death, never quite coming to a solution. If you have to attend a meeting with a Spanish firm, bring a good dose of patience along with your PowerPoint presentation. Also, especially with traditional Spanish businesses, hierarchy is extremely important and only top-level managers can make final decisions. This can cause additional delays if you are meeting with intermediaries.

For better or worse, Spain is not the capitalist juggernaut that the United States is. A good many people would rather have their nights free, weekends off, and lots of vacation time than be at the top of their field. One of the best things about Spanish culture is that free time comes before business. But when you're actually engaged in business here, this attitude can lead to some teeth-gritting moments. As Friday arrives, expect very little work to get done. And if there is a *puente,* one of the very frequent long weekends on the Spanish calendar, you may not be able to get anything at all done until it is over.

In Spain, the customer *isn't* always right—and if you offer to pay someone a little extra to have a service performed your way, you'll probably get absolutely nowhere with the tactic. The way someone offers you a service is the way you'll get it—no frills, no extras, no amendments. When one American wanted to shoot a television show in a certain Sevilla restaurant on a Monday night—a night when the place was typically closed—the owner flatly turned the producer down. So, of course the American explained that the restaurant would get free publicity and all that was required was opening the doors and turning on the lights. That point was met with the response, "I don't need publicity—I have enough customers and I *don't* open on Mondays." The producer was left speechless and the show was shot elsewhere. Americans are often always looking for a way to do something more efficiently or more cost-effectively. Spaniards, on the other hand, are more apt to do things exactly how they have always been done, because, well, Spain is different.

Finally, don't expect to grab a sandwich and eat it at your desk. Most Spanish companies have a two-hour break for lunch and staff generally head out to a leisurely lunch, go home for a break, or get in a workout at the gym. And many meetings happen over lunch. If you'll attend a lunch meeting, expect wine to be flowing during the meal followed by brandies or liqueurs after. A dinner meeting may not start until after 9 P.M. and will surely finish in the wee hours of the morning.

The Job Hunt

Arriving in Spain with employment set up is the ideal scenario, but if you're not in that lucky position you still have options. The most important thing to know is that speaking English is a plus, but speaking Spanish is a must. In addition to being one of the world's three most widely spoken languages, it's the language of business in Spain. Even in multinationals where much of the work is in English, you'll need to speak Spanish in order to interact with your coworkers. If you're less than fluent in Spanish, your job opportunities will be severely limited.

Keep in mind, the majority of employers will require that you be legal to work in Spain with the appropriate visa for *cuenta ajena,* or company work.

© BEA MORA

Many Spaniards dream of winning the Spanish lottery and never working again.

However, there are many success stories of Americans who found companies willing to sponsor them for the visa (see the sidebar, *Visa Success Stories* for a sampling). Though it is by no means easy, it can be done and it all starts with the job hunt.

First off, forget your résumé. In Spain, you'll need a curriculum vitae, normally called a CV. It should begin with a personal section that includes the usual data—your name, local address, phone number, and email—as well as some details that would never be required in the states—your birth date, marital status, and a scanned photo. But be aware, age discrimination does exist in Spain. If you are over 35, unless you are applying for a senior management position, it is probably a good idea to leave your birth date off and make sure your picture shows your youngest side. Employment and Education sections should be formatted in reverse chronology, with your most recent experience first, and it should feature the same kind of information you would include in an American résumé. Note that some Spanish companies will want proof of your education. It is best to have a copy of your college transcripts on hand, just in case. The CV should also include a section on language proficiency—beginner, intermediate, or advanced—and it is best to be honest about your level lest you find yourself in an interview with someone you can't speak to. Computing and other technical skills should appear under their own heading. Finally, most Spaniards include an interests section listing their hobbies or sports. Especially if you have any unique pastimes, definitely include this. Don't worry about the "one-page" rule; CVs generally run 2–3 pages depending on experience. And of course,

TEACHING ENGLISH IN SPAIN

Much has been said and written about how to become an English teacher in Spain. The amount of information is staggering, sometimes contradictory, and often confusing. Reflecting on several years of experience teaching English in Madrid, I will try to clear up some of the most basic questions.

What skills do I need? Communication skills, interpersonal skills, patience, and a sense of humor to start. It also helps to be outgoing. Organization is also a plus as you'll have to plan classes, administer tests, and manage any administrative tasks related to your job. You don't necessarily need to know Spanish, and in fact some academies will insist that you never use Spanish in the classroom. However, you do need to know English. That may seem obvious, but just speaking English is not enough. You'll have to know phrasal verbs and past tenses, gerunds and infinitives. If grammar was never your strong point, you'd better hit the books before you try to start teaching.

Should I take a teacher training course? For as many teachers that say you should, others will say it is not necessary. In my case, I never took a course and have not once had a problem finding teaching jobs. If you are a DIY-er or really good with grammar, you can probably also get away without doing a course. But, there are some benefits beyond learning grammar. You'll also learn how to plan classes, prepare materials, and conduct classes. In addition, job prospects and, in some cases, pay tends to increase if you hold a certificate from a teaching course.

When choosing a course, you'll run across an alphabet soup of acronyms. TEFL simply means teaching English as a foreign language and while many academies offer TEFL certificates, there is no one set standard for these. On the other hand, CELTA (Certificate in English Language Teaching to Adults) and TESOL (Teaching English to Speakers of Other Languages) are certificates granted in accordance with the British Council and Trinity College London respectively. Is one better than the other? Not necessarily. Some British academies may request CELTA or TESOL, but in general any certificate you earn will be valid when job seeking.

You should do some research on TEFL academies before leaving the U.S., but I would highly suggest you do not enroll or commit money to any school before arriving in Spain. Visit the academies once you are here, shop around for a good location and price, and if you can, speak to some graduates to get their feedback. One word of advice: Be very wary of any course that demands you complete long hours of unpaid teaching in order to graduate. A few teaching hours are essential to get your feet wet, but it should be nothing more than that. Finally, many of the larger academies offer free in-house training to their new hires, eliminating the need for a paid course.

How do I get started? If you do not take a course, you can get started like myself and many others did – job hunting. Jobs are posted online in TEFL forums and in English-language periodicals as well as in the usual classified sources.

In most cases, it will be nearly impossible to land a job teaching English in Spain while you are still in the States. You have to be here to make the contacts and go on the interviews. One exception worth noting is the Spanish Ministry of Education's North American Language and Culture Assistants program which places over 1,000 North Americans in public schools throughout Spain. The job is to assist the teachers in English activities and it comes with both a paycheck and a visa! Search for the program at www.mepsyd.es. And note – some unscrupulous employment agencies have been selling this program for a fee to unwitting applicants. This is a free program, you only need to apply and be accepted.

Can I get work without a visa? In theory, no. In practice, yes. While it is illegal to hire a worker who does not hold a work visa, it happens all the time. There is greater demand for native English teachers than there are native English teachers in Spain. Some academies ostensibly do not hire teachers without working papers and a very, very few will sponsor working papers, but you can always teach on your own to private clients without working papers.

Who should I work for? Your options are academy, agency, or yourself. An academy is often the best way to get started. You'll have access to materials, free training, and a support group of other teachers. The drawback to working in an academy is generally low pay. Agencies are individuals or small offices that book teachers. They handle the contract with the client – usually a company – and pay you separately. You'll have little to no support, but agencies often hire teachers without papers. Working for yourself means running your own business and all that entails. The upside is selectivity of your classes and higher pay rates.

How much will I get paid? This varies widely depending on location, type of job, type of client, etc. In an academy in Madrid in 2008, you could expect €11-15 to teach in-house classes and €15-18 for company classes. Agencies were paying €18-25 and freelance teachers were commanding €20-35. In general, company classes pay higher than in-academy classes. And the further you have to move from the center of the city, the higher the pay. If you are freelancing, you can charge companies higher than you can charge individuals – but you will have to be legal in order to bill a company.

Where can I get more information? There are many excellent online resources including the super portal Expatriate Café (www.expatriatecafe.com) which focuses on teaching English in Spain. Madrid Teacher (www.madridteacher.com) is based in Madrid, but there are lots of interesting articles on the teaching industry in Spain. Dave's ESL Café (www.eslcafe.com) is a mega-site offering all kinds of information on teaching English.

DAILY LIFE

it should be in perfect Spanish. Have a Spanish friend help out or hire a translator to prepare it.

Now, on to the job hunt. As in the U.S., the Internet has become the first resource for job hunters. One of the biggest job portals in Spain is InfoJobs (www.infojobs.net) which lists tens of thousands of jobs throughout Spain and is updated daily. You can upload your CV and establish a free account to help you keep track of your applications. Other Spanish-language job sites include www.monster.es, www.infoempleo.com, and www.trabajo.org with links to specialized job search databases. When searching for jobs that require English, type the word "English" in the *clave* (keyword) box. There are many sites in English, some more reliable than others. Try www.recruitspain.com to start. The websites of both Spanish and American papers are also good resources; for American papers, put "Spain" in the keyword box. The popular bulletin board site Craigslist (www.craigslist.org) has sections focused on cities throughout Spain. The Spanish site, Loquo, www.loquo.com, is very similar in structure to Craigslist and has sections focused on even more cities throughout the country. Both are excellent job resources.

The Instituto Nacional de Empleo (National Employment Institute) or INEM is a service of the Ministry of Work and Immigrations and can match people with a broad range of permanent positions. Their regional offices have bulletin boards with postings, resource libraries, and employees willing to lend you a hand. However, many people have commented that foreign residents take a back seat to Spanish citizens with the INEM. And, note that INEM is also the unemployment agency for Spain, handling issues of *paro* (unemployment) and benefits. By law, before offering a foreigner a job, a company should post the position with INEM, allowing the agency a chance to see if any unemployed Spaniard meets the requirements.

Several companies specialize in temporary positions; Adecco (www.adecco.com) and Manpower (www.manpower.es) are two of the larger ones. If you have a very specialized profile or a high level position, consider a *cazatalentos* (headhunter). There are several prestigious firms operating in Spain including Hays Executive (www.haysexecutive.com) and Ray & Berndtson (www.rayberndtson.com). Also, check out the websites of international companies with presence in Spain. Often, jobs will be listed right on their website.

And of course, there is the old standby—newspaper classifieds. In addition to looking through the *clasificados* in *El País* (www.elpais.es) and other national newspapers, don't miss *El Mercado de Trabajo* (www.mercadodetrabajo.com), a weekly paper that targets people looking for work, and global papers such as the *International Herald Tribune*. Local English-language periodicals are also good sources, especially *In Madrid* (www.in-madrid.com) and *Barcelona Metropolitan* which maintains the useful classified service, Catalunya Classified (www.catalunya-classified.com).

If you're persistent and keep your search as wide as possible, you'll have a good chance of success. Fair or not, you'll have one extra thing working in your favor. U.S. citizens have a reputation for being hard workers, and go figure, that's something most employers really like. On the other hand, labor laws mean that companies have to offer jobs to Spanish nationals first, European Union citizens second, and lastly anyone else—and that can make things rougher for Americans. Finally, don't forget the all-important *enchufe*. Connections will get you everywhere in Spain. Use them to the fullest. Family members, friends, friends of friends, people you meet on Spain forums—are all potential connections to your dream job.

INTERVIEWS

Job interviews can be good, bad, and ugly, and I'm referring to those in the United States. That's also true in Spain. You might hit if off with your potential boss, or you may sweat through your Armani suit—that's just a universal fact of job hunting. The basic rules are the same in both countries, arrive early, be prepared with information on the company and relevant questions, and dress neatly. A tailored suit is highly suggested for both men and women and, if you can afford it, a designer label. Spain is a country very much in love with labels and your good taste will be noted in the interview. As in the states, keep your hair and makeup conservative and neat. Finally, be sure to have crisp, clean copies of your CV tucked away in your leather portfolio (a briefcase is overkill). Other documents to have on hand, depending on the job, include letters of reference or introduction, academic degrees or certificates, a portfolio of work for creative types, and business cards if you have them.

The key difference in Spanish interviews is that it's unlikely that you'll know what salary is attached to a job before you're interviewed. And that magic number may not be mentioned even once during the interview. While salary might be the number-one question on your mind, don't blurt it out. Wait until the job has been offered before asking about pay. Once the job has been offered, you can and should negotiate—ask around to find out what the standard rate is for your type of job. However, don't be shocked to see that your salary offer is lower than you had hoped. Salaries in Spain lag well behind those in most other Westernized nations. It is a sad fact of life but one you have to accept if you want to live here. Also, keep in mind two important terms: *salario bruto* is your gross income before tax and social security; *salario neto* is your net income after deductions. Salaries are normally paid in 14 payments—12 monthly plus two extra in June and December.

BENEFITS AND CONTRACTS

If they like you and you like the salary, you could very well be facing that all-important piece of paper—your work contract. There are a few things to know before you sign it. First, is the contract for permanent or temporary work? A permanent contract is called *indefinido* and it makes you eligible for many benefits under law, including job security. Temporary contracts come in many forms—training, seasonal work, substitution for employees—and must adhere to various regulations. However, as you've already started to figure out, Spain is different, and the tremendous difference between the two kinds of contracts has nothing to do with what the contract actually stipulates regarding your job and salary.

More than 75 percent of workers under 25 have temporarty contracts, and that's not a sign that they're viewed as untrustworthy—instead, it has everything to do with the law. When a worker with an *indefinido* contract is fired, the company has to pay a lot of money. The exact amount is worked out in an equation based on the duration of employment and the reason for the dismissal, and is generally 45 days pay for each year worked with a maximum of 42 monthly payments. This means that an employer might have to pay a fired worker a full salary for several years after the person was let go.

Unfortunately, this law, designed to protect workers' rights, is hurting the system as a whole. No company wants to be saddled with an inadequate member of staff so in order to dodge that bullet, temporary contracts have become the norm. Under those circumstances, workers can be let go without penalizing the employer. The terms within short-term agreements are the same except for the duration of employment. The hitch is that such contracts can only be renewed for up to three years. After that time period, the employee must either be hired as a permanent worker or fired altogether. I wish I could tell you that at that point, bosses hand out *indefinido* contracts like it's Christmas morning but unfortunately, that's not always the case. After three years, many employees are let go. You may have no choice but to accept a temporary contract, if that is all that is being offered to you. If you are planning on staying in Spain only for a few years—no problem. But, if you want to make a long-term life here, you'll have to work hard to land a permanent contract.

Your Spanish work contract also entitles you to all kinds of benefits. First off, kiss your substandard HMO plan goodbye and welcome to Spain. If you're legally working a full-time job and you earn more than €421 a month, then your employer has to pay social security benefits on your behalf. This gets you access to the health care system which offers all residents and workers free, full-service medical coverage. You'll also be covered for work-related injuries, disability, unemployment, and pensions. If you fall ill, your employer will cover the first few days of your illness, provided you have a *baja* (sick notice) from your doctor. After a certain number of days, social security will then kick in, paying your salary until you are well. Longer illnesses are evaluated and covered in part depending on many factors including how long you've worked and the possibilities of your recovery.

As a contracted employee, you'll also receive an unimaginable (by U.S. standards) number of paid days off. Start with 30 days of paid vacation—yep, a full month—guaranteed by law. Normally, it is the month of August, but larger firms allow some flexibility in your vacation dates. In addition, there are another 14 days of paid national holidays, plus several days of regional holidays. If you get married, you get 15 days of paid leave to celebrate. And if you have a baby, mom gets four months of paid maternity leave, while dad gets 13 days paid paternity. There are also days off for administrative tasks, moving, and a host of other reasons. And in summer, many companies offer *jornada intensiva,* a compressed workday, normally ending at 3 P.M. If all of this free time makes you wonder how Spaniards ever get any work done, you're not alone. Despite persistent stereotypes of lazy, *mañana, mañana* Spanish workers, the truth is that they are some of the hardest workers in Europe. The working day may officially be just nine hours long, but once you move here, you'll meet many Spaniards who regularly work well over ten per day.

Labor Laws

The Estatuto de los Trabajadores (Workers' Statute), established in 1980 and amended most recently in 1990, mandates many aspects of the employer-employee relationship including contracts, working conditions, and the roles of labor unions. However, not everyone with a job benefits from this law. Part-time and seasonal workers enjoy few of the advantages outlined in the statute. Of course those working illegally (and they are many) have no legal protection whatsoever.

WORKERS' RIGHTS

The standard work week is 40 hours and the standard working day is nine hours. However, this timeframe is merely a benchmark and it can vary according to the type of job you have. In practice, most Spaniards work many more hours per week, both due to heavy workload and, in the case of companies with shortened summer hours, as a compensation for those early afternoons off. Overtime, *horas extraordinarias,* if you qualify for it, is limited to 80 hours a year. If your work conditions stray from the standard, they should be clearly written into your contract.

© NIKKI WEINSTEIN

checking the inventory at a neighborhood store

Discrimination based on gender, race, religion, age, marital status, sexual orientation, union membership, or social standing is illegal. Likewise, people with disabilities have equal employment rights and cannot be discriminated against provided that they are able to do the work in question. Children under 16 years old cannot work, and anyone younger than 18 is subject to special laws regarding overtime, night work, and hazardous conditions.

The law also protects the right to unionize and each industry has its own union with both national and regional branches. The unions help insure that working conditions, the practices of hiring and firing, and the details within labor contracts are all being adhered to. Though there are dozens of unions, the Comisiones Obreras (CCOO) and the Unión General de Trabajadores (UGT) wield a lot of power, often setting the labor standards for the country.

MINIMUM WAGE

Just as in the United States, Spain's minimum wage is pathetic—just €600 per month as of January 2008. Considering the high cost of living, particularly in cities like Madrid, Barcelona, and Valencia, the wage will barely—if at all—keep you afloat. Most Spaniards who are surviving on this sum, live with family and have minimal expenses. An expat does not generally have this option. If it looks like your only job options are those paying minimum wage, make sure you have a slush fund back home or prepare to seriously pinch your *céntimos.*

FINANCE

For over a century, Spain had a currency called the peseta. Neighboring France produced francs, and Italy used the lira. All that changed when Spain, along with several other European Union (EU) members, became the first nations to adopt the euro. The implementation of a single currency was big news and its ramifications are still being felt. The common currency suddenly opened up markets as business, people, and capital could move more freely between member countries. The EU, and Spain with it, had become one union under the euro.

Despite the rosy rhetoric from politicians and pundits, the adoption of the euro was not without backlash, at least in Spain. Most of it derived from the dreaded *redondeo,* or rounding-up effect. On January 1, 2002, when the euro went into effect, a single euro was worth 166.386 pesetas. When merchants took out their calculators to make their peseta–euro conversion, they found a pesky decimal point left over. So what did they do? You guessed it—they rounded up. Overnight, prices on everything from a can of corn to a new car

DECLARING MONEY

Before you try walking through customs with a duffle bag full of Ben Franklins, there are a couple things that you should know. You can breeze in and out of the country with cash, checks, and even gold bars that amount to €6,000 or less. But if you try the same thing with larger amounts, you might land in big trouble. You can in fact move that amount of money across the Spanish border, but you have to declare it. The government merely wants to know that everything is above board and that you're not an international drug dealer.

If your bank account was filled in small, undeclared increments and you need to re-export a large sum of cash, you should also declare it just to keep everything on the up-and-up. Here's how you take care of business: When entering Spain with gobs of money – that means €6,000-30,000 – you'll have to fill out a B-1 form at customs. For amounts greater than €30,000, non-EU residents have to receive prior approval to send or receive the cash. You can ask permission of the Dirección General de Transacciones Exteriores by simply completing a B-2 form at your local Spanish bank.

So will you face a real mess if you accidentally forget to declare the cash? That depends on whether or not you think that having several thousand euros confiscated constitutes a mess. If you do, you should make a mental note to fill out the required forms.

were jacked way up. A cup of coffee that cost 100 pesetas on New Years' Eve was nearly 167 pesetas (or one euro) the next morning. Talk about a hangover. And the kicker? The big players did not round up. When it came to salaries, neither private industry nor the Spanish government were willing to take a dive—workers' paychecks were converted to the decimal point. Thus, the cost of living went up, but take-home pay remained the same. Not a good way for the new currency to win fans. Even today, many Spaniards are bitter about the conversion, convinced they got the short end of the *palo*.

That sounds dire, right? It's really not. And all but the most curmudgeonly of old fellas sipping *sol y sombra* (an early morning concoction of brandy and anisette) at the corner bar readily admit that the overall effect of the euro—and EU membership—on Spain has been *muy positivo*. Following the implementation of the euro, the pace of Spain's economic expansion was much stronger than other euro-zone countries. That's a particularly big achievement given that for almost the whole of the 20th century, Spain was viewed as a backwater compared to the rest of western Europe. At one point, things were so bleak in Spain that thousands of Spaniards were forced to emigrate to neighboring countries in order to earn money. By 2008, boasting the ninth largest economy in the world, those dark days were long gone.

Of course, 2008 was also the year that Spain's economic *burbuja* burst and as of the writing of this book, the country was in the grips of an economic crisis. In fact, let me get the disclaimer out of the way right now. All the information in this chapter is based on Spanish reality just before the economic fall. So, if you find out that your *café con leche* costs €1 more than I mention below, please don't blame me. Remember, it's the economy *tonto!*

Cost of Living

In March of 2008, the Spanish real estate supersite Kyero (www.kyero.com) released data on the cost of living for foreigners in Spain. Excluding housing expenses, the total for a couple was €644 per month. I wish they did my budgeting as my Madrid-based family of three rarely shells out less than €1,300 per month (and no, my five-month old baby doesn't account for the extra 700 euros). Then again, my English-teaching friend Tanya from Baltimore confessed that her minus-rent living expenses were less than €300 (of course she does know a thousand different bars where the tapas are free!)

What all this number yakking proves is that living in Spain doesn't come with a clearly printed price tag. Where you live, how you live, who you live with—all play a role in your daily costs in Spain. Will it be more than you paid in the states? Well, if you are coming from a tiny town in rural America—probably. If you are coming from New York, L.A., or Chicago—you will be convinced you hit the low-cost life lottery. In fact, the Swiss bank UBS put each of those American cities above both Madrid and Barcelona in its 2008 ranking of the world's most expensive cities. Of course, with Madrid at number 22 and Barcelona at 26, you can be sure that these are the two priciest places to live in Spain. Their big city costs are rivaled only by the prices in resort meccas such as Ibiza and Mallorca. Towns in those regions attract masses of wealthy tourists and expats, so not surprisingly restaurants, entertainment outlets, and landlords charge a lot for everything from food to homes. In smaller cities such as Granada, Valencia, and Sevilla, prices dip into the mid-range, while small-town life in Spain can be had for bargain-basement prices. Then again, if you live in a big city, you can usually find actual bargains. Smaller towns, simply due to the laws of supply and demand, often charge higher prices for basic goods.

Which brings us to the price of daily necessities in Spain as compared to the United States. Statistically speaking—and by that I mean based on my opinion and that of the expat friends I asked—the following are cheaper in Spain: food and drink—both in the market and out on the town; medical and dental care; prescription drugs; health insurance; and household utilities. Things you'll find pricey in Spain compared to back home include: clothing, especially undergarments, swimsuits, and athletic footwear; household furnishings and linens (excluding anything purchased at IKEA); beauty and hygiene products; oil and gas; and Internet access. A lot of other things are about the same: public transport; gyms and yoga studios; hair salons; office supplies; cleaning and other household products. And, it pays to keep in mind that a sale in Spain has nothing in common with its American cousin—the ultra-discounted super sale. Spain holds *rebajas* (sales) twice a year, in late summer and after the winter holidays, and this means that maybe they will bust out the 30 percent off signs. You'll never see the juicy 75 percent off and more deals you get back home.

Keep costs down by shopping at the local market.

© CANDY LEE LABALLE

Remember our friend the euro? Well, this is the last factor I'll mention that will really impact your Spanish cost of living. If you are paid in U.S. dollars while you are living in Spain, then you better get cozy with the conversion rate. The days of the one-dollar-to-one-euro exchange rate are way gone. The euro has taken the lead for the last several years and as of the writing of this book in late 2008, €1 bought $1.41. That's no problem if you are earning euros. If not, your cost of living will jump up a notch so it's worth doing the math in order to figure out the real cost of things. But don't think you've got it made if you are making euros. What you save on the exchange rate can easily be offset by the sad fact that Spanish salaries are markedly lower than those in the United States. In fact, Spain boasts some of the lowest salary figures in Europe. That means, unless you are a well-paid executive or simply wealthy, you'll want to keep an eye on your budget regardless of your paycheck currency.

BALANCING YOUR BUDGET

In order to balance your budget, you'll have to keep costs down. That means knowing where to shop and how to find the best *gangas* (cheap deals).

One of your biggest expenses will be your monthly basics—food and household and hygiene products. You can fill your basket by hitting a one-stop *hipermercado* (superstores) or trailing your own *carro* (shopping cart) around your neighborhood shops. In the former, you can pretty much get whatever you need which makes shopping fast and easy. The cheapest superstores include Alcampo, Eroski, and Mercadona. The most expensive store in this category is El Corte Inglés. But to call this icon of Spanish culture merely a store is a grave understatement. The oldest—and only—department store in Spain, El Corte offers everything from green peas to D&G jeans. You can get your hair cut, have lunch, try on wedding gowns, find the fixings for paella, decorate your bedroom, update your wardrobe, even book a cruise. And, the best part? There is always one near you—the stores are ubiquitous throughout Spain. The one drawback is price. El Corte Inglés (and its grocery store sidekick Hipercor) has some of the highest prices in Spain. After you've lived here a while, you'll swear yourself off of filling up their green-and-white bags. But, like a New Years' Day dieter, you'll soon be dipping into the El Corte cookie jar. The place is just too dang convenient.

A little less convenient, but a whole lot more fun are the mom-and-pop shops in your neighborhood. Visit the *drogería/perfumería* for household and

Prices hang alongside Spain's iconic legs of ham.

© NIKKI WEINSTEIN

hygiene items. The *ferretería* will have nuts and bolts, pots and pans, hardware and tools. The *panadería* will bake your daily bread and the *carnecería* will carve up your *carne* (meat). Each neighborhood will also have a *mercado* (market) lined with stalls selling fresh fruit and vegetables, ocean-fresh fish and seafood, cured meats and cheeses, chicken and eggs, and even stalls dedicated to key-making, knife-sharpening, and clothes-altering. Patronizing these types of shops takes time—several visits per week—but it is the best way to really integrate into your new *barrio*. And of course, budget in mind, *barrio* shops and markets tend to be cheaper than supermarkets. Just one bit of advice; when you enter, call out *¿Quién es el ultimo?* (who is last?) to find your place in line.

Another great way to get to know your new home is through its restaurants. And, in Spain, this can be done deliciously on a budget. There is little reason why a meal out for two with wine has to exceed €30, tax and tip included. Of course, you can easily shell out in excess of triple digits per person—Spain is home to Ferran Adrià and his world-famous El Bulli in Cataluña as well as a few dozen other world-renowned restaurants—but by choosing basic goodness over haute style, you can definitely include dining out in your Spanish budget. One excellent option is to take advantage of the *menú del día* (menu of the day). Spanish culture places great importance on lunch and all restaurants, no matter their nighttime prices, will offer a three-course lunch with drink and dessert for around €10. Granted, it's more than a sandwich costs— but it's a great way to eat like the locals do. In the evening, you can also keep dining costs down by *tapeando* (going out for tapas). Expect to spend €12–20 per person including drinks.

Wine and beer quickly pad a dining bill in the United States but those items are super cheap in Spain—a glass of wine or beer is on average €1.50; a decent bottle of Rioja can be had for as little as €10. Some more dining costs: coffee and tea are rarely more than €1.50; a *caña* (small glass of beer) is about €1 and a Coke, €2; a *bocadillo* (sub sandwich) is usually around €3; breakfast including coffee and a pastry is €2.50; a slice of Spanish *tortilla* (potato omelet) is €2. One other point when dining out—tipping is not required. Waiters and bartenders are paid a normal living wage, they don't rely on tips. In addition, many restaurants include a small service charge in their prices. The bottomline is that you never have to calculate 15 percent of the bill again—a euro or two is more than sufficient as a thank-you for good service.

All those cheap eats may put a *talla* (size) or two on your hips, which means you'll eventually have to buy new clothes. In general, clothing in Spain is more expensive, but you can find some deals if you know where to look. The *hipermercados* mentioned above often stock inexpensive clothing alongside their groceries—much like the famous "marts" back home. These are great for kids clothing and basics like T-shirts and socks. If you are bit more fashion-forward, there are a few chains with decent fashion-for-euro ratios. Zara, H&M, Mango, and Springfield are four good bets and they are everywhere in Spain. Expect a pair of jeans for around €40, sweaters for €30, coats for €80, and sundries like scarves, hats, and gloves for an average of €10. Of course, if you are not limited by pesky things like a budget, you can spend as much as you want in Spain. Doorkeeper-guarded shops offering Prada, Boss, and Loewe are ready to fill your closets for about the same prices you'd expect back home. On the fringes of most big Spanish cities, you'll find outlet malls, offering discounted deals on high-end fashion. If you are fan of thrift stores, you'll be pretty disappointed; *tiendas de segunda mano* are few and far between. One small chain with shops in Madrid, Barcelona, and Granada is Humana, which funnels profits from their used clothing sales into social programs in Africa.

Banking

It's more than advisable to open a Spanish bank account—in most cases it's a necessity. In Spain, people view checks as being almost as obsolete as horses and buggies. Most all of your household service providers—mobile phone, gas, electric, Internet—will require that your bills be paid via *transferencia bancaria* (bank transfer). Many landlords also require payment this way. In fact, bank transfers are the most common method to exchange money in Spain. In addition, most bank accounts will come with a *tarjeta de débito* (debit card) which you can use in shops, restaurants, for online purchases—anywhere you'd use a credit card.

OPENING AN ACCOUNT

First, you'll have to choose a bank to join which may lead you to wonder what is the difference between a *banco* and a *caja*. The first is a standard bank as you know it and the second is usually a savings entity, however the difference between the two isn't in the services but in the ownership. Savings banks don't have shareholders; they were founded with charity in mind, and profits are invested in cultural, educational, and social projects—some of the best museums in Spain are funded by *cajas*. A few of the more popular banks are Banesto, BBVA, Banco Popular, and Banco Santander, but there are hundreds. If you are unsure where to start, check with your local expat community or

© CANDY LEE LABALLE

La Caixa is a popular bank.

an online expat forum. In Madrid, the owner of the forum www.multima-drid.com banks at a local La Caixa. His good relationship with the staff there caused him to recommend that branch to the forum members and many of them opened their accounts there. As a result, that branch knows how to deal with foreigners. If you are in a small town or even a small community of a big city, your banker may not speak English, nor know the requirements for a foreigner opening an account.

If you are a legal resident of Spain, you can open a *residente* account; you'll need to bring your resident card with your NIE, *número de identificación de extranjero* (foreign resident identification number), as proof. If not, you can open a *no residente* account using your passport. You may also be asked to provide a *certificado* or *carta de no residencia* which proves you are not a legal resident in Spain. You can obtain it at your local police station with your passport. You'll have to fill out a few forms and then return a few days later to pick it up. Alternatively, you can ask your bank to apply for the certificate for you; many will for a fee. However, I did write "may" above and that is because many banks ignore, overlook, or just don't seem to know about this requirement. Check a local online expat forum for advice on banks that do and don't request this document. Also, be aware that while the nonresident account is intended for foreigners who do not reside in Spain for more than 183 days per year, many illegal residents have held such accounts for years. However, your bank may report your status as an account holder to the Spanish authorities, particularly *hacienda* (the tax office) if you are moving large sums of money through your account.

When setting up your account, bear in mind that Spaniards have two last names. Many Americans have discovered that the bank erroneously filed their records under their middle names—undoubtedly innocent mistakes in which bank employees mistook middle names for last names. In order to avoid unnecessary confusion, just use *nombre* (first) and *apellido* (last) names on your account.

There are several different types of *cuentas* (accounts). A *cuenta corriente* is most similar to a U.S. checking account (minus the use of checks). It is basically for individuals or families who do everyday basic banking. Depending on the bank (and, also the person helping you at the moment), you will have different types of fees—for opening the account, monthly maintenance, card fees, and more. This can amount up to €100 per year, with nonresident accounts slightly higher. Because the fees are so variable, shop around and ask questions in the bank. If you have a *nómina* (salary), you can have it directly deposited into your account and that normally eliminates all fees. You can also set up all of your monthly bills to *domiciliar* (direct debit). Again, this is the preferred payment plan for your service providers.

A *cuenta de ahorros* (savings account) may or may not come with interest. Recently, many banks in Spain have begun offering rates of up to 5 percent. Again, shop around. A savings account often does not allow for direct deposit or direct debit and many do not issue debit cards. Instead, you'll receive a *libreta* (savings book) which you can use at the bank to *ingresar* (deposit) or *sacar* (withdraw) money from your account. In addition, there are accounts designed for the self-employed, business owners, and a host of other situations depending on the bank. You can also request credit cards, apply for loans and mortgages, and other services such as an *aval bancario* (bank guarantee) at your local bank.

If your account came with a direct debit card you can use it at any *cajero automático* (ATM) throughout Spain (and the world), however your fee will vary based on where you use it. If you use the card at an ATM located at a branch of your own bank, there is no charge. If you can't find your local bank, then check the back of your card to see what *red* (network) your bank belongs to. ServiRed and 4B are two of the largest networks in Spain and as long as you use an ATM within your network, your fee will be reasonable (less than €2). Withdraw *dinero* from outside of your network and you will be hit with a fee up to €5.

CURRENCY

Though I've heard rumors of some Spanish banks offering accounts in dollars or pounds, the odds are pretty good that your bank will deal in euros. You should know that one hundred *céntimos* amounts to one euro and coins are easily distinguished at a glance. Each one is a different size, some are copper-colored, others look silver, and a few appear gold. Coin money comes in denominations of 1, 2, 5, 10, 20, and 50cents, single euros, and two euros. Be careful with the euro coin, it may look like a quarter, but it is worth at least six times as much. The designs on one side of the coins indicate the

A one euro coin may look like a quarter, but it's worth about six times as much.

country in which the money was minted. Paper money is uniform throughout the whole of the EU—there's nothing country-specific about it. It is also sized and colored to be easily recognizable with just a quick look into your wallet. The bills come in denominations of 5, 10, 20, 50, 100, 200, and 500 euros. Most ATM machines give out bills up to 50 euros and you'll rarely receive anything higher. If you do have notes of three digits, do not expect corner shops, bars, or taxi drivers to break them for you. Carry smaller notes for these purposes.

One note about money (and numbers in general) in Spain. Locals use a comma where Americans use a period and vice versa. So, you may write down €10,000.00 to mean ten-thousand euros; a Spaniard will write €10.000,00 for the same amount.

Exchange Rates

Exchange rates are fickle. Don't assume that the amount of euros you can buy for a $20 bill on a given Monday will be the same by next Thursday. Many people still think that the dollar and the euro have a one-to-one exchange rate but in fact they don't—the euro has been stronger for the past few years. If you intend to wire dollars into your Spanish bank account, they'll be transferred to euros at the day's exchange rate and thus it's a good idea to transfer more money when the rate works in your favor. If you don't do that and you instead wire money at a low moment for the dollar, you can lose a fair amount in the process of a simple bank transaction. Moreover, if you don't keep up with the exchange rate you won't know what you're truly spending on anything. There are several rate calculators available on the Internet.

If you brought dollars with you into Spain, you can change them at a bank or a *cambio* (exchange office). Banks will offer the current exchange rate offset by a small fee. Exchange offices tend to charge much higher fees therefore they are best avoided. If you are living in Spain on your U.S. dollars back home, you can take out what you need in euros from any ATM. Though this will get you the best of the daily exchange rate, both the machine where you remove the money as well as your bank back home will charge you a fee. Therefore, it is best to find out the largest amount you can remove at a time so as to avoid multiple withdrawals and multiple fees.

Taxes

The Spanish dread paying taxes as much as anyone and just a short time ago tax evasion was so common in Spain, it was almost the norm. The system is less lenient today. The government penalizes tax dodgers with stiff fines and that has decreased evasion. Historically, taxation was lower in Spain than the EU average. That's still true although the disparity is smaller than it once was.

Although it's important to understand the Spanish tax system, bear in mind that laws are regularly amended and your individual finances and residency status can change things dramatically. The best way to handle a brand-new and completely foreign set of tax laws is to consult a professional who can help you stay within the guidelines of the law and even work the system in your favor.

SPANISH TAXES

The Spanish tax year runs January 1–December 31 and taxes must be filed between May 1 and June 20. The necessary forms for filing must be purchased. Some are sold in *estancos* (tobacco shops). Others are available exclusively from the *agencia tributaria,* commonly known as *hacienda* (the tax office).

Three separate branches of the government have the right to impose taxes: the central government, autonomous regional governments, and local municipalities. However, income, capital gains, wealth, and inheritance taxes—four of the biggies—are all paid to *hacienda.*

Ultimately, individuals might be responsible for paying as many as 17 different kinds of taxes including a garbage tax for property owners and a motor vehicle tax that applies to car owners. Even the tourist lounging at a Marbella resort will end up paying a chunk of change to the government in the form of IVA, or *impuesto sobre el valor añadido* (value-added tax). Restaurants and hotels tack on a 7 percent IVA, and the tax is bumped up to 16 percent for retail goods, rental cars, and even services such as utilities. The general rule mandates that the tax on necessary goods such as food and medicine drops to 7 percent, but anything deemed unessential is taxed at 16 percent.

Direct income taxes called *impuestos sobre la renta de las personas físicas* (better known as IRPF) are due yearly and are assessed a bit differently based on whether or not you are a resident. For tax purposes, you're a resident if you live in Spain for 183 days out of the year or if the majority of your financial interests are in Spain. In either of those cases, you must pay income taxes on both earned and unearned incomes (the latter category includes investments, etc.). However, deductions are permissible and the rate of taxation can range 24–43 percent depending on your net income. Now for some good news: You need not file at all if your taxes are being withheld and you earn less than €22,000. Nonresidents are required to pay tax on any earnings acquired in Spain; the rate is currently set at 25 percent of earnings.

If you own property, you'll have to pay the annual *impuesto de bienes inmuebles* or IBI (property tax) to the municipality where your home is registered— the rate fluctuates according to the cadastral value of the property. (That's the official value of the property and it's typically much lower than market value). Factors such as location and size of the land also affect the amount owed.

If all that sounds confusing, it is. So much so that even Spaniards regularly put their tax issues in professional hands. Hence the popularity of a place called the *gestoría*. There is not really an equivalent in the states. A *gestor* is a type of administrator that serves as a liaison between you and the Spanish government. They can file papers, do small-scale accounting, and handle most basic bureaucratic tasks. They often offer legal advice, but they are not lawyers. They also regularly offer accounting advice, but they are not accountants. However, as long as you are dealing with basic issues—personal income tax, property tax, self-employment tax—a *gestor* can help. They can spare you the burden of trying to figure out a tax system wholly unfamiliar to you, and they also know the system well enough to save you money. Many specifically cater to English-speaking expats. Find a *gestor* the way you would a lawyer back home—personal recommendation.

AMERICAN TAXES

All U.S. citizens and residents must file their annual income tax forms regardless of where they live. However, that doesn't necessarily mean that you have to pay U.S. taxes. If you spend the majority of your time in Spain, it's the place where you earn your income, you're a tax resident, and your total Spanish income is $87,600 or less, you do not have to pay U.S. income taxes thanks to the Foreign Earned Income Exclusion. If you're worried that you'll be doubly taxed on an income exceeding that amount, you can relax. Spain and the United States have a treaty to avoid double taxation. The details of that law are complex and you should speak to an accountant to know how to handle that. If you really must have local IRS assistance, pack your bags and head to Paris. The U.S. Embassy there has a full-time IRS assistant for Americans living overseas (http://france.usembassy.gov/irs.html). In addition, Publication 54 on the IRS website (www.irs.gov) covers the basics of taxation for Americans abroad.

Most bilingual accountants in Spain are more familiar with U.K. tax laws than they are with U.S. ones, but there are a few exceptions. One solution is to seek out financial assistance within the United States. A number of U.S. accountants specialize in taxes for expatriate people. Despite the ocean dividing Spain and the states, working with an American accountant is easily done thanks to email and Skype.

DAILY LIFE

COMMUNICATIONS

The advent of cell phones and the Internet have completely changed the way we communicate when abroad. If you have a tri-band cell phone and net-searching laptop, you can be up and chatting with folks back home as soon as you hit Spanish *tierra*. If not, you may still need to look for a few *monedas* (coins) and plug them into a pay phone. Either way, once you get settled in Spain, setting up your own personal communications system is just a matter of a few phone calls, the exchange of some euros, and yes, being Spain, a bit of red tape. Internet service may take a while to install, especially if you are living somewhere off the beaten path. But getting a cell phone is pretty painless and tapping into the local media is as easy paying a visit to your corner *kiosco* (newsstand).

Telephone Service

Spain's country code is 34 and precedes any Spanish number that's dialed from abroad. To call Spain from the United States, dial 011 + 34 + number. If calling another country from within Spain, 00 must be added before the country code and number. To call the United States, dial 001 + area code + number. All *fijo* (landline) numbers in Spain begin with nine and the first two or three numbers indicate the city or town being called, similar to area codes in the states. Common codes are Barcelona: 93; Bilbao: 94; Cadiz: 956; Granada: 958; Madrid: 91; Malaga: 952; Palma de Mallorca: 971; Sevilla: 95; and Valencia: 96. Cellular-phone numbers in Spain always start with six. 900 numbers are toll-free, whereas 901 and 902 numbers charge a fee. Unfortunately, most of the customer service numbers for big companies like RENFE, some hotels, and airlines are 902 numbers. 906 numbers are used for psychic hotlines, erotic chat, and other euro-eating calls.

TELEPHONE COMPANIES

Though there are several companies involved in the telecommunications business in Spain, **Telefónica** (www.telefonicaonline.com, tel. 1004) is the grand-daddy. Until recently, this multinational monster was the only national phone company and although it privatized in 1997, it still owns almost all of the country's phone infrastructure—lines, cables, antennas, routers. It also still operates like a state-owned monopoly, which results in the company's well-deserved reputation in two key areas—high prices and bad service. Customer service is extremely erratic—if you don't like the answer one agent gives you, call back, you'll likely get another response altogether. A good trick is to demand to speak in English. This will get you an agent who will then coordinate all the details of your call with the appropriate departments. But be aware, in almost all dealings with Telefónica, you'll find that the customer is never, ever right, regardless of circumstances. Complaining to the company will get you almost nowhere. If you have truly bad service, you can lodge a complaint with the Oficina de Atención al Usuario de Telecomunicaciones, the country's telecommunications watchdog (www.usuariosteleco.es).

Slowly and surely, competitors are starting to make headway into Telefónica territory, but they are having more success in some areas than in others. For example, the companies that are now offering *líneas* (landlines), must still rout their service through Telefónica and that means long waits for installation and sometimes sketchy service. Still their presence is making Telefónica shed off some of its bullying practices and offer better service

DAILY LIFE

and prices. Competitors have found more luck in providing service—calling plans, Internet, and television. The top alternative telecommunications company in Spain is **Orange** (www.orange.es, tel. 1414), a division of the telecommunications giant France Telecom, which is also one of Spain's top three cellular companies. Others include **Ono** (www.ono.es, tel. 1400), **Jazztel** (www.jazztel.com, tel. 1565), and a host of others that suddenly appear on the market and disappear just as quickly. Do not be swayed by ads offering amazing deals, do your homework and research your potential provider—some are plagued by problems. Finally, have patience;

Orange is one of Spain's top cellular operators.

alternative providers almost always have long delays—up to a month—for the installation of their services.

LANDLINES

All that said, like it or not, you more than likely will have to deal with Telefónica if you want good phone service in Spain, particularly in rural areas. Installation of a new Telefónica line can cost up to €200 (sometimes higher for nonresidents), but—again, due to competition—they now regularly offer deals with *alta gratis* (free installation). It is a good idea to seek out a deal before you sign up—the never helpful customer service staff will not inform you about any offers.

You do not have to be a legal resident of Spain to set up a phone line (though higher prices may apply if you are not). You only need your passport, proof of your address such as a lease or deed, and a bank account number to set up payment. With this, you can set up a line in one of three ways: visit one of the company's many stores; dial tel. 1004 from any telephone to order installation (ask for an English-speaking agent); or visit www.telefonicaonline.com and click on *alta de línea*. Do not order phone service through sites claiming to broker for Telefónica—these are more than likely scams. The company assures a wait of 7–10 days before installation. In big cities, it often occurs faster, even on weekends. However, others end up waiting for up to a month. It's impossible to predict what your wait will be. Also, be sure to turn down their offer of *teléfono en alquiler* (renting a phone). The fee to do so is a minimum of €3 per month and it is easy to see that in a few months, you've paid more than the cost of the phone. Say *no, gracias,* and buy your own phone in an electronics or department store.

Your monthly *factura* (bill) for the line alone will be between €18 and €30, depending on which deal you got when you signed up. The bill will arrive every two months and more than likely will be deducted directly from your bank account. The option to pay in cash at either a Telefónica store or a bank is also available, though less usual. If you have other services with Telefónica such as Internet or cable television, those fees will also appear on your bi-monthly bill.

If you choose to set up your *linea* with another company, again, you can visit their store, call their toll-free number, or enter their website. As with Telefónica, you will need ID, proof of address, and a bank account.

CALLING PLANS

Tarifas (rates) are both competitive and wildly fluctuating. All of the companies offer a variety of *tarifa planas* (set rate plans) and at a minimum, you should be able to get one that offers free calls to other landlines and free national calls. Calls to *móviles* (cell phones) and international destinations can range from a few *céntimos* up to a euro, and again that rate will fluctuate greatly with the deal you secure. If you will make a lot of calls to a particular international destination, inquire about *descuentos* (discounts) to that location. All of the companies offer some such service which usually involves a minimal monthly fee in exchange for a low per-minute rate. Of course, with the popularity of Skype and other free Internet dialing options, dialing +001 from a landline seems a bit antiquated. And speaking of rates, you need to know that many *tarifa planas* are based on the hours of consumption. Calls made during peak hours (daytime and weekdays) usually cost more than calls made during off-hours (evenings and weekends). Finally, keep in mind that all of these providers often package their calling plans with any combination of Internet service and cable television. Check out the full package before making your choice.

DAILY LIFE

Cell Phone Service

One of the first things you should do upon arriving in Spain is to get a *móvil* (cell phone). The three main *operadores* (providers) are **Movistar** (www.movistar.es, tel. 1485), a divison of Telefónica, **Orange** (www.orange.es, tel. 1414), and **Vodafone** (www.vodafone.es, tel. 1444). The easiest way to set up service is to visit one of the ubiquitous shops run by these three companies. Or, you can do price comparisons by visiting a reseller that offers all three services such as The Phone House, El Corte Inglés, or FNAC.

However, before you can even get to that step, you first have to decide if you want a *contrato* (monthly contract) or a *prepago* (pay-as-you-go) plan. Technically, a cellular company will not give a contract to someone who does not have legal residence in Spain; if you are *sin papeles* in Spain, you have no choice but to go *prepago*. In practice, anything goes and it all seems to depend on the knowledge of the person who sets up your account. With a contract, you are billed monthly for your *tarifa plana* plus any calls you made. This amount will be taken out of your bank account automatically—paying on your own is not an option. With pay-as-you go, your cell number must have an amount of *saldo* (credit) on it to make calls. To get credit, you *recargar* (recharge) your phone by purchasing a minimum amount of minutes for your number. This can be done in many places including your cellular provider's stores, department stores, *locutorios* (private call centers), grocery stores, ATMs, and even some restaurants. You can always switch a pay-as-you-go plan to contract once your residency is established.

CELL PHONE RATES

Each provider offers a dizzying array of *tarifa planas* (set rate plans)—for those that speak during the day, during the night, for business, with friends who share the same provider, and so on and so on. It is a good idea to check out the various offers to see which best meets your needs. If your bill ends up being more than you thought, you can easily switch to another plan. Rates vary wildly depending on your provider and plan, but expect the most expensive rates to be daytime calls to cell phones covered by another provider. These could reach as high as €.50 per minute. Calls within the same provider network are often the cheapest. In addition, for each call you make you will be charged for an *establecimiento de llamada* (call connection), which runs around €.13. Text messages, SMS, generally cost €.15. But again, all of this is highly dependent on your specific rate plan. One nice surprise for Americans using cell phones in Spain—the receiver never pays for the call. Calls are charged in their entirety to the person making the call, whether it is being made from Spain or the United States.

CELL PHONES

Each cellular company offers new clients a free or deeply discounted cell phone with service. In return, you sign a contract agreeing to stay with that company for a minimum of 18 months. Breaking off service sooner results in a hefty fee, usually over €100. You'll undoubtedly recognize many of the same phone models that are popular in the United States and may think about just bringing over your American phone to use here. However there is one crucial difference: unless you have a GSM/GPRS compatible U.S. model, your old phone from home is no good in Spain. Spain, like much of the world, uses these systems. If your American phone is of the tri-band variety, then it should work fine. However, to use it on a local phone network, you'll have to get it *liberado* (unlocked), or released from your previous network. You can do this at any of the many small phone shops around Spain. Look for a sign advertising *se libran móviles*. The cost will be around €10. You'll also need to purchase a Spanish SIM card. They are sold anywhere cell phones are sold or through www.spainSIM.com run by an American based in Madrid. Finally, if you are an iPhone addict, know that Movistar is the official service provider in Spain. Of course, if you are a wily sort, you can probably figure out how to get around that requirement and hack your phone to use with other servers.

Internet Service

A 2007 Eurostat survey found that only 45 percent of Spanish households had Internet service. That doesn't mean that it's hard to find Internet providers, but the choices are thinner than elsewhere and some of the remoter parts of the country don't yet accommodate DSL lines—called ADSL in Spain. And, compared to other countries, Spain's Internet rates are quite high—considerably higher than in the U.S. You can get an incredibly in-depth overview of ADSL service in Spain by visiting the Spanish forum, www.adslzone.net and searching for *"comparativa,"* a comparison chart detailing packages, costs, and quality of service for each of the major Spanish ADSL providers.

The major ADSL providers cross over with the telephone and cellular providers listed above and include: Telefónica, Orange, Vodafone, Jazztel, and Ono. They each offer a variety of ADSL packages that vary in terms of bandwidth (the faster you go, the more you pay) and that you can combine with any

DAILY LIFE

Until you get your Internet installed, you'll need to visit an Internet café.

number of services (landline, calls, television). Of course, this means that prices vary wildly but for even the cheapest service, you are looking at a minimum of €40 per month, often plus the charge for the landline. Again, do your homework. Compare prices and quality of service before making a final choice.

Most providers will give you *alta gratis* (free installation) and often a free router. Be sure and confirm the price of the router before you sign up and, as with phones, do not accept a rental contract—you'll end up paying many times over what the router is worth. When you do sign up with a provider (again in a shop, by phone, or via Internet), you'll get an appointment with a service technician to install the service. If you are lucky, your doorbell will be ringing in just a few days, if you are not, it could be up to a month or more before you get installation. Telefónica, despite their downfalls, is often the quickest to get your installation done. Finally, a word to Mac lovers—Spain is not Mac friendly. Though that is slowly changing, if you have a Mac, expect your installation tech to have at least some level of confusion. Do an Internet search on "Macs in Spain" to learn what kind of quirks you can expect and how to resolve them.

If for some reason there is no ADSL service in your area, that old dinosaur dial-up is still around. The same companies that offer ADSL can hook you up with dial-up service; ask for *Internet básico*. The service can be contracted solo or in combination with a calling plan. Again, depending on the *tarifa plana* you choose, the actual connection fee may be free or just a few euros per month, but you will be charged per minute for usage and that can really rack up your bill. In addition, some companies have hourly restrictions and limit the amount of time you can spend online each month.

While you are waiting for your service to get up and running, you can always connect to the Internet at a *cibercafe;* even the smallest towns will have at least one. Surf time is usually charged by the hour, though some places such as the copy center chain **Work Center** (www.workcenter.es) offer the option to buy time in bulk with an *abono* (multiuse ticket). When using public cyber cafés, be aware that they are notorious breeding grounds for thieves who take advantage of their victim's online distraction to make off with their goods. Keep your bag on your lap or wrapped around your leg and be vigilant. Just because someone is chatting on the web at the computer next to you does not mean that they are not a thief.

Wi-Fi is still not as available in Spain as in the United States. You may find a network in the area of your hotel, but it will more than likely be locked. Prices run from free to exorbitant, depending on the owners. Many cafés in bigger towns now offer Wi-Fi free to their clients. Be on the lookout for Wi-Fi hotspots as you do your sightseeing or ask at the tourist office.

Post Office and Couriers

Most *correos* (post offices) are open on weekdays 8:30 A.M.–8:30 P.M., though in smaller towns, they may close down for a two-hour lunch midday. Weekend hours are normally 9 A.M.–1:30 P.M. Locations and exact hours can be found at www.correos.es.

© CANDY LEE LABALLE

Look for the bright yellow mailboxes if you want to send a letter.

Within Spain, a normal letter or postcard costs €0.31 to send while postage for the same to the United States is €0.78. Letters can also be sent *certificado* (registered) for an additional charge of a few euros. There is no urgent or express service to the United States, but don't fret, normal post times run just 5–10 days to the states, a bit slower for packages. The price of postage normally increases slightly each January. To buy *sellos* (stamps), there's no need to trek all the way to the post office and wait in line—most *estancos* (tobacco shops) also sell stamps. They are easily identified by their maroon signs with the word *tabacos* written in yellow. Deposit your mail in any of the bright yellow mailboxes that line city streets.

If you're desperate for a same-day or next-day delivery, several courier companies will be happy to comply—for a cost. **FedEx** (www.fedex.com) and **DHL** (www.dhl.es) both have offices throughout Spain. Spanish-owned couriers include **MRW** (www.mrw.es) and **Seur** (www.seur.com).

If you will be receiving items from the states, you should have no problem with letters and very small packages. Larger packages can lead to a few headaches. First, if you are not home, the mail person will leave a slip of paper for you directing you to the nearest post office where you can retrieve your package—bring your ID. Second, *aduana* (customs) has the right to open any package coming in from abroad and impose duty taxes accordingly. No doubt there is some official formula for levying these taxes, but it seems pretty random to the citizen. Spanish customs has been known to levy taxes on used products from shoes to cameras while letting other, newer, more valuable products just slip through. At a minimum, they will levy a tax on packages that show a documented value of more than $100. One way around this is to have the person mailing the package to remove any price tags from the products being mailed and to list the items on the shipping slip as "used goods" with a value of less than $100. You still may get taxed and if you do, you will be expected to pay the tax directly to the post office when you retrieve the item. Don't even bother trying to fight this. You'll be in for a long battle that you will undoubtedly lose. Pay up and shut up is the only way you'll get your package.

Media

Despite the international image of a laid-back *fiesta y siesta* culture, Spain is a nation of news junkies. In addition to national television and radio news broadcasts, there are dozens of news analysis shows, talk shows, and gossip programs. In print, you can find just as many newspapers and magazines snaking out along the sidewalks from the ubiquitous corner *kioscos* (newsstands). Expect taxis and buses to have a news program blaring and everyone from the butcher to the woman sweeping your stairs will have an opinion on the news of the day. In Spain, you won't ever have to wonder what's going on in the rest of the world (unless you want to, of course!).

NEWSPAPERS

The Spanish press is readily available in newsstands on nearly every city street corner and free daily newspapers litter the subways throughout the day. The

PINK AND WHITE AND READ ALL OVER

Nothing can help you jump into the office water-cooler talk like a dutiful study of the *prensa rosa* (pink press, a.k.a. gossip news), and a thorough examination of sports news doesn't hurt either.

Spain's ample *presna rosa* provides heavy doses of romantic rumors and tales of the rich and famous (and inexplicably tan). It's likely that you'll begin your studies by staring at strangers in pictures and wondering who all those lovelies splashing in the Ibiza waves actually are. Don't worry. You'll soon have names memorized down pat and be able to jump right into the latest chatter about Isabel Pantoja, Francisco Rivera, Ana Obregón, Belén Esteban, and Eugenia Martínez de Irujo.

If the idea of reading these gossip rags leaves you cold, well, scoff if you must but conversations about the most recent soccer match and juicy celebrity pairings erupt all around – in the office, on the metro, at cafés. If you want to join in, these magazines and papers can give you the background you'll need.

Here are the details: *iHola!* is the grande dame of gossip rags – it is big and glossy and full of carefully composed photos of European royalty and Spanish celebrities posing in their very posh homes. It also covers weddings, baptisms, and social events of the upper crust of Spanish society. For gossip that's a little cruder but a whole lot more fun, check out *Diez Minutos, Cuore,* and *iQué Me Dices!,* which translates as "What Are You Telling Me!" Full of photos of embarrassing celebrity moments – thigh cellulite and underarm sweat are very popular – as well as articles on whether or not a celebrity has gotten plastic surgery, which celebrity is sleeping with whom, and lots of other rumors presented as facts.

The sports pages will give you all the latest *fútbol* news as well as a heavy dose of gossip on team owners, managers, and of course players – Messi, Torres, Iker, Raúl, Etoo. *Sport* delivers a hefty dose of information on exactly what its name promises and it hits the newsstands every day. *Marca,* another athletics-only paper, is also a daily and it seems to be the reading material of choice in bars and trains around the country. *AS* amps up the sports with sexy *señoritas* in barely-there wear.

Spend enough time pouring over these pages and you'll soon be able to wax on about the small but entertaining happenings throughout Spain – in other words, you'll be in the pink.

DAILY LIFE

three main national newspapers are *El País* (www.elpais.es), *El Mundo* (www .elmundo.es), and *ABC* (www.abc.es). And as in the U.S., political leanings drive their coverage. *El País* leans left, *El Mundo* right, and *ABC* even further right. Other top national papers include the very left *Público* and the right-ish *La Razón.* There are also a host of regional papers, the most popular being *La Vanguardia* and *El Periódico* in Cataluña, *El Correo* in País Vasco, *Diario Sur* in Andalucía, *La Voz de Galicia,* and *Diario de Navarra.* There are also newspapers dedicated to sports—a Spanish obsession—including *Marca* and *AS,* and to business including *Expansión, La Gaceta de los Negocios,* and *Cinco Días.* For a complete guide to leisure activities, pick up the *Guía del Ocio,* which covers everything from where to eat to what is playing at the cinema.

ENGLISH LANGUAGE PRESS

If you are feeling a bit nostalgic for English-language newspapers and magazines, fear not. The newsstands in major cities and tourist areas of Spain (especially the coasts) sell current international press alongside the Spanish. You can easily find *USA Today,* the *International Herald Tribune* which regularly pairs up with Spanish paper *El País* to offer an English version of the Spanish news, and *The Wall Street Journal.* Occasionally, you'll find a *New York Times, Washington Post* or another U.S. paper, but they're usually a few days old and sell for inflated prices. British papers such as *The Guardian* are also readily available. Easy to find English-language magazines include *Time, Newsweek,* and *The Economist.*

It may be a few days old, but international press is available.

© CANDY LEE LABALLE

Most of the major cities, especially those with large expat populations, have local papers and magazines in English. You'll find copies at tourist offices, hotels and youth hostels, Irish pubs, and language schools. In Madrid, look for *In Madrid,* in Barcelona, *Barcelona Metropolitan,* in Andalucía, *The Olive Press,* and on the coasts *Costa News,* which prints papers for several of the Mediterranean coastal communities.

TELEVISION

Just as in the U.S., television is a national obsession in Spain. Nearly every bar and restaurant will have one or more blaring all day and by night, you can see the blue glow of the screen emanating from windows all over the country. Though Spanish television scheduling has a heavy dose of *prensa rosa* (gossip) programs, far too many reality shows—*Gran Hermano* is just as gratuitous as *Big Brother*—and a penchant for dubbed versions of American "hits" like *Walker, Texas Ranger,* there is hope with cutting edge documentary programs, award-winning Spanish series, and in-depth news coverage. Though some channels broadcast their programming in *dual* (dubbed and in original version), most programming will be in Spanish—Homer still sounds like Homer in Spanish, but House of the same-named show sounds like a linebacker when compared to his original New England whine. If you really need English-language TV, cable and satellite television offer a wide-range of American programs and movies.

There are five main national channels. TVE1 and TVE2 are owned by the Spanish state, while Antena 3, Cuatro, Telecinco, and La Sexta are wholly private. There are also dozens of regional channels. Digital terrestrial television (DTT) has also become quite popular and as long as you have the receptor (available quite cheaply at any electronics store) you can get dozens of more channels including CNN+, the Disney Channel, and 40 Latino, a Spanish music video program.

Currently, the main cable and satellite companies are Canal Plus and Digital Plus. The main telephone providers also provide pay TV service including Telefónica Imagenio and Orange TV. Channels are as diverse as you'd expect in the U.S., from family programming and sports to movie channels and pornography. Receiving international channels requires satellite or Sky digital equipment—getting that is not usually a problem although those living in apartments sometimes need the approval of building management to install it. Try Spain-based Sky's the Limit (www.skysthelimit.tv) for more information.

Finally, don't think about lugging your American television to Spain. Like the rest of Europe, the country uses PAL, while the U.S. uses NTSC. A good television in Spain will run you a minimum of €300—a lot less if you buy one *segundamano* (secondhand). Videos and DVDs from the U.S. are also NTSC and will only work if you have a multisystem video or DVD player in Spain.

RADIO

Radio is hugely popular in Spain and considered one of the most influential media outlets in the country. Hundreds of radio stations broadcast daily. Radio Nacional de España (RNE) controls the state-owned stations including Radio 1, a talk format with a focus on news, politics, and society, Radio 3 which emphasizes culture and features some acclaimed world music shows, the all-news, all the time Radio 5, and Radio Clásica, a classical music station.

The very popular Cadena SER is mainly talk radio with an emphasis on politics, culture, and sports; it is also considered the voice of left-leaning Spain. On the right, is COPE, owned by the Catholic Church and home to some of the most radical right-wing broadcasters in the country. The most popular music stations include Los 40 Principales, KISS FM, and M80 Radio. Find local dial settings in the "Cartelera" section of the *El País* daily newspaper. To listen in English, check the website www.englishradio.co.uk for a current listing. The bulk of English-language radio stations are based on the Mediterranean coasts, the Balearic Islands, and the Canary Islands. Top broadcasters include Wave 96 FM (www.wave96fm.com) and Radio Europe Mediterraneo (www.rem.fm).

WEBSITES

Dozens of expats across Spain have set up online guides to getting the most out of the country. Use them to track down anything from English-speaking hairdressers to advice on how to set up a language academy. These are also the best places to get insider information on the whats, wheres, and hows of everything related to living in Spain. Some general Spanish sights worth perusing prior to your trip are the fact-packed www.spainexpat.com, www.justlanded.com, and www.idealspain.com. More locally based information can be found at sights such as Madrid's www.multimadrid.com or www.madaboutmadrid.com and Barcelona's www.barcelonaconnect.com. A quick Internet search will reveal many more. For news and views on Spanish life, try www.expatica.com and click on Spain. Another site where Spanish news of the day is translated into English is www.typicallyspanish.com. Finally, to really get an insider's perception of living in Spain, run a search on "blogs in Spain." You'll find Americans blogging about everything from raising their children in Spain to building a pilgrim refuge on the Camino de Santiago. Live vicariously through them, then plan your own blog detailing your adventures as an expat in Spain.

TRAVEL AND TRANSPORTATION

Some say Europe is a continent for train travelers, but they're really talking about the Europe of a bygone era. Although Spain's train service is far superior to its U.S. counterpart, the country's enormous web of roads is also intricate and far-reaching, and it seems as though new roads are always under construction. Cars are commonplace—arguably too commonplace as cities throughout Spain suffer vicious *atascos* (traffic jams) day and, in the case of Madrid, night. But unlike in L.A. or Detroit, there is an alternative. Spain's public transportation is excellent. All the country's major metropolitan areas have extensive subway, bus, and regional train lines that make getting from one corner of the city to another a piece of *tarta*. But perhaps that's leaping ahead. Before you even think about how you'll get around Spain, you'll have to handle just getting into the country.

© ALFONSO MORCUENDE

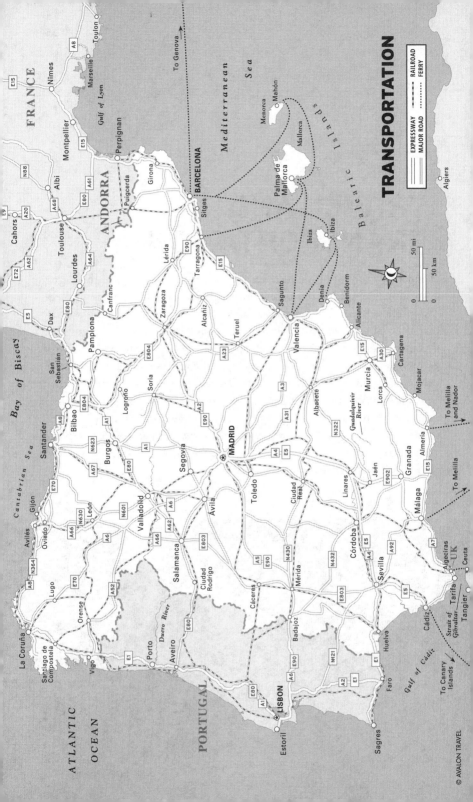

By Air

For its size, Spain has a lot of international airports including those in Barcelona, Málaga, and Palma de Mallorca. But chances are good that Madrid's Barajas airport—the most trafficked in the country—will be your hub when flying in and out of Spain. The city's position in the dead center of the country makes it an ideal jumping-off point to destinations throughout Spain, and most national flights go via Madrid. In fact, the country's largest airline, **Iberia** (www.iberia.es), is based in the airport's Richard Rogers–designed Terminal 4. Information on Barajas and all other airports—including flight arrival and departures, facilities, and airport transfers—can be found at the website of **AENA,** the organization that manages the country's airports (www.aena.es).

When traveling around Spain, don't automatically rule out flying. Iberia as well as several other Spanish-owned airlines including **Spanair** (www.spanair .com), **Air Europa** (www.aireuropa.es), and **Vueling** (www.vueling.com) offer regular discounted flights to points throughout the country and beyond. Keep your eyes out for *ofertas* (deals) and you could find a flight from say, Barcelona to Santiago, for under €50.

All the major U.S. airlines run flights in and out of Spain. If you will be returning regularly to the same place, you might consider signing up for a miles program and sticking with one airline—eventually you'll earn a free flight home (it took me four years of regular trips on US Airways, but I did it). Several deep-discount, no-frills airlines offer cheap flights from Spain to other points in Europe. These include **RyanAir** (www.ryanair.com) and **Easy Jet** (www.easyjet.com), but beware both of these airlines have racked up consumer complaints for excessive delays and as the 2008 financial crisis was panning out, both were showing signs of folding.

To find deals, check out sales advertised in newspapers or just walk into any *agencia de viaje* (travel agency)—there are plenty of them around. Don't overlook the Internet either. Spanish-based online bookers include **Rumbo** (www.rumbo.es), **Viajar** (www.viajar.com), **eDreams** (www.edreams.es), and **Atrapalo** (www.atrapalo.com).

The same airport security restrictions that apply in the United States, also apply in Spain including restrictions on flying with liquids—if you jet off to La Rioja for a wine tour, be sure to store your vino in your checked-in luggage. You'll also have to go through security before accessing the boarding areas, and yes, the security personnel are as, um, exasperating as they are stateside. I was recently reprimanded for not removing my shoes as I approached the security checkpoint at the Madrid airport. On the return flight in Palma de

Mallorca, I did remove my shoes and the *agente* yelled at me, saying that I shouldn't remove my shoes unless asked.

By Train

Spain boasts an impressive network of trains that crisscrosses the country with thousands of miles of track. The main operator is Red Nacional de los Ferrocarriles Españoles, better known as **RENFE** (www.renfe.es), which goes pretty much to all major cities in the country—smaller villages and rural areas have less coverage. You can almost set your watch by the trains as they generally leave on time. The trains are also mostly well kept and clean with adequate bathrooms, dining cars, and sleeping berths (for a price of course).

Ticket price varies greatly depending on the type of train and the seat class. The cheapest train between Madrid and Barcelona will cost under €40 for tourist class—but you are looking at nine hours of travel. The AVE high-speed train between the two cities starts at just over €100 but takes less than three hours. RENFE's star train is the AVE, *alta velocidad española,* which zips along at 300 kilometers (186 miles) per hour. The AVE network is rapidly being expanded throughout Spain but cities currently connected include Madrid, Barcelona, Zaragoza, Sevilla, and Málaga. You pay for speed though—AVE ticket prices are considerably higher than other trains and they do book up especially on *puentes* (long weekends), so reserve ahead.

Other *larga distancia* (long-distance) trains include Talgo, Altaria, and Euromed, depending on your departure and arrival points. You'll have to spend time on the RENFE website or with a travel agent to find the best train for your budget—the variety of fares is bewildering. But in general, the more stops the train makes, the slower it will be, and the cheaper the ticket. Fewer stops equals faster travel and higher prices.

Trains connect all cities in Spain.

© CANDY LEE LABALLE

Seat classes include *club* (first class), *preferente* (business class), and *turista* (tourist class). Prices and services vary incrementally with each, however tourist class doesn't mean you'll be slumming it. Even the cheapest seats tend to be comfortable and roomy and though there is no service, you'll be just a few cars away from the bar car where you can stock up on snacks and drinks. One nice perk—prices are not over-the-top just because it is a train; you'll only notice a very slight increase from what you'd pay in a *barrio* bar. For overnight trains, there is the option to upgrade to a sleeping berth. *Cama gran clase* is a private sleeper with its own shower, *cama preferente* is also private but offers only a sink, *litera,* which translates to bunk is a shared sleeping car with up to six bunks. They can be either all male, all female, or mixed.

If you buy your tickets early—at least 15 days in advance—through the website, you will get up to 60 percent off the regular fare—but expect bewildering exceptions. Adults over 60 and people with disabilities can qualify for a *tarjeta dorada* which offers discounts of 25–40 percent. Those under 26, with a *carnet joven* (youth card) issued by their local town hall can get 20–25 percent off. Children are also eligible for discounted fares.

You can purchase your train *billetes* (tickets) directly at the train station, through the RENFE website (though for your first purchase, you'll have to pick your tickets up in person, after which you can print them at home), or from any travel agent. If you are in a rush, or traveling out of a very busy station such as Madrid's Atocha or Barcelona's Sants, you may want to think twice before buying your ticket from the station. You may end up in such a long line that you'll watch your train come and go before you get to the *taquilla* (ticket window). If you find yourself in this situation, check to see if there is an *agencia de viajes* in the station. If so, you can probably get your ticket there with no wait, though you'll be charged a few euros for the privilege. You cannot purchase tickets aboard any train and if you are caught without a ticket, you'll be charged a few euro fee at best or be kicked off the train at worst.

But RENFE is not the only train game in town. Chugging along the northern coast of the country, Ferrocarriles de Vía Estrecha, **FEVE** (www.feve.es), is a narrow-rail train that hugs the rugged coasts from País Vasco to Galicia. It is slow, stops in every town imaginable, and offers an up close view of some of Spain's most ruggedly beautiful regions. If you live in this area, you make take it for day trips; if you travel here, you should consider a few days of riding the Spanish rails.

By Bus

Anyone who's ever been on a Greyhound knows that bus travel is never as relaxing as going by train. However, it's a lot cheaper, it's often faster, and sometimes in Spain it's the only option. If you're headed to a tiny town without a train station, you may have to take the bus to get there. But don't worry, unlike the scary tin can coaches that crisscross the back roads of America, Spanish buses are clean and comfortable. Seating is assigned, air-conditioning is assured, and there is usually a movie (albeit in Spanish). Not all buses have bathrooms however, so if you go frequently, be sure and book a bus with an *aseo*. Most buses stop every two hours at a rest stop—hustle off quickly before super long lines form at the bathrooms and snack bar. For a luxury experience, upgrade to *gran clase* if it is available. Often for less than €10 more, you'll enjoy a supersized seat, an on-bus hostess, magazines, plus free snacks and drinks. *Normal* fare often includes several stops on the way; *express* is usually direct and costs a bit more.

The main problem with Spanish bus travel is that there are dozens of companies in operation. Unless you are at the bus station, where destination information is posted, you'll need to know what bus company goes where in order to book your trip. The one-stop bus-booker **Movelia** (www.movelia.es, tel. 90/233-5533) is helping out with an online bus ticketing service in English. If you do know the bus company, you can also often book tickets directly through their website. **Alsa** (www.alsa.es) and **Avanza** (www.avanzabus.com), also known as Auto Res, are two of the biggest companies. Check the local tourist website for your destination under *Cómo llegar* (how to arrive) to determine which bus company travels there.

Larger towns may have more than one bus station, so you'll have to know which one your bus is departing from. Smaller towns may not even have a station—the bus will pull up in front of a café or bar and it will depart from the same place. In such cases, tickets can likely be bought inside or nearby—ask a local.

Apart from holiday travel, you probably won't have to buy your ticket in advance but you should arrive at the station with ample time to battle the long lines—it is very exasperating to watch your bus depart while you are stuck in line. It's always less expensive to buy *ida y vuelta* (round-trip) although if you won't be returning the next day, you should make sure that the ticket is still valid for the return leg—sometimes they expire quickly.

By Car

In big cities like Madrid, Barcelona, and Valencia, excellent public transport eliminates any need for owning your own car. Americans who've been attached to the steering wheel of a car since the age of 16, are thrilled to find they don't need one in Spain—no car notes, no insurance payments, no scrambling for a parking spot. Still, a car can be an asset particularly if you have a family or live on the outskirts of town. And of course owning your own *coche* means you can leave for weekend trips at a moment's notice. Then again, renting a car is a cheap enough option for that. Read on and then make your decision.

If you've never driven a stick shift, now is the time to learn. The vast majority of cars available to buy or rent in Spain are *cambio manual;* automatics are very rarely available and then only by requesting them ahead of time. If renting, the cost will also be a bit higher. You should also get used to small cars. In Spain, less is more and cars are usually small enough to navigate medieval streets and slip into tiny parking spots. Though you'll see your share of Mercedes, Volkswagen, Renaults, Toyotas, and BMWs in Spain, you'll also get used to ultratiny cars like the 8-foot long Smart car or the 10-foot Mini. The most popular carmaker is the Spanish brand, Seat, which offers a wide range of affordable compact cars named for Spanish cities—Toledo, Altea, Léon.

Whether you rent or own, you'll have to fill 'er up and for that you'll need to visit a *gasolinera* (gas station). They run pretty much the way they do in the U.S. In big cities, you'll have to pay first, in smaller towns not. You'll also see a plastic glove dispenser near the pump. Use them; Spaniards consider it poor hygiene to pump with bare hands. Of course, the biggest difference is cost. Fuel prices in Europe have always been considerably higher than in the states. In addition, you'll pump liters not gallons, so multiply each liter by 3.75 to get a rough estimate of how many gallons you're pumping. If your car takes *gasóleo* (diesel)—and many Spanish cars do—you'll shell out a tad less. Of course prices fluctuate dramatically according to oil tariffs, taxes, international relations, and even between gas stations. However, as a general rule a 98-octane breed of *gasolina* is the most expensive. Stations are located throughout cities and every few kilometers on the country's highways with Repsol and Cespa being the two most popular companies.

ROADS AND HIGHWAYS

The Spanish highway system is wonderfully maintained with an extensive network of new, wide highways throughout the country. That said, some of the secondary roads and old highways are in a dreadful, even dangerous state.

DRIVING QUIZ

While this quiz isn't as rigid as the government's, it covers a few basics you'll need to know when you hit the road. So buckle your seat belts, start your engines, and take out your number-two pencils.

1) In the trunk of your car, you should have a spare tire, tools, and what else?

A. a flare gun

B. a sleeping bag in case you have a breakdown and need to spend the night in your car before help arrives

C. two red warning triangles

D. windshield-wiper fluid

2) If you wear glasses, what should you keep in your car?

A. maps with extra-large font

B. a little screwdriver for emergency repairs

C. reading material to keep you occupied in traffic jams

D. an extra pair of glasses

3) Who must wear a yellow reflective vest when exiting their vehicle on the side of a highway?

A. everyone

B. drivers under 21

C. children

D. anyone with a medical emergency

4) Who has to wear seatbelts?

A. children younger than 10

B. everyone in the car

C. people in the front seats

D. people in the backseats

5) What kind of cellular phone can you use while driving?

A. That's a trick question – you can't use a cellular phone in the car.

B. the kind that have digital cameras so you'll be prepared if you see something scenic

C. hands-free ones

D. Nokias

Answers: 1) C. 2) D. 3) A. 4) B. 5) C.

Traffic tends to be fast-moving except upon entering or leaving cities during rush hour or on Friday nights out of town and Sunday afternoons in.

An early point of confusion when you hit the roads are the various names held by a singly roadway such as the A-7/E-15. Additionally, locals, restaurants, and hotels, may call a road by its end points such as the Madrid–La Coruña road. Here is a run down of the basic names and what they mean:

Carreteras nacionales (national highways) are indicated by an "N" and the number in white lettering on a red background. They radiate from Madrid across the country. The principal roads are indicated by Roman numerals (though some maps use the numerical equivalent) and are often called by their end points, so the N-I is locally called the road to San Sebastián, N-II is the road to Barcelona, N-III is Valencia, N-IV is Cádiz, N-V is Badajoz, and N-VI is La Coruña.

Autopistas are toll *(peaje)* roads and are indicated by the abbreviation "AP." They are among the nicest, best-maintained roads in Spain. They are also relatively free of traffic as the tolls are fairly high—a distance as short as Valencia to Alicante costs over €12. Spaniards either can't or won't pay the fees and therefore jam the national roads instead. *Autovías* are nontoll highways and are indicated by the letter "A." Some Spanish highways are also European roadways and therefore have an "E" name as well, such as the E-5 which runs from France down to Andalucía. Regional roads often begin with the letter "C" or the first two initials of the province through which the road runs and they are usually older, windy roads.

On any road, a sign reading *cambio de sentido* (change of direction) indicates an opportunity to turn around via an overpass or underpass. If you're on a main road and you run into trouble, be it a flat tire or an overheated engine, know that emergency telephones are planted on the side of the road every five kilometers. Just pick up the receiver and you'll automatically be connected to the local police department. If you want to use your cellular phone instead, just dial the operator and ask for *auxilio en carreteras* (roadside assistance). If you're able to, park your car on the side of the road, don your mandatory yellow reflective vest, place emergency triangles 100 feet (30 meters) behind and in front of your car and then—and this part is very important—head well away from passing cars. It's not safe to sit in your vehicle while you're waiting for help to arrive.

DRIVING

Spain has historically ranked among the most deadly European countries for drivers. In 2007, *Forbes* magazine ranked Spain 13th of the European nations

READING THE SIGNS

Most road signs in Spain are self-explanatory and a few – such as **Stop** and **Yield** – are even the same. Still, plenty of mysterious ones are out there. To American eyes, one sign suggests driving off a dock, another appears to encourage drag racing, and yet another suggests turning in two directions at once. As you might have guessed, the real messages in those pictures are more logical than they appear. Here's a breakdown of a few of the stranger ones.

The shapes signs take are no arbitrary detail; they specify what sort of sign you're reading. A diamond indicates priority, red triangles warn you of an upcoming change in the road or danger, and blue-rimmed circles tell you of a particular rule. Circles with red borders specify a restriction – the pictures in those signs indicate what you *shouldn't* do. Simply put, blue means, "do the thing in the picture" and red means, "*don't* do it." The most crucial element to note is that you won't see a diagonal slash through a circle when a sign indicates a prohibition. Instead, the circle will merely have a red margin.

So given that information, let's revisit that sign of a car driving off a pier. The picture is on a red-bordered, triangular sign, so the shape and color signify a warning. What exactly does it mean? A dock is nearby and you shouldn't drive off of it. (Sound advice.) What about the apparent drag racing sign – the one of two cars depicted side-by-side in a red-rimmed circle? That means no passing; and if you see a circular sign with the same image and a diagonal slash through it, you're exiting the no-passing zone. How about the picture of two arrows pointing in different directions? Traffic moving in the direction of the red arrow has to yield to traffic coming from the other direction.

While we're demystifying signs, let's talk about speed limits. A

in terms of road fatalities—93.7 per million residents. However, much is being done to lower the number of accidents in Spain. In July of 2006, the Spanish government passed a new set of regulations concerning driving, *carné por puntos,* basically a points system. All drivers are assigned 12 points (new drivers 8) which can be lost for a variety of infractions—speeding, not wearing a seat belt, driving drunk—and can lead to an eventual revocation of your driving license. There has also been a reduction of speed limits around major cities and an increase in alcohol check points. In 2006, there were 3,367 driving-related fatalities; in 2007 that number dropped to 3,082. Though fairly modest, the fact is that driving safety is now very big in the minds of the public thanks to aggressive campaigning by the Dirección General de Tráfico, the Interior Ministry office that oversees roads, driving, and traffic issues in Spain.

That said, when you do hit the road you may be shocked at the driving habits of Spaniards—they make New York taxi drivers seem tame. Be prepared to drive defensively. Road rules are pretty much the same as you'd expect stateside

© CANDY LEE LABALLE

If you come across this sign while driving, you are going the wrong way!

number in a circular sign will tell you what the speed limit is, and a number with a diagonal slash through it tells you that you've left the speed limit's zone. A circular sign with a number on a shaded background tells you the recommended minimum speed.

Now that you know how to interpret the more baffling signs, it's a good idea to follow their directions – if you don't, you can expect other drivers to beep their horns, shake their fists, and shout out that you're *loco* (crazy) – or less printable things!

and illustrated signs usually have clear meanings. You'll see that speed limits, passing zones, mountain passages with dangerous curves, and the like are all fairly well marked.

Rules of the Road

Speed limits depend on the type of road, and speed limits as well as speedometers are in kilometers. The upper limit is 120 km/h (about 75 mph) on highways and 50 km/h (30 mph) in towns. You are not allowed to stop on the shoulder of a highway except in the case of an emergency. Breaking any Spanish driving regulation can result in an on-the-spot fine (starting around €90) or, for serious infractions such as drunk driving, arrest. Things to know before getting behind the wheel in Spain:

• Driver must be at least 18 regardless of whether he/she possesses a license from their own country.

- Everyone in the vehicle must wear seatbelts.

- Children younger than 12 must ride in the backseat unless the front seat is fitted with safety equipment or a car seat.

- Drivers may only use cellular phones with a hands-free system.

- Those who wear glasses must keep an extra pair in their car.

- For more details on driving in Spain, visit the blog *Driving in Spain* (http://drivinginspain.blogspot.com).

Getting Stopped by the Police

Most highway and road infractions are handled by the Guardia Civil (the Civil Guard) one of the three branches of national law enforcement (the Policia Municipal and the Policia Nacional are the others). You can be stopped for one of two reasons—a mandatory police check of all passing vehicles or for an infraction committed on your behalf. In both cases, utmost respect should be used as your first defense against receiving a *multa* (ticket). If you are stopped at a mandatory control, do whatever the police ask you to. Most likely it will be an alcohol check and if you are asked to take a breathalyzer and refuse, you can be arrested. If you are stopped for a driving infraction, you may or may not have to pay the fine on the spot. If so, you should receive a receipt that you can later use to contest the fine if you wish. If you are asked to step outside of the car, be sure to first put on your yellow security vest (by law it should be inside your vehicle and easily accessible). Typical infractions that can result in your being pulled over include:

- Driving more than 30 km/h (19 mph) above the speed limit

- Driving while under the influence of drugs or alcohol (the legal blood-alcohol limit is 0.05 percent)

- Refusing to take a Breathalyzer test

- Exceeding the number of people permitted to ride in the car by 50 percent

- Reckless driving

- Passing on the right

- Driving at night with the lights off

Driver's Licenses

If all those rules seem like a lot to remember, don't worry, your mandatory driving course and test will drill them (and hundreds more) into your brain. But, you say you've been driving for over 20 years in the traffic-clogged streets of Boston? Tough luck. The United States and Spain do not have a agreement for the validation of U.S. driving licenses. You can drive on your stateside license for up to six months, but once you pass that mark as a legal resident of Spain, you must get a Spanish *carné de conducir*. This means enrolling in a Spanish driving school and taking the Spanish driving test. Before going into those details, note that many Americans who do not own cars in Spain and rent very infrequently, often just leave their residence card at home and rent on their American passport and U.S. driver's license, claiming to be a tourist. It works, but if you have an accident, it is not the police you will have to worry about, but the insurance companies who will look for any loophole to escape responsibility and your renting as a tourist when you are actually a resident fits the bill. Follow this procedure at your own risk.

If you will be buying a car in Spain, then there is no option but to get your Spanish license. That means finding a local *autoescuela* where you can prepare for both the practical and theoretical tests. The course will run you around €800, though if you fail the test or have to repeat courses, you could easily be looking at four figures. If you see schools advertising courses for as low as €150, you can bet that doesn't include hourly driving fees, testing fees, and a variety of other requirements. Most Americans whiz through the practical test which will be conducted in the school's vehicle. The theoretical test is another *historia*. There are over 600 rules contained in the *Manual de Normas de Circulación y Seguridad Vial* (Spanish driving regulations) and you need to know them all—first aid, vehicle maintenance, engine mechanics, payloads, towing specifications. In addition, the multiple-choice test is written in a deliberately twisted version of Spanish designed to trip up Spaniards. One American described it as worse than the GRE. Another said it was tougher than his Michigan bar exam. They are not exaggerating. You can register to take the test in English in some locations—check with your driving school for more info. You can find English-language study materials at http://english.test-autoescuela.com. You will also need an eye and medical exam which is little more than a formality and can also be facilitated by your driving school.

Parking

Parking in the major cities can be a real nightmare. Each city will have its own very specific regulations for parking on the street and they are strictly

© CANDY LEE LABALLE

Mopeds are a common sight on Spanish streets.

enforced—a parking *multa* (ticket) can cost up to €90. If you are unsure about where you can and can't park, consider a *aparcamiento* (parking garage), easily identified by a large white "P" on a blue background. Parking fees vary greatly depending on location but expect a minimum of €.50 per hour.

If you do decide to park on the street, learn the local laws. For example in Madrid, green lines on the ground mean that only residents can park there. Blue lines mean anyone can park, but you'll have to pump some coins into the nearest *parquímetro* (parking meter) to get a ticket to display in your car window. Maximum parking time is 1.5 hours and you don't have to pay on Saturday afternoons, Sundays, or holidays.

Of course, once you've been in Spain a while, you'll see that Spaniards regularly break all parking rules, both legal and common sense. Double-parking is very usual. If you find your car hemmed in by a double-parker, lean on your horn a few minutes—the driver should be within earshot. And if you are tempted to double-park, don't go far and keep your ears open for the sound of someone's impatient horn. In the south of Spain, it is common for a person who is double-parking to leave their brake off. This allows anyone hemmed in by their car to simply push it out of the way. You'll also eventually run into someone who will guide you with exaggerated hand gestures into a legal parking spot on the street. They will expect a small tip for their "help." Though illegal and extremely frustrating, there is little that can be done. Give them a euro or spend the rest of the day worrying what type of damage they will do to your car.

The worst that can happen if you are illegally parked is that your car is towed away. The *grúa* (tow truck) will take your car to the closest car pound—*depósito de coches*. Call tel. 092 to find out the exact location. The amount of the fine varies depending on the size of the car and how long it has been impounded. Expect fees to start at well over €100 and to increase at an hourly rate of at least €1. Be sure to bring your driver's license, identification card, and any vehicle documents that were not in the car when it was towed. Also bring a wad of cash as not all pounds take credit cards.

BRINGING YOUR CAR INTO SPAIN

If you move to Spain with the intention of getting residency and the appropriate visa to do so, you can include your car in your personal belongings that you ship over. You'll have to shop around for shipping companies, and expect to pay in the thousands for one. Technically, as it is your personal property, you should not have to pay taxes, however there are always various exceptions and it is best if you hire a *gestor* (administrator) to handle the paperwork and taxes. Another option is to hire an expert in car importation such as Barcelona-based **Car Import in Spain** (www.carimportinspain.com) run by a British expat who has specialized in importing cars and re-registering them in Spain since 1988. You will also have to have the rear lights on the car changed from red to amber and some internal engine wiring modified to European standards. A local mechanic should be able to do that, or you could refer to Car Import in Spain. Finally, you have to get Spanish car insurance. **Línea Directa** (www.lineadirecta.com) and **Genesis** (www.genesis.es) are two of the more popular providers.

BUYING A CAR

To buy your own car, you'll need *residencia* in Spain. If you do have it, buying is fairly easy, although cars in Spain are slightly more expensive than their U.S. counterparts. That's mainly due to the sales tax. In addition, in 2007 a tax for carbon emissions was added with environmental polluters like SUVs and 4x4s getting the hardest hit. If you buy through a dealer, you can sign on to a monthly payment plan which will be financed by a bank. The dealer will also take care of all paperwork and guide you through the process.

You can also buy a *coche segundamano* (used car). Be sure to use the same precautions you would back home—look for a car that is still within its warranty period or get a good mechanic to inspect it. A good place to find one is through the English-language press as many expats buy new when they arrive, then sell a few years later when they return home. Though you can handle the purchase of a used car yourself, if your Spanish is not up to par, think about hiring a *gestor*. The sale can begin when the seller provides you with original copies of the *permiso de circulación* (an official log detailing chassis number, make and model, year of first registration, and most importantly the name and address of the current owner), a valid *inspección técnica* (technical inspection), also called the ITV, and the most recent *impuesto sobre vehiculos* (vehicle tax) showing that the taxes are up-to-date. Beware, if you buy a car with outstanding taxes, you will become responsible for paying them. Each of these documents should have the same name and address as the person who is selling the car— ask to see their identification. Both seller and buyer then must visit the local Jefatura de Tráfico (office similar to an American DMV) to file for a change of title for the vehicle. Bring several copies of all documents as well as copies of both of your DNIs. Normally they accept cash only, so bring lots. Once this is done, and the car is in your name, you can take your proof of ownership to your local *ayuntamiento* (town hall) and register the car.

To legally drive your car, you will also have to have it insured. At all times you are behind the wheel, the following documents must be with you:

- Driver's license

- *Permiso de circulación*

- *Fichas technicas* (the technical specifications of the car, included with the vehicle)

- Proof that your vehicle taxes have been paid

- Valid insurance documents

- Your NIE or residence card

In addition, vehicles must also have:

- A reflective yellow jacket

- Two warning triangles

- Spare glasses (if you need them for driving)

- Spare tire and the tools to replace it

Public Transportation

Spain has excellent public transport and even the smallest town will have some type of service. The *transportes* (transportation) department of each town generally offers a monthly *abono* (pass) which will entitle you to unlimited rides on the city's buses, subways, trams, and/or commuter trains. Though the process is a bit different in each town, in general, you can buy the actual pass itself at any *estanco* (tobacco shop); bring two passport-sized photos and your ID. Then, purchase the monthly ticket from a kiosk in the subway station or other location; just ask a local.

SUBWAYS

Many cities, including Barcelona, Bilbao, Madrid, and Valencia are served by excellent subway systems called Metros. Each offers inexpensive, fast transport around the city. When you arrive in each city, be sure and get a free *mapa de metro* from the nearest tourist booth or a metro station. Before embarking on a metro trip, read up on the system so you know what to expect. The easiest way to find your way around is to locate where you are on the metro map, then locate where you want to go. You'll have to devise a connection route between the two points. Metro lines are always named by a color, a number, and/or their end points. So Madrid's line 3 is yellow and is also called *Moncloa–Villaverde Alto*. To determine which track you need to catch, find your destination and then look where that line ends. As you figure all this out in the metro station, be especially wary of your surroundings. Pickpockets thrive on the confusion that metro systems create. Consult your map with your back up against the wall.

transferring through a metro station in Madrid

© ALFONSO MORCUENDE

COMMUTER TRAINS

Major cities are connected to their satellites and suburbs via local *Cercanías* trains operated by RENFE (www.renfe.es/cercanias). Tickets

DAILY LIFE

usually cost less than €10 as the distances are short. These trains tend to be hard-seated and make frequent stops and rarely come equipped with bathrooms. If you are traveling during rush hour, you may not even get a seat, but prices are dirt cheap and the service is fast.

BUSES

All major cities are served by extensive bus systems and these are often the best way to get around town. However, as with the national buses, the bus system can be very confusing. Part of the problem is that stops and end points are named for various places in the city. If you don't know the city, it is hard to figure out the routes. Your best bet is to get a *plano de transportes* (transport map) from the nearest tourist office.

TAXI

Though they once suffered a bad reputation for rudeness and overcharging, Spanish *taxistas* (taxi drivers) have improved greatly—thanks in part to the government and tourist boards who have pushed through extensive reforms. If your Spanish is nonexistent, don't try telling the driver the address, he won't understand you. Have the address of your destination written on a piece of paper that you can give him. If you have a map, you can point it out on the map as well—though most taxis come equipped with GPS these days.

Official fares are posted in the back seat of the taxi in Spanish and English. There are almost always surcharges for airport pickup/drop-off, luggage, and traveling at night or on holidays. In some cities, set airport rates apply. In-city trips rarely top €10, making taxi travel in Spain a bargain compared to New York, London, or Paris. Be sure and have small bills available; though bound by law to break anything up to a €20, drivers often ask you to pay with small bills especially if the fare is low. Drivers are not obligated to break a €50 bill and if you present one, the driver may insist that you get out and find change while he/she keeps the meter running. Tipping is not required, but it is usual to round the fare up to the nearest euro.

Once you settle into Spain, you will eventually run into an unscrupulous driver who will attempt to rip you off. The most common way is by not turning on the meter—a serious offence, punishable by a fine against the driver. If this happens to you, point to the meter and insist. If the driver refuses, get out of the cab. He cannot force you to pay as there is no record of the charge. One way to insure proper service is to ask for a *factura,* or bill.

PRIME LIVING LOCATIONS

© CANDY LEE LABALLE

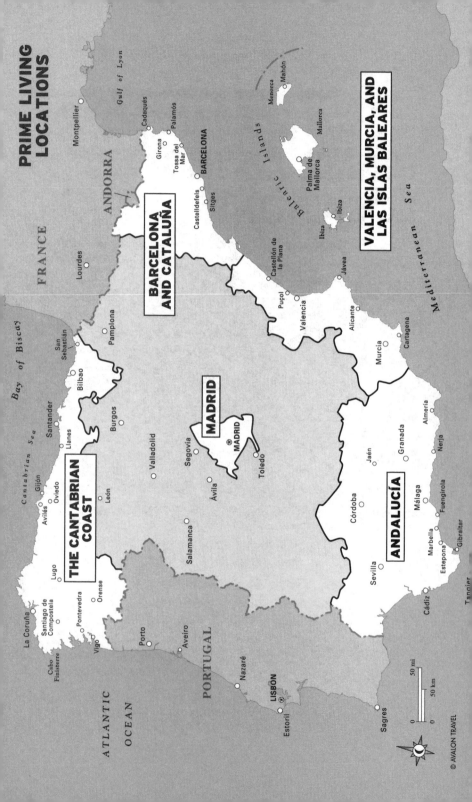

PRIME LIVING LOCATIONS

FRANCE

ANDORRA

BARCELONA AND CATALUÑA

THE CANTABRIAN COAST

MADRID

ANDALUCÍA

VALENCIA, MURCIA, AND LAS ISLAS BALEARES

ATLANTIC OCEAN

Bay of Biscay

Cantabrian Sea

Gulf of Lyon

Balearic Islands

Balearic Sea

Mediterranean Sea

PORTUGAL

Montpellier
Lourdes
Pamplona
San Sebastián
Bilbao
Santander
Llanes
Gijón
Avilés
Oviedo
Lugo
La Coruña
Cabo Finisterre
Santiago de Compostela
Pontevedra
Orense
Vigo
Porto
Aveiro
Nazaré
LISBON
Estoril
Sagres
Tangier
Cádiz
Sevilla
Estepona
Marbella
Gibraltar
Fuengirola
Málaga
Nerja
Córdoba
Jaén
Granada
Almería
Cartagena
Murcia
Alicante
Jávea
Valencia
Puçol
Castellón de la Plana
Sitges
Castelldefels
BARCELONA
Tossa del Mar
Girona
Palamós
Cadaqués
Menorca
Mahón
Mallorca
Palma de Mallorca
Ibiza
Ibiza
Burgos
Valladolid
León
Salamanca
Ávila
Segovia
MADRID
Toledo

0   50 mi
0   50 km

© AVALON TRAVEL

OVERVIEW

One of the first things you notice about Spaniards is that they always live in the best city, the best *pueblo,* the best *barrio.* Their hometown has "the best—chorizo, tapas bars, nightlife, apple cider, paprika, wild boars, potatoes—in Spain. It is a country full of people very proud of where they are from and I am not talking about the big *país.* Rarely will you hear someone boast about being Spanish; no, they break it down to the smallest geographic decimal point—they are Andaluz (from Andalucía), or better yet, Sevillano (from Sevilla, a region of Andalucía). Foreigners seem to quickly adopt this attitude and pretty much any expat you talk to will tell you that they've found the country's most idyllic spot—and the funny thing is they're often right (after all, unlike the Spaniards who were born here, the expats have chosen to live where they live). And, you'll have that choice too (unless you are being sent to Spain by your company). With some soul-searching and a little planning, you too can end up living in the best place in Spain. So, tune out the advice from both Spaniards and expats alike and tune in to what you really want in

your new Spanish *hogar*. Crave slow-country living way off the beaten path? Maybe the craggy coast of Galicia is for you or perhaps a whitewashed village surrounded by olive groves in Andalucía. Looking for resort living with sun-soaked beaches stretching as far as you can squint—consider the Mediterranean coast or maybe the Islas Baleares. Need the buzz and bustle of a world-class city? Then Madrid or Barcelona is for you.

And of course for each urban haven you find, you'll find comfortable suburbs surrounding them—just don't call them *surburbios,* this grammatical false friend actually means "poor community" and many of Spain's suburbs are anything but. Call them *ciudades dormitorios* (bedroom communities), *urbanizaciónes* (residential developments), or simply *pueblo* (village). There are a few other key differences between Spanish suburbs and the American version of split-level, clapboard houses with working fireplaces, emerald green lawns, and a white-picket fence thrown in for good measure. In Spain, freestanding houses—called *chalets*—exist but are usually as luxurious as their name suggests. Instead, attached townhouses—called *casas adosadas*—are the norm. Amenities like swimming pools or tennis courts are either public or private in the United States—whereas in Spain they're often shared among the members of a given community. Finally, Spanish suburbs are often not made up of houses at all, but massive apartment blocks.

One thing's for sure: Spain offers dozens of possibilities to suit any lifestyle. Here is an overview of the most popular options.

MADRID

Spain's capital appeals to both young and old, urbanites and suburbanites, Spaniards and expats. It garners as much devotion as New York does among New Yorkers—though Madrid has been inspiring poets and writers for at least six hundred years before the Big Apple was founded! Madrid is fast and glorious, centuries old and cutting edge too. It is the seat of Spanish politics and finance, the center of Spanish culture and art. There's no doubt that Madrid has drawing power, but add to the list the notorious nightlife and it's little wonder that people from even the remotest corners of Spain choose Madrid when they seek out big-city life. If you have young children, you'll find life easy in any part of the city, but you'll also discover more space on the well-connected outskirts of the city. There you'll find houses rather than apartments, peace and quiet rather than the noisy riot of traffic and street life, more grass and less pavement—heck you can even get a glimpse of the stars that the bright lights of the capital drown out. However, plenty of folks prefer to live in the smack center of the urban action. Whichever you choose,

© CANDY LEE LABALLE

a Madrid bar famous for its shrimp

just be aware—not only is Madrid the country's most popular city, it's also the most expensive.

BARCELONA AND CATALUÑA

More than any other Spanish city, Barcelona is cosmopolitan—from its Roman roots to its internationally acclaimed architecture. Home to one of Spain's largest expat communities, the city's streets teem with globe-hopping jet-setters, dream-seeking immigrants, and hordes of expats from English teachers to executives, artists to artful dodgers. And why not? The city offers a little bit of everything—culture and history, finance and funk, nature and nightlife. In fact, Barcelona's location is one of its biggest draws—basking on a lovely stretch of Mediterranean, just a quick train ride from the mountains. Families also do well in Barcelona; the city offers top-notch international schools and parks and kid-friendly culture abound. But all this urban glory comes at a hefty price and Barcelona is second only to Madrid in cost.

Barcelona is also the capital of Cataluña—which any local will tell you, is *not* España! Older than Spain itself, Cataluña is a proud region of enduring tradition and a distinct tongue—Catalan (you'll have to learn it if you move here). One of the most popular spots for expats is the Costa Brava, an area of intense natural beauty where the lumbering Pyrenees tumble dramatically into the sea. It is dotted with everything from glitzy resorts to sleepy seaside *pueblos*. South of Barcelona, Sitges is a popular spot among beach lovers, partiers, and commuters who want a little distance from the big city. The town mellows out

© CANDY LEE LABALLE

a pastry shop in Barcelona

during the off-season but in the summer months it's in full swing and that's precisely what so many Sitges residents adore about their home.

VALENCIA, MURCIA, AND LAS ISLAS BALEARES

Valencia is the place to be if you want the convenience of big city life without the madness of a huge metropolis. It's the country's third-largest city and though it's not exactly beautiful, it compensates by throwing great parties (particularly Las Fallas de San José, a fiery fiesta held every March). It also offers heavenly stretches of Mediterranean beach, a world-renowned Arts and Science center, ample inner-city parkland, and paella that can't be beat. Houses and apartments cost less than the going rate in both Barcelona and Madrid and the expats who live here often boast that their lifestyle is not only more affordable than for residents of other cities, it's also more peaceful. Just outside the city, you can find commuter towns with sprawling villas and a few solid international schools to boot. From Valencia, traveling south along the Costa Blanca, dodge the concrete high-rises to find bucolic, coastal towns and small urban areas such as Altea, Denia, and Alicante. The population along this stretch of Spain is growing quickly and property prices reflect its popularity.

Continue along the coast and the region of Murcia unfolds. Traditionally a land of seafarers and farmers, Murcia was not much of a tourist draw and as a result avoided some of the worst of the coastal overdevelopment. This has proved to be irresistible to expats looking for a some authentic Spain still near the sea and in recent years, Murcia has had the fastest growing expat community in the country.

Some people forgo the mainland for life on the nearby Islas Baleares. Sitting in the Mediterranean Sea, less than 100 miles off the coast of Valencia, these four islands offer the stuff dream vacations are made of—miles of powder-white beach, acres of upscale resorts, and every amenity you can imagine from top-rated restaurants to high-end shopping. In fact, much of the islands' fame and fortune comes from its draw as a tourist hot spot (nightlife on the islands is legendary). However, the islands also offer diverse lifestyle options from big-city living in Palma de Mallorca to laid-back life along lonely coves in Menorca. And, with a very well-established expat population (mainly English and German), you'll also find international schools, shops, and support networks.

ANDALUCÍA

When people conjure up an image of Spain, it is often Andalucía they picture—whitewashed villages, colorful flowers crammed in cool patios, the sound of flamenco in the streets. More or less, Andalucía fits this image. Throughout the region—which borders both the Mediterranean Sea and the Atlantic Ocean—the weather is hot in the summers, temperate in the winters, and the pace of life is decadently slow. But it is so much more than the stereotypes. Sevilla and Granada—the area's two biggest cities—offer the culture, commerce, and commotion you'd expect from any Spanish urban center, yet they are entirely different from one another. Sevilla exudes a stately elegance and, not surprisingly, it's a tad conservative. Granada is a bit rougher around the edges; it's more casual, attracts younger people, and has a more intimate air to it.

The Costa del Sol is Spain's most famous tourist magnet and it attracts hordes of expats, most seeking a vacation of sun, sand, and sangria. Still, plenty of people find this coast alluring enough to stick around for good, and they have an easier time at adapting than those who live elsewhere in Spain. Some communities are almost entirely populated by northern Europeans, and you could end up in a town where speaking Spanish is optional. Is this a plus? A minus? You decide. You'll find plenty of international schools and amenities that range from the useful (wide-aisled grocery stores, a plethora of English-speaking doctors) to the out-and-out deluxe (mud wraps, golf courses, and decadent meals).

© MEGAN CYTRON

farmland bordrering the Cantabrian Sea in Asturias

THE CANTABRIAN COAST

Running along the Bay of Biscay from the French border out to the Atlantic Coast, the Cantabrian Coast offers desolate beaches, soaring mountains wrapped in mist, ancient villages, and deep green forests. In fact, the area is known as the Costa Verde, the Green Coast, and it offers a year-round temperate climate (though umbrellas and rain boots are a necessity), a thriving industrial sector, and a world-renowned surf culture fueled by the fierce waves thrown up from the tumultuous waters. The coast stretches through four autonomous regions of Spain. The most famous is the País Vasco (Basque Country) which is home to arguably Spain's loveliest city—San Sebastián, an elegant seaside town famed for its crescent-shaped beach and its delicious cuisine. The small regions of Asturias and Cantabria are defined by the sea and the mountains, rural living and ancient history. It is an area that attracts few expats, though Oviedo and Santander—both modestly sized cities—do offer an inexpensive, urban lifestyle for those seeking it. Galicia comprises the northwest corner of Spain and with its craggy coast, deep fjords, and misty interior, many consider it the most beautiful area of the country. You can definitely get lost way off the beaten path here. Or, you can choose city life in thriving towns such as Santiago, La Coruña or Pontevedra. Wherever you set your roots in Galicia, you'll always be close to the peaceful, rugged beauty that characterizes the area.

MADRID

Madrid is as vibrant and forward looking as it is infused with reminders of the romantic, old Spain that Cervantes wrote about in *Don Quixote*. Walking from the worn cobblestones of Plaza Mayor to the screaming glitz of Gran Vía, it is hard not to be dazzled by the contrasts. The city built Europe's largest Royal Palace and adopted a peasant farmer as its patron saint. Three of the world's greatest art museums—the Prado, the Reina Sofía, and the Thyssen—are clustered on one of its grandest streets—Paseo del Prado. A few blocks away cloistered nuns bake sweets following a 16th-century recipe. Every year it throws one of Europe's most audacious gay pride parades and a few months later it herds sheep down the same streets.

Founded as a Moorish fortress around the 10th century, Madrid wasn't much of a town until 1561 when King Felipe II made it his royal capital based on little more than its location in the exact center of Spain. Courtesans and culture followed, sparking the birth of modern Madrid as we know it today. By European standards, it was a late start, and many point out that this city

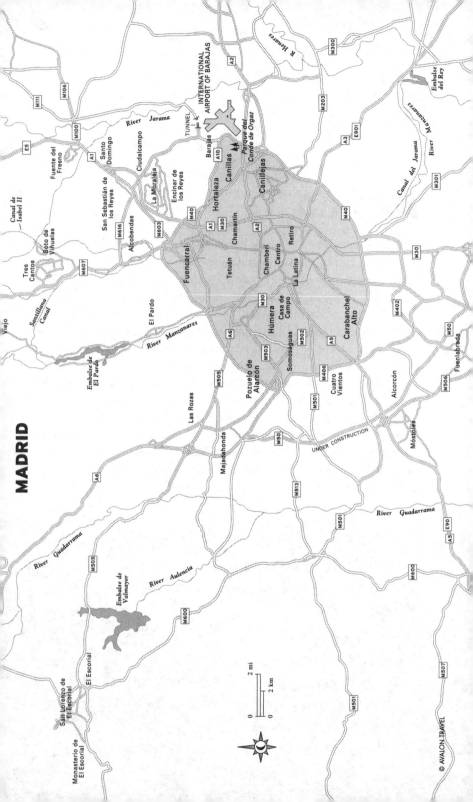

lacks the history-steeped physical beauty of places like Paris and Rome. This is a fair point, although even a cursory visit shows that Madrid has plenty of architectural triumphs to boast of. Yet Madrid has an altogether different appeal, and for those who choose to live here, it's one that's equally as powerful as outward appearance. Madrid truly *feels* like the center of Spain. By day the it sizzles with activity—home to over three million people (over seven including the suburbs), the seat of the Spanish government, and the center of Spain's financial world—traffic is thick and the noise incessant. Come evening, not much changes. Whole families spill out into the plazas, restaurants fill to bursting, and *madrileños* (as Madrid residents are called) take to the streets. World-famous for its raucous nightlife, with one bar for every 100 residents, Madrid is as vibrant at 3 A.M. as it is at 3 P.M.

Given all its enticements, many Americans (and in fact people from all over the world—Madrid has one of the highest immigrant populations in Spain) have chosen to make Madrid a long-term home. This means you can easily find a community of expats to fall in with, making your transition to Spain much easier. I've lived here nonstop since 2003, and I've celebrated Thanksgiving each year with various groups of Americans. However, Madrid doesn't have the sprawling, all-English communities that you might find along the Mediterranean. If you live just a few blocks outside of the main central neighborhoods, you are apt to find yourself the only English speaker around. This fact will offer you ample opportunity to mix into the city's predominant culture, and for most people living abroad that is the main point of the experience.

Finally, if you are sure you want to live in Spain but don't really know where to start, Madrid is your easiest jumping off point. Yes, it is the country's most expensive city, but it also offers the most amenities—from an English-speaking subculture to higher employment opportunities. And, if you are looking to work as an English teacher while you figure out your next move, Madrid has some of the highest pay rates in the country.

The Lay of the Land

Madrith (as the locals pronounce it) sits on the Spanish *meseta* (tableland), a high, flat stretch of fertile earth that's insanely hot and dry in summer and bitterly cold but sunny in winter. Perched over 2,000 feet above sea level, it is also Europe's highest capital. As a result, the Madrid air has a clarity and shimmer that has inspired writers and artists for centuries. And when people say that Madrid is in the center of it all, they truly mean it. The city isn't just

SUNDAY BRUNCH LA LATINA STYLE

In the warmer months, right as the Sunday morning flea market El Rastro is winding down, the plazas and streets of La Latina start plumping up with hordes of laid-back *madrileños* looking for a few beers, a few snacks, and a really good time. For decades, this impromptu Sunday afternoon street party has been a neighborhood phenomenon. In the last few years, as La Latina has become the address of choice for Madrid's creative community, the crowds have become hipper, edgier, and much, much bigger. It is not uncommon to see actors like Javier Bardem or directors like Pedro Almodóver weaving through the throngs.

The action is centered on Plaza San Andrés right in front of the Iglesia de San Andrés. If the sun is out, hundreds of people will be sprawled about in designer sunglasses sharing beers right from liter-sized bottles. They used to be accompanied by hippie drummers and the occasional drag-queen flamenco singer, but the church priest put a stop to all that. Seems all the hand-clapping was disrupting the services.

The tiny Plaza Humilladero, just next door, is the place to see and be seen. The truly cool set up at bar El Bonanno, a miniscule place that is unfathomably popular. The no-name tapas bar on the corner of Calle Cava Baja is also famous for its large, free tapas – get there early for a helping of paella. The other main stomping zones are Calle Almendro and Plaza de la Paja, though all of La Latina's bars and restaurants will be packed from about 2 P.M. to sunset. Do like the locals and go from bar to bar, having one *caña* here, one *vino* there. Just be sure to graze on tapas as you go along.

In 2003, Madrid city government made it technically illegal to drink in public streets and the bars all have signs to that effect. It doesn't hold back these crowds though. The bars don't seem too worried either. People go out of their way to return glasses and plates to the bars and you'll usually see a waiter or two collecting glassware from the tops of parked cars which are used as improvised tabletops. If the driver comes along, people just pick up their glasses, and wait for the next "table" to pull up.

the figurative heart of the country—it literally *is* the geographic middle of Spain. The sprawling square Puerta del Sol marks the spot and it's known as "kilometer zero." From that nucleus, the nation's six most important highways unfurl towards points throughout Spain. When you're driving along in Andalucía or Galicia and you come across a kilometer mark on the side of the road, the number you see tells you just how many kilometers you are from Puerta del Sol—the absolute center of Spain.

Just north of Sol, you'll find the Gran Vía. This broad avenue, lined with restaurants, shops, and businesses and teeming with pedestrians merges into the ritzier Calle de Alcalá. A historic route once considered Europe's most magnificent street, Calle de Alcalá has plenty of bragging points such as the 19th-century Banesto building and the Círculo de Bellas Artes, which hints at a kind of modernism that's more commonly seen in Barcelona. These streets bisect the city into southern and northern halves. The Paseo de la Castellana further divides the city into east and west. La Castellana, as it's known locally, is a major thoroughfare holding up to eight lanes of traffic, but it is also one of the city's loveliest boulevards, bordered for most of its length with tree-lined walkways, colorful gardens, outdoor cafés, and playgrounds.

Where to Live

The living options in a city as big and bustling as Madrid are nearly unlimited— from grungy artist havens to centuries-old barrios to clean, sprawling suburbs. It would be impossible to cover them all here, so what follows is a listing of some of the more popular expat choices. No matter where you live—city center or suburbs—you'll find everything you need right in your new barrio. Madrid is a huge urban space and people live and work in all neighborhoods. After years of living here, I am still amazed that on any given evening, on any given street, anywhere in Madrid, every single café you pass will be full of people. Of course, *madrileños* do not subsist on café culture alone and no matter your neighborhood, it will be dense with grocery stores, Internet cafés, restaurants, boutiques, cell phone stores, shoe repair shops, fresh fruit markets, and the ever present *chino*. Literally meaning "Chinese," these practically 24-hour shops are usually run by people hailing from Asia—hence the less than politically correct name. The outlying communities and suburbs will also have all of those amenities plus one-stop supercenters and malls—the only difference is that you might have to reach those places on wheels rather than on foot.

Price can more or less guide your choice of Madrid casa. In the city center, apartment shares can be had for as low as €350 per month, though €500 is around average. To rent a place on your own, expect an average of €700 for a one-bedroom, €1,000 for two (of course, depending on location, amenities, and luck, your price could be lower or much, much higher). Buying a house in Madrid is going to start at the lowest around €190,000 for a dinky one-bedroom in an undesirable part of town. Midrange is around €250,000, and everything else goes up from there. Upscale barrios and the better suburbs start around €400,000 and go up. Of course, keep in mind that this book was written as the housing market was crashing and Spain's economy with it. Prices as of publication were sliding.

THE CENTER
The barrios (neighborhoods) that make up Madrid's old city center blend into one another, yet manage to retain their own distinctive personalities. **Puerta**

del Sol and **Gran Vía** are famous throughout Spain and are places you'll grow to know well if you're living anywhere near Madrid. Together they make up the city's commercial hub and tourist nucleus. This part of town is always crowded, often exciting, and decidedly not the place for those with acute noise sensitivity. **Puerta del Sol** (or just "Sol") is home to Madrid's proud symbol—*el oso y madroño,* a statue of a bear eating fruit from a tree. Sol also marks the place where a city gate once stood thus giving the area its name, "door of the sun." Prices here are a real mix, with lots of low rent places mixed among some of the most expensive housing in the city. The better barrios near Sol include: **Barrio de las Letras,** Cervantes's old stomping grounds—it includes the delightful pedestrian street Huertas and the tapas mecca of Plaza Santa Ana; and, **Ópera,** which runs from Sol to the Palacio Real (Royal Palace) and includes some of old Madrid's most spectacular buildings as well as its most elegant plaza—Plaza de Oriente. Both of these areas are midpriced to high on the Madrid housing scale.

The always buzzing Gran Vía cuts a swathe from the neighborhood of Argüelles in the West to Salamanca in the East. Madrid's "Great Way" is an architectural buff's delight lined with extraordinary early 20th-century buildings. The avenue is also a dizzying buzz of commercial activity with retail shops and restaurants for all budgets, massive city cinemas, and eateries from ice cream parlors to fast food places. Up top are some of Madrid's most exclusive apartments; if you want to live here, you'll need a penthouse-sized pocketbook to do so.

To the south of Sol is the lively barrio of **La Latina.** It boasts ancient cobbled streets, gourmet wine bars, and a reputation as the place to be on Sunday afternoon when beautiful bohemians (and everyone else) spill out of the zillion bars for a (weekly) impromptu street party. The area around Plaza de la Paja, is known as Madrid de Los Austrias and is quite arguably the most

© CANDY LEE LABALLE

For centuries, Spanish shepherds have herded their sheep through the center of Madrid.

MADRID'S *LA MOVIDA*

You've probably heard of **Pedro Almodóvar** already – the filmmaker famous for creating candy-colored stories of sexually liberated women, transvestites, pregnant nuns in preposterous situations – think *Women on the Verge of a Nervous Breakdown, Tie Me Up, Tie Me Down,* and *All About My Mother.* When the latter won the Oscar for Best Foreign Film, presenter Penelope Cruz famously cried "Pedroooo!" You've also probably heard that people either love his work or they hate it. But what you might not know is that Spain's most famous director was part of an entire movement in the late 1970s and early 1980s.

While Americans might likely remember that era for Duran Duran and football-worthy shoulder pads, it was a bold period of cultural liberation in Spain. Franco was dead and buried, blatant sexuality and subversive creativity began to blossom, and *la movida* was born. Mainly centered in Madrid, it was an explosive backlash to years of political oppression that expressed itself in good old counterculture-style rebellious and riotous fun. And what better way to have fun than through creative expression, sexual freedom, and consuming vast amounts of alcohol and drugs? Almodóvar was there at the center of it.

The great director started out as part of a cross-dressing glam rock duo and not long after that, he was running around the city with a Super 8 camera. His early flicks give a good dose of the *movida* spirit. In *Pepi, Luci, Bom and Other Girls on the Heap, Labyrinth of Passions,* and *Dark Habits* Almodóvar depicts drug-taking nuns, cross-dressing judges, and explicit, kinky sexuality. It's not hard to catch his drift – Franco's Spain was decidedly gone and 40 years of repression was bursting through all cultural boundaries. This was especially true regarding gays and lesbians. The *movida* was a much-needed catalyst for gay liberation in Spain – during the dictatorship it was a crime to be gay.

In its heyday, the *movida* inspired magazines and art galleries, and the central figures of the movement occupied city bars until the wee hours. Madrid first got its reputation as an all-night party town during this era – a reputation still very much alive and well. Two popular bars are holdovers from that time – El Sol and La Vía Lactea.

Though the movement itself is over, many of the *movida* movers-and-shakers are still contributing to Spanish culture – actress Carmen Maura, singer Alaska, photographer Alberto García-Alix, and of course Almodóvar. However, where *la movida* most keenly endures is in its historical importance. As highly regarded as the 1960s counterculture movement in the U.S. or the punk emergence in the U.K., *la movida* hailed Spain's entrance into the modern world and promised unlimited social, sexual, and creative opportunities for the Spanish generations that followed.

PRIME LIVING LOCATIONS

impressive old barrio of Madrid. The name refers to the 16th and 17th centuries when the Hapsburg dynasty ruled Spain. At that time, the city didn't extend much beyond this barrio, and many of the nobles lived along these very streets. Plaza Mayor is a highlight of this area. Built in the 16th century,

© CANDY LEE LABALLE

A street in the working-class barrio of Lavapiés.

Madrid's grandest plaza has hosted bullfights, Inquisition trials (and executions), and coronations. Today the plaza continues to be a central meeting spot for tourists and locals alike and many dozens of apartments are located right in the square. La Latina is one of the most desirable addresses among the oversized Ray-Ban–wearing set and both rentals and home prices are quite high here.

Just a bit farther south, **Lavapiés** is considered the most multicultural neighborhood in the city, and one of the most historic. In the middle ages, its twisting, narrow lanes were home to Madrid's Jewish quarter. Though more than a little dilapidated these days, Lavapiés is rich with atmosphere and a heavy dose of funk. This is *the* barrio for both immigrants (Americans, French, Moroccan, African, Pakistani, Chinese), left-leaning Spaniards, and all kinds of artists. Expect Indian restaurants, art galleries, women-only sex shops, Arabic pastry shops, storefront theaters, and alternative bars side-by-side with the traditional Spanish restaurants, shops, and markets that have stood here for decades. It is high on the list of living locations for young, single expats—English teachers, freelancers—it helps that rental and home prices are lower than elsewhere in the city—though just slightly. Though beware, Lavapiés has earned a reputation as one of the roughest corners of town—its gritty charms are not for everyone.

North of Gran Vía is a maze of streets and plazas that make up two of

Madrid's liveliest barrios. To the west of Calle Fuencarral is the barrio of **Malasaña;** to the east lies **Chueca.** Traditionally, these two neighborhoods have a
lot in common—narrow streets lined with ancient shops, vegetable markets,
and neighbors of all ages going about their daily bustle. Throughout both
you'll find writers lingering at marble tables in belle epoque cafés, *señoras* in
housecoats mopping stoops, and blue-jumpered construction workers tucking
into fat slices of *tortilla* at corner bars. More recently, distinctive personalities
have emerged. Malasaña is a bit gruff, with a tough-kid attitude, albeit a kid
with a skateboard, an addiction to techno, and the money to spend on upscale street clothes. Chueca is not only the center of Madrid's gay and lesbian
life, it is also achingly hip, brimming with trendy shops, exclusive salons, and
daring restaurants. Malasaña still offers affordable housing, though it is rising
quickly, while Chueca has high prices to match its high style.

NORTH OF CENTER

The Paseo de la Castellana passes through some of Madrid's poshest neighborhoods as it rolls north through the city. Unlike the neighborhoods in the
buzzing center, these barrios attract more families and more corporate transfers. The streets of Salamanca and Recoletos radiate elegance and not only
because of the designer stores that line them—the Parque del Buen Retiro
with its 300-acres of manicured gardens borders this area, the 19th- and early
20th-century buildings are more like minipalaces with elaborate wrought iron
balconies, marbled stairways, and intricate stained glass windows, and the restaurants are among the most renowned in Spain. Yet, for all its magnetism,
these barrios are blissfully quiet at night. Living in these refined airs doesn't
come cheap, though if you look intently, bargains can be found.

Across La Castellana lies **Chamberí,** an ideal spot for those who don't want
to be in the middle of the city but also don't want to be far from it. It is a
charming, low-key barrio of tree-lined streets, sidewalk cafés, storefront boutiques, and corner markets. Housing prices are higher—firmly midrange to
high for Madrid.

Other popular residential barrios that are still in the city include **Chama-
rtín,** which sprawls around Madrid's train station of the same name. Its tidy
streets lined with modern apartment buildings, smart row houses, and cozy
private villas make it a very popular spot with families, both Spaniard and
expat. Quite similar, but a bit more upscale is **Arturo Soria,** a favorite barrio
for up-and-coming *empresarios* (business leaders), many of them expats, and
their young families—Bugaboo strollers vie for sidewalk space. Many of those

babies will grow up attending the International School of Madrid which is located here. The nearby barrio of **Parque Conde de Orgaz** also attracts many foreigners with apartment blocks, terraced houses, and a Montessori school. Property prices in these areas start midrange and go up from there.

SUBURBAN MADRID

As with most major cities, Madrid is surrounded by a network of small towns that offer the best is suburban living. The benefits are clear—proximity to all that Madrid has to offer, but in an environment that is decidedly family focused with more spacious properties, easy access to parks and nature, and a whole lot of tranquility. More than four million residents call Madrid's outer district home.

Very close to the northernmost point of Madrid city limits are **Alcobendas** and **San Sebastián de los Reyes,** both offering an upscale lifestyle to middle- and upper-income residents. Expect international and bilingual private schools, luxury malls (as well as the best outlet shopping in Madrid), quality sporting and recreation facilities, lush parks, and a variety of housing (attached houses, apartment complexes, villas) at prices from high to the sky. Alcobendas in particular attracts well-heeled residents to its **La Moraleja** area—one of the most exclusive addresses in Spain. It is home to Madrid's moneyed classes as well as quite a few celebrities, both Spanish and international; this is where superstar couple David and Victoria Beckham set up house when he played for Real Madrid. There are private golf courses, world-class spas, gourmet restaurants, and quite a few American expats. La Moraleja is one of the top relocation spots for American executives and diplomats, many with children enrolled at one of the several private schools located here—International College Spain, Runnymede College, or the regrettably named but quite prestigious, Colegio Brains. Housing options are mainly attached duplexes, chalets, and mansions and prices are as high as you'd expect.

A little farther north from the city center, **Santo Domingo, Ciudalcampo,** and **Fuente del Frenso** have detached houses for less than they cost in La Moraleja. But these homes have another price: the agonizing 30–50 minute drive to the city center. When you aren't coming or going behind the wheel of a car, this part of town is a pleasant place with decent shopping, a few local clubs with golf courses, tennis courts, and even horseback riding.

Pozuelo de Alarcón, Majadahonda and **Las Rozas** are three popular options located about 30 minutes northwest of the city. They each offer a comfortable middle- and upper-class environment of attached homes, upscale apartment

© CANDY LEE LABALLE

a gardened terrace in the old center of Madrid

complexes, communities of private villas and chalets, as well as very good private schools—Pozuelo de Alarcón is also home to the American School of Madrid. This trio of towns is particularly popular with white-collar types who need to be close to the city for work, but want the tranquility of village living for their families. Property prices tend to be on the high end for Madrid.

To the south are working-class, utilitarian towns dominated by massive block apartment buildings, ample parks, mom-and-pop shops, sprawling malls, a couple of good public universities, and of course, IKEA. **Leganés, Mostoles, Alcorcon,** and **Getafe** offer relatively low-cost living within half an hour of the city. And, you don't need a car to get to them—the southern suburbs are well connected to Madrid by both subway and commuter train. The drawback is very few private or bilingual schools.

Getting Around

It doesn't take long to get a feel for the city's layout—Madrid is compact and easily navigable. If you live in the old center, you can get pretty much anywhere by foot. If you need to go a bit farther, the city is covered by an extensive system of subways, buses, and commuter trains. Details of all three, including maps and suggestions on how to get from point A to point B can be found at Consorcio Transportes Madrid (www.ctm madrid.es).

One of the benefits of living in Madrid that Americans mention most is not

PRIME LIVING LOCATIONS

needing a car. Unless you live out in a distant suburb or have kids to haul out to private schools, you can get by very easily without using a car. If you want to make a road trip, there are several car rental agencies in Madrid, usually offering good prices for weekend rentals. If you do choose to have a car, be ready to deal with one major downer—traffic, particularly coming into and out of the city. The congestion is so excruciating that many who commute to work spend about two hours in their cars every day. And if you are renting for a weekend escape, know that the backups on Friday evenings out of town and Sunday evenings into town are legendary. Have lots of CDs and a good dose of patience to deal with it.

METRO

One of the fastest ways to travel throughout the city is via Madrid's very modern metro (subway system). The recipient of a major expansion in the past few years, the metro has 16 lines and hundreds of *paradas* (stops), covering the entire city as well as many of the bordering towns (aka suburbs). In fact, most people identify where they live, work, or are going by what station is closest to that location. So maybe you live by Bilbao, but work near Gregorio Marañón. The system runs 6:30 A.M.–1:30 A.M. 365 days a year and during peak hours, trains come every 3–4 minutes. And unlike the subway systems in London or New York, Madrid's system is blissfully simple. Each line has a single start and a single finish— no trying to figure out if you want this train or the next. The lines are identified by colors, numbers, and sometimes names. So line 3 is also known as the yellow line, line 2 is red, but line 12 is MetroSur. Get a free *plano de metro* (map) at any metro station and you'll essentially have the transport key to the city (alternatively visit www.metromadrid.es). One drawback, though the newer stations are equipped with elevators, most older and central

© CANDY LEE LABALLE

The Metro is a speedy way to get around town.

stations are not—making the metro a pain for people pushing baby strollers and a near impossibility for wheelchair users.

BUSES

Madrid's buses cover more ground than the metro but they are a bit more difficult to figure out—you have to know the city fairly well to know the location of any given bus stop. Buses are identified by number and points of origin and arrival, so Bus 25 is also known as Ópera-Casa de Campo. Hours of operation are 6 A.M.–11:30 P.M. daily and you'll rarely wait more than 10 minutes for one to come. If you need a bus after hours, there are several night buses known as *buhos* (owls); most originate in Plaza de Cibeles.

COMMUTER TRAINS

Madrid also has an extensive commuter train system, the Cercanías, which is a very fast way to whip through the city and often the only way to get out to the suburbs. There are stations throughout Madrid, but the main terminals are the city's two major train stations—Atocha in the south and Charmartín in the north.

COST OF PUBLIC TRANSPORT

Pricing for all three forms of public transportation is quite inexpensive compared to other European capitals. Prices are determined by the zone in which you are traveling. Everything within Madrid city limits is considered Zone A and many expats spend years only moving within this zone. Moving outward from the city, there are seven additional concentric zones and to travel into them via public transport requires additional costs. In Zone A, a metro, bus, or commuter train ticket costs just €1 for a *sencillo* (single) trip. Save money by purchasing a Metrobús ticket valid for 10 trips via subway or bus for just €7.40. (Note, these prices were valid in December of 2008, but they usually increase nominally each January).

If you will be a daily traveler on public transport, it is time to think about an *abono mensual* (monthly pass). A Zone A pass allows unlimited travel throughout the city of Madrid for the entire month and currently costs €46, with prices increasing for the other zones. People under 26 and senior citizens receive heavy discounts on their passes, and kids under four always ride for free. But be aware, you cannot buy your actual pass in any station—instead you will need to take proof of ID (your passport is fine) plus two passport-sized photos to any *estanco* (tobacco shop). For a little over €1, they will issue

Madrid street signs point the way.

your pass. With this, you can buy your monthly ticket, which you must keep with your pass, in most stations. But note, the passes are only good for the actual calendar month—not 30 days—and can only be bought within five days of the first of the month. If you haven't bought a pass by the 6th, then you will be back to using the 10-trip strip.

BARCELONA AND CATALUÑA

Cataluña (Catalunya) begins in the eastern part of the Pyrenees mountains—that imposing wall of natural beauty that kept Spain isolated for centuries. From there, the region tumbles towards the Mediterranean Sea, down along the dramatic Costa Brava, through Barcelona and the golden sands of the Costa Dorada, where it abuts the border of Valencia. This part of Spain became an artistic hothouse back when local boys Pablo Picasso, Joan Miró, and Salvador Dalí earned their reputations. Today, the region maintains its forward-thinking legacy and its international standing as an artistic hub (though the artistic daring has moved to the plate thanks to Ferran Adrià, the world's most famous chef).

But what inspired the surrealists, the cubists, and the culinary madmen alike is the same thing that draws expats and tourists by the plane load—breathtaking natural beauty. The idyllic beaches stretch for miles offering

© CANDY LEE LABALLE

glistening sand and golden sun nine months out of the year. And then there's Barcelona—the pride of Cataluña. Cosmopolitan and vibrant, fashion forward and sophisticated, edgy and affluent, Spain's second largest city is one of the most attractive in the world. In fact, it is so enticing that it has the highest number of resident foreigners in all of Spain and a good many of them are Americans.

But before considering a move here, you must know, Cataluña is more than a geographic destination. It is also a deeply rooted culture with its own traditions and language, both of which are fiercely protected and passionately promoted. The Catalan (Català) language is taught in schools, used in print and press, and serves as the official language of the local government. Catalans are known for hard work, shrewd negotiations, and frugal habits. A popular saying, *"El Català de les padres fa pa,"* means "A Catalan can make bread from stones" and is an accurate metaphor. No other region in Spain is wealthier or more industrious. However, Cataluña's nose-to-the-grindstone attitude is matched by its throw-your-hands-in-the-air frivolity. Catalan popular customs are full of charming, even quirky, traditions from human castle builders to fire-spewing dragons, solemn folk dances to barbecued onion festivals.

Barcelona

When speaking of world-class cities, Barcelona falls off the tongue as easily as Paris, London, and Rome. Sure, Madrid, with at least a million more inhabitants is Spain's capital city, but it is beautiful Barcelona that captures the imagination. With streets lined with Gaudí's curve-crazy structures, Roman ruins, and medieval plazas, Barcelona is a place that inspires and awes. Just ask Woody Allen—his 2008 film *Vicky Cristina Barcelona* is as much a love letter to Barcelona as his early films were to New York. As capital of the autonomous region of Cataluña, it is also the guardian of Catalan culture and tradition. Even as the city's trendiest denizens push the boundaries of cutting edge in food, fashion, and fun, Barcelonans still find time to head down to the plaza in front of the cathedral on Sundays and dance the ancient Catalan dance called *la sardana*.

But Barcelona is also business. One of the most affluent cities in Spain, it has thriving manufacturing and service sectors and a highly trafficked international port. Barcelona is a major destination for companies looking to expand into Spain and dozens of top multinationals have locations here. It is also a very important location for international fairs and conventions thanks

THE SPIRIT OF INDEPENDENCE

If Cataluña is your destination, there's one thing you need to know: This may be Spanish land now but it is not truly Spain...this is **Cataluña.** Cataluña is unique and its rich history attests to that point.

Around 15 B.C., the Romans built a military camp near Mont Taber, a hill that once stood in modern-day Barri Gòtic. Barcino was not much more than a walled encampment – nearby Tarragona was the real Roman powerhouse in the region. In the 5th century, the Visigoths sacked the city. Two centuries later, the Moors arrived. In 801, the Franks who ruled the areas of France and Germany captured Barcelona. The city and its surroundings served as a buffer zone between the Frankish empire in the North and the Moors in the South. Christened the Marca Hispania, the area corresponded with Cataluña's current boundaries and some historians attribute the origins of Catalan culture and language to this era.

With its enviable port, Barcelona grew in power and wealth over the next five centuries. As it did, it achieved greater independence from the Franks and by the 10th century it was its own nation-state, eventually adopting the Generalitat form of governmental self-rule. Operating out of the Drassanes naval yards, it became one of the mightiest seafaring powers in the Middle Ages with territories as far flung as Italy and Greece.

In 1479, Fernando, King of Aragón married Isabel, Queen of Castile, in a union that would change not only Spain, but the world. Barcelona was no exception. The royal pair limited Catalan power by authorizing only one port to deal with the New World, Sevilla, and Barcelona was prevented from doing the two things it did best: sailing and commerce. In 1561, when Madrid was named capital of Spain, Barcelona's fate as the second city of Spain was sealed. In 1714, Spanish rule took over completely; the Generalitat was abolished and Catalan language and culture were curtailed.

In the 1930s, after making a couple of pushes for nationhood, the powerful revolutionary spirit of Cataluña was redirected to the Spanish Civil War effort. Barcelona became the capital of Republican Spain (which favored regional independence), a move that brought bombing raids and fierce attacks upon the city from the Franco-led Nationalist forces. The Republicans eventually lost the war and when Franco took control of the country in 1939, he punished Cataluña vehemently. Thousands were shot in the war's aftermath, and the Catalan language was outlawed in public. Catalan town and street names were changed to Spanish, and all talk of independence was forcibly silenced.

Spain moved from a dictatorship to a parliamentary monarchy shortly after Franco died in 1975, and at that point the status of Generalitat was once again granted to the area. In 1980, Jordi Pujol, a conservative who had been imprisoned under Franco's rule, became the president of Cataluña. Streets and signs have returned to Catalan, and the language today has a strong place in classrooms, on television, on the radio, and in the streets. Although Cataluña remains under the Spanish flag, as recently as 2006, the Catalan government approved the Estatut d'autonomia de Catalunya (a statute of autonomy), greatly increasing their ability for self-rule. It still may be Spain, but there is no denying that Barcelona and Cataluña are Catalan, historically and culturally, heart and soul.

to its sprawling Fira Barcelona meeting hall. All this indicates that Barcelona is a good place to get a job, right? Well, that depends. The higher up you are on the executive food chain, the better chances you'll have of getting by with English only, Spanish at a minimum. Underlings and others will have to speak Spanish and at least some Catalan if they hope to get their *peu* in the door. However, the English-teaching and services market is a lively as it is in Madrid and if you work for yourself, you can choose your own language.

THE LAY OF THE LAND

Barcelona is located on the Pla de Barcelona (the Barcelona plain), about half-way between France and the region of Valencia. The city is snug between the Mediterranean Sea and the Serra de Collserola mountains (its highest peak, Tibidabo, provides the city's most popular scenic overlook). The always buzzing Plaça de Catalunya is a good way to orient yourself in the city. To the south of it lies Ciutat Vella, Barcelona's oldest area. It sprawls towards the Mediterranean Sea and is divided by Las Ramblas into the neighborhoods of El Raval to the west and Barri Gòtic and El Born to the east. Here you'll find a jungle of medieval lanes, gothic churches, trendy boutiques, and sidewalk cafés sitting beside Roman ruins. Along the seashore, Barceloneta offers neighborly tapas

© CANDY LEE LABALLE

one of Barcelona's outdoor markets

bars, excellent seafood, and a still seamy side despite the onslaught of gentrification. At the other end of the beach (some would say of the world), Vila Olímpica offers shiny (almost) new streets lined with luxury apartments and some of the city's more acclaimed restaurants. North of the plaza, L'Eixample unfolds in a precise grid of broad blocks lined by magnificent mansions including several designed by modernist madman Antoni Gaudí. Other areas include Montjuïc, a seaside mountain on the west of the city, Gràcia, a working class barrio and expat hive, and Zona Alta, a verdant residential area of stately homes and peaceful city living.

SANT JORDI: SPAIN'S VALENTINE

Forget Saint Valentine! If you want a holiday to celebrate love and romance in Cataluña, look no further than the region's patron saint, George – known by his Catalan moniker, Sant Jordi. When **Diada de Sant Jordi** (St. George's Day) rolls around every April 23, Catalan women celebrate by giving their fellas books, and in return the guys give roses to their sweeties. The event is no small thing – publishers specifically work their schedules in order to launch new titles on that day, and the entire city is transformed into a blanket of vendors hawking books and blooms. By all means, jump into the festivities by handing out love tokens, but before you do, there are a few more things to know about Saint George.

Rumor has it that the guy was a quite a dragon-slayer but in fact, the word "dragon" was possibly (some say probably) a misunderstanding of Roman emperor Diocletian's name. The despotic ruler was fiercely anti-Christian and Saint George was a pretty religious man as you might have already guessed. It's believed that Diocletian eventually had Saint George (a Roman soldier) beheaded for defending Christianity. Still, the story of Saint George versus the dragon is a romantic one and is a common motif in Cataluña. Gaudí even depicted it on the facade of his famous Casa Batlló in Barcelona's Eixample district.

As it turns out, Barcelona is not the only place that appreciates the saint. He's also the patron saint of Portugal, England, Germany, Lithuania, the Greek army, knights, archers, boy scouts, and sufferers of skin diseases. Despite all that devotion, on Valentine's Day, 1969, Pope Paul VI deemed the worship of George optional, but in 2000, Pope John Paul II plucked him from the sidelines and put him back on the Saints' calendar.

It's also worth noting that Shakespeare, Cervantes, Wordsworth, and Rupert Brooke all died on Saint George's day – April 23. Perhaps that's just a coincidence but it's an awfully convenient one. After all, you'll now have a few good wordsmiths to consider when shopping for books for your main squeeze.

Local Language

Catalan and Castilian Spanish are official co-languages here but the local government seems hell-bent on ensuring Catalan is just a little more official. Street signs, official documents, and several daily newspapers and television stations are in Catalan. Everything else is in Spanish, and everyone does speak it. However, speaking Catalan is essential if you want to be more than a *guiri* (slang for foreigner). One of the biggest complaints that expats have about living in Barcelona is that it is tough to make friends with the Catalans. At least part of that is language—you can easily live here speaking only English and/or Spanish, but speaking Catalan will open doors for you. Another part is that the sheer size of the expat community here makes it too easy to build a life in English—there are English bookstores, many bars and restaurants owned and staffed by English speakers, and several English magazines. While this is a great cushion against culture shock—and in fact, many expats never leave these circles—if you plan on living here for the long-term, make the effort to learn Catalan. And, if you have kids, be aware that public school subjects are taught in Catalan, not *castellano*. Of course, Barcelona also has several good private schools where English is the language of instruction. The bottom line is like this: For the short-term, you can survive on English, in the mid- to long-term, Spanish is sufficient, for permenant residency, Catalan is a good idea.

WHERE TO LIVE

When people daydream of living in Barcelona, they often imagine a high-ceilinged walk-up with wrought iron balconies hanging over a medieval alleyway lined with fresh fruit markets, cozy cafés, *cava* (Catalan sparkling wine) bars, and impossibly chic shops. Don't worry, there is plenty of that to go around and at prices from kind of cheap to way up high—all depends on the grunge to glam ratio you go for. But thanks to Barcelona's housing expansion in recent years, modern places are easy to come by, especially as you move away from the center. And of course, there are a few exclusive communities of spacious homes, walled gardens, and Mercedes-clogged driveways—priced as you would expect.

Living in one of the world's most storied cities is cheap compared to living in other storied cities like New York, London, or Paris. A rented room in a flat can be had for as low as €250 per month, though €400 is around average.

©CANDY LEE LABALLE

El Born is Barcelona's trendiest barrio.

PRIME LIVING LOCATIONS

To rent a place on your own, expect an average of €700 for a one-bedroom, €1,000 for two (of course, depending on location, amenities and luck, your price could be lower or much, much higher). Buying a house in Barcelona is going to start at the lowest around €180,000 for a one-bedroom *a reformar* (in need of renovation). Midrange is around €250,000, and everything else goes up from there. Upscale barrios and the better suburbs start around €300,000 and go up. Of course, keep in mind that this book was written as the housing market was crashing and Spain's economy with it. Prices as of publication were sliding (though Barcelona real estate has long been one of the best investments in Spain so I wouldn't expect too much of a slide). What follows is a brief overview of some of the more popular choices for expats—it is in no way a full presentation of the variety of Barcelona's barrios.

Old City Center

Barcelona's old city center, **Ciutat Vella** in Catalan, is about as old as Spain gets. It was founded in Roman times as Barcino and 2,000-year-old ruins are scattered throughout this area like crumpled napkins on the floor of a tapas bar. But don't be alarmed if you don't notice them at first, the Ciutat Vella is such a jam-packed jumble of "ooh" and "ahh" sights, that it is easy to overlook a Roman ruin or ten. Start with Las Ramblas. One of the most recognizable streets in the world, it is jammed with third-generation flower stalls, canary sellers, cubist tile work, human statues, belle epoque cafés, hawkers of fake Tous bags, hucksters, pickpockets, and people people people everywhere.

Step off the Ramblas in either direction and you'll find more of the same, plus moody medieval alleyways, artisan cheese shops, Catalan wine bars, artist-in-residence galleries, sidewalk cafés under gothic spires, museums. In short, this is the sort of place conjured up when Americans think of Old World Europe. Can't you just imagine yourself picking up the day's produce at the world-famous Mercat Boqueria then hustling down the narrow cobbled lane towards home? You aren't alone, the Ciutat Vella is probably the number-one destination for expats arriving in the city. But be aware, all the wonderful things that give this area such ambience do not entice expat residents alone. Expect tourists at your doorstep every day, and at their side, the thieves that rob them. Noise is incessant, the charmingly narrow lanes impossible for driving, and at night, the delightful medieval plazas fill up with drunken modern-day revelers. For long-term living, this barrio is a better bet for younger, single expats than those with children.

The Ciutat Vella is broken up into three distinct neighborhoods, Barri Gòtic, El Born, and El Raval. **Barri Gòtic** borders the eastern side of Las Ramblas

© CANDY LEE LABALLE

lamposts designed by Gaudí

and is the city's political center—Plaça Sant Jaume is home to both the Palau de la Generalitat (the seat of the regional government) and city hall. It houses the Museu d'Història de la Ciutat which takes visitors deep underground to the Roman foundations of the city. Full of stone lanes barely an arms-length wide, this thriving medieval maze is one of the most romantic in Spain.

Crossing Vía Laietana brings you into **El Born** (also known as La Ribera, Sant Pere, and Santa Caterina). While still maintaining the same medieval air as its gothic neighbor, this barrio bristles as the city's new-found haven of hip. It is loaded with the kind of boutiques, jewelry shops, and art galleries that require serious credit limits. In between are trendy eateries, classy cocktail bars, laid-back sidewalk cafés, and the world's most expansive collection of Picassos. The barrio, anchored by the imposing 14th-century Santa Maria del Mar cathedral, was once little more than a marketplace full of wholesale shops and creaky-tabled cafés. If you squint behind your black-framed glasses, you'll still find a bit of that old-time Born in traditional cafés and shops.

On the western side of Las Ramblas lies **El Raval,** once the city's seediest district. French literary bad boy Jean Genet once described it as a bohemian, cutthroat, poverty-stricken slum. The southernmost parts of the barrio, especially around the plaza named for the author, still fit that description. However, in the northern end, artists, hippies, and expats have taken over. Bohemian cafés and trendy restaurants ring the Rambla del Raval, a long, wide plaza lined with palm trees, benches, and one very fat black cat. The Museu d'Art Contemporani de Barcelona, a massive modern art complex, has enlivened the surrounding blocks with galleries and art festivals. Meanwhile, the barrio still serves as the number one destination for the city's immigrant population, particularly Pakistani, North African, and Filipino.

Rental prices are wildly skewed in the Ciutat Vella. There are tons of dumps on the market where for little more than the price of a Custo Barcelona sweater,

lank one-bedroom facing some centuries-old water pipes (door
ed by hall-dwelling junkies included). On the other hand, luxe
digs are wildly available, especially in El Born and in the newer properties in
El Raval. Purchasing prices throughout Ciutat Vella are firmly in the mid to
high range for Barcelona.

On the Seafront
Bordering the old center, **Barceloneta** is a triangular wedge of tidy, tightly
knit streets teeming with colorful apartment blocks, seafood restaurants, dive
bars, and lots of lively street life. Built in the mid-1800s as an attempt at urban
planning, the barrio quickly became the residence of choice for the city's seafaring residents. Despite encroaching gentrification, Barceloneta still manages
to hang on to its authenticity—see the local celebration which has revelers
burying sardines in the sand. It is a popular choice with young Barcelonans
and expats alike, however due to its spitting distance to the Mediterranean
and the beach, housing prices have been skyrocketing in recent years. Great
deals are still possible (more for renters than buyers), but in general expect
prices on the higher end of midrange.

A little more than 15 years ago, **Vila Olímpica** was an ignored, industrial stretch of land. Thanks to the 1992 Summer Olympics which turned
this area into an Olympic village, it's now a vibrant neighborhood wrapped
around an upscale port. Some 2,000 apartments built to house athletes have
been converted into upscale properties with shared gardens, parks, and pools.
Port Olímpic, which hosted Olympic sailing events, is now a luxury marina
peppered with popular bars (some are too popular as hosts of anything-goes
bachelor and bachelorette parties) and several of the city's most acclaimed restaurants. Property here is newer and more spacious than that in older parts
of Barcelona and is very popular with middle-class Spanish families. Expect
both rental and purchase prices on the higher end for Barcelona.

North of Center
By the late 19th century, Barcelona was growing too big for its Gothic britch-
es. It needed an expansion, a word which translates as *ensanche* in Spanish,
eixample in Catalan. A then-novel grid of orderly blocks, their corners cut off
to let in the sun (and give room to turning horse-drawn carriages) was laid
out in large swath of land north of Plaça de Catalunya. Almost immediately,
rich locals snapped up lots in L'Eixample and spared no expense in building
their elaborate mansions. Luckily for architectural history, this coincided with
the beginning of the Catalan *modernisme* movement began. The result is a

wealth of whimsical structures—La Pedrera, La Sagrada Família, La Manzana de Discordia—that make this neighborhood one of the most visited sites in Spain. Despite this, the bulk of **L'Eixample** (eye-SHAM-plah) is residential. Expect old Barcelona families as well as up-and-coming new ones. Unlike the old center and seaport, these streets are also quite quiet at night making it a good choice for early-rising professionals and anyone with kids. The one exceptions is "Gayxample," a multiblock area on the left side of the barrio that is home to a thriving gay and lesbian community and some of the liveliest late-night bars and clubs in the city. (Note, locals think of L'Eixample in terms of right (Eixample Dreta) and left (Eixample Esquerra). Rental prices vary based on amenities (a terrace with a view over La Sagrada Família can double the rent) but expect the mid to high range. Purchase prices also vary but tend to be on the high side.

Until the 20th century, the working class barrio of **Gràcia,** just north of L'Eixample, was its own working-class village. Home to factory workers and the poorly paid, it was a hotbed of Catalan nationalism. Today, many of the factory workers have been replaced by Converse-wearing hipsters and the fervent nationalist attitude by a pervasive bohemian air. Gràcia is extremely popular with expats—Americans, Brits, Africans, Middle Easterners—who have carved out their own niches in Gràcia. The result is a roiling cultural pot of Lebanese restaurants, English-language cinemas, artist workshops, alternative bars, hip couples pushing expensive strollers, and lifelong residents soaking up the sun on benches. However, before moving in, be aware that many

a pastry shop in the working-class barrio of Gràcia

© CANDY LEE LABALLE

PRIME LIVING LOCATIONS

of Gràcia's sun-dappled plazas give way to booze-soaked parties at night. Visit your potential home at night before plunking down your euros. Despite its popularity, bargains can be found for both rentals and purchases, however in general expect midrange prices.

On the northern reaches of Gràcia is **Parc Güell,** one of the most delightful spots in Barcelona. Designed by Gaudí, it features undulating benches, multicolored mosaics, and one oversized, very photogenic salamander. The area around the park is hilly and many of the apartments offer spectacular views. As a result, prices here are higher than in other areas of Gràcia.

Moving north, Zona Alta translates into "upper zone" and that doesn't just refer to the hilly terrain. The neighborhoods that make up this zone— **Gervasi, Sarrià, Pedralbes,** and **Tres Torres**—are among Barcelona's most privileged addresses. Think sprawling single-family homes, luxury apartment villas, and enough mansions to meet the needs of Barcelona's moneyed set. As you can guess, it is a very popular spot for expat families from diplomatic and executive circles.

There are numerous benefits to living here, especially for families—consider parks, community pools, and the best international schools in the city including the Benjamin Franklin International School. Zona Alta is just a 10-minute drive to the center of the city but is easily accessible by buses and trains (convenient for the many housekeepers and nannies that head out here daily to work). Yet for all those residential boons, Zona Alta still has an urban edge complete with gourmet restaurants, upscale shops, cultural venues, and a smattering of Gaudí works. About the only drawback to Zona Alta is that it attracts many foreign families who are based in Barcelona temporarily—making it a bit too transient to develop a neighborly vibe. Prices, as you can guess, run from the high-end of high to through the terra-cotta–tiled roof.

Suburbs

Sant Just and **Esplugues de Llobregat**—two adjacent neighborhoods—are so close to Barcelona that they could be considered part of the city. Located on a hilltop, they offer breathtaking vistas of the city. Rent and housing prices are high, but the good news is that you do get what you pay for. Most homes are detached or semidetached and many are downright luxurious. The American School of Barcelona is located here, making it particularly popular for American families.

Castelldefels, located on the coast just 11 miles south of Barcelona, is a big hit with expatriates. Even though it pulls in hordes of tourists in warmer months, rental and home prices have remained relatively stable which is good news for those who choose to live here. The excellent train service is another bonus—it takes about 20 minutes to reach the city center. Unfortunately, travel by car is less convenient and rush-hour traffic can keep commuters on the road for as long as one hour in each direction. Foreign families put up with that headache in order to enjoy the town's attractions as well as the opportunity to enroll their children at the British School of Barcelona which is located here.

Romans lived in **Sant Cugat del Vallès** and in the 8th century the town housed a Visigothic monastery. But much of the evidence of that assorted history was razed when the Moors invaded the area. There are still hints of the early past in Sant Cugat—including a medieval monastery—but more than anything, the town is a comfortable (if slightly pricey) suburb that caters to year-round residents and is particularly popular with families both Spanish and increasingly international. Both apartments and houses are available, and the prime access to public transportation is one of the greatest benefits to living in the area—commuter trains depart for the 30-minute trip to the city every five minutes or so. Driving, the commute is slowed by traffic but it usually takes just a little more than half an hour to reach Barcelona by car. Property for rent or purchase will cost you on the high-side for Barcelona, but the payback is space for your money and easy access to some of the loveliest natural scenery in the forests of the Collserola mountains.

GETTING AROUND

With an extensive network of subways, trams, commuter trains, and buses, Barcelona shuttles its residents to just about any point in the city and beyond easily, quickly, and cheaply. The Barcelona transport site (www.tmb.es) offers all the details you could want but search for "Get On the Move" unless you want to get lost in the site. Even the suburbs are well-connected by public transport, however most suburban Barcelona dwellers prefer the convenience of a car for quick jags into the city and for hauling around kids. Of course, as in every other major city in Spain, traffic is a major *problema* which impacts the benefits of driving.

In addition to the metro, bus, and commuter train system detailed below, Barcelona has a couple of short tram lines and funiculars leading up to the hilltops of Montjuïc and Tibidabo. The city is also a major stop on the national and international rail lines and Barcelona–Sants is the main hub. In addition, inner-city commuters can use Bicing (www.bicing.com), a subscription bike-rental service with hundreds of bikes available for daily use at points throughout the city.

Metro

Barcelona's efficient metro (subway) has six lines, each identified by number and color (Line 1 is red, Line 2 is purple, etc.) as well as by its endpoints. So, line 2 is also called Paral.lel-Pep Ventura. Most businesses include the closest metro stop in their addresses and you'll soon discover that the metro system is a great way to orient yourself in the city. The metro operates 5 A.M.–midnight Monday–Thursday and Sunday, 5 A.M.–2 A.M. Friday, and 24 hours on Saturdays and the weeknight before public holidays. Ticket machines are located in the *boca* (mouth) of the metro stations and are easy to use, especially when you select the "English" function. Some stations also have a staffed counter, but don't expect the attendant to speak English.

A word of caution. The metro stations—especially busy ones like Catalunya and Passeig de Gràcia—are feeding grounds for pickpockets. Be sure and practice common sense on the metro, meaning hands on your purses, wallets in front pockets, and backpacks turned around to the front. Even expats who've lived years in Barcelona occasionally fall victim to a metro pickpocket.

Buses

Barcelona's city buses are efficient and inexpensive and cover much more ground than the metro does. However, they are more complicated to figure out. You have to know the city fairly well to find your line or your stop. The Barcelona transport site (www.tmb.es) can help, but your best bet is to ask your new neighbors for help. Timetables vary, but buses generally run 6 A.M.–11:30 P.M. After hours, 17 Nit Bus lines provide service 10:30 P.M.–5 A.M.; most pass through Plaça de Catalunya.

Commuter Train

Barcelona has a far-reaching network of commuter trains called Ferrocarrils de la Generalitat or FCG (www.fgc.cat). The main stations are in Plaça de Espanya and Plaça de Catalunya and from these points you can move throughout Barcelona and beyond to the suburbs. As with the buses, it is a bit confusing to figure out at first. Get a map and study it, then ask a neighbor for help.

Cost of Public Transport

The cost of public transportation in Barcelona is inexpensive compared to other European capitals. Prices are determined by the zone in which you are traveling and everything within city limits is considered Zone 1. Moving outward from the center there are five more zones, each with increasing prices.

A single ride on the metro, bus, or train costs €1.35. A T-10 ticket gives you

10 journeys (metro, bus, or commuter train) for €7.70 in Zone 1. However, if you will be a regular user of public transport, there are several options to save money. The T-Month is valid for unlimited travel on public transport for 30 days from date of purchase (€47.90 for Zone 1). A T-50/30 allows 50 journeys in a 30-day period (€31.50 for Zone 1). Families can travel together with the T-Familiar, which offers 70 trips within 30 days (€45.40 for Zone 1). T-Trimestre allows unlimited trips for 90 days from the date of purchase (€131.50 for Zone 1). There are discounted tickets for those under 21 and kids under four ride for free. If you get caught without a ticket, the minimum fine is €40. You can buy tickets in the station, but they're also sold at newsstands, tobacco shops, and some ATMs.

Costa Brava

Snaking along the Catalan coast towards France, the Costa Brava offers some 150 miles of Mediterranean-lapped beaches and cliff-backed inlets. The name Costa Brava means "wild coast" and most of it is just that—rocky and tumultuous. After all, this is where the majestic Pyrenees Mountains tumble into the sea. The result is deeply green cliffs soaring high above craggy shores pocked with coves, inlets, whitewashed fishing villages, Romanesque churches, and a few spectacular Greek ruins. It is a haunting, seductive combination that inspired artists including Dalí, Picasso, and Chagall. It has also proved attractive

The Costa Brava is riddled with pint-sized beaches tucked into dramatic coves.

to those more interested in indulgence than inspiration. Mass tourism arrived here in the 1950s and since then many seaside villages were swallowed up by concrete high-rises, all-inclusive megahotels, and boardwalks lined with neon-lit disco-pubs. A sad case in point is the once-sleepy Lloret de Mar which today draws hundreds of thousands of tourists in search of sun, sand, and all-you-can-drink sangria. However, you can still find some spots relatively free from the ravaging effects of mass development.

The Costa Brava attracts a large retiree community from the UK and northern Europe but younger expats are drawn here too, probably because it's ideal for outdoor enthusiasts. Winter ski resorts are tucked into the nearby mountains, hiking trails wind through the area, and some of the world's top bicyclists train here. Of course, the sea also offers its pleasures from sailing and sunning to some of the best scuba diving in Spain.

THE LAY OF THE LAND

The Costa Brava runs the length of Girona, one of four provinces that make up Cataluña (the other three are Barcelona, Lleida, and Tarragona). It is snug between the Pyrenees mountains and the Mediterranean Sea and stretches from the French border almost to Barcelona. The mild Mediterranean climate promises sunny summers and cool, wet winters. The average temperature is around 60°F but July and August can get broiling. In winter, it is too cold to swim, but still nice enough for walks on the beach. Winter also brings with it the Tramontana, a wild wind that has over millennia carved much of the wild landscape of the seaside cliffs.

Local Language

While Catalan is even more broadly spoken in the small towns of Cataluña than in Barcelona, much of the Costa Brava is dependent on tourism and expat populations. That means, English is quite common and you can easily get by with that alone. Of course, to make living easier—dealing with doctors, plumbers, grocery clerks—Spanish is essential. Learning some Catalan is a good idea if you want to mingle with the locals—and a real plus if you plan to live here for the long-term, but it's not an absolute necessity.

WHERE TO LIVE

The variety of living options on the Costa Brava is diverse. Want a built-in pool and gourmet restaurants? You got it. A sleepy fishing village? Check. An off-the-path hideaway above the sea? That too. Your best bet before moving here is to do your research and that should include a trip or two up and down the coast by car. To find a deal on a house, look at property away from the water—prices drop considerably as you move inland. However, access to water is one of the most sought-after features of a home along the Costa Brava and the prices below are for such properties. If renting, know that prices can be quite reasonable 10 months of the year but many landlords prefer to reserve the right to rent for much higher prices in July and August. Clarify this before signing a contract.

Tossa de Mar

Painter Marc Chagall fell in love with Tossa de Mar when he visited in the 1930s. He christened it Blue Paradise and if you squint past the buzzing holiday resorts, you can see what he meant. Shimmering in the sun high above the town are the 12th-century walls and turrets that make Tossa one of Cataluña's best preserved medieval cities. The area tucked into the arc made by the walls is the Vila Vella (old town), a moody labyrinth of tiny cobbled streets. However, like nearby Lloret, Tossa couldn't resist the lure of tourist dollars and the village boasts a newer section that caters to the drink-till-you-drop holiday set. Some say the expansion is a blessing, others claim it's a curse, but the good news is that while old and new Tossa are adjacent, they're still separate. A seaside two-bedroom apartment costs €200,000–400,000. A multiroomed villa with built-in pool and views to the sea starts around €500,000 and goes up from there. Two-bedroom rentals start as low as €700.

Palamós and Sant Antoni

Sitting on the edge of a wide turquoise bay of the same name, the small town of Palamós offers the best of the Costa Brava; the medieval fishing village is near the mountains and thanks to protected areas that restrict development, the area has been preserved from tourism's more ravaging effects. While it does attract plenty of tourists, it mainly caters to year-round residents. Palamós also nourishes a hearty local economy thanks to its fishing port, the busiest on the Costa Brava—the locally caught *gambas* (shrimp) are coveted throughout Spain. At night, the restaurants and bars surrounding the port are the place to be! While housing can be found in the old medieval center of town, many families, expats and locals alike, opt to live in the bordering town of Sant Antoni de Calonge which offers modern developments including upscale apartments and villas. A two-bedroom apartment near the beach sells for around €250,000–450,000 while a lovely gardened villa can exceed €1 million. A month's rent on a two-bedroom place starts at a reasonable €600.

L'Estartit

Like so many towns on the Costa Brava, L'Estartit offers an impossibly wide stretch of golden sand running along the sapphire sea, dusky grey and green hills rising up just a few miles inland, and smack in between, row after uninspiring row of blocky all-inclusive holiday resorts, English pubs, and Chinese buffets. However, L'Estartit compensates for all that with a wealth of surrounding natural beauty. The coast in this area is called Montgri after the mountains that take root here. It is rugged and wild and dotted with dozens of beaches, coves, and the Baix Empordà Wetlands, a protected natural reserve. However, the most spectacular natural feature in L'Estartit are the Illes Medes, a tiny archipelago of islands just off the coast. This protected collection of rocky islands is home to some 1,000 species of marine life and a glorious kaleidoscope of sea flora. Millennia of turbulent sea crashing against the soft limestone of the islands has also resulted in a cathedral of underwater caves. Naturally, they draw divers from all over the world and many expats have set up diving businesses here.

Just inland lies **Torroella de Montgri,** L'Estartit's sleepy sister. Though the two towns are governed as one, Torroella has more in common with a traditional Catalan town than a Costa resort. It boasts a 14th-century Gothic church, a Renaissance monastery with a Tuscan-style cloister, and above the town, nestled in the foothills of the Montgri massif, the Castell Montgri, a Romanesque-Gothic castle dating to the 13th century. The nearby foothills are riddled with excellent biking and hiking trails.

A two-bedroom near the beach starts as low as €190,000. Prices are about the same in Torroella but you have more options for a finding a detached house inland. Two-bedroom rentals in both places run between €400 and €700.

Roses

Sitting at the northern tip of the impossibly blue Gulf of Roses, the resort town of Roses offers breathtaking views of what can really be described as a *costa brava* (wild coast)—deeply green with wild tufts of rock rising from the sandy coves far below. Flowing into the bay beneath the town is a turquoise swath of clear, calm water dotted most days with fishing and pleasure boats. This perch was sought after as far back as 776 B.C. when the Greeks set up the town of Rhode here. Nearly eight centuries later, the Romans moved in and still later, the Christians. The remains of their 11th-century Romanesque fortress still loom over the town. Down below, some 2.5 miles of fine, sandy beach and dozens of crystal clear coves has led to the development of a buzzing little resort. Of course, if you are even slightly interested in food, you know that Roses is also the home of the world's most famous restaurant, El Bulli, run by the world's most visionary chef, Ferran Adrià. It is also home to a very buzzing expat community and you can join them for around €500 per month to rent a two-bedroom or €180,000–300,000 to buy. A villa with a view can start at well over €1 million.

Cadaqués

Many swear that the loveliest village on the Costa Brava is Cadaqués—a cluster of brilliant white buildings surrounded by olive groves and hugging a turquoise bay dotted with colorful fishing boats. The town is a tangle of narrow alleyways lined with wrought-iron window grilles draped in colorful flowers. In warmer months, these tiny streets buzz with art galleries, artists workshops, boutiques, and bars that manage to be both rustic and arty. The stretch of coast from Roses to Cadaqués is one of the most rugged on the Costa Brava and the turbulent landscape has prevented the type of resort development seen farther south which suits the town's 2,700 full-time residents just fine. Yet, tourists do triple the population in July and August, drawn to the picturesque beauty of the village as well as its artistic legacy—Salvador Dalí lived and worked here and the fantastical home he built has put the village on the tourist map. You can get your own two-bedroom spot on Cadaqués' map for €175,000–400,000. Rentals start as low as €600.

Cadaqués is one of the prettiest villages on the Costa Brava.

Girona

Okay, it is not technically on the Costa Brava, but Girona (Gerona in Spanish) is a short drive inland and one of the loveliest cities in Spain. Spread over a clutch of hills at the confluence of the rivers Onyar and Ter, the city has 2,000 years of history including artifacts from Romans, Jews, Moors, and even Charlemagne's army which once beset the city. The Jewish quarter dates back to the 9th century and is one of the most atmospheric in all of Spain.

Founded by the Romans as Gerunda, it was a fortress point on the Vía Augusta, the ancient road from Rome to Cadiz. Visigoths later ruled it, then the Moors in quick succession. Charlemagne's Frankish troops captured the town in 785 and made it one of the courts of Cataluña. Despite another brief occupation by the Moors, Girona remained firmly under Christian control. In the 11th century, it was declared a city under the Crown of Aragón. From the 9th century onwards. From the nineteenth century onwards, Girona's Jewish populations flourished, economically, socially, and intellectually. Many scholars believe that it was in Girona that the mystical branch of Judaism called Kaballah was born. By the 14th century, widespread anti-Semitism had spread across Spain. In 1492, the Jews were forced to either convert or leave the country. Girona's Jewish quarter, the Call, was built over and lost for six centuries. Historians, with the help of the Catalan, local, and Israeli governments have located and recovered much of it and today the Call is one of Girona's top attractions, as well as the center of much research into Cantaluña's and Spain's medieval Jewish populations. Today, the city also serves as a training base for the world's best cyclists—Lance Armstrong owns a home here. They are attracted to the area's rolling hills and temperate climate which is perfect for training. Just a few minutes from the city center, tranquil roads lead up into the foothills of the Pyrenees or ramble down toward the coast.

One of the biggest pluses for expats is that Girona is big enough to offer culture, cuisine (a couple of Michelin-starred restaurants are here), and easy connection to the rest of the country (there's an airport and major train hub) but small enough to feel neighborly with just over 86,000 residents. If you want to join them, two-bedroom apartments start as low as €150,000 and go up to over €400,000—amenities, views, and neighborhood location are the fluctuating factors. A two-bedroom rental runs €500–700.

GETTING AROUND

It is possible to live in the Costa Brava without a car. The villages mentioned above are all connected to Barcelona and Girona via a system of buses mainly run by the bus companies Sagales (www.sagales.com) and Sarfa (www.sarfa.com). And the city of Girona is well connected to the rest of Spain via an international *aeroport* (www.aena.es) and a major train station (www.renfe.com). However, if you want the freedom to move about, lug the kids to school in Barcelona, or make your evening reservations at El Bulli, you'll need a car. The AP-7/E-15, also known as the *Autopista del Mediterráneo,* connects Barcelona and Girona and continues on into France. The C-31 winds along the Costa Brava and offers some truly spectacular (and often knuckle-whitening) views.

Sitges

South of Barcelona runs the Costa Dorada (Golden Coast) and its star resort town is Sitges. Just 22 miles from Barcelona, this seaside jewel offers miles of

excellent beaches, a picturesque medieval quarter, and a sprinkling of Modernist buildings. Once a sleepy fishing village, it stepped into the limelight as the resort of choice for wealthy Barcelonans in the early 20th century. Many of the current residents still commute to work in the city. The town has also gained fame as one of Europe's premier gay and lesbian resorts and it is *the* summer Spanish resort of choice for the young, gay, and beautiful. Ditto during the town's annual Carnival celebration. Called Carnestoltes in Catalan, this event, like all carnivals round the world, has its roots in Catholicism. However, here those roots have been bleached

Human towers called *castellers* are a festival tradition in Cataluña.

blonde and dressed in a gold lamé thong. The rest of the year, Sitges is almost sleepy and its 26,000 year-round residents are just fine with that.

THE LAY OF THE LAND

Although the landscape of Costa Dorada is not considered Spain's finest—the scenery is flatter and less varied than it is in other areas—the beaches are some of the best in Spain. They extend for miles and the sand is fine and golden (hence the area's name, the Golden Coast). The Ebro River delta lies at the southern end of the coast, and the protected area attracts hundreds of birds. To the north, the Garraf National Park offers both hiking and mountain biking.

Local Language

You are still in Cataluña despite the English-speaking drag queens! If you want to live here full time, Spanish at a minimum will make that living a whole lot easier. If you really want to ingratiate yourself to your neighbors, learning Catalan is a good start. That said, if you are here for the short-term, the international flavor of this town makes surviving on English alone a possibility.

WHERE TO LIVE

The buzzing center of town attracts a mix of people from young singles to retirees—it's conveniently located to stores, schools, coffee shops, and the beach. An apartment in the center of Sitges costs about the same as in Barcelona: around €600 for a low- to midrange two-bedroom apartment and €1,400 for the high end (with great variance depending on amenities and proximity to the beach). To buy a two-bedroom place, expect to shell out €300,000 or more.

If you're more interested in a single-family house, Zona Vinyet and Leventina are popular spots. The first area lies south of the church and the latter is to the church's north but both are scenic, good for families, and priced similarly. Rent on a two-bedroom starts around €1,200 and shoots up from there. About the lowest you'll find to buy will be €600,000 and most properties top the €1 million mark.

GETTING AROUND

You don't absolutely need a car in Sitges—the city is compact and easy to navigate on foot (or by bus if you live on the edge of town), but of course, you'll have more freedom to explore the area if you do have your own transportation. If you work in Barcelona (or just need the occasional cultural infusion of the big city), you can get there easily and cheaply via RENFE (www.renfe .es/cercanias/Barcelona). There are dozens of trains every day between 6 AM and midnight and the ride takes approximately 40 minutes.

VALENCIA, MURCIA, AND LAS ISLAS BALEARES

Inset map (top left)

Mediterranean Sea

Mallorca

Menorca

Ibiza

Baleares Islands

Fornells
Ciutadella de Menorca
Mahón
Pollença
Calvià
Capdepera
Peguera
Bay of Palma
Santanyí
Palma de Mallorca

San Antonio
Santa Eulària des Ríu
Ibiza
Formentera

Main map

Amposta
AP7
Morella
N232
Vinarò
Benicarló
N340
Peñíscola
E15
Costa Dorada

Cuenca
N420
Ademuz
Mora de Rubielos
Castellón de la Plana
Villarreal
Burriana
Costa del Azahar
AP7

N330
Sierra de los Bosques
Segorbe
Sagunto
Gulf of
Puçol
MONASTERIO DEL PUIG
Valencia

Embalse de Contreras
Utiel
Liria
Moncada
C234
Rocafort
Cheste
Chiva
A3
VALENCIA
Catarroja
La Albufera
Silla
E901
A3
Requena
Buñol
Picassent
Benifaió
N332
Sueca
Algemesí
Cullera
Sierra de Martes
Alzira

La Roda
Casas-Ibáñez
River Júcar
N330
Tabernes de Valldigna
Gandía
Ayora
Játiva
Canals
To Las Islas Baleares
Denia
Albacete
N332
A31
Almansa
N430
Oteniente
N340
River Serpis
E15
Jávea
AP7
Benitachell
Moraira
Ayna
A30
Yecla
Villena
Alcoy
Sierra de Aitana
Altea
Hellín
N344
River Vinalopó
Jijona
Benidorm
Sierra de Salinas
Elda
Costa Blanca
Aspe
Novelda
Cieza
Alicante
Caravaca de la Cruz
River Segura
A30
Elche
N332
Laguna de Hondo
Mula
Orihuela
Guardamar del Segura
Mediterranean Sea
A7
Salinas de Torrevieja
Torrevieja
Murcia
E15
El Pilar de la Horadada
Alhama de Murcia
Parque Regional de Carrasco y El Valle
San Javier
A30
Vélez-Rubio
A91
Lorca
Mazarrón
Cartagena
AP7
Costa Cálida

0   20 mi
0   20 km

© AVALON TRAVEL

VALENCIA, MURCIA, AND LAS ISLAS BALEARES

Hugging the Mediterranean coast south of Cataluña, the regions of Valencia and Murcia are known jointly as Levante, meaning "from the East." Inland, the landscape is dominated by mountains and fertile *huertas* (farmland) including vast groves of the world-famous Valencian oranges. Moving towards the coast, the land is riddled with wetlands such as Albufera, a bioreserve which also happens to be the best place in the region for paella. The coasts—particularly the shimmering Costa Blanca—are blessed with some of the longest, finest, whitest beaches in all of the Mediterranean. Though several areas been "resorted" to death, other places like Altea and Jávea are dreamy little Mediterranean towns, drawing healthy expat communities.

The biggest city in the region, Valencia is both medieval and modern, and, during the festival of Las Fallas, absolutely wild. Down the coast, the seaside city of Alicante is just as sizzling, but on a much smaller scale. Keep

curling south along the sea and you come to the province of Murcia, a hilly, fertile stretch of land which has recently emerged as a hot spot for relocating expats. They are drawn to its Baroque jewel of a capital, Murcia City, its ancient seafaring town Cartagena, and one of the more unique features on the Mediterranean, Mar Menor, a vast saltwater lagoon separated from the sea by a long, thin slip of sand.

Just off the Levante coast, the Islas Baleares glimmer in the Mediterranean Sea, enticing tourists and foreign residents by the shipload. They offer endless beaches of powder-fine sand, irresistible bays of clear, turquoise waters, coasts pockmarked with cozy coves, and spectacular caverns carved by millennia of wind and water. All that nature is balanced by a healthy dose of urbanity from the big city of Palma de Mallorca to the upscale resorts located throughout the islands.

Valencia

If you mention the name Valencia to a Spaniard, you might be asked to specify which Valencia you mean. Perhaps you're talking about the city itself, but you might also be referring to the province or even the region. There's no need to scratch you're head over that—it can easily be explained. The region of Valencia (officially called Comunitat Valencia) is one of Spain's 17 autonomous regions. It is further divided into three provinces, Castellón, Valencia, and Alicante. The city of Valencia is the capital of the both the province of Valencia and the region of Valencia. It is also Spain's third largest city. Castellón and Alicante also have their own provincial capitals which—you guessed it—share the same name as their regions. But no matter how you slice it up geographically, this is an enticing area. Expect whitewashed villages glistening in the Mediterranean sun and sprawling expat communities, fragrant pans of paella simmering on sidewalks and a local addiction to a milky drink called *horchata,* miles of bucolic orange groves, and the noisiest festivals in all of Spain.

THE LAY OF THE LAND

Valencia's coasts have been the area's biggest draw since back when the Romans first founded Valentia (the modern-day city of Valencia). Running along the province of Castellón, the coast is called Costa del Azahar (the Orange Blossom Coast), along Valencia it is simply Costa de Valencia, and along Alicante it is the famed Costa Blanca (White Coast). The name draws as much from the sugar-white beaches as it does from the many whitewashed villages overlooking the sea. Although the coast is known for broad stretches of beach, don't assume that if you buy a house on these waters you'll find powdery sands outside your front door. In some places, the surf crashes onto rocks. Inland from the coast lies a large plain that yields an abundance of oranges and slowly rises into pine-covered hills where almonds grow.

Local Language

Valencia is officially bilingual and people speak both Spanish and Valenciano (nearly identical to Catalan). Valencia's brand of regionalism isn't as political as what you'll find in Cataluña but you can expect to see street signs, public transport information, and official documents in Valenciano. Nonetheless, Spanish is still the dominant language here and if you make this your home, you can get by with that. If you put down roots in a very large expat community, you may be able to survive for years on only English. However, as always, if you want to get to know your new neighbors beyond a mumbled *"hola"* in the hallway, Spanish is essential and a bit of Valenciano quite beneficial.

VALENCIA CITY

Bustling Valencia is often overlooked when dreams of living in Spain are conjured up. Third in size behind Madrid and Barcelona, more reserved than sloe-eyed Andalucía, and more urban than the nearby coastal towns, Valencia just doesn't stir the imagination. It should. Along with all of the amenities of big-city life—a healthy economy, museums, cutting-edge cuisine, rollicking nightlife—Valencia offers an evocative gothic quarter, miles of sandy beaches, and arguably the most spectacular aquarium and science center in the world, La Ciutat. Throw in beautiful parks, architecture from medieval to ultramodern, and a mild climate year-round and you have a nearly perfect hometown. The city's profile was ratcheted up a few notches by the 2008 America's Cup which brought big-time expansion to the city's beachfront as well as millions of euros to the city's coffers.

Where to Live

The heart of Valencia is a circle of medieval streets called **Ciutat Vella** (Old City). It can be roughly divided into four zones. **Ayuntamiento** is a bustling mix of commerce and residential living. It is home to city hall, the bullring, the train station, and some spectacular baroque architecture. **El Mercat** refers to the cluster of streets surrounding the rambling Mercat (central market), which opened in 1928 and since then, has pulled in hordes of shoppers in search of edibles as basic as fruit and vegetables, and as adventurous as

ALL ABOUT PAELLA

Without question, paella is Spain's most famous contribution to the world's table – even edging out tapas. Unfortunately, the uninitiated think paella is nothing more than glorified pilaf with a little yellow coloring. Even worse, outside of Spain – and, shamefully, within as well – what is served as paella *is* just glorified yellow pilaf. To enjoy this ubiquitous dish at its most delicious, fragrant, savory best, it will help to know a few facts.

Let's start with the name. It is pronounced pie-AY-ya and the word is actually Valenciano for "pan." As the dish has become synonymous with the name, the broad, flat handled pan used to cook paella is now called the *paellera*. Paella's origin goes back to the rice field workers of Valencia. They created paella as a simple one-pot lunch dish cooked over an open fire using whatever local products were close at hand.

Today, it is one of the most versatile, emblematic dishes in Spain and a worldwide favorite for festive dinner parties.

Paella always starts with rice and the rice from Valencia's Albufera region is the most acclaimed in the country. It is so special, that it even has its own *denominación de origen* (appellation) which carefully monitors the harvesting and processing of the rice. Albufera rice forms the basis of much of Valencia's *arroces* (rice dishes), including paella, which is only one of many different rice-based dishes.

The two main ingredients of paella are rice and olive oil with saffron being a close third. After that, ingredients vary widely depending on the region, the season, and the chef's whim. The dish that started it all is simply called *paella valenciana* and it is traditionally made of rabbit, *ferraduras* (a broad green

paella pans for sale in Valencia.

bean), and a handful of snails. Paellas are usually served "dry," that is, without any type of sauce or liquids. Many other rice dishes are "wet," or *caldoso* (served with stock).

The best place to guarantee a good rice dish is at an *arrocería*, or rice restaurant. Nearly every town in Spain will have at least one. And the time of day to have it is lunchtime; Spaniards consider it too heavy to eat for dinner. Paella and other rice dishes are often only offered for a minimum of two people (a good sign that the paella is being made to order for you). The *paellera* will be brought to your table and set in the center. Traditionally, Spaniards eat directly from the pan, though restaurants now almost exclusively place plates down for individual servings. You may notice the waiter or your Spanish dining companions scraping up the bits stuck to the bottom of the pan. This caramelized rice is considered the highlight of the dish and even has its own name, *socarat* (so-KA-raht).

Now that you know the basics, you can really enjoy an authentic *arroz*; here are a few suggestions for getting started. As the Valencians say, *Bon Profit!*

- *arroz a banda* – cooked with seafood and stock and served *a banda* (apart) in two courses

- *arroz al horno* – cooked in the oven in a terra-cotta pot, often with sausages and meats

- *arroz con costra* – baked in an

Paella: it's what's for lunch.

oven with a variety of meats, chickpeas, and an egg crust

- *arroz negro* – black rice with squid ink and calamari, often served with aioli

- *caldero* – served in a soupy base, common in Murcia

- *fideuà* – "paella" made with short, fat noodles instead of rice, common in Cataluña

- *paella de marisco* – with seafood, usually a variety plus monkfish

- *paella de peix* – with fish only

- *paella mixta* – a meat and seafood combination

- *paella valenciana* – with rabbit (or chicken) and broad beans

© CANDY LEE LABALLE

a corner café in the Mercat area of Valencia

eels and barnacles. This somewhat seedy neighborhood is jammed with old apartment buildings, alternative bars, and tiny restaurants with upscale illusions. **Catedral** is the area of nicer buildings and businesses that surround the cathedral and the adjacent squares Plaza de la Virgen and Plaza de la Reina. The cathedral is a majestic monument that shows off Valencia's history with its mix of Romanesque, baroque, and Gothic styles and, if you believe the local ecclesiastical hype, houses the real, honest to God, Holy Grail (so why weren't any Indiana Jones films set here?)

Rounding out the Ciutat Vella is the most atmospheric quarter of Valencia—Barrio del Carmen. El Carme, as the locals call it, is a medieval warren of enchanting alleyways, colorful buildings with flower-laden iron balconies, and quiet, tree-lined plazas. Long a mecca for Valencia's bohemian crowd, El Carme boasts more than its fair share of modern boutiques, artist galleries, trendy restaurants, and the city's most boisterous nightlife.

Given the diversity of living options (new lofts, old walk-ups, restored palaces) within such a small space, property prices in Ciutat Vella vary wildly. In general, a decent two-bedroom runs €600–1,000 to rent; €275,000–600,000 to buy.

The small towns surrounding Valencia function as city suburbs and you can find beautiful villas with mountain and sea views, orange groves close by, and in some cases, metro access to the city center. Some of the most sought after housing is in **L'Horta Nord,** along the coast north of the city.

Los Monasterios—a housing development near Puçol, about a half-hour north of Valencia's city center is perched on a hill offering magnificent sea views. American expats with young children often choose this neighborhood because it is home to both the American School of Valencia and Caxton College, a prestigious British school. Prices in Los Monasterios tend to be some of the highest in the area. Forget about two-bedrooms, this is a community of chalets and multiroomed luxury apartments. Expect to shell out a minimum of €400,000 to buy. If you are renting, prices start around €1,500.

Rocafort is about 15 minutes from the city center, about 20 minutes from the beach, and home to Cambridge House Community College, one of the best British schools in Spain. It is a town of detached houses and villas, most with swimming pools. A two-bedroom home begins at around €200,000 and goes up from there. Rent on a home would start about €900. Adjacent **Campolivar** also pulls in scores of young families, many of them wanting to enroll their children in Los Olivos, a bilingual English-Spanish primary and secondary school. Homes in Campolivar rent for about €1,000–€2,000 per month. Purchase prices begin around €250,000.

Lliria, 15 miles northwest of the city, was originally a weekend retreat but in recent years it's become a coastal suburb to Valencia. Metro connection to the city is a tremendous boon and buses also serve the area. Homes in the area are all detached and they're mainly villas. Two-bedroom homes begin selling at around €180,000; rentals, if you can find them, start around €1,000.

Getting Around

Valencia has an excellent system of public transport that includes buses, subways, trams, and commuter trains. The bus system is run by Empresa Municipal de Transportes (www.emtvalencia.es) and maps can be found online. A single trip is €1.25 or you can buy a 10-trip BonoBus for €6. The subway is called the metro (www.metrovalencia.com) and is easily identifiable by the lowercase red "m" that marks the stations. There are six lines and dozens of stops covering the whole of the city and some suburbs. Line 4 of the metro is above ground to the beach and is locally called the "tram." The cost depends on the zone in which you are traveling. The city center is Zone A and a single ticket is €1.40, a BonoMetro of 10 trips is €6.50. A 30-day Abono Transporte offers unlimited rides on buses and metro for €37.40—you'll have to buy a €4 ID card first. Valencia City is also well connected to its suburbs and further out provinces via the Cercanias (commuter train) run by RENFE (www .renfe.es/cercanias/Valencia).

COSTA BLANCA

If you find this sweep the Mediterranean coast magnificently alluring, you won't be alone—the Costa Blanca is one of Spain's most popular shores. It draws tens of thousands of tourists annually and is home to several sprawling expat communities. What draws them in? The weather to start. The sun shines for about 320 days a year and the average temperature is a lovely 62°F. The World Health Organization named the coast's climate one of the healthiest in the world. Moreover, the crime rate is low, the number of amenities is high, and have I mentioned that the area is magnificently alluring?

So what's the drawback? Quite simply, too much of a good thing. In the 1960s and 1970s, much of the coast underwent severe overdevelopment. Benidorm has had the worst of it and the city with its stunning beaches and lovely sea views is a jungle of skyscrapers, megadiscos, and squat cement hotel complexes. Rising real estate prices and conservationist outcry has somewhat stemmed the tide of overbuilding, but the Costa Blanca still remains the land of the package tour—rock-bottom, all-inclusive deals that include ridiculous quantities of booze. You've heard about the ugly, drunken, sunburned tourist? This is their Spanish ground zero.

Nonetheless, the Costa Blanca still has enough charms to make it worth a transatlantic move. And the upside of the development boom is convenience. Whatever you want, you can find here—from gourmet restaurants to Reiki massage. The massive expat community means you can easily find English-speaking doctors and lawyers, English press, and a support network of expats who've been here, done that long before you arrived. But, venture just a little ways off the beaten path and you'll find bits of the Costa Blanca that are still rustic and remote. What follows are a few places that offer a good balance of Costa Blanca beauty and Costa Blanca bustle.

Where to Live

With a population of just over 29,000, **Jávea** (Xàbia in Valenciano) is one of the more sizable small towns on the Costa Blanca, yet it retains an air of seclusion. Perhaps that's because it is sheltered by the hulking Mount Montgó to the west. Its enticements include a scenic old port and modern marina, a rambling medieval quarter centered on a 14th-century church, and a long, inviting expanse of beach. Throughout the town you'll find galleries, restaurants, and shops stocked with products from home (okay, from the UK). Sailing, scuba diving, and other water sports are widely available and the nearby Montgó Nature Park offers some very challenging hiking trails—if you make it to the top of the mountain, you may be able to see clear out to the Islas

Baleares. There are also two international schools—Laude, The Lady Elizabeth School and Xàbia International College. The town offers a wide range of apartments, townhouses, and villas and prices vary depending on how close you are to the sea. In general, monthly rent on a two-bedroom apartment is €500–900. To buy the same, expect to pay no less than €150,000 on the low end, and upwards of €250,000 on the high. Villas and town houses begin around €300,000 and the sky is the limit.

People come to **Moraira** for numerous reasons—the beach access, the quaint atmosphere of a traditional fishing village (the afternoon fresh fish auction is a highlight of daily life here), or to live in one of the least populous towns on the coast. Yet despite its small size, Moraira has a lot to offer from a stunning old quarter and a range of restaurants, to idyllic beaches nestled into coves and a strong expat network. Strict zoning laws keep the town unspoiled. Rather than high-rises, you'll find townhouses, apartments, and villas. However, the price of a little beach and quiet is steep. Monthly rent on a two-bedroom begins around €600. Purchase prices for the same average around €220,000. Add a pool, a terrace overlooking the sea, and other amenities, and expect to spend a minimum of €400,000.

Altea, a whitewashed village wrapped around a hilltop overlooking the sea, is widely considered the loveliest town on the Costa Blanca. Long an artist's colony, there is a decidedly bohemian air here especially when summertime art festivals take over the medieval central plaza. Running from the plaza in all directions are tiny streets curling down the hill. They are dotted with postage stamp–sized gardens lush with flowers and broad-leafed trees. At almost every turn, you'll find an expansive view over the deep blue of the Mediterranean, Altea's fishing harbor down below, or the craggy shadows of mountains all around. There is a good-size expat community here and with it, gourmet restaurants, fish-and-chips pubs, and nearby English schools including

© CANDY LEE LABALLE

PRIME LIVING LOCATIONS

a cobbled, climbing street in the old part of Altea

the Waldorf La Marina School and Costa Blanca International College, both 20 minutes away in Benidorm. You'll have a choice between settling into an apartment in the town or a villa in one of the surrounding developments such as Altea Hills. A two-bedroom in town rents for about €600 and sells from €150,000 on the low end and up to €1 million on the high-end. Rent for villas starts around €800 monthly and purchase prices start at €400,000 and can exceed €1 million easily.

Although **Benitachell** is just a five-minute drive from the beach, it's considered an inland town. Surrounded by almond trees and pretty hills lined with scenic walking trails, the town is a bit more low-key than the coastal resorts and a lot more Spanish. Still, golf courses, restaurants, and cultural outlets catering to foreigners are less than a 15-minute drive away, including a newly opened Laude School, a prestigious British school. Rent for a two-bedroom apartment starts at €500, purchase price starts at €200,000. Of course, luxurious chalets can be had for much more.

The harbor town of **Alicante** (Alicant in Valenciano) is an urban utopia on the resort-clogged Costa Blanca. The Romans called Alicante Lucentum, "city of light," and when you see the purity of the blue sky and the ethereal haze of one of the city's nearly 360 days of sun, you'll understand why. With its marvelous seaside esplanade, charming medieval quarter, bustling city center, and easy access to gorgeous white-sand beaches, Alicante is perfect for expats who want Spain's sun-and-sand lifestyle, but can't live without the bustle of the city. With a population of 330,000, Alicante is the second biggest city in Valencia province but small enough to feel neighborly. Those *vecinos* will mainly be Spaniards so speaking Spanish is more of a necessity than in other spots on the Costa Blanca. Valenciano is often used on official signs and documents, but it is by no means the dominant tongue.

Seafront properties along the Playa de San Juan are among the city's most desirable homes, as are any lodgings in the city center. Monthly rent for a two-bedroom will cost you at least €600. To buy the same, expect to pay at least €200,000. Rent on a villa begins around €1,000 and €300,000 and up to buy.

Getting Around

Though you can survive without a car in Costa Blanca, life will be a whole lot easier with one, particularly if you live outside of a town. To zip around the coast with confidence, know that the AP-7/E-15 highway (toll in parts) runs along the coast from Valencia to Alicante. At times the highway merges with the old, two-way road N-332. Get used to hearing all three names used interchangeably.

If you prefer public transportation, Alsa (www.alsa.es) runs daily buses from Valencia to Alicante with several stops along the way. In addition, a narrow-gauge train operated by FGV Tram (www.fgvalicante.com) runs along the coast between Dénia and Alicante.

Murcia

Lying in Spain's southeast corner, the region of Murcia features 105 miles of spectacular Mediterranean coast called the Costa Cálida. It means "warm coast" and it is just that, warm, sunny, and very enticing. However, until recently, the area was pretty much off the map for relocating expats—hidden behind the glitz and glam of the nearby by Costa Blanca. All that began changing in the late 1990s when Murcia experienced a huge influx of foreign residents—Britons chief among them. Population growth in Murcia has been more than double that of the national average in Spain for the past several years and today there are lively expat communities throughout the regions.

THE LAY OF THE LAND

Ever since the Moors laid down an irrigation system a millennium or so ago, Murcia has been a vital *huerta* (farmland). Despite high temperatures and a deficit of local water, it is one of the biggest suppliers of fresh fruit and vegetables to the rest of Spain and beyond. This long tradition of farming has kept much of inner Murcia unspoiled by development and away from the coast, the landscape unfurls in a mosaic of desert, mountain, and miles and miles of farmland that is refreshing in its rural calm. Around the northern-lying towns of Yecla and Jumilla, acres of vineyards have recently begun producing award-winning wines. Expect dusty one-road towns dominated by medieval castles and churches as well as the region's bustling capital, Murcia.

Along the Costa Cálida, terra-cotta–colored hills give way to the unbearably blue Mediterranean. It is dotted by whitewashed villages and towns as well as the buzzing port city of Cartagena, whose name recalls the Carthaginians who set up base here over 2,240 years ago. The coast features the Mar Menor, a vast saltwater lagoon lying alongside the Mediterranean. It is home to one of the ritzier resort areas on the coast and is popular with both foreigners and Spaniards.

Local Language

On the coasts, you can find communities where English seems to have supplanted Spanish as the main language. However, if you live here for the long-term, Spanish will greatly help you, not only in daily life (doctors, teachers, shopkeepers) but also in making local friends. If you live in inner Murcia, Spanish will be essential. Older locals also speak their own dialect called Murciano, a version of Valenciano (which derives from Catalan). Some rural villagers even speak an ancient patois called *panocho,* which is incomprehensible to Spanish speakers.

WHERE TO LIVE

Where you live in Murcia will be driven by what you want. A laid-back beach lifestyle with easy access to shops, schools, and English speakers? You want the coast. A big city experience in a deeply Spanish setting? Cartagena and Murcia city comply. A rambling old *finca* where all you can see is farmland and the occasional medieval castle? Head inland my friend.

Costa Cálida

Cartagena is the biggest city on the Costa Cálida and has an enviable position on a wide harbor opening onto the Mediterranean. It is so well suited to seafaring that is has been used as such for millennia—Carthaginians and Romans both had naval bases here. Spain has followed suit and Cartagena is the current home of the Spanish navy. Walking around the lovely old center of town can feel like being stuck in an archaeological site—you can barely turn a corner without running into a centuries-old monument—Roman, Punic, Moorish, medieval. Add to that a busy business center, a vibrant university, and some very lovely beaches, and you have a perfect little Spanish town. Expats are drawn to both the city center and the adjacent small towns and developments that make up the metropolitan area, such as tony **Tentegorra** where the Alpha-Omega British School is located. A two-bedroom in the old city center can start as low as €550 to rent and €100,000 to buy. A well-appointed villa on the outskirts will run an average of €400,000 with great variance depending on amenities and views.

Just 14 miles north of Cartagena, the **Mar Menor** is one of the most exclusive resort areas in Spain. The area is named for a saltwater lagoon that runs along the Mediterranean. Mar Menor means "small sea" and at 65 square miles, it does indeed feel like a sea. Up to 20 feet deep and filled with a very still, tranquil body of warm, salty water, Mar Menor has drawn health-seekers to its curative waters for centuries. The 15-mile strip of land lying between the sea and the lagoon is called La Manga and is home to many resorts, high-rise buildings, and world-class golf courses—La Manga Club is the most comprehensive boasting many popular bars and restaurants.

Along the shores of the Mar Menor are several towns that draw expats—**San Pedro del Pinatar, San Javier, Los Alcazares.** A two-bedroom rental can start as low as €500 and zoom past four figures (but be careful when renting, many landlords want to reserve the right to rent out during summer months for exorbitant prices, clarify all details in your contract before signing). A two-bedroom to buy can start as low as €180,000; a lovely detached villa at €400,000.

South of Cartagena, **Mazarrón** is a traditional fishing village that is very fast becoming an expat colony. It's divided into two urban clusters—the seaside port and the little town just inland. Despite its newfound popularity, it is still far enough from the bustle at Mar Menor to feel slow and unhurried. The picturesque port, bobbing with colorful fishing boats, gives way to more than 20 miles of unspoiled beaches riddled with coves. A two-bedroom apartment rents for €400–800 and can be bought for as low as €120,000. A multiroomed villa with a sea view will set you back a minimum of €250,000.

Inner Murcia

The capital of the region of Murcia is also called **Murcia** and it stands some 30 miles inland. With 433,000 residents, it is Spain's seventh largest city, yet the fact that it is not on the coast has traditionally kept both tourists and expat residents away. That is changing, in part due to reasonably-priced housing, and, well, the lack of tourists and expats. It is a catch-22 but one you want to be part of if you are looking for a bit of authentic Spain with a big city feel close to the sea. The city center is lined with ornate sienna-colored buildings dating from the 19th century while its three universities ensure the streets are always buzzing. Adjacent to the city are small towns and suburbs that extend the population to nearly 750,000, a size that ensures any amenity you want is readily available, including the highly-rated private school, El Limonar International located in lovely **El Palmar.** To rent a two-bedroom in the city, expect a minimum of €550 to rent and €150,000 to buy. A detached villa in El Palmar can set you back upwards of €250,000.

Lorca is an area in the southwest of Murcia stretching from the Mediterranean Sea into a terra-cotta–colored landscape of desolate hills and medieval castles. Its biggest city (also named Lorca) is known for its wealth of baroque structures and an impressive 13th-century castle. Some 90,000 people call the city home and the result is all the amenities you'd expect from a bustling small town. On the coast, the centuries-old port town of **Aguilas** has a resort vibe but on a much lower key than what you'd find farther up the coast. Nearby are some of the most undeveloped beaches on the Spanish Mediterranean. Both towns are renowned for their over-the-top fiestas and carnivals as well as their burgeoning expat communities. Though with an entire regional population of just 130,000, you can still find a quiet, unspoiled piece of Spain to call your own here. *Cortijos,* spacious Spanish villas on a large plot of land, are particularly popular in this region and can be had starting at €170,000.

Las Islas Baleares

Just 120 miles off the Costa Blanca shoreline, lie the islands that make up Las Islas Baleares (Balearic Islands in English, Illes Balears in Catalan). The gorgeous beaches, craggy coasts full of coves, pine forests, gentle mountains, and mild climate of these Mediterranean gems have enticed settlement since way, way before our time. In fact, prehistoric monuments on Menorca date back to 2500 B.C. A couple of millennia later and the foreigners invaded—first Phoenicians, then Carthaginians, Romans, Moors, and Turks. In the 3rd century, the Catalans took over, introducing the language which is still in use today. For most of the 1700s, Menorca was under British rule. Spain regained full control of the islands in 1802, however foreign invasion didn't end just because other countries stopped taking over.

a hidden cove on Mallorca

Up toward 10 million tourists visit the islands annually seeking good times under the Mediterranean sun. Over the years, many of those visitors have decided to stay. Of the one million permanent residents, an estimated 10 percent are foreign expatriates—British, German, and northern Europeans chief among them. An estimated fifth of the property in Mallorca is foreign owned.

Yet, despite these high numbers, the islands have fended off some of the more ruinous effects of development and it is still possible to find rolling landscapes dotted with orange, almond, and olive trees, picturesque small towns boasting Gothic cathedrals and medieval plazas, and of course, spectacular died-and-gone-to-heaven beaches. Of course, around the Bay of Palma in Mallorca and San Antoni in Ibiza, you'll more likely be dazzled by high-rise buildings, brash resorts, and monster crowds than by the natural wonders that brought them all here in the first place.

THE LAY OF THE LAND

The four largest islands—Mallorca, Menorca, Ibiza, and Formentera—combined with the smaller islets comprise 3,125 square miles of land surrounded by sapphire, Mediterranean waters. The first three of the islands are the most populated and Mallorca (Majorca in English) is the largest. Its 2,260 miles of landmass includes the buzzing capital of the islands, Palma de Mallorca. Not far from the northwest coast, the land rises up into the Serra de Tramuntana, a mountain range full of walking trails with peaks reaching over 4,000 feet. The eastern coast is crammed with tourist developments that take advantage of the expanse of fine-sanded beaches.

Ibiza has emerged as the glitziest, the most stylish, and the most decadent of the islands. Its techno clubs are famed worldwide and draw young beat-and-booze seeking tourists by the disco-load. But the island is more than its famous clubs, offering upscale club culture amid stunning natural scenery. In addition to gorgeous beaches and secluded coves, Ibiza boasts a laid-back countryside riddled with deep-green pine trees, scrubby hills, and olive, almond, and fig groves. Its capital, Ibiza City, is a thriving town with one of the most picturesque ports in the islands.

Menorca (Minorca in English), the farthest away and the least developed, seems oblivious to all the fuss. Battered for millennia by a wind named *tramontana,* the island boasts untouched coves, unspoiled landscapes, and an island-wide designation as a UNESCO Biosphere Reserve. It also offers city living in its endpoint towns of Mahón and Ciutadella.

Local Language

Catalan and Spanish are the official co-languages of the Islas Baleares, and you can expect Catalan on street signs, some television and print media, and in public schools (though not to the exclusion of Spanish). Spanish is widely spoken and you won't have a problem if you can manage in this language. Of course, due to the islands' heavy dependence on tourism, English is also quite common and you can usually run into a few expats who've managed in their native tongue just fine for years.

WHERE TO LIVE

Money and motive should guide your decision on where to live in the Islas Baleares. If urbanity is your thing, Palma is the place to be, though Ibiza City, and the small towns of Mahón and Ciutadella can also comply. Upscale beach life can be found on any of the coasts, while a more low-key vibe is best sought after in Menorca. Getting away from it all is easy in the islands—just head inland, where the lack of sea views has warded off both development and tourism. Regarding money, just have lots of it and you should be able to make the transition to Balearic island life without problem.

One point to keep in mind is seasonality. From mid-June to mid-September, the Baleares swell with tourists. Prices in restaurants and shops can double or triple and space on the sand becomes scarce. The plus side is the sizzling vibe as streets, restaurants, bars, and nightclubs fill to bursting. Of course, many locals loathe this and make a pretty penny by renting their homes out for the season while they repair to somewhere quieter. Things slow down considerably in the off-season and in winter, many businesses shut down. Though it might be a bit too chilly for the water, there is still enough sunshine to enjoy a stroll on the beach blissfully free from sun-worshipping hordes.

Mallorca

With more than 400,000 residents, **Palma de Mallorca** offers the kind of big-city sophistication you'd expect on the mainland. Its old quarter is a charming blend of Gothic architecture and baroque touches. But as one of the most cultured in the islands, it also offers museums and galleries, gourmet restaurants and buzzing nightlife, and a local yacht club that is considered Spain's most prestigious—a reputation helped by the fact that it's the home of King Juan Carlos's annual regatta event. Palma (as locals call it) also offers a well-developed expat population. This means it is easy to find English-speaking doctors, therapists, and yoga instructors in the area. If you have children, there are also several good international schools near town including Baleares International School.

Homes in and around Palma do not come cheap and the sky is the limit depending on the amenities and proximity to the sea you want. A two-bedroom apartment in the old part of town will rent for €700–1,000 a month. Purchase prices begin at about €200,000 on the *very* low end and there is no limit on the upper end.

Although expatriates usually congregate around high-rise, low-brow resort areas such as Calvià, Bay of Palma, Peguera, and Santa Ponça, expats seeking something more tranquil should head to the western side of the islands. Traversed by the Serra de Tramuntana, a rugged

taking home the groceries on a street in Sóller

PRIME LIVING LOCATIONS

rise of mountains that follows the coast from d'Andratx in the southeast to Pollença in the north, this area is billed by the local government as *la otra Mallorca* (the other Mallorca). It offers the kind of natural beauty that will silence even the most jaded of nature lovers. This is where the English poet Robert Graves set up house, and many have followed in his footsteps. Lovely living options close to the shore include the towns of **Valldemossa, Deià,** and **Sóller,** as well as dozens of villages farther inland. A two-bedroom rental in this area will run €600–1,200 (all dependent on amenities and proximity to the sea). If you want to buy, a two-bedroom apartment in town can start as low as €200,000; a multiroomed villa overlooking the sea can be had starting at around €450,000 and exceeding many millions from there.

The northeast section of the island is home to several big-time resorts offering all the amenities you could want from luxury spas to tennis courts. If you choose to live in one of the smaller towns near a resort such as **Alcúdia** or **Portopetro** (on the east coast), you'll be able to disappear into a relatively pastoral setting while being conveniently close to those amenities. Monthly rent on a two-bedroom will run €800–1,000, and upwards of €180,000 to buy. Spacious villas rent for about €1,500 per month and begin selling around €500,000.

Ibiza

Ibiza is the island known around the world for its all-night culture. For this very reason tourists flock to it while some potential residents shy away. Most of the party-seekers head to the resorts and megaclubs that cluster around the sprawling beach of San Antoni and though many expats call this club-crazy town home, it is very easy to find a tranquil life away from the neon lights and big beats. A good option is the northern part of the island, particularly in the vicinity of **Sant Joan,** which has recently emerged as a hippie haven of alternative living. Two-bedroom rentals run €500–€1,000. A two-bedroom apartment in town can be bought for as low as €160,000, while a small villa starts around €275,000 and can exceed six figures.

If you still need big city amenities and also want easy access to Ibiza's charms from the natural to the manmade, head to **Ibiza City.** Overlooking a busy harbor, this ancient town features soaring medieval walls, whitewashed architecture, and cobbled lanes. Yachting is big fun in Ibiza City and the marina shows off a host of sleek sailboats. In addition to the clubs, you'll find top-notch restaurants, sporting activities (on land or in water), and great shopping— especially during the summer months. Property is costly and you can expect to pay about €800 or more for a two-bedroom rental, while the same sort of home can fetch €250,000 and upwards on the market. A villa might rent for €1,800 a month, or sell for €450,000 and up, up, up.

Menorca

The second largest of the Balearic Islands, Menorca (also spelled Minorca) is also the least developed. Less hustle and bustle than Mallorca and Ibiza, it offers a truly laid-back Mediterranean lifestyle. Follow a dusty road anywhere on the island and you are sure to be stunned silent by the craggy cliffs falling off into the crystal clear sea and the long, white beaches etching along the coast like fine lace. But it is hardly desolate. With a population near 90,000, two midsized cities, and amenities including good medical facilities, choice restaurants, and a few international schools, you do not have to give up all the comforts of home (though forget about finding a cinema that does not dub its films!)

The capital **Mahón** (also known as Maó) boasts a bustling port, a clutch of tidy Georgian townhouses (a legacy from when the British ruled the island), and a sprawling gin factory. Rent on a two-bedroom apartment in the city will begin around €600. Two-bedroom price tags usually begin around €200,000. Prices are a tad cheaper in **Ciutadella,** the former capital and a place with a rustic, old town and captivating harbor. However, one of the joys of Menorca is its slow-paced way of life and that means heading away from the citites. If

MENORCA'S PREHISTORIC RUINS

Menorca has one of the richest collections of prehistoric monuments in the Mediterranean with over 200 sites and thousands of ruins, the oldest dating to 2500 B.C. Archaeologists usually divide the prehistory of Menorca into three epochs: pre-Talayotic, Talayotic, and post-Talayotic.

Pre-Talayotic culture is the oldest and some of the most important remains from this era are the burial monuments called *navetas*, mass tombs that resemble upturned boats. The Naveta des Tudons is the best known of these structures. Around 1400 B.C., Talayotic culture took root. This period is characterized by the building of stone towers or *talaiots*. Also dating from this era are the *taulas*, megalithic stone T's made by hoisting a massive granite beam upright and topping it with a large stone slab laid horizontally. The Talatì de Dalt, just outside of Maó, has one of the most impressive examples, rising to 10 feet.

The Talaiots also left behind thousands of remains from houses to cisterns. The most important Talayotic sites on the island include Trepuco and Talati de Dalt near Maó, and Torretrencada and Torre Llafuda near Ciutadella. The most extensive sites, having produced the most remains and clues into this prehistoric world, are on the Western side of the island and include Torre d'en Gaumes and Torralba d'en Salord. The island of Mallorca also has several Talaiot sites. The post-Talayotic period occurred after other cultures entered the islands and the Talaiots adopted outside building techniques. By the time the Romans arrived, the Talayotic era had ended.

you relocate to the vicinity of a resort you can have both tranquility and easy access to the amenities of a town. One example is **Fornells,** located on a stunning bay that swoops deeply into the northern coast of the island. It is a lovely little village of whitewashed houses with bright blue windowsills lining well-worn cobbled streets. In the 17th century, this was a favorite entrance point for pirates and parts of the massive castle that was erected to prevent this still stand guard over the bay today. A villa here will rent for a minimum of €900 monthly. To buy the same, expect to start at €400,000.

GETTING AROUND

The only train transportation throughout the Balearic Islands is in Mallorca, and the train is just a notch up from the one in Disney World. In other words, it's a good idea to have a car on the islands. Ferries between islands and to the mainland take cars (for a fee) and you'll find it enormously useful—almost necessary—for getting around.

Ferry services to the Costa Blanca, Valencia, and Barcelona run frequently through the summer, while in the off-season the boats come and go more sporadically. Each of the main islands has its own airport with connection to Spain and several European capital cities.

PRIME LIVING LOCATIONS

ANDALUCÍA

When people imagine Spain, it's usually Andalucía that comes to mind—pastures of olive trees rolling out towards the horizon, sleepy cities where Moorish flourishes mingle with Gothic architecture, orange trees, flamenco guitar, whitewashed towns, and a cold glass of *jerez* (sherry) washing down a slice of *jamón*. Modern Andalucía is all that and more—Sevilla and Granada in particular are vibrant urban centers with busy business districts, Michelin-starred restaurants, and sprawling satellite communities.

Andalucía's climate is just as diverse, ranging from Spain's driest and sunniest in Almería to its wettest and greenest in the Sierra de Grazalema. It offers the country's highest mountains in the Sierra Nevada where you can ski in the morning and then head downhill two hours for a swim in the Mediterranean. Its seaside is home to the protected reserve of Cabo de Gata and the concrete jungles of the Costa del Sol. All that splendor spreads over about 558,000 square miles and eight individual provinces—Almería, Granada, Jaén, Málaga, Cádiz,

Córdoba, Huelva, and Sevilla. Just keep in mind, each of these provinces has a capital city that shares its name, so clarify when someone is speaking about Sevilla or Granada, if they mean the city or the province.

The coasts attract the bulk of foreigners who move to Andalucía, especially the notorious Costa del Sol which is jam-packed with spas, golf courses, marinas, and villas. However, the cities' enchanting way of weaving history and modernity together have attracted their share of expatriates, too, and you'll enjoy yourself there if you're looking to settle into an authentically Spanish place.

Sevilla

"Sevilla doesn't have an ambience. It is ambience," James A. Michener once wrote. No statement could be more apt. More than any other city, sloe-eyed Sevilla evokes the sensuality of Andalucía—orange blossoms and Moorish arches; the clattering of castanets and the whish of a flouncy polka-dotted skirt; the crescendo of *"Ole!"* rising from the bullring and the grandeur of medieval towers rising from a jumble of whitewashed buildings. Sevilla gave birth to some of the sultriest, bawdiest, most unforgettable lovers of literature—*Carmen, Don Juan,* and *The Barber of Sevilla.* Spain's beloved painter, Diego Velázquez (of *Las Meninas* fame) was born in Sevilla and Miguel de Cervantes did time in prison here, where rumor has it, he began *Don Quixote.* Yet, all this history, palpable as it is, is just a part of modern-day Sevilla. The city is also one of the most prosperous towns in Andalucía with thriving industries in shipbuilding, food processing, construction, pottery, silks, and of course, tourism.

Moorish arches overlook a garden in Sevilla.

© CANDY LEE LABALLE

THE LAY OF THE LAND

Sevilla is in the southwestern part of Andalucía, an inland city surrounded by farms that grows olives, almonds, fruits, and vegetables. The nearby hills are gentle and the sun is strong. Summer temperatures are on average in the mid to high 90s, although there are always a few skin-scorching days in July and August where the mercury tops three digits. Winter is far gentler and temperatures rarely dip below the mid-40°F range. The Río Guadalquivir bisects Sevilla into two sections with most of the city's historic treasures on the eastern side. The Avenida de la Constitución runs through the center of town—it's a broad avenue of banks, shops, cafés, and offices, and it cuts a modern line through a patch of historical landmarks. Head to the northern end of the avenue and you'll reach Plaza Nueva, the border to the city's premier shopping district. South of Plaza Nueva you'll hit the cathedral, the Alcázar, and Barrio Santa Cruz—a romantic 13th-century jumble of whitewashed lanes.

WHERE TO LIVE

The city is filled with old buildings that are as beautiful as they are dilapidated, yet you can also find historic places that have been impecabbly renovated. Not surprisingly, newer buildings have appeared as the city has grown, and Spaniards typically go for the modern digs while young foreigners are all too pleased to snap up a vacancy in **Barrio Santa Cruz.**

El Centro is the throbbing central heart of Sevilla and its liveliest commercial district. The best shopping will be right outside your front door, as will theaters and cinemas, restaurants and nightlife, outdoor cafés and people-filled plazas. Add the fashionable Calle Sierpes and stately old buildings to the mix, and it's no shock that people like living around here. You can expect to pay about €800 to rent a two-bedroom apartment and a minimum of €280,000 to buy.

You'll pay about the same prices for aged charm in Barrio Santa Cruz but be warned: What you gain in atmosphere, you *might* lose in quality. Aged charm is another way of saying "old," and while some buildings are in prime condition, others are not. Crazy wiring, skittish water, and cracked-tile floors are pretty common. However, all but the dumpiest of places will have been updated enough for phone lines and DSL. And don't forget, those narrow lanes are not meant for driving. If you have a car, you'll also have to rent a spot in a nearby parking garage. Yet, most who live here say the sacrifices are worth waking up every day to a magical maze of whitewashed walls draped in colorful bougainvillea, wrought iron street lamps, colorful doors with intricately carved knockers, twisting cobbled streets, surprisingly lush patios, and ancient, cozy plazas.

On the west side of the Río Guadalquivir sits the old barrio of **Triana,** a lively warren of narrow cobbled streets and winding alleys. Though not as picturesque as Santa Cruz, this barrio makes up for it with less tourists and more of a local village-within-a-city feel. Triana has long been a center of glazed tile production, and the fruits of the local labor are handsomely displayed on the surrounding buildings. It is also nicknamed the "cradle of flamenco" and some of the most authentic flamenco bars are located here. A two-bedroom starts about €700 to rent and €250,000 to buy.

Nervión is one of the most sought-after neighborhoods in Sevilla, especially for young families. About a half-hour walk from the center, it is a neighborhood of wide avenues and well-maintained older buildings. It is home to many businesses, the city's two train stations, and even a piece of an old Roman aqueduct. Apartments with two bedrooms start at €750 and sell for a minimum of €180,000.

HOW THE *OESTE* WAS WON

Not only is the Andalusian region of **Almería** home to Europe's only desert, it also claims honest-to-goodness Hollywood fame. During the 1960s, the somewhat backwards region became a Spanish outpost for Tinseltown glitz when directors and stars came here to film big-budget films. Almería offered an irresistible combination of cheap labor and spectacular landscape – the mild, malleable desert of Tabernas. It could double as the American West, Saudi Arabia, even Africa. And it did in films like *A Fist Full Of Dollars, The Good, The Bad and The Ugly, A Few Dollars More, The Man With No Name, Lawrence Of Arabia, Cleoptra,* and *Doctor Zhivago.*

Between 1965 and 1973, over 150 films were made in Almería. Clint Eastwood, Raquel Welch, Brigitte Bardot, Peter O'Toole, Henry Fonda, and Charles Bronson took the starring roles, the Native Americans were played by *gitanos* (gypsies), and Spaniards filled the credits as extras, assistants, and technicians.

By the 1970s, film work in Almería had tapered off considerably due to rising costs, though a few big-budget productions were filmed in the desert in the 1980s – *Conan, the Barbarian, Never Say Never Again,* and *Indiana Jones and The Last Crusade.*

Today the biggest evidence of Almerí's Hollywood heyday are two theme parks built up around some of the original sets from several of the many Westerns shot here. At Mini Hollywood and Western Leone you can take a stagecoach ride, swing through the doors of an old West saloon, and witness gunslingers dueling throughout the day.

GETTING AROUND

The traffic in Sevilla would make the Dalai Lama slam the horn and sputter in rage, so if you plan on using your own wheels to get around town, be prepared for frustration. Another note of caution for car owners: Be careful with street parking as the city is known for break-ins. While renting a parking space is an additional expense, it might just be a worthwhile one. Fortunately, a car is only necessary if you'll be using it to get around outside of the city. Within Sevilla itself, you'll find a good system of public transportation, plenty of taxis, and your own two feet can get you far—the city is compact.

Granada

From the evocative old Moorish quarter of the Albaicín to the gypsy caves of Sacromonte to the hundreds of bustling tapas bars spread deliciously all over the city, Granada entices all the senses. A local saying concludes, "there is no worse fate than to be blind in Granada" and that is so very true. Consider the Alhambra. This 13th-century Moorish fortress is arguably the most beautiful building in all of Spain, many say of the world. The enormous red edifice sits high on a hill, and until you lay eyes on its detailed stuccowork and gurgling fountains for yourself, you might believe that people are exaggerating when they say that the place is the stuff of fairy tales. But, the Moors' architectural flourishes don't end with the Alhambra. They're visible throughout town, from latticed windows to curved archways. History is alive in this Andalusian city.

Yet step away from the historic district and you'll find traffic jams and highrises that are entirely 21st century. With a population of 238,000, Granada is a decent-sized city with a busy commercial center, a university that provides a good dose of culture, and famously fun-loving residents that keep the tapas bars full round the clock.

THE LAY OF THE LAND

The city of Granada is the capital of the province of the same name and it sits on a fertile plain called La Vega. Though it lies barely 40 miles inland from the coast, the city is defined more by the Sierra Nevada mountains which stand guard over it. Even days when the sun bakes the streets with a heat fierce enough to send everyone scrambling for shade, peaks with snowy

Tapas approach religion in Granada.

summits can be viewed in the distance. The mountains are also one of the top spots for skiing in Spain and keep the local economy thrumming through winter. Stretching south from the mountains are the rolling hills and green valleys of Las Alpujarras. They are dotted with whitewashed Andalusian villages and are ideal for rustic day trips. The weather in Granada is pleasant some 10 months out of the year. In July and August however, the heat can be deadly—most locals abandon the city for vacation during this time.

The city of Granada is laid out amorphously with a dense cluster of streets in the city center. The two central streets, Gran Vía de Colón and Calle Reyes Católicos, merge at Plaza Isabel La Católica. At that point, the main avenue continues its beeline for Puerta Real in the southwest. To the northeast the same street runs up to Plaza Nueva, near the Alhambra, the Albaicín, and the narrow Río Darro.

WHERE TO LIVE

Like Sevilla's Barrio Santa Cruz, Granada's **Albaicín** is the most romantic spot in the city. Sloping up a hillside in a jumble of whitewashed buildings, it is the center of the old Moorish Granada dating back some thousand years. It is honeycombed with narrow cobblestone streets, secluded plazas bursting with bright flowers, mosques rebuilt as churches, and the horseshoe-shaped arches so distinctive in Islamic art. The barrio is flanked by the Río Darro, creating a natural border. The upper reaches of the barrio offer the most spectacular views of the Alhambra in the city. But all that atmosphere comes at a cost—most of the buildings are old, very old, and may not be updated to modern expectations, particularly regarding wiring and appliances. This is also no place for a car, traffic is restricted, parking is extremely limited, and the narrow alleyways knuckle-whitening. This is also not a place for the weak of heart or thigh. The streets are steep and the hills many. On the plus side, after a few months of hauling groceries up your street, you are guaranteed buns of steel. A two-bedroom apartment starts as low as €650 to rent and €160,000 to buy. A multiroomed townhouse can start around €250,000 and exceed seven figures depending on amenities and views.

Barrio de Realejo, a 10-minute walk from Plaza Nueva, shares much in common with Albaicín, but is just a smidgen less popular with tourists. It is, however, quite popular with residents, particularly young families, expatriates, and art-

a narrow alleyway in the Albaicín

ists. In addition to being one of the most tapas bar intensive zones in all of Spain, the barrio is also lined with cafés, restaurants, shops, and markets. The apartments in Barrio Realejo are both a bit more spacious and cheaper than the homes in Albaicín. Rental on a two-bedroom starts around €500. To buy the same, you'll spend an average of €200,000.

Around the spacious and elegant **Plaza Bib-Rambla,** the commercial center of the city unfolds. This is where you'll find a plethora of banks, businesses, and bustling purpose. It is also home to the 16th-century cathedral, some spectacular Moorish structures, part of the University of Granada, and traditional shops selling everything from leather-tooled sandals to embroidered shawls. A two-bedroom apartment in the area rents for €600–1,000 and the same sort of unit will sell for €200,000 and up.

GETTING AROUND

Owning a car in Granada is a luxury, not a necessity—and considering the nonstop traffic, expensive parking, and tiny, twisting streets, it is a pain-in-the-butt luxury at that. The city is compact enough that you'll be able to walk most places, but if not, there is also a solid network of buses, including minibuses that snake through the Albaicín.

Costa del Sol

Up until the 1950s, the Costa del Sol was a rugged stretch of coast as sleepy as could be, full of battered fishing villages and tumbledown towns. Then two key factors changed all that forever. Cheap land and unregulated development. Starting in the 1950s through the 1970s, developers built sprawling resort towns all along the Costa del Sol. High-rise after high-rise went up with little to no government intervention. After all, poverty was still the norm in Spain and tourism looked like a way out. As the resorts went up, tourists duly followed, drawn to the coast's 300-plus days of sunshine and 200 miles of Mediterranean seafront. Over the years, thousands of those tourists decided to stay and the Costa del Sol is now home to a 300,000-strong expat community, comprised mainly of Brits and Germans. It is possible to spend a week on the Costa del Sol and not hear Spanish spoken at all. In fact, if you are looking for the "real" Spain; this is not it. This is the real *costa,* where sun and sand are complemented by Irish bars, theme parks, golf courses, glittering casinos, all-you-can-eat Chinese buffets, and miles of concrete. Thousands of expats are just fine with that, but if you seek something a little more Spanish, read on for a few jewels amidst the *costa* chaos.

THE LAY OF THE LAND

It wasn't dubbed the sun coast for nothing, and in a place with sunshine almost year-round, the land is bound to be a little dry. That said, some areas are surprisingly verdant thanks to a complex network of irrigation systems. You'll also find patches of forests with pines and cork oaks, which adds welcome contrast to the more arid sections of land. The coast itself borders the province of Málaga running along the Mediterranean Sea southward from the city of Nerja to the tip of the Iberian peninsula. Here the Mediterranean meets the Atlantic at the Strait of Gibraltar, a tumultuous nine-mile wide stretch of water separating Europe from Africa.

Just inland you'll find small mountain ranges; the Sierra Bermeja rises behind Estepona, Sierra de las Nieves provides Marbella with dramatic scenery, and the Axarquía range edges the eastern part of the region. Best of all, the mountains protect the coast from northern winds, ensuring a balmy year-round climate. Winter temperatures almost never dip below the high 40°F range, and summer highs max out in the 80s.

WHERE TO LIVE

The options are many when choosing a Costa del Sol casa to call your own. Inland, lovely whitewashed towns like Ronda and Mijas are very laid-back, very lovely, and very Spanish. And the capital city of Málaga offers big city culture from ancient monuments to modern art right on the beach. However, most expats beeline for the coast when choosing a home. Skipping over concrete playpens like Torremolinos, there are a number of lovely seaside towns offering a good balance between *costa* urbanity and *costa* utopia.

On the eastern end of the Costa del Sol, Nejer is a bit less developed than many towns farther down the coast (partly because its beaches are pebbly). The buzzing towns of Fuengirola and Estepona are reminders that you are still in Spain; you can find an English-speaking hairdresser and after your cut, go tapas-hopping with the locals. Marbella is where to go if you've got cash and like flash; it is the most exclusive and expensive stretch on the Costa del Sol.

Nerja

Of all the Costa del Sol resort towns, Nerja has borne the brunt of its tourist development the best. The old town, sitting above the Mediterranean, offers slow-moving Andalusian grace with whitewashed buildings, pocket-sized gardens, and a handful of Spanish tapas bars. The Balcón de Europa (balcony of Europe) offers breathtaking views out over the sea and up to the Sierra de Burno mountains. Stretching in either direction from the balcony are long, wide promenades, perfect for a *paseo* (stroll) along the beach. Nerja offers several fine beaches including the spectacular Burriana, though they tend to be rockier than others along the Costa del Sol. There are also many coves and caves to explore and nearby mountains to climb.

With a population of 22,000, Nerja is small enough to feel quaint

flowers on the façade of a house on the Costa del Sol

© CANDY LEE LABALLE

PRIME LIVING LOCATIONS

LA COSTA DE LA LUZ

While the Costa del Sol has gotten all the fame – and skyscrapers and megaresorts and English-speaking communities – nearby Costa de la Luz has kept itself a bit of a mystery. Running from Tarifa – the southernmost tip of Europe – along the provinces of Cádiz and Huelva to the Portuguese border, the "Coast of Light" is in no way immune to development, it has just had a whole lot less of it. That is due in part to the wind that blows so strongly here and also to the colder waters of the Atlantic which lap these shores. But whatever the reasons, the result is a heady dose of traditional España right along one of the loveliest coasts in the country. It rambles along wild, nearly undeveloped beaches, sleepy whitewashed villages, pastures where *toros* (fighting bulls) graze, acres of grapes destined to become *jerez* (sherry), and even another country – the British outpost of Gibraltar. This is not the Andalucía of jaw-dropping Moorish monuments nor all-inclusive resorts. The charms are subtler here, hidden within the weave of everyday life – the smell of fish frying, the rattling clap of flamenco pouring out of a tinny radio in no-name bar, the low roar of horse hooves on the sand, the dark-eyed smile of a child kicking a soccer ball against a whitewashed wall.

The seasons are mild. With 300 days of sun, the average temperature is just 57°F, though in summer, the mercury edges up to the 90s. Winters can be bone-chilling. The most distinctive feature of the weather along the Costa de la Luz is the Levante, a strong easterly wind that blows most days, some much stronger than others. It thrills the wind and kite surfers down near Tarifa, but legend has it that it can make locals go crazy. When someone

a rustic beach on La Costa de la Luz

© CANDY LEE LABALLE

yet large enough to offer the basic amenities you'll need. Thanks in particular to the estimated 2,600 British residents, you'll find markets stocked to foreign tastes as well as a range of bars and clubs, some of which will undoubtedly make you think of merry old England. A few miles to the east of town is the Almuñecar International School lying in the province of Granada

Although the seafront and western part of Nerja have the monolithic apartment blocks so frequently seen along this coast, farther back from the water

has a bad day or acts out of character it's always blamed on Levante.

In addition to wonderful beach towns like Bolonia, Caños de Meca, Zahara de los Atunes, and Conil, the Costa de la Luz is home to:

Tarifa: It is at Tarifa, just seven miles from the coast of Africa, that the turbulent Atlantic and tranquil Mediterranean meet. This clash of two of the world's proudest bodies of water has given rise to roiling waves and swooping winds that have led to Tarifa's nickname as the "City of Wind." Though it long kept holidaymakers at bay, the wind proved irresistible to extreme sport fans and the beaches north of town have become Europe's biggest wind and kite surfing destination. Tarifa also happens to be a perfect little Spanish village. Whitewashed buildings, a winding maze of old streets, medieval ruins, sandy beaches, a harbor lined with seafood restaurants, and hopping tapas bars.

Cádiz: Considered the oldest city in western Europe, Cádiz is a magical maze of old cobbled lanes bursting at their cracked edges with palm trees and sweet-scented jasmine. At any turn, you may end up under a medieval archway or standing atop a Roman ruin, and then quite suddenly, the narrow crook of the street gives way to a sea view. Surrounded on two sides by the Atlantic Ocean and on the third by the Bay of Cádiz, the 3,000-year-old city has a vibrant port that has made it self-sufficient for millennia. Unlike many Andalusian towns, Cádiz has not had to turn to tourism for economic sustenance. As a result, it is refreshingly laid-back, even quiet – despite the bustling port. Except of course in February, when the city throws Europe's most raucous Carnival party.

Jerez: No matter where you go in Jerez de la Frontera it's hard to get away from the influence of the distinctive straw-colored wine named for the city. Sherry (in Spanish, *jerez* like the city) has been produced at least since Roman times. Just a few miles inland from the coast, Jerez offers a typically Andalusian warren of cobbled streets, lively tapas bars, dancing horses, and of course, dozens of wine bodegas.

Coto de Doñana: This national park comprises both sandy dunes and swampy wetlands and makes up one of western Europe's largest road-free areas. The region is protected for good reason – it's downright stunning. The delta waters flood the place in the winter and drop dramatically during spring, leaving marshes and cork oak trees in their wake, and providing an ideal resting spot for thousands of birds exhausted from their spring and autumn migrations.

you'll find villas and other styles of homes that blend more seamlessly with the environment. A two-bedroom villa can run €600–1,000 per month, depending on amenities and views. If you want to buy an equivalent property, it will go for no less than €200,000.

Fuengirola

Once a laid-back fishing village, this Costa del Sol town has unfortunately succumbed to high-rise development and package tour mania. Downtown feels like any nameless resort town. Menus come in four languages, beers come in steins, and everyone speaks English. However, just inland from the beach, the local Spanish population is as Andalusian and traditional as anywhere else in the region. This is ecstatically demonstrated during the October Feria del Rosario, a typically Andalusian festival which brings out the local *señoritas* dressed in flouncy skirts, carnations tucked behind their ears. Couples parade around town on horseback, attend bullfights, and dance until dawn.

With 25 percent of the population of 63,000 coming from outside of Spain, the expats too offer lively cultural options. One prime example is the Salon Varietés, an expatriate theater group that stages productions in English throughout the year.

Most expats look for homes on the east side of town in Los Boliches, and some sections such as Riviera del Sol seem to be almost entirely populated by British residents. That can be a real plus if you want to move to Spain without breaking open a grammar book, but if speaking Spanish is high on your list of things to do, you might want to steer clear. The going rate for rent on a two-bedroom apartment in town is about €500–800 a month. To buy the same, expect to pay at least €150,000 and as much as €225,000. Beachfront properties are only slightly more.

Estepona

Under the gaze of the Sierra Bermeja mountains, Estepona (pop. 60,000) is one of the very few places along the Costa del Sol that is completely and authentically Spanish. For evidence of that (or just a good time), check out the daily fish market on the western end of the promenade where the local trawlers auction off their loot. That's no tourist show; Estepona has one of the largest fishing fleets on the coast.

Development has been kept in check, so the beach, Playa de la Rada, has foregone colossal hotels in favor of a scenic promenade and a row of flowerbeds and palm trees. Further inland, the historic portion of town is a car-free, cobbled network of streets with the lovely Plaza de Las Flores as its core. At the western edge of town, you'll find a busy marina and a lighthouse.

In town, expect to pay at least €550 a month for a two-bedroom apartment. The same sort of property sells for around €200,000. A villa on the outskirts of town will rent for €750 or more, and such a home can be yours for €350,000 and up.

A few miles west of Estepona, you'll find one of the toniest resorts in

Spain—**Sotogrande.** This privately owned development is home to some of the most expensive properties in Spain. Located not far from the rock of Gibraltar (technically in the region of Cádiz), Sotogrande stretches from the Mediterranean Sea back into the rolling foothills of the Sierra Almenara encompassing some eight square miles of mansions, golf courses, polo grounds, and tennis courts. It is also home to a yacht-filled marina and the Sotogrande International School. Forget two-bedroom places, the luxury properties here—whether apartments or detached homes—come with several bedrooms and baths, and the prices are steep. Expect to rent from €1,200 per month at the lowest and to buy from €400,000 and on up into the millions.

Marbella

In the years after the Civil War, Marbella was a rough-around-the-edges fishing village, bristling with lazy charm, cheap land, a warm year-round climate, and amazing sea views. In the 1950s and 1960s, spurred on by Prince Alfonso de Hohenlohe-Langenbur, a visionary businessman of royal descent, the town transformed into the playground of choice for Europe's rich and famous. Before long, it was crammed with Hollywood starlets, Arabic sheiks, and various levels of royalty from around the world. Today, it is still a hot spot for Spain's *famosillos* (celebrities), Saudi royalty, and a handful of Hollywood hotshots—Antonio Banderas, Bruce Willis, and Michael Douglas all own mansions here. Their yachts clog the harbor and the country's top gossip rags cover their parties and social events in glossy 10-page spreads. However, unless you are packing some serious buying power and the elusive Spanish clout known as *enchufe* (contacts), you probably won't get access to their world. Stretching for miles on either side of the city are the private resorts, members-only restaurants, and guarded compounds where the Marbella aristocrats do their gossip-making. To join this exclusive enclave, a rental (if you can find one) can start around €5,000 per month, with purchasing prices well into the millions.

Mere mortals prefer the **Casco Antiguo** (Old Village), a labyrinth of pedestrian, cobblestoned streets thick with laid-back Andalusian charm. Still partially enclosed by Moorish walls, the heart of this part of town is the lovely Plaza de los Naranjos which, true to its name, is full of orange trees. It is steps away from the Puerto Deportivo, where the marina is packed with yachts and the bars and clubs pulse with feverish activity until the wee hours of the morning. A few kilometers west, **Puerto Banus** feels like Miami beach—fancy cars, fancy people, and fancy restaurants all vying to be the fanciest. When the celebrities do come out to play, it is here, though more often than not, the

a beachside casa at sunset

port is clogged with rich tourists—mainly European—hoping for a glimpse of the glittering high life. When not seeing and being seen, they shop at Fendi, Versace, Dolce & Gabbana, Roberto Cavalli, Dior, and Jimmy Choo.

If you choose to live in the center, you'll almost inevitably live in an apartment. Some units are in high-rises, others in smaller buildings with just a few floors and a grand old door leading to the street. Health clinics, stores, and restaurants will be right in your neighborhood. A two-bedroom apartment here rents for about €800 and up per month, and sells for a minimum of €250,000 and way, way up. Similar properties in Puerto Banus will rent for €1,000 and up and sell for €350,000 and up.

You'll find more spacious properties in the outlying communities, such as **San Pedro, Nueva Andalucía,** and **Nagüeles** on the west side of town. These communities are highly sought after for their lovely villas, proximity to the city center, and international schools including Aloha College and the International College of San Pedro. A two-bedroom apartment starts at €900 to rent, and €300,000 to buy. A multiroomed villa begins around €1,000 to rent and €400,000 to buy.

The east side of town is where you'll find **Los Monteros** and other lovely residential developments. This area is slightly cheaper than the west-side communities, but it's by no means a bargain. Rent on a two-bedroom apartment begins around €800 and sales start at €300,000. A villa will start at €900 to rent and €350,000 to buy. The English International College is located nearby.

If you really want the good life in Marbella, head to Paradise, **El Paraiso** that is. Ten minutes west of the city, this beachside community is one of the most prestigious in Marbella—and that is saying a lot. In addition to an award-winning golf course, the community offers a health clinic, shops, restaurants, and of course, several options for deep-tissue massage or private Pilates classes. Villas typically come with all the frills and that is reflected in the prices. Rent for a two-bedroom apartment costs a minimum of €1,000. Purchase prices begin at €300,000 and can exceed the million mark. Villas rent for approximately €1,200 a month, and to buy, you will spend a minimum of €450,000.

GETTING AROUND

Maybe in the cities of Marbella or Málaga, you can get by without your own wheels, but everywhere else in the Costa del Sol a car will be a necessity. For longer trips, you will be well-connected on the coast. Málaga is a major transport hub, home to both a buzzing international airport and a major train station—the high-speed AVE train connects Málaga to Madrid in under three hours. The AP 7 highway runs the length of the coast from Málaga city down past Estepona.

THE CANTABRIAN COAST

THE CANTABRIAN COAST

Running from the Pyrenees mountains and the French border across to the craggy cliffs overlooking the Atlantic Ocean is one of the lushest landscapes in all of Spain—the Cantabrian Coast. The rain in Spain does not fall mainly on the plain—it falls here, leaving in its wake the greenest landscapes in all of Spain. Locals call it Costa Verde (Green Coast) and while green is the dominate color splashed across the four autonomous regions of País Vasco, Cantabria, Asturias, and Galicia, there is whole lot more to the palette—deep blue seas and steely blue skies, white frothy waves and golden sand beaches, stone gray Romanesque churches and deep, dark cliffs. The coast runs for some 300 miles along the Cantabrian Sea (also called Bay of Biscay in English and Mar Cantábrico in Spanish) and is followed just inland by soaring mountain ranges—including the spectacular Picos de Europa.

© CANDY LEE LABALLE

A BASIC BASQUE PRIMER

Geography

Though the País Vasco is one of the 17 autonomous regions of Spain, culturally, historically, and linguistically, it is part of Euskadi (collection of Basques) which includes the three provinces of País Vasco (Vizcaya, Guipúzcoa, and Álava) plus northern Navarra. These Spanish Basque lands are part of a greater historical territory called Euskal Herria which also includes three regions in the French Pyrenees – Zuberoa (Soule in French), Behe Nafarroa (Basse-Navarre), and Lapurdi (Labourd). Euskal Herria is located in the western Pyrenees between France and Spain and bordered by the Cantabrian Sea. This region is comprised of some of the most spectacular landscapes in Europe, but also some of the most rugged – a fact which has kept the Basques geographically isolated for millennia.

History

Archaeology indicates that the current Basque lands have been inhabited since the late Paleolithic era of the Stone Age – anywhere from 10,000 to 40,000 years ago. Modern research suggests that current Basques are descended from the peoples who lived during this time. In fact, some theorists have proposed that the Basques descend directly from Cro-Magnon man. How the ancient Basques got into this region is unknown, but the Romans, who were never able to subjugate the Basque, documented their presence as distinctive tribal cultures. The Basques later fought off the Visigoths and the Moors, keeping their heritage relatively free from the influence of invading cultures. The combination of impassable terrain, fiercely independent Basque behavior, and a perception that the Basques were barbarians, proved not worth it for potential invaders.

One influence that did infiltrate the Basque culture was Christianity. It probably arrived with the Visigoths in the 3rd or 4th century. Prior to that time, the Basques were a pagan culture, but by the Middle Ages, the Basques were devoutly Christian. In fact, one of Christianity's most venerated figures, Iñigo de Loyola who founded the Jesuits, was Basque.

During the Spanish Reconquista, the Basques were a confederacy of aligned tribes. They were often under the political rule of other groups including the Franks and the Kingdom of Navarra. As the various kingdoms were consolidated into one nation, the Basque lands eventually fell under the command of Spain. During this time, the Basques were granted charters that allowed for a strong measure of autonomy and self-rule. The origins of this sovereignty date to a 1513 statute enacted by Fernando I of Aragón. Subsequent kings ratified this statute, which today is the basis for Basque claims to autonomy, mainly as a means of ensuring Basque loyalty to the Spanish nation.

By the 19th century, many of the charter rights were being chipped away by the central Spanish government, which was eventually met by full-fledged Basque nationalist resistance, and led to the founding of the first Basque nationalist political party Eusko Alderdi Jeltzalea (EAJ) in Basque (Partido Nacionalista Vasco [PNV] in Castilian Spanish). By 1931, Spain was in the throes of political turmoil. When the second Spanish republic was installed, it granted autonomy to Cataluña. This galvanized the EAJ-PNV into action and they voted for their own autonomous rights. In 1936, the Spanish republic officially granted autonomy to a Basque region that included only the provinces of Vizcaya and Guipúzcoa (Álava and Navarra declined participation). The new Basque government adopted their own flag and installed an army. Of course, by this time, the Civil War had begun. The Basques supported the Republican forces because the Republicans supported regional autonomy. Franco's Nationalist forces retaliated with vicious attacks on Basque lands including the infamous air raid attack on the town of Guernica in April of 1937. Following Franco's victory and the installation of his dictatorship, Basque culture and language were oppressed, often violently. Legitimate political entities such as the PNV continued to operate, however, within the terms of Franco's regime.

ETA

In 1959, **Euskadi Ta Askatasuna,** or ETA, was formed by radicals who felt the PNV was too moderate in its opposition to Franco. The group's goal was to create an independent state for the Basque people, and their means of achieving this goal have been extremely violent. Both the European Union and the United States have labeled ETA a terrorist group, a feeling held by many Spaniards and Basques as well.

In March of 2006, ETA declared a cease-fire for the first time in its history. The socialist-led government (PSOE) responded cautiously with an attempt at creating a dialogue, a move that was mercilessly attacked by the right-wing opposition party (PP). The cease-fire didn't last long as the group set off a December 2007 bomb in the parking lot of Barajas airport in Madrid killing two civilians who were napping in their cars. Since that time, several more assassinations and bombings have been carried out. The government has since increased arrests of ETA members and outlawed political parties with links to ETA. However, in January of 2009, ETA celebrated 50 years of their existence by issuing a statement that they would continue to fight for Basque freedom.

ETA violence and issues of Basque separatism rarely affect tourists or important touristy areas such as San Sebastián. The Basque people themselves take living with these possibilities with a grain of salt – you'll more likely be hit by lightning than struck down in an ETA attack. Do keep in mind however that ETA and Basque nationalism are very volatile subjects. Families and friends have been sharply divided on this difficult matter for over five decades. It is unwise for an outsider to speak about it casually.

Basque Culture

Since Franco's death and the 1981 installation of democracy, Basque culture has enjoyed a resurgence. Basque traditions have been revived including folklore, regional dances, music, and the popular sport, *pelota,* played with a ball and wooden racquet-like object. The Herri Kilorak, a series of Paul Bunyan-type events including competitions for chopping wood, tossing bales of hay, and stone lifting have also become a regular feature of Basque society. Perhaps the strongest resurgence of Basque culture has been the language. The Basque tongue (called *euskara* in Basque) is the official co-language of the region and you'll have to pick up a bit of it if you plan on living in the area long-term. In the meantime, making the effort to learn and use simple phrases such as *kaixo* (hello, KAI-sho), *agur* (goodbye, ah-GOOR), and *eskerrik asko* (thank you, eskay-REEK as-KOH) is a much appreciated gesture of respect and friendliness.

Though there are a handful of big cities in this area—San Sebastián, Bilbao, Oviedo, Santiago de Compostela—the Cantabrian Coast is mainly known for its wild beaches, pint-sized fishing villages, ancient stone ruins, and the most revered cuisine in all of Spain. While foreign residents are drawn to both extremes, it is often easier to make a move into this region by starting out in a city. Once you've got the language (or in the case of País Vasco—languages) down, have had a chance to explore the region, make some contacts, and find the perfect little stone casa to make your own, you can move on to more remote realms.

País Vasco

Though it is geographically and politically an entity of Spain, País Vasco (Basque Country) is culturally, historically, and linguistically, part of the Euskadi (collection of Basques) which include the three provinces of País Vasco plus part of Navarra. Archaeology indicates that the area has been inhabited since the late Paleolithic era of the Stone Age—anywhere from 10,000 to 40,000 years ago. Over the millennia, the Basques developed into a distinctive tribe with a stronghold over their lands. They fended off the Romans, the Visigoths, the Moors, and managed to stay neutral throughout much of the Spanish Reconquista. After years of oppression under the Franco dictatorship, the Basques experienced a resurgence of regional pride. However, with it came a very ugly side—the rise of Euskadi Ta Askatasuna (ETA), a terrorist group that resorts to horrific violence in its bid for independence from Spain.

Despite this political backdrop, País Vasco is quite safe. In fact, locals enjoy their lives with an unbridled fervor—best experienced in the local festivals. In January, San Sebastián explodes in noise as thousands of drummers take to the streets for the annual **Tamborrada.** In August, Bilbao lets loose with **Semana Grande,** a two-week long celebration featuring nonstop street parties and a competition of rural sports including chopping wood, tossing bales of hay, and stone lifting.

One of the biggest draws of this region is its food and if you love good eating, País Vasco will delight you on a mealtime basis. Local chefs have elevated traditional dishes to culinary heights with a New Basque cuisine that has the international gastronomic press dizzy with praise—San Sebastián holds 14 Michelin stars, more per capita than any other city in the world. However, traditional Basque cuisine is equally wonderful, based on impeccably fresh seafood, seasonal produce, local game, and subtly flavored sauces.

Long-lingering lunches are the norm in this food-obsessed culture, but so are the delicious snacks called *pintxos*. Imagine the scene. 9 PM at a bar somewhere in the País Vasco. It is a typical Spanish scene—legs of ham hanging from the walls, wooden tables crowded with plates and glasses, lots of people crowded around the bar—until you lean in to order a drink. The entire length of the bar covered in platter after platter of beautiful prepared *pintxos*—jamón and tomato on toast, crab tartlets, cod-stuffed red peppers, fresh marinated anchovies, wild mushroom omelet, shrimp with aioli, monkfish with leek, duck breast with pear. As one platter is finished, the bartender lays out another. This is a *pintxo* bar and if you move to this part of Spain, *txikiteo* (going out for *pintxos)* will be a very delicious part of your weekly routine.

Finally, one key difference between the País Vasco and the other regions on the Cantabrian Coast—Cantabria, Asturias, and Galicia—the País Vasco is considerably wealthier. It has a long history of industry and very developed local economies. If you will be job-seeking, País Vasco offers more opportunities; if you plan on setting up a business, you'll have more access to infrastructure, supplies, and potential clients. The flipside is that País Vasco is more expensive than its neighboring regions and in fact, the city of San Sebastián is only just behind Madrid and Barcelona in cost of living.

THE LAY OF THE LAND

País Vasco is divided into three provinces, Vizcaya (Bizkaia in Basque), Guipúzcoa (Gipuzkoa), and Álava (Araba) and is home to 2.2 million people. The coast, lying between the Cantabrian Sea and a stretch of mountains is moist, green and mainly temperate, and the coast is defined by the many deep estuaries that reach into the land. Inland, the Alavesa plains unfurl in rolling fields and farmland. Farther south, the Ebro River valley unfolds. This is wine country, specifically Rioja Alavesa—or the Rioja wine harvested and produced on the Álava side of the Ebro River. On the southern side lies the region of La Rioja.

Year-round, País Vasco has a milder climate than much of Spain. Summer brings the warmest weather, with daytime averages around 75°F; however nights are chilly even in July and August. Winter hovers around 40°F and fluctuates quite a bit with cold air from the Atlantic. Fall and winter bring quite a bit of rain to the entire area and the wind can whip up waves as high as a three-story building. In fact, year-round the waves along the Basque coast are formidable and the region is an international hot spot for surfing.

Local Language

The Basque language (called *euskara* in País Vasco) is a linguistic puzzle

PRIME LIVING LOCATIONS

that has challenged researchers for decades. It predates Indo-European tongues and has some links with ancient languages of Central Asia and pre-Arabic languages of northern Africa. Because of the millennia-long isolation of the Basques in their remote valleys, the language has retained its own structure and phonology—unique in all the world. Outlawed under Franco, it has come back with a vengeance. It is the official co-language (with Castilian Spanish) of the País Vasco and an estimated one million people speak it.

Do you need to learn it? Probably. Especially in bigger cities, everyone speaks Castilian—often with each other, too—so if you can manage in Spanish, you won't have a problem communicating your daily needs. However, regional emphasis has been placed on Basque in recent years, and increasingly more young people are mastering it. The language is also commonly used in government offices, on public announcements, and on street signs. Therefore, if you live here for the long-term, it is a good idea to learn Basque. Not only will it endear you to the locals, but speaking it well can ease social situations.

If you have a child in the school system in País Vasco, you'll have to contend with the language on another level. In theory, parents can choose to have their children educated entirely in Spanish, in Spanish with Basque as a compulsory subject, in a mix of Basque and Spanish, and in Basque with Spanish as a compulsory subject. In reality, the majority of students in the region are enrolled in the latter. If you are in an area with limited schooling options, your children may end up in a Basque school.

WHERE TO LIVE

While País Vasco offers a variety of living options from rural to coastal, urban to off-the-beaten path, this book focuses only on the main cities on the Cantabrian Coast, San Sebastián and Bilbao. Barely 90 miles long, the coastal area is small enough to offer the best of Basque living—roaring seas, silvery beaches, medieval fishing villages, gourmet restaurants—no matter where you are based. But having a city address means you can also get the best of the city from speedy DSL connections to good private schools.

San Sebastián

San Sebastián (pop. 183,000) is a bit of unexpected grace in the middle of one of Spain's most rugged coasts. Hugging the Bay of La Concha, the town is protected from the full force of the Cantabrian Sea by the bay and its looming Isle of Santa Clara. Its eastern edge is guarded by the thickly wooded Mount Igeldo while the twin peak of Mount Urgull stands over the west. Between the

Dining at a *pintxo* bar is a way of life in País Vasco.

two runs **La Concha** beach. Lined by a broad promenade, the golden beach is one of the loveliest spots in a city of immense loveliness.

The compact **Parte Vieja** (Old Quarter) is tucked alongside the sheer climb of Mount Urgull. Over a thousand years ago, this neighborhood comprised the whole of San Sebastián and though the narrow streets still bear a medieval air, the Parte Vieja burned to the ground several times, most recently in 1813. Lined with *pintxo* bars, classic cafés, shops, and home to the city's Bretxa market, where the region's top chefs convene each morning to have first go at the day's fresh fish and produce. It is definitely the liveliest part of the city and a big draw for both locals and expats. That said, the crowds on the street can grow riotously loud on summer evenings, and that's something to consider if you're sensitive to noise. A two-bedroom apartment here starts at €1,000 per month to rent and €300,000 to buy.

Along the banks of the River Urumea, the newer part of San Sebastián unfolds—if you consider the 19th century new. The elegant apartment blocks along the river are majestic testaments to a lovely era long gone and a highly sought after address in town. In this area, also called **Centro Romántico,** you'll find excellent pedestrian shopping zones, restaurants and bars packed with locals, and the lush little Plaza de Gipuzkoa, an oasis of green in the middle of a bustling commercial zone. A two-bedroom apartment starts around €850 to rent and €300,000 to buy.

Cross either the Puente de Zurriola or the Puente Santa Catalina to get to the cozy little neighborhood of **Gros,** home to some of the most-acclaimed *pintxo* bars in town and the Playa de la Zurriola, a favorite beach for surfers. It is also home to the glowing cubes of glass called the Palacio de Congresos de Kursaal, a multifunction space which hosts the annual San Sebastián Film Festival. Rent starts around €900 and purchase prices begins around €350,000.

Bilbao

Nestled in the deep folds of the coastal hills of the País Vasco and hugging the undulating banks of the River Nervión as it spills out into the coast's deepest estuary, Bilbao (pop. 355,000) has long been this region's busiest city. Founded in 1300, the town was an important trading port, shipping iron and wool to northern Europe. By the 1800s, the city was one of Spain's wealthiest. Industrialization continued through the Franco regime with many car manufacturing plants settling in the region. Prosperity was great, but so was damage to the city. The surrounding mountains captured the vile exhaust from the hundreds of factories and plants, and the city went about its business under a gloomy cloud of pollution and indifference. Bilbao soon became the ugly stepsister to San Sebastián's fairytale beauty.

All that changed with the opening of the Guggenheim Museum in 1997. The Frank Gehry–designed building with its swirling titanium facade, became an instant cultural landmark and drew over 1.5 million visitors its first year. Inspired by a gust of creativity, commerce, and confidence, the city turned its hardworking attitude towards cleaning up Bilbao. The gritty docks along the river were converted into parks, housing, and cultural centers. British architect Norman Foster designed the city's new subway system. Spanish architect Santiago Calatrava built a new airport and a footbridge across the river. The city polished up its Casco Viejo (Old City) and connected it to the Guggenheim with a sleek tram system. At the same time, Basque cuisine was ascending to the top of gastronomy ratings and foodies worldwide were aiming their forks at local tables. Bilbao was ready, serving up a delicious roster of internationally renowned chefs and world-class restaurants. It is one of Europe's greatest comeback cities and an exciting place to live.

the old train station in Bilbao

One of the most atmospheric neighborhoods is the **Casco Viejo,** a warren of narrow, cobblestone streets that form the medieval heart of Bilbao. The 14th-century streets teem with boutiques, bars, and bakeries. At its center, Plaza Nueva, a broad arcaded walkway, is home to several popular *pintxo* bars and a Sunday flea market. On the edge of the Casco Viejo, along the river, stands the Mercado de la Ribera the largest covered market in Europe and a lively center of commerce in Bilbao. A two-bedroom apartment starts at €700 to rent and averages €250,000 to buy.

The **Abando** district is an elegant grid of streets built in the 19th century and crisscrossed by several diagonal boulevards. They are lined with cafés, restaurants, shops, and some spectacular mansions. If that exceeds your tastes, there are also row after row of graceful apartment buildings. Rent on a two-bedroom apartment runs €800 and up and costs on average €400,000 to buy.

Bilbao's metropolitan area is home to over 600,000 residents and many of the surrounding towns are located right on massive Bilbao estuary. One nice option is **Getxo,** only 10 minutes from downtown Bilbao by subway. This waterfront town of 85,000 boasts lovely 19th-century mansions and apartment buildings, a popular boardwalk offering casual restaurants and *pintxo* bars, and easy access to several beaches. The American School of Bilbao is located about five miles minutes outside of the Getxo. There is also a curious *puente colgante* (hanging bridge) that you may use to get from one side of town to the other if you live here. A two-bedroom rental starts €850 per month and the same will sell for no less than €250,000.

GETTING AROUND
Both San Sebastián and Bilbao lend themselves to a leisurely life without a car. San Sebastián is compact and walkable and has an extensive bus service. Bilbao has excellent public transport including buses, trams, and a subway system which connects to nearby towns and beaches. However, if you want to take off on day trips, a car is a necessity. Whether you buy one or choose to rent occasionally really depends on how far out of the cities and how often you want to go.

PRIME LIVING LOCATIONS

Galicia

Comprising the northwest corner of the country, Galicia is Spain's most surprising landscape. Forget all your notions about the russet plains of central Spain, the golden sands of Costa Blanca, and the whitewashed villages of Andalucía, Galicia is green Spain where the hills roll out in a thick blanket of velvet and everything is alive. It is also wet Spain where rain falls most days and locals say "Rain is art." Looking upon Galicia's impressionist landscape of muted shades—slate-blue sky, gray-tinged clouds, moldering granite buildings, and a thousand shades of green—it is hard to argue.

This is also coastal Spain, where the land ends in a tumble of dramatic cliffs over the tempestuous point where the Atlantic Ocean meets the Cantabrian Sea. An eternity of tumult between land and sea has resulted in Galicia's most distinctive feature—its estuaries (*rías* in Spanish). These narrow fingers of ocean seep inland bringing calm waters, natural fishing ports, and beautiful beaches—there are over 750 beaches along the Galician shoreline.

Inland Galicia, the land is mountainous, thick with ancient forests and untamed valleys. It is colder in the winter, hotter in the summer, and more desolate year-round than the coasts. Agriculture feeds both the local culture and the economy, and on some of the steepest plots of land, plowing is done by oxen rather than tractors. Grapes are one of the most successful local crops, and Galician white wines, particularly *albariño,* are revered throughout Spain.

Of course, Galicia's biggest claim to fame is the **Camino de Santiago.** Since its founding, nearly 1,000 years ago, the Camino has drawn millions of pilgrims to Santiago de Compostela, the burial place of Santiago (Saint James), apostle and patron saint of Spain. Today, Santiago remains one of Spain's most vital cities and is the capital of Galicia.

THE LAY OF THE LAND

Geography keeps Galicia isolated. The Miño River to the south creates a natural border between the Spanish province and Portugal, while the Cordillera Cantábrica (Cantabrian Mountains) buffer Galicia from Spain's broad, central plateau. Thus Galicia stands apart, looking out over endless waters where the Atlantic Ocean meets the Cantabrian Sea. The province breaks down into four regions: La Coruña, Pontevedra, Orense, and Lugo—each named for its capital city. Galicia is also well defined by its estuaries and the Rías Altas comprises the northern coasts of Galicia from the Atlantic shore in La Coruña, snaking around to the Cantabrian shores of Lugo. The Rías Baixas comprise the southern coast running down to Portugal.

If you choose to make Galicia home, pack your raincoat and umbrella—this is Spain's rainiest area and the drops fall some 300 days per year, most viciously in spring and winter. Still, the region has nothing on England and the sun shines plenty, especially in the summer when temperatures can hover around 70°F. In winter, temperatures rarely go below 40°F on the coast; inland they can dip below freezing and bring with them heavy snow.

Local Language

Like Catalan and Basque, Gallego is a regional language of Spain. However, unlike its linguistic cousins, it is not so politically charged. Though it is the official co-language of the region, Gallego is not used as much in day-to-day conversation as Castilian Spanish. Only if you get way off-the-beaten path will you notice a shift with more rural dwellers speaking Gallego. However, if you plan on living here long-term, it would be wise to shore up your Spanish with a little bit of Gallego.

WHERE TO LIVE

There are about as many living options in Galicia as there are shades of green. Maybe you'd prefer a seaside home on one of Galicia's many *rías* where you can watch trawlers pull in their catch every afternoon and dine on that same fish that very evening. Or you could do like many starry-eyed expatriates and buy a rambling old stone home inland to fix up for yourself or run as a B&B. If you want a little of all of the above, yet still need a big city location for work, school, or sanity, Galicia is home to some bustling urban centers including Santiago de Compostela, La Coruña, and Pontevedra.

Santiago de Compostela

Of all the legends in Galicia, the one that founded Santiago de Compostela is the most notorious. As the story is told, the body of Santiago (Saint James) was brought to Galicia by stone boat after he died in Jerusalem. Once on land, the apostle's body was carried inland and buried in what is today Santiago de Compostela. The grave was forgotten until 813, when a star led a religious hermit to it. What perfect timing! The Reconquista was just beginning and the Christian forces needed a saint to rally around. Santiago was proclaimed the patron saint of Christian Spain, and a church was built on the spot. Soon, the *campus stellae* (field of the star)—from which the name Compostela is derived—became a bustling town as Christians from across Europe made their way over the Pyrenees and through the peninsula to pay homage to Santiago. Their footsteps wore the path of the Camino de Santiago that generations of

© CANDY LEE LABALLE

Santiago's famed cathedral rises above the city's neighborhoods.

pilgrims still follow today. However, modern pilgrims soon find out that it is the city that holds the true magic.

Santiago de Compostela (Santiago for short) shimmers in the distinct medieval hues of gray and stone. In addition to its imposing thousand-year-old cathedral, the city's **Casco Viejo** (Old Center) is so full of historic buildings that it has been designated a UNESCO World Heritage Site. But Santiago is no museum. During the school year, the place is alive with the activity of university students. During the summer months, they are replaced by tourists. Both groups amp up the city's population of 93,000 and ensure that Santiago is abuzz with cultural events, restaurants, bars, boutiques, and just about any perk of modern life you could want.

If you want to live among history in the Casco Viejo, or a bordering neighborhood, you won't be alone. This is one of the most sought-after addresses in the city and the prices reflect that—while they're relatively inexpensive by Spanish standards, they're costly in Galicia. A two-bedroom apartment will rent for about €600 and sell for €200,000 and up. However, many places in this area are sold *a reformar* (to renovate) which translates into prices as low as €140,000.

Look outside the center for more modern housing and quieter surroundings. Southwest of Plaza de Galicia, you'll find a smart, residential zone filled with shopping, schools, and comfortable homes. Prices are about the same as they are in the city center. For something more rural, head just a few minutes outside of the city to a surrounding neighborhood such as **Teo,** an upscale residential zone located amid green rolling hills. There is a good international school in the area, Chester College, and plenty of new housing, most of it detached homes and chalets. You can rent one for as low as €700, to buy you'll spend a minimum of €280,000.

La Coruña

Flinty New Englanders will feel right at home in La Coruña—an attractive, maritime city situated on a piece of terra firma thrust out into Atlantic waters. Located in the Rías Altas, the city is part of Galicia's most breathtaking sweep of land. Just southwest of the city, you'll find the Costa da Morte (Coast of Death), a piece of coast mercilessly ravished by the Atlantic Ocean. It earned its macabre name eons ago when ship after medieval wooden ship sunk in its impetuous waters. Ancient Celtic legends say that whole villages have even been captured and sunk by these waters. The scenery is as magical as the myths, full of theatrical cliffs, mist-soaked skies, churning seas, wild gray beaches, and some of the loveliest tangerine sunsets you'll see in your life.

The city of La Coruña has its own myth-filled origin. It says that Hercules founded the city when he killed one of his enemies here. A lighthouse was eventually built over the victim's body. The facts are nearly as impressive. The Torre de Hércules (Tower of Hercules) lighthouse was actually built in the 2nd century by the Romans and it is the oldest, working lighthouse in Europe.

La Coruña is the second largest city in Galicia with 244,000 residents (over 400,000 counting the metropolitan area). Their friendly demeanor is a soothing counterpart to the city's dramatic location, surrounded by the roiling waves of the Atlantic. Its size means that La Coruña can also offer pretty much anything you will need from groceries to gourmet restaurants while the oceanfront location means miles of lovely beaches within walking distance of the city center.

Some of the most popular places to live in town can be found on La Coruña's isthmus, which leads to a large headland where the **Ciudad Vieja**—the oldest part of the city—is located. The lively Plaza María Pita is the heart of this area and it is filled with stately arcades, popular cafés and bars, and city hall. The Avenida de la Marina, a wide seaside avenue, is another popular area and its *galerías* are among the most photographed sites in La Coruña. These white-framed glass balconies were added to the old stone buildings facing the sea in the 19th century to allow residents to enjoy as much sun as possible while keeping out the rain and wind. To rent a two-bedroom in either of these zones, you can pay as low as €500. To buy the same will start at about €200,000.

Pontevedra

With a population of 80,000, Pontevedra is big enough to be considered a small city—one with a long, colorful, maritime tradition. Christopher Columbus's boat, the Santa María, was built and set sail from these waters, and perhaps that's why a local fable claims that Columbus was born in Pontevedra. (As of press time, the Italians had yet to comment.) Fishing is still a vital part of the local economy today, and mussel farms are scattered throughout the area.

The city is situated in the greater province of Pontevedra which is located in the Rías Baixas, the lower estuaries of the Galician coasts. This area is markedly greener, tamer, and warmer than the Rías Altas. The city is located at the end of the expansive Ría de Pontevedra. All around are broad beaches of fine sand facing the calm waters of the *ría*. Within the city, the Lérez river helps delineate the **Zona Monumental** (the old city center). The tangle of cobbled streets are lined with imposing granite buildings in styles from baroque to neoclassical and it is hard to walk more than a block without stumbling upon a lovely old plaza full of lively cafés. This lively, yet historic, ambience makes this one of the most popular places to live in Pontevedra. A two-bedroom apartment rents for about €500 a month, and prices begin around €180,000 to buy. If you want to be in the city but prefer a quieter residential zone, consider looking for a place in the new town. The stately city gardens, Jardines de Vicenti and Alameda, add a whiff of green to this area just west of the historic district. Prices here are about equal to those in the old quarter.

GETTING AROUND

Galicia's larger towns are compact enough to walk in though the rain may send you scurrying for the bus. If you plan ahead and are a bit flexible, you can also move around the coastal areas pretty well via public transportation. However, keep in mind that Galicia is mainly rural and amenities, cultural opportunities, and the best beaches are spread out, far from mass transit. If you want to head off to the interior at a moment's notice to take in a cheese festival or go trout fishing, you'll really need a car.

Asturias and Cantabria

Let's get one thing straight. Asturias is the one and only piece of Spain that was never conquered by the Moors—and yes, it matters. Asturianos are proud of that history. It means the region was Spanish before Spain even existed, and that distinguishes it from the rest of the country. Yet in many ways, Asturias is linked to the areas that surround it. The Celts kicked off the region's history around the 6th century B.C., and that's something that Asturias has in common with Cantabria—the region to the east. In fact, Castro de Coaña in Asturias is one of the country's best-preserved examples of a Celt fortified town.

Both Asturias and Cantabria are situated on the Cantabrian Sea in a particularly rumpled stretch of coast of imposing cliffs and inviting coves. The beaches are some of the loveliest in the country—silvery white and flanked by velvety green hills—with names like Playa del Silencio, the Beach of Silence. Add a backdrop of snowcapped mountain peaks riddled with crystal clear mountain streams coursing through dramatic gorges and you start to get an idea of just how unexpectedly breathtaking this region is.

Lining the coast, you'll find fishing villages, a few of which have evolved into summer resorts, while others have grown into industrial ports. The mountainous interior is dotted with fertile pastures and rustic villages filled with pre-Romanesque churches, and the stone homes and the rustic *hórreos*

PRIME LIVING LOCATIONS

© CELLAR TOURS / WWW.CELLARTOURS.COM

The Asturias flag flies on a boat on the coast of Asturias.

(raised, wooden granaries) so typical of the region. The inland regions are also ideal for dairy farming—an unusual benefit in Spain where summer temperatures typically grow too hot for cows—the potent blue cheese Cabrales hails from here where it is cured in caves in the mountains. This is also *sidra* (hard cider) country and locals have been brewing it since the 8th century. Learning to *escanciar* (pour *sidra* from over your head) is a fun goal for new residents to pursue.

THE LAY OF THE LAND

The autonomous regions of Asturias and Cantabria run for some 230 miles along the Cantabrian coast. The interior is dominated by the Cordillera Cantábrica (Cantabrian Mountains) which runs east-west nearly parallel to the sea. The most spectacular of the mountains are the Picos de Europa which rise suddenly and severely to nearly 9,000 feet just a few miles from the shore. Though a relatively small range, the Picos are some of the most dramatic and treacherous in the world. Within they offer clear glacial lakes, ancient Romanesque churches, and pint-sized villages of stone houses tucked into verdant valleys.

All those pastures and meadows need water to stay so green, and it's no surprise that Asturias and Cantabria see their share of rain. Winter is the wettest time of year but the sun shines a lot in summer when temperatures average in the high 70°F range. In winter, the temperature dips into the low-to-mid 40s and the interior can get very heavy snowfall.

WHERE TO LIVE

Many are drawn to this area with the idea of disappearing into rural bliss in the interior or settling in a tiny seaside fishing village. The bustling coastal resort towns offer a bit of both worlds—remote charm but ample amenities. If this sounds like you, consider Ribadesella, Asturias which hosts an international canoe festival on the Río Sella—one of the biggest rivers in the region. The delightful port town of Llanes, is another option. The most popular resort in Asturias, it boasts a medieval city center and a dramatic stretch of coast pockmarked with pristine beaches, secluded coves, and a few very active blowholes. In Cantabria, the village of Castro-Urdiales is one of the coast's most scenic fishing ports, boasting a fine beach, excellent seafood, and a very dramatic Gothic church. Comillas, is one of Cantabria's busier coastal towns—and among its most lovely. It offers a medieval city center surrounded by impressive Catalan *modernisme* architecture including a sunflower-covered house by Gaudí.

However, for all these towns' winning points, they slow down considerably off-season, with many shops and restaurants shutting down entirely. If you want proximity to the best of Asturias and Cantabria without depriving yourself of basic services (and human company), you would do better in a larger city—one that offers its own set of diversions, a host of amenities, and is still just miles from the region's lush natural beauty. Oviedo and Santander are very good options. Oviedo and its surroundings have been declared a UNESCO World Heritage Site for its impressive 1,100-year-old pre-Romanesque churches. Santander has a distinctive, upper-crust charm and a dream location right on a stunning

living way off the beaten path in inner Asturias

bay. And as capitals of Asturias and Cantabria respectively, they are bustling hubs of commerce, well connected to the rest of Spain.

Oviedo

The capital of Asturias, Oviedo (pop. 200,000) is a pleasing blend of medieval and modern. It is compact and easily walkable with a pedestrian historic quarter and a bustling cultural scene including cutting-edge restaurants, lively festivals, and a large university that has been educating locals since around 1600. However, the real treat in Oviedo is its collection of pre-Romanesque buildings which are dotted throughout the city and had a recent cameo in the 2008 Woody Allen film *Vicky Cristina Barcelona*. In fact, Oviedo is quite enamored with the filmmaker and wandering among the cobbled city streets you'll find a life-sized statue of Allen complete with bronze-carved glasses.

Oviedo's main street, Calle de Uría leads straight from the train station to the city's old section by way of the Campo de San Francisco, a grassy park. The old town's collection of sites includes Plaza de la Constitución and the rambling Mercado El Fontán. Locals and tourist alike flock to Calle Gascona, known locally as the "boulevard of cider" because it is home to several boisterous

a busy plaza at lunchtime in Oviedo

siderías (cider houses). An address here is well sought after and a two-bedroom rental will start around €600 per month and €200,000 and up to buy, depending on location and amenities.

If you want more tranquil surroundings, the communities of **La Fresneda** or **Soto de Llanera,** barely 10 miles outside of the city, are popular options. They both offer detached houses, recreation facilities, and close proximity to The English School of Asturias, one of the few international schools in this area. Rental on a small home will start around €800 and the purchase prices for the same begins around €250,000.

Santander

Although the fire that raged through Santander (pop. 183,000) in 1941 reduced a good amount of the town to ashes, it was rebuilt into an elegant city with fine properties, and an active port on a pretty marina. The capital of Cantabria, the city has been a popular resort since King Alfonso XIII took to vacationing here in the 1900s, and sun-seekers and surfers still flock to the city when the days grow warm and the local population is considered one of the more upscale in Spain.

Santander is laid out in a long, amorphous strip along the northern side of the Bahía de Santander, and it reaches out to the Península de la Magdalena where the English-styled Palacio de la Magdalena looms over the spot where the bay meets the Cantabrian sea. The entire 24 hectares of the peninsula have been converted into a park where seniors play cards under shady trees, young people rent bikes, and families bask in the view. Just north of the peninsula, the lovely Sardinero beach unfolds. It is one of the most chic spots to catch rays, and the barrio of El Sardinero itself is a well-heeled enclave.

Residential areas are spread throughout the city, and should you want to settle in the town's center where the cultural life is most vibrant, you'll find

THE PICOS DE EUROPA

They're not the highest mountains in Europe and they're not even the tallest ones in Spain, so how is it that the Picos de Europa get away with being dubbed *the* mountains of Europe? There's justice in that badge. The stalwart crags in Spain's north country managed to throw the advancing Romans for a loop and centuries later, the natural, limestone wall blocked the advancing Moors. They may be relatively small in stature, but the Picos de Europa helped change the course of European history.

The mountains were christened by sailors who, when returning to Europe, saw the peaks rising up over the horizon. At the sight of the snowy hills, the sea-weary crews knew that they were home. These days, the summits are part of one of Spain's largest natural parks. Within the Picos, you'll find spectacular gorges, steeplelike peaks, verdant green valleys, medieval stone villages, cheese-curing caves, and crystal clear rivers and lakes.

Lying very close to the coast, the Picos de Europa span Asturias, Cantabria, and León. They soar suddenly up to 8,000 feet in under 13 miles. The effect is almost surreal, with the snow-covered peaks towering above the beaches and surrounding pasture land. Three river gorges divide the range into three tremendous massifs: Andara in the east, Urrieles in the center, and Cornión in the west. Across the range, there are 200 limestone peaks rising 6,500 feet above sea level with drops of up to 7,550 feet. The highest summits are in the central section, with three rising above 8,000 feet. There are three towns at the foot of the mountains that are popular base camps: Cangas de Onís, Arenas de Cabrales, and Potes (over the border in Cantabria). The mountains were formed by glacial action and the combination of millennia of glacial movement combined with slightly acidic rain on the limestone peaks resulted in erosion that led to the development of an immense underground drainage system full of caves. The deepest yet explored goes down over 4,500 feet.

Opportunities for outdoor activities abound: rock climbing, spelunking, backcountry skiing, horseback riding, mountain biking, four-wheel drive treks, fishing, and so on. Each of the main towns has tour operators and mountaineering stores where travelers can get maps or set off on guided treks. Most hotels in the area can also arrange activities or package tours for their guests. For those who prefer to ponder nature, there are countless quaint historic inns, cottage rentals, and bed-and-breakfasts sprinkled throughout the Picos. Most have views of the mountains and outdoor patios where visitors can breathe it all in.

The weather in the Picos is notoriously fickle. You may step out in short sleeves and warm temperatures only to find yourself shivering under a damp, cold fog a few hours later. Even the summer months feature a few chilly, cloudy days, but keep in mind that July and August are the traditional vacation months for Spain and thousands of Spaniards flock to the Picos during these months.

PRIME LIVING LOCATIONS

two-bedroom apartments renting for about €600 a month. To buy a comparable place will cost you anywhere between €160,000–300,000. Homes in Sardinero are more expensive and, although the area does have some independent homes, most people live in apartments. A two-bedroom runs €900 a month to rent and a minimum of €300,000 to buy.

GETTING AROUND

While both Oviedo and Santander have solid bus services that link the various neighborhoods in the city, a car is a vital asset for the same reason it is throughout the Cantabrian Coast. Although you can be

© CANDY LEE LABALLE

Colorful fishing boats are a common sight all along the Cantabrian Coast.

self-sufficient and reasonably entertained in the cities proper, you'll inevitably want to escape to a secluded beach or mountain village or make a shopping trip out to IKEA. And that means a car.

RESOURCES

Embassies and Consulates

UNITED STATES

Before moving to Spain, a visit to one of the Spanish Consulates in the United States is often essential. At the time of this writing, all Spanish consulate websites were "under construction," though general information can be found in the Ministry of the Interior's very confusing site (www.maec.es). Search for *"embajadas y consulados."*

CONSULATE GENERAL OF SPAIN IN BOSTON

31 St. James Ave., Suite 905
Boston, MA 02116
tel. 617/536-2506 or 617/536-2527
fax 617/536-8512
cog.boston@mae.es
Jurisdiction: Maine, Massachusetts, New Hampshire, Rhode Island, Vermont.

CONSULATE GENERAL OF SPAIN IN CHICAGO

180 N. Michigan Ave., Suite 1500
Chicago, IL 60601
tel. 312/782-4588 or 312/782-4589
fax 312/782-1635
conspainchicago@sbcglobal.net
Jurisdiction: Illinois, Indiana, Iowa, Kansas, Nebraska, North Dakota, South Dakota, Ohio, Kentucky, Michigan, Minnesota, Missouri, Wisconsin.

CONSULATE GENERAL OF SPAIN IN HOUSTON

1800 Bering Dr., Suite 660
Houston, TX 77057
tel. 713/783-6200
fax 713/783-6166
cog.houston@maec.es
Jurisdiction: New Mexico, Oklahoma, Texas.

CONSULATE GENERAL OF SPAIN IN LOS ANGELES

5055 Wilshire Blvd., Suite 960
Los Angeles, CA 90036
tel. 323/938-0158 or 323/938-0166
fax 323/938-2502
cog.losangeles@mae.es
Jurisdiction: California (Imperial, Inyo, Kern, Los Angeles, Orange, Riverside, San Bernardino, San Diego, San Luis Obispo, Santa Barbara and Ventura counties), Arizona, Colorado, Utah.

CONSULATE GENERAL OF SPAIN IN MIAMI

2655 Le Jeune Rd., Suite 203
Coral Gables, FL 33134
tel. 305/446-5511
fax 305/446-0585
cog.miami@mae.es
Jurisdiction: Florida, South Carolina, Georgia.

CONSULATE GENERAL OF SPAIN IN NEW ORLEANS

2102 World Trade Center
2 Canal St.
New Orleans, LA 70130
tel. 504/525-4951 or 504/525-7920
fax 504/525-4955
conspneworleans@correo.mae.es
Jurisdiction: Alabama, Arkansas, Louisiana, Mississippi, Tennessee.

CONSULATE GENERAL OF SPAIN IN NEW YORK

150 East 58th St., 30th Floor
New York, NY 10155
tel. 212/355-4080
fax 212/644-3751
cog.nuevayork@mae.es
Jurisdiction: New York, Connecticut, Delaware, Pennsylvania, New Jersey.

CONSULATE GENERAL OF SPAIN IN SAN FRANCISCO

1405 Sutter St.
San Francisco, CA 94109
tel. 415/922-2995
fax 415/931-9706
conspsfo@mail.mae.es
Jurisdiction: Alaska, California (except southern part), Hawaii, Idaho, Montana, Nevada, Oregon, Washington, Wyoming, and American possessions in the Pacific.

CONSULATE GENERAL OF SPAIN IN WASHINGTON, D.C.

2375 Pennsylvania Ave., N.W.
Washington, D.C. 20037
tel. 202/728-2330
fax 202/728-2302
cog.washington@mae.es
Jurisdiction: Maryland, Virginia, West Virginia, District of Columbia, North Carolina.

SPAIN

Only the embassy in Madrid and the consulate general in Barcelona can handle passport issues; the consulate agencies can provide basic support and forms. Information on consular services in Spain can be found at the embassy website.

UNITED STATES EMBASSY

C/Serrano, 75
28006 Madrid
tel. 91/587-2200
fax 91/587-2303
http://madrid.usembassy.gov

U.S. CONSULATE AGENCY FUENGIROLA (MÁLAGA)

Avda. Juan Gómez "Juanito," 8
Edificio Lucía 1-C
29640 Fuengirola (Málaga)
tel. 95/247-4891
fax 95/246-5189

U.S. CONSULATE AGENCY LA CORUÑA

C/Juana de Vega, 8, Piso 5, izquierda

15003 La Coruña
tel. 98/121-3233
fax 98/122-8808

U.S. CONSULATE AGENCY LAS PALMAS

Edificio ARCA
C/Los Martínez Escobar, 3-Oficina 7
35007 Las Palmas
tel. 92/827-1259
fax 92/822-5863

U.S. CONSULATE AGENCY PALMA DE MALLORCA

Edificio Reina Constanza, Porto Pi, 8-9D
07015 Palma de Mallorca
tel. 97/140-3707
fax 97/140-3971

U.S. CONSULATE AGENCY SEVILLA

Plaza Nueva 8, 2, E2-4
41001 Sevilla
tel. 95/421-8751
fax 95/422-0791

U.S. CONSULATE AGENCY VALENCIA

Dr. Romagosa, 1, 2, J
Valencia 46002
tel. 96/351-6973
fax 96/352-9565

U.S. CONSULATE GENERAL BARCELONA

Pso. Reina Elisenda de Montcada, 23
08034 Barcelona
tel. 93/280-2227
fax 93/280-6175
http://barcelona.usconsulate.gov

Planning Your Fact-Finding Trip

TRAVELING IN SPAIN

The official website of the Spanish Tourism Board is www.spain.info—it is incredibly complete, if a bit cumbersome to maneuver. In addition, each autonomous region, province, city, and most towns, have their own tourism websites. These should be key when planning your trip.

The following websites are all privately owned, some with profit-making in mind, and are quite exhaustive.

www.justspain.org
www.red2000.com/spain
www.sispain.org
www.travelinginspain.com

RESOURCES

GUIDED TOURS

Gastronomy Tours

CELLAR TOURS
C/Infantas, 27
28004 Madrid
tel. 91/521-3939
info@cellartours.com
www.cellartours.com
Cellar Tours offers luxury wine and gourmet tours throughout Spain. Their website is also a great resource for information about Spanish wines. Tours are also offered in Italy, Portugal, and Ireland.

VINTAGE SPAIN
C/Burgos, 9, 4, B
09200 Miranda de Ebro (Burgos)
tel. 94/731-0126
info@vintagespain.com
www.vintagespain.com

Bike Tours

BIKE SPAIN
Plaza de la Villa, 1
28009 Madrid
tel. 91/559-0653
info@bikespain.info
www.bikespain.info
Pablo and his crew of guides lead daily excursions around Madrid and longer bike tours throughout Spain—their trips through La Rioja wine country are particularly popular.

CICLOTURISME I MEDI AMBIENT
C/Impressors Oliva, 4-A
17005 Girona
tel. 97/222-1047
info@cicloturisme.com
www.cicloturisme.com
Bike tours in the rolling hills of Girona—where Lance Armstrong trains—with an emphasis on ecological awareness.

Adventure Tours

IBERIAN WILDLIFE TOURS
Apto. 59
39570 Potes (Cantabria)
tel. 94/273-5154
teresa@iberianwildlife.com
www.iberianwildlife.com
A British resident in the Picos de Europa leads wildlife and walking tours through some of Spain's loveliest landscapes.

RANCHO HUERTA DEL BATÁN
Apto. 31
29100 Coín (M,#135>laga)
tel. 95/245-5010
info@horseridingspain.com
www.horseridingspain.com
Horse-riding vacations in Andalucía run by a British-Dutch couple who are members of the Andalusian Equestrian Federation.

Cultural Tours

ICONO SERVEIS
C/Muntaner, 185, 1-2
08036 Barcelona
tel. 93/410-1405
info@iconoserveis.com
www.iconoserveis.com
This association of certified guides offers very unique culture and history tours in Barcelona and Cataluña.

TOUR GUIDE IN SPAIN
Urb Bahia de Denia
C/Llac Maracaibo, 3
Apto. 127
03700 Denia (Alicante)
tel. 60/718-4008
kellyodonnell@tourguideinspain.com
http://tourguideinspain.com
A Chicago native resident in Spain for over 20 years offers tailor-made cultural and history tours.

Making the Move

LIVING IN SPAIN
www.allthingsspain.net
www.escapeartist.com/Live_In_Spain
www.euroresidentes.com
www.expatica.com/es
www.iberianature.com
www.mocaenboca.tv
www.spainexpat.com
www.spainlawyer.com
www.spanishfiestas.com
www.spanish-living.com

www.typicallyspanish.com

HOUSING CONSIDERATIONS
www.eyeonspain.com
www.idealista.com
www.kyero.com
www.loquo.com/en_us
www.property-net-spain.com
www.spanishrealestateforum.com

Language and Education

SPANISH INSTRUCTION IN SPAIN

International House
International House (www.ihspain.com) has locations throughout Spain—call individual schools for bookings.

INTERNATIONAL HOUSE BARCELONA
C/Trafalgar, 14
08010, Barcelona
tel. 93/268-4511
spanish@bcn.ihes.com

INTERNATIONAL HOUSE CÓRDOBA
Rodríguez Sánchez, 15
14003 Cordoba
tel. 95/748-8002
info@academiahispanica.com

INTERNATIONAL HOUSE COSTA DE LA LUZ
C/José Castrillón Shelly, 22
11150 Vejer de la Frontera (Cádiz)
tel. 95/644-7060
info@lajanda.org

INTERNATIONAL HOUSE MADRID
C/Zurbano, 8
28010 Madrid
tel. 91/319-7224
spanish@ihmadrid.com

INTERNATIONAL HOUSE PALMA DE MALLORCA
Plaza de Cort, 11
07001 Palma de Mallorca
tel. 97/172-6408
ihpalma@pal.ihes.com

INTERNATIONAL HOUSE SAN SEBASTIÁN
C/Mundaiz 8,
20012 San Sebastián
tel. 94/332-6680
info@lacunza.com

INTERNATIONAL HOUSE SEVILLA
Albareda, 19
41001 Seville, Spain
tel. 95/450-2131
clic@clic.es

INTERNATIONAL HOUSE VALENCIA
C/La Nave, 22
46003 Valencia
tel. 96/353-0404
info@espanole.es

Escuela Oficial de Idioma
Though you'll have to go through some bureacracy to get into these Official Language Schools run by the government, once admitted you'll enjoy high-level instruction at very low prices.

ESCOLA OFICIAL DE IDIOMES BARCELONA
Avda. Drassanes, s/n
08001 Barcelona
tel. 93/324-9330
www.eoibd.cat

ESCUELA OFICIAL DE IDIOMA DE MADRID
C/Jesús Maestro, 5
28003 Madrid
tel. 91/533-5802
www.eoidiomas.com

ESCUELA OFICIAL DE IDIOMA DE SEVILLA
C/Dr. Fedriani, 21
tel. 95/565-6869
http://sevilla.eeooii.org
www.eoidonheo.org

ESCUELA OFICIAL DE IDIOMA DE SAN SEBASTIÁN
C/Zemoria, 24
tel. 94/32-86311
www.eoidonheo.org

INTERNATIONAL UNIVERSITIES
EUROPEAN UNIVERSITY (BARCELONA)
C/Ganduxer, 70
08021 Barcelona
tel. 93/201-8171
www.euruni.edu

INSTITUTO DE EMPRESA (IE)
Business School (one of the top-ranked MBA programs in the world)
C/María de Molina, 11
28006 Madrid
tel. 91/568-9600
www.ie.edu

INSTITUTO DE EMPRESA (IE) UNIVERSITY
Campus Santa Cruz la Real
C/Cardenal Zúñiga, 12
40003 Segovia-Spain
tel. 92/141-2410
www.ie.edu/university

ST. LOUIS UNIVERSITY MADRID
Avda. del Valle, 34
28003 Madrid
tel. 91/554-5858

Health

PRIVATE INSURANCE COMPANIES
Here are a few of the most popular companies that insure foreigners living in Spain as well as a fully licensed Spain-based English broker who will set up your policy for no fee at all—the insurance companies pay him directly, no cost to you.

MAINLY HEALTH PLANS
David Harris Geritie
C/Vizconde de Valoria 7
19210 Yunquera de Henares (Guadalajara)
tel. 60/952-2300
www.mainlyhealthplans.com

ADESLAS
www.adeslas.es

ASISA
www.asisa.es

CIGNA
www.cigna.es

DKV
www.dkvseguros.com

MAPFRE
www.mapfre.com

SANITAS
www.sanitas.es

SAFETY
You can find out the correct number to dial for any emergency by calling national operator information at tel. 11818.

Here are some additional numbers to be aware of:

AMBULANCE
tel. 061

AMBULANCE, FIRE DEPARTMENT, AND/OR POLICE
tel. 112

COMISIÓN DE INVESTIGACIÓN DE MALOS TRATOS A MUJERES (COMMISSION OF INVESTIGATION INTO THE ABUSE OF WOMEN)
tel. 90/010-0009

FIRE DEPARTMENT
tel. 080 or 085
A few parts of the country use a different number. Upon moving to a new place, find out the correct number in your area.

POLICE DEPARTMENT NONEMERGENCY
tel. 091 or 092

Finance and Legal Matters

CASTRO, SUEIRO & VARELA
C/Alcalá, 75, 1
28009 Madrid
tel. 91/577-5020
fax 91/431-5931
www.csvabogados.com
Lawyer Marco Bolognini (mbolognini@ csvabogados.com) handles foreign investment activity and the setting up of businesses in Spain for this firm, one of the most prestigious in Madrid. Spanish, English, French and Italian are spoken.

JOSÉ MARÍA POLLOS HERNÁNDEZ
C/Lope de Rueda, 3-1
28009 Madrid
tel. 60/763-3858
An excellent lawyer in Madrid experienced with immigration issues.

LAWBIRD LEGAL SERVICES
Edificio Alfil
C/Ricardo Soriano, 19-4
29600 Marbella
tel. 95/286-1890
fax 95/286-1695
ifv@lawbird.com
www.lawbird.com

Full-service law firm dealing with any legal matters an expat in Spain might encounter—immigration, taxes, purchasing a home, setting up a company. The website—along with their informative site—www.belegal.com—is chock-full of useful information.

LTF, LEGAL, TAX, AND FINANCIAL ADVISORS
C/Goya, 38, 5 izquierda
tel. 91/426-1173
alejandra.pastor@ltfadvisors.com
This is a popular law firm for small to mid-sized expat-run businesses in Madrid. They also offer *gestor* (administration) services.

STRONG ABOGADOS
C/Balmes,173, 2-2
Barcelona 08006
tel. 93/215-5393
pstrong@strongabogados.com
www.strongabogados.com
Another full-service firm offering business services—starting or relocating businesses in Spain, labor law, taxation—as well as individual legal services.

RESOURCES

Communications

TELEPHONE AND INTERNET

Though Telefónica is the main phone company in Spain, many other telephony companies repackage Telefónica services and bundle them in packages including home phone, cell phone, Internet, and cable television.

JAZZTEL
tel. 1565
www.jazztel.com

MOVISTAR
tel. 1485
www.movistar.es

ONO
tel. 1400
www.ono.es

ORANGE
tel.1414
www.orange.es

TELEFÓNICA
tel. 1004
www.telefonicaonline.com

VODAFONE
tel. 1444
www.vodafone.es

EXPRESS MAIL SERVICES

DHL
tel. 90/212-2424 or 90/212-3030
www.dhl.es

FEDEX
tel. 90/210-0871
www.fedex.com/es

MRW
tel. 90/230-0400
www.mrw.es

SEUR
www.seur.com

UPS
tel. 90/288-8820
www.ups.com/europe/es

Travel and Transportation

BY AIR
AEROPUERTOS ESPAÑOLES Y NAVEGACIÓN AÉREA (AENA)
tel. 90/240-4704
www.aena.es
All of Spain's airports are operated by this organization and full details of each airport as well as regularly updated flight information is available on their website.

BY TRAIN
RED NACIONAL DE LOS FERROCARRILES ESPAÑOLES (RENFE)
tel. 90/224-0202
www.renfe.es.
RENFE runs the country's exhaustive train network as well as the Cercanías (commuter trains) in the major cities.

BY CAR
REAL AUTÓMOVIL CLUB DE ESPAÑA (RACE)
tel. 90/240-4545
www.race.es
Similar to AAA in the United States, this century-old organization offers information on all aspects of driving. It has offices throughout Spain as listed on its website.

Prime Living Locations

MADRID
www.aboutmadrid.com

THE AMERICAN WOMEN'S CLUB OF MADRID
www.awcmadrid.com
www.descubremadrid.com

THE INTERNATIONAL NEWCOMERS CLUB OF MADRID
http://incmadrid.com
www.in-madrid.com
www.madaboutmadrid.com
www.multimadrid.com

Real Estate Agents

AGENCIA ASTORGA
C/Luchana, 40, 2E
28015 Madrid
tel. 91/308-0761
www.agenciaastorga.com

AGINSUR API
C/Francisco De Rojas, 5-1
28010 Madrid
tel. 91/446-1111
www.aginsur.es

COLDWELL BANKER LAS ROZAS
Av. Iglesia, 6
28231 Las Rozas (Madrid)
tel. 91/636-3780
www.coldwellbanker.es

UNICA INMOBILIARIA
C/Jorge Juan, 78 5C
28009 Madrid
tel. 91/576-0101

Relocation Agencies

CROWN RELOCATIONS
C/Camino Ancho s/n
Polígono Industrial Gitesa
28814 Daganzo de Arriba (Madrid)
tel. 91/878-2410
www.crownrelo.com

RELOCATIONS ESPAÑA
C/Arturo Soria, 263 B
28033 Madrid
tel. 91/384-3900
www.relocationspain.com

SPANISH RELOCATION NETWORK
Av. Ahones, 8B dcha.
28043 Madrid
tel. 91/388-7777
www.spanishrelocation.com

BARCELONA AND CATALUÑA

THE AMERICAN SOCIETY OF BARCELONA
www.amersoc.com
www.barcelona-metropolitan.com
www.barcelonaconnect.com
www.barcelona-tourist-guide.com
www.bcn.es
www.extraguide.de

Real Estate Agents: Barcelona

ALTING GRUPO INMOBILARIO
Torre Barcelona
Av. Diagonal, 477
08036 Barcelona
tel. 93/505-4040
www.alting.com

BOURGEOIS SERVICIOS INMOBILARIOS
C/Selva de Mar, 7
08019 Barcelona
tel. 93/415-3535
www.ebourgeois.com

FINCAS OCCIDENTE
C/Castillejos, 31 Local C
08190 Sant Cugat del Valles (Barcelona)
tel. 93/675-1848
www.fincasoccidente.com

FORCADELL INTERNATIONAL REAL ESTATE CONSULTANTS
Pl. Universitat, 3
08007 Barcelona
tel. 93/496-5400
www.forcadell.com

Relocation Agencies: Barcelona

BARCELONA RELOCATION SERVICES
Psg. Gràcia, 52 ático
08007 Barcelona
tel. 93/203-4935
www.barcelona-relocation.com

CROSSING CULTURES
C/Josep Carner, 5
08193 Bellaterra (Barcelona)
tel. 93/580-8729
www.crossing-cultures.com

ERES RELOCATION
Av. Diagonal 598, 3-1
08021 Barcelona
tel. 93/200-1476
www.eresrelocation.com

OLYMPIC ADVISORS
C/Platon, 6, ático
08021 Barcelona
tel. 93/414-4000
www.oasl.net

Real Estate Agents: Costa Brava

BCI-BRACA CASA REAL ESTATE
Pl. St. Pere, 3
17480 Roses (Girona)
te. 97/215-4030
www.bci-immobilien.de

CATALAN LIFE PROPERTIES
Carrer Sant Llorenç, 25A
17220 Sant Feliu de Guíxols (Girona)
tel. 97/232-7311
www.catalanlife.com

COLLECTION PROPERTIES
C/Josep Tarradellas, 1
17310 Lloret de Mar (Girona)
tel. 97/236-9505
www.costabrava.de

VAN DEN HOUT ENTERPRISES
C/Roger de LLúria, 85
08009 Barcelona (Spain)
tel. 60/932-1308
www.vdhenterprises.com

Real Estate Agents: Sitges

FINQUES FARRERAS
Psg. de la Ribera, 10
08870 Sitges (Barcelona)
tel. 93/894-4851
www.afarreras.com

KEY STAR
Po. de la Ribera, 27
08870 Sitges
tel. 93/811-4614
www.keystar.org

VALENCIA, LAS ISLAS BALEARES, AND MURCIA

http://costacalida.angloinfo.com
www.alicante-spain.com
www.balearics.com
www.costablanca.org
www.costablanca-news.com
www.costacalida.com
www.roundtownnews.co.uk
www.thisisvalencia.com

Real Estate Agents: Valencia City

RAWLINS HOLDEN VALENCIA
C/San Vicente de Paul, 19
46160 Lliria (Valencia)
tel. 96/202-8218
www.rawlinsholden.com

VALENCIA PROPERTY
C/Virgen del Rosario, 31 bajo
46185 La Pobla del Vallbona (Valencia)
tel. 90/274-7425
www.valencia-property.com

VILLAS VALENCIA
Apartado 37
46119 Naquera (Valencia)
tel. 96/168-0025
www.villasvalencia.com

Real Estate Agents: Costa Blanca

BTB
C/Arquitecto Urteaga, 31
03730 Jávea (Alicante)
tel. 96/579-3059
www.btb.es

MOLINO VILLAS
Centro Comercial Kristal Mar, 24E
03724 Moraira (Alicante)
tel. 96/649-2335
www.molinovillas.com

Real Estate Agents: Murcia
DREAM SPAIN
C/Pantano de Talave, 11
El Carmoli
30368 Los Urrutias (Murcia)
tel. 62/654-4987

**HARTLAND PROPERTY
CONSULTANTS**
C/Pinos, 5
30368 Cartagena (Murcia)
tel. 96/813-4784
www.hartlandproperty.com

Real Estate Agents: Las Islas Baleares
Some of the agents on the Balearic Islands work in specific sections, while others work throughout the whole of the islands. Here are a few that have developed good reputations.

BALEARIC PROPERTIES
Via Pollentia, 3
07460 Pollensa (Mallorca)
tel. 97/153-2221
www.balearic-properties.com

MALLORCA DOMIZIL
C/Isaac Peral, 19
07157 Puerto de Andratx (Mallorca)
tel. 97/1674-767
www.mallorca-domizil.com

**MIA-MALLORCA PROPERTY
AND INVESTMENT**
C/Hostalets, 1
07181 Portals Nous (Mallorca)
tel. 97/167-9025
www.mia-mallorca.com

ANDALUCÍA
www.andalucia.com
www.exploreseville.com
www.surinenglish.com
www.theolivepress.es
www.vivagranada.com

Real Estate Agents: Sevilla
INMOBILIARIA ESTADIO
Av. Luis de Morales, 22, 3B
41018 Sevilla
tel. 95/453-7528
www.inmobiliariaestadio.com

MASTER PROPIEDAD
Av. Ramón Carande, 8
41013 Sevilla
tel. 95/470-9175
www.masterpropiedad.com

Real Estate Agents: Granada
INTERCENTRO INMOBILIARIA
C/Elviroa, 111 bajo
18010 Granada
tel. 95/820-2078
www.inmobiliariaintercentro.com

OASIS SERVICIOS INMOBILIARIOS
C/Navas, 20, 1
18009 Granada
tel. 95/822-8930
www.aloasis.com

Real Estate Agents: Costa del Sol
PANORAMA
Edificio Centro Expo
Búlevar Príncipe Aflonso Hohenlohe, s/n,
29600 Marbella (Málaga)
tel. 95/286-3750
www.panorama.es

PASSEPARTOUT ANDALUZ
Pasaje Brazales, Milenio A13
29649 Miraflores, Mijas-Costa (Málaga)
tel. 66/162-6298
www.pamarbella.com

SCANDISOL COSTA DEL SOL
C/Santa Ana, 11
29680 Estepona (Málaga)
tel. 95/279-2296
www.scandisol.com

THE CANTABRIAN COAST
www.aboutsantiagodecompostela.com
www.asturiaspicosdeeuropa.com

RESOURCES

www.basquecountry-tourism.com
www.galiciaguide.com
www.lavozdeasturias.es
www.santanderspain.com
www.turismodecantabria.com
www.whatsansebastian.com

Real Estate Agents: Paás Vasco
FINCAS ABANDO
C/Colón de Larreátegui, 35
48009 Bilbao
tel. 94/661-3131
www.fincas abando.es

INMOBILIARIA ORTUONDO
Gran Vía, 58
48011 Bilbao
tel. 94/442-2058
www.ortuondo.com

INMOBIRA
Av. Tolosa, 5, 3
20018 San Sebastián
tel. 94/345-5432
www.inmobira.com

VALENCIAGA AGENCIA
C/Churruca 3,1
20004 San Sebastián
tel. 94/343-0784
www.valenciaga.es

Real Estate Agents: Galicia
BK PROPERTY
C/Arida, 174
36980 O Grove (Pontevedra)
tel. 65/597-0660
www.bkproperty.com

FONTELA 2000
C/Alcalde Pérez Ardá, 51-53
tel. 98/128-2073
www.fontela2000.com

GALICIA PROPERTY NET
Edificio San Francisco, Portal 2, 3-A
C/Fray Luis Rodriguez
15200 Noia, (La Coruña)
tel. 68/755-2497
www.galiciaproperty.net

Real Estate Agents: Asturias and Cantabria
AGENCIA RODRÍGUEZ INMOBILIARIA
C/San Bernabé, 2 1
33002 Oviedo
tel. 98/521-6869
www.agenciarodriguez.es

DISTRITO INMOBILIARIO
Av. Reina Victoria, 15, bajo
39003 Santander
tel. 94/231-8281
www.distritoinmobiliario.com

Glossary

abierto *open*
abono *pass, coupon book*
aquí *here*
avda. *avenida*
ayuntamiento *town hall*
C/or calle, *street*
caña *small draft beer*
casi *almost*
cecina *dry cured beef*
d.o. *appellation (for wine, food)*
enchufe *contact or inside information*
gobierno *government*
gran *great*
jamón *spanish cured ham*
jerez *sherry*
marcha *to go out at night*
morcilla *blood sausage (usually smoked)*

mundo *world*
nada *nothing*
nunca *never*
parador *state-run luxury hotel*
pl. *plaza*
playa *beach*
tapeo *to go out for tapas*
tarde *afternoon*
tiempo *weather*
todo *all*
todos *everyone*
tortilla *spanish potato omelette*
vamos *let's go*
vida *life*
vino blanco *white wine*
vino tinto *red wine*

Spanish Phrasebook

Too many new arrivals to Spain make mistake of thinking that everyone will speak English. In reality, the lack of English spoken in the country makes it a great place for both English teachers looking to earn euros and students of Spanish seeking language immersion. Part of the problem was that under the rule of Franco no languages other than Castilian Spanish were allowed to be used. All films and television shows were dubbed into Spanish—a practice still in use today—meaning that few people got to hear other languages spoken. Another problem is the school system. English (and other language) teachers were rarely speakers of the language themselves and thus lessons were grammar-focused rather than focused on actual usage. Finally, Spaniards are a proud people and are reticent to embarrass themselves by speaking poorly. Even the most fluent speakers of English will swear up and down that they don't speak a word. What this all comes down to is one thing—you'll need

some basic Spanish to get acclimated in the country and eventually you'll should become fluent. And one word of advice, attempting to speak even a little Spanish will be appreciated and can make the difference between a cold reception or a warm welcome. The best phrase you can learn is, *lo siento, no hablo castellano* (low SEE-en-toe, no a-BLO kas-TEE-ya-no), "I'm sorry, I don't speak Castilian Spanish." It lets the listener know that you can't speak their language, but you are respectful enough to acknowledge it. The worst thing you can do is just approach someone and start speaking English, it comes off as rude and insensitive.

Spanish commonly uses 30 letters—the familiar English 26, plus four straightforward additions: ch, ll, ñ, and rr, which are explained in "Consonants," below.

PRONUNCIATION

Once you learn them, Spanish pronunciation rules—in contrast to English rules—don't change. Spanish vowels generally sound softer than in English. (Note: The capitalized syllables below receive stronger accents.)

Vowels

a like ah, as in "hah": *agua* AH-gooah (water), *pan* PAHN (bread), and *casa* CAH-sah (house)

e like ay, as in "may:" *mesa* MAY-sah (table), *tela* TAY-lah (cloth), and *de* DAY (of, from)

i like ee, as in "need": *diez* dee-AYZ (ten), *comida* ko-MEE-dah (meal), and *fin* FEEN (end)

o like oh, as in "go": *peso* PAY-soh (weight), *ocho* OH-choh (eight), and *poco* POH-koh (a bit)

u like oo, as in "cool": *uno* OO-noh (one), *cuarto* KOOAHR-toh (room), and *usted* oos-TAYD (formal form of you); when it follows a "q" the **u** is silent: *qui* kay (what); when it follows an "h" or has an umlaut, it's pronounced like "w": Argüelles are-GWAY-yez (neighborhood in Madrid)

Consonants

b, d, f, k, l, m, n, p, q, s, t, v, w, x, y, z, and ch pronounced almost as in English; h occurs, but is silent – not pronounced at all.

c like k as in "keep": *cuarto* KOOAR-toh (room); when it precedes "e" or "i," pronounce **c** like th, as in "this": *cerveza* thair-VAY-sah (beer), *encima* ayn-THEE-mah (atop). Note that this lisping "th" is unique to Spanish in Spain and is not used by other speakers of Spanish.

g like g as in "gift" when it precedes "a," "o," "u," or a consonant: *gato* GAH-toh (cat), *hago* AH-goh (I do, make); otherwise, pronounce **g** like h as in "hat": *giro* HEE-roh (money order), *gente* HAYN-tay (people)

j like h, as in "has": *Jueves* HOOAY-vays (Thursday), *mejor* may-HOR (better)

ll like y, as in "yes": *toalla* toh-AH-yah (towel), *ellos* AY-yohs (they, them)

ñ like ny, as in "canyon": *año* AH-nyo (year), *señor* SAY-nyor (Mr., sir)

r is lightly trilled, with tongue at the roof of your mouth like a very light English d, as in "ready": *pero* PAY-doh (but), *tres* TDAYS (three), *cuatro* KOOAH-tdoh (four).

rr like a Spanish r, but with much more emphasis and trill. Let your tongue flap. Practice with *perro* (dog), *carretera* (highway), and Carrillo (proper name), then really let go with *ferrocarril* (railroad).

y sounds like the English y except when being used as the Spanish word for "and," as in "Alfonso y Susana." In such case, pronounce it like the English ee, as in "keep": Alfonso "ee" Susana

z is pronounced like a soft th as in "pith": *zapato* tha-PAH-toe (shoe), Zaragoza tha-ra-GO-tha (capital of Aragón).

Accent

The rule for accent, the relative stress given to syllables within a given word, is straightforward. If a word ends in a vowel, an n, or an s, accent the next-to-last syllable; if not, accent the last syllable.

Pronounce *gracias* GRAH-the-ahs (thank you), *orden* OHR-dayn (order), and *carretera* kah-ray-TAY-rah (highway) with stress on the next-to-last syllable.

Otherwise, accent the last syllable: *venir* vay-NEER (to come), *ferrocarril* fay-roh-cah-REEL (railroad), and *edad* ay-DAHD (age).

Exceptions to the accent rule are always marked with an accent sign: (á, é, í, ó, or ú), such as *teléfono* tay-LAY-foh-noh (telephone), *jabón* hah-BON (soap), and *rápido* RAH-pee-doh (rapid).

NUMBERS

zero *cero*
one *uno*
two *dos*
three *tres*
four *cuatro*

five *cinco*
six *seis*
seven *siete*
eight *ocho*
nine *nueve*
10 *diez*
11 *once*
12 *doce*
13 *trece*
14 *catorce*
15 *quince*
16 *dieciseis*
17 *diecisiete*
18 *dieciocho*
19 *diecinueve*
20 *veinte*
21 *veintiuno*
30 *treinta*
40 *cuarenta*
50 *cincuenta*
60 *sesenta*
70 *setenta*
80 *ochenta*
90 *noventa*
100 *ciento*
101 *ciento y uno* or *cientiuno*
200 *doscientos*
500 *quinientos*
1,000 *mil*
10,000 *diez mil*
100,000 *cien mil*
1,000,000 *millón*
one half *medio*
one third *un tercio*
one fourth *un cuarto*

DAYS AND MONTHS

Monday *lunes*
Tuesday *martes*
Wednesday *miércoles*
Thursday *jueves*
Friday *viernes*
Saturday *sábado*
Sunday *domingo*
today *hoy*
tomorrow *mañana*
yesterday *ayer*
January *enero*
February *febrero*
March *marzo*

April *abril*
May *mayo*
June *junio*
July *julio*
August *agosto*
September *septiembre*
October *octubre*
November *noviembre*
December *diciembre*
a week *una semana*
a month *un mes*
after *después*
before *antes*

TIME

What time is it? *¿Qué hora es?*
It's one o'clock. *Es la una.*
It's three in the afternoon. *Son las tres de la tarde.*
It's 4 A.M. *Son las cuatro de la mañana.*
six-thirty *a las seis y media*
a quarter till eleven *a las once menos cuarto*
a quarter past five *a las cinco y cuarto*
an hour *una hora*
the morning *la mañana*
the early hours of the morning *la madrugada*
the afternoon *la tarde*
the night *la noche*

GREETINGS AND BASIC EXPRESSIONS

Most Spanish-speaking people consider formalities important. Whenever approaching anyone with a question, do not forget the appropriate salutation — good morning, good evening, etc. The greeting *hola* (hello) can sound brusque standing alone.

Hello. *Hola.*
Good morning. *Buenos días.*
Good afternoon. *Buenas tardes.*
Good evening. *Buenas noches.*
How are you? *¿Cómo está usted?*
Very well, thank you. *Muy bien, gracias.*
Okay; good. *Bien.*

RESOURCES

Not okay; bad. *Mal* or *fatal*
So-so. *Más o menos.*
And you? *¿Y usted?*
Thank you. *Gracias.*
Thank you very much. *Muchas gracias.*
You're very kind. *Muy amable.*
You're welcome. *De nada.*
Goodbye. *Adios.*
See you later. *Hasta luego.*
please *por favor*
yes *sí*
no *no*
I don't know. *No sé.*
Just a moment, please. *Un momento, por favor.*
Excuse me, please (when you're trying to get attention). *Disculpe* or *Con permiso.*
Excuse me (when you've made a mistake). *Perdone.*
Sorry. *Lo siento*
Pleased to meet you. *Encantado/a. (male/female)*
How do you say...in Spanish? *¿Cómo se dice...en español?*
What is your name? *¿Cómo se llama usted?*
My name is ... *Me llamo...*
Do you speak English? *¿Habla usted inglés?*
Is English spoken here? *¿Se habla aquí el inglés?*
I don't speak Spanish well. *No hablo bien el español.*
I don't understand. *No entiendo.*
Would you like ...? *¿Quisiera usted...?*
Let's go to ... *Vamos a ...*

TERMS OF ADDRESS

When in doubt, use the formal *usted* (you) as a form of address.
I *yo*
you (formal) *usted*
you (familiar) *tu*
he/him *él*
she/her *ella*
we/us *nosotros (all males or mixed gender); nosotras (all females)*

you (plural, formal) *ustedes*
you (plural, familiar) *vosotros (all males or mixed gender); vosotras (all females)*
they/them *ellos (all males or mixed gender); ellas (all females)*
Mr, sir *señor*
Mrs, madam *señora*
Miss, young woman *señorita*
wife *mujer* or *esposa*
husband *marido* or *esposo*
friend *amigo (male); amiga (female)*
boyfriend; girlfriend *novio; novia*
son; daughter *hijo; hija*
brother; sister *hermano; hermana*
father; mother *padre; madre*
grandfather; grandmother *abuelo; abuela*

GETTING AROUND

Where is ...? *¿Dónde está...?*
How far is it from ... to ...? *¿Cuánto hay de...a ...?*
How many blocks? *¿Cuántas cuadras?*
Where can I find ...? *¿Dónde puedo encontrar...*
the bus station *la estación de autobuses*
the bus stop *la parada de autobuses*
Where is this bus going? *¿Adónde va este autobús?*
the taxi stand *la parada de taxis*
the train station *la estación de ferrocarril*
Suburban railway *las cercanías*
the port *el puerto*
the ferry terminal *el terminal de los ferrys*
the airport *el aeropuerto*
I'd like a ticket to ... *Quisiera un billete a ...*
first (second) class *de primera (segunda) clase*
roundtrip *ida y vuelta*
single; one-way *sencillo*
reservation *reservación*
baggage *equipaje*
Stop here, please. *Pare aquí, por favor.*
the entrance *la entrada*
the exit *la salida*

the **ticket office** *la taquilla*
(very) near; far *(muy) cerca; lejos*
to; toward *a; hacia*
by; through *por*
from *de*
the right *la derecha*
the left *la izquierda*
straight ahead *todo recto*
in front of *delante de*
beside *al lado*
behind *atrás*
the corner *la esquina*
the stoplight *el semáforo*
a turn *una vuelta*
right here *aquí*
somewhere around here *por aquí*
right there *allí*
somewhere around there *por allí*
street; avenue *calle; avenida*
highway *la carretera*
bridge *el puente*
toll *el peaje*
address *la dirección*
north; south *norte; sur*
east; west *este; oeste*

AT THE GAS STATION

gas station *gasolinera*
gasoline *gasolina*
unleaded *sin plomo*
fill it up, please *llénelo, por favor*
(flat) tire *neumático (desinflado)*
air *aire*
water *agua*
oil (change) *(cambio) de aceite*
grease *grasa*
breakdown *avería*
My...doesn't work. *Mi...no funciona.*
car battery *batería*
radiator *radiador*
alternator *alternador*
generator *generador*
tow truck *grúa*
repair shop *taller de reparaciones*

ACCOMMODATIONS

hotel *hotel*
Do you have any rooms available? *¿Tiene habitaciones libres?*

May I (may we) see it? *¿Puedo (podemos) verla?*
How much is it? *¿Cuánto cuesta?*
Is that your best rate? *¿Es su mejor precio?*
Do you have anything cheaper? *¿Tiene algo más barato?*
a single room *una habitación sencilla*
a double room *una habitación doble*
double bed *cama de matrimonio*
twin beds *camas gemelas*
with private bath *con baño*
hot water *agua caliente*
shower *ducha*
towels *toallas*
soap *jabón*
toilet paper *papel higiénico*
blanket *manta; frazada*
sheets *sábanas*
air-conditioned *aire acondicionado*
fan *ventilador*
key *llave*
manager *gerente*

FOOD

I'm hungry *Tengo hambre.*
I'm thirsty. *Tengo sed.*
menu *carta*
to order *pedir*
glass *vaso*
fork *tenedor*
knife *cuchillo*
spoon *cuchara*
napkin *servilleta*
drink *bebida*
alcoholic drink *copa*
coffee *café*
tea *té*
drinking water *agua pura; agua potable*
bottled carbonated water *agua mineral con gas*
bottled uncarbonated water *agua sin gas*
beer *cerveza*
red/white wine *vino tinto/blanco*
butter *mantequilla*
milk *leche*
juice *zumo*
cream *nata*

RESOURCES

sugar *azúcar*
cheese *queso*
snack *bocado*
breakfast *desayuno*
lunch *almuerzo*
daily set menu *el menú del día*
dinner *cena*
small snacks served with drinks *tapas*
meal-sized version of tapas *ración*
small filled sandwich *montadito*
the check *la cuenta*
eggs *huevos*
bread *pan*
baguette *barra (de pan)*
salad *ensalada*
fruit *fruta*
watermelon *sandía*
banana *plátano*
apple *manzana*
orange *naranja*
lime *lima*
lemon *limón*
olives *aceitunas*
onion *cebolla*
beans *judías*
lettuce *lechuga*
potato *patata*
fries *patatas fritas*
tomato *tomate*
carrot *zanahoria*
fish *pescado*
trout *trucha*
cod *bacalao*
tuna *atún or bonito*
sea bass *dorada*
sole *lenguado*
hake *merluza*
salmon *salmón*
sardines *sardinas*
shellfish *mariscos*
squid *calamares*
shrimp *camarones*
prawns *gambas*
king prawns *langostinos*
crab *cangrejo*
mussels *mejillones*
octopus *pulpo*
(without) meat *(sin) carne*

chicken *pollo*
pork *carne de cerdo*
beef; beefsteak *carne de vaca; bistec*
chop *chuleta*
fillet *pechuga*
loin *lomo*
leg *pierna*
bacon *beicon or tocino*
sausage *chorizo*
ham *jamón*
paella *paella*
omelette *tortilla*
potato omelette *tortilla española*
pie *empanada*
fritters *churros*
biscuit; cookie *galleta*
ice cream *helado*
cake *pastel or tarta*
almond nougat *turrón*
fried *frito*
roasted *asado*
barbecue; barbecued *barbacoa; a la parilla*
grilled *a la plancha*
oven-baked *al horno*

SHOPPING

money *dinero*
exchange bureau *oficina de cambio*
What is the exchange rate? *¿Cuál es el tipo de cambio?*
How much is the commission? *¿Cuánto cuesta la comisión?*
Do you accept credit cards? *¿Se acepta tarjetas de crédito?*
money order *giro postal*
ATM *cajero automático*
How much does it cost? *¿Cuánto cuesta?*
What is your final price? *¿Cuál es su último precio?*
expensive *− caro*
cheap *barato*
more *más*
less *menos*
a little *un poco*
too much *demasiado*

MAKING THE MOVE
border *frontera*
customs *aduana*
immigration *inmigración*
visa *visado*
inspection *inspección*
passport *pasaporte*
profession *profesión*
marital status *estado civil*
single *soltero/a (male/female)*
married; divorced *casado/a;*
divorciado/a (male/female)
widowed *viudado/a (male/female)*
insurance *seguro*
title *título*
drivers license *carnet de conducir*

HEALTH
Help me please. *Ayúdeme por favor.*
I am ill. *Estoy enfermo/a. (male/female)*
Call a doctor. *Llame a un doctor.*
Take me to . . . *Lléveme a . . .*
hospital *hospital*
drugstore *farmacia*
pain *dolor*
fever *fiebre*
headache *dolor de cabeza*
stomachache *dolor de estómago*
burn *quemadura*
cramp *calambre*
nausea *náusea*
vomiting *vomitar*
medicine *medicina*
antibiotic *antibiótico*
pill; tablet *pastilla*
aspirin *aspirina*
ointment; cream *pomada; crema*
bandage *venda*
cotton *algodón*
sanitary pads *compresas*
tampons *tampones*
condoms *preservativos; condones*
birth control pills *píldoras*
anticonceptivas
toothbrush *cepillo de dientes*
dental floss *hilo dental*
toothpaste *pasta dentífrica*
dentist *dentista*
toothache *dolor de muelas*

FINANCE AND LEGAL MATTERS
I'd like to open an account,
please. *Quisiera abrir una cuenta por*
favor.
checking account *cuenta corriente*
savings account *cuenta de ahorros*
I would like to withdraw
money. *Quisiera sacar dinero.*
I would like to deposit
money. *Quisiera ingresar dinero.*
deposit *depósito*
mortgage *hipoteca*
loan *préstamo*
accountant *contable*
lawyer *abogado*
notary *notario*
taxes *impuestos*
value added tax *IVA – impuesto sobre*
el valor añadido
title deeds *título de propiedad*

COMMUNICATIONS
long-distance telephone
call *llamada de larga distancia*
I would like to call . . . *Quisiera llamar*
a . . .
collect call *llamada a cobro revertido*
person to person *persona a persona*
credit card *tarjeta de crédito*
post office *correo*
letter *carta*
stamp *sello*
postcard *(tarjeta) postal*
air mail *correo aereo*
registered *registrado*
money order *giro postal*
package; box *paquete; caja*
string; tape *cuerda; cinta*

HOUSING CONSIDERATIONS
I am interested in buying/renting
a . . . *Me interesa comprar/alquilar*
un/a . . .
house *casa*
villa *chalet*
apartment *piso*

terraced house or townhouse *casa adosada*
plot of land *parcela*
real estate agent *inmobiliaria*
real estate agency *agente inmobiliario*
Are you licensed? *¿Es autorizado?*
suburbs *afueras*
private community *urbanización*

Does it have a . . .? *¿Tiene un . . .?*
yard *jardín*
garage *garaje*
swimming pool *piscina*
parking spaces *aparcamientos*
How many square meters is it? *¿Cuántos metros cuadrados es?*
Where is the town hall? *¿Dónde está el ayuntamiento?*

Suggested Reading

Over the centuries, Spanish writers have compiled volumes on their country, and foreign authors have also had quite a bit to say about Spain. When it comes to the printed word, you can find endless amounts on just about everything Spanish—history, art, recipes, poetry, novels, and more.

FICTION AND POETRY

Bly, Robert, translator. *Times Alone: Selected Poems of Antonio Machado.* Middletown, Connecticut: Wesleyan University Press, 1983.

Burns, Jimmy. *A Literary Companion to Spain.* London: John Murray (Publishers) Ltd., 1995.

Cervantes, Miguel de. *Don Quixote.* London: Penguin Books, 2001

Gordon, Noah. *The Last Jew.* New York: St. Martin's Griffin, 2002.

Hemingway, Ernest. *Death in the Afternoon.* New York: Touchstone Books, 1996.

Hemingway, Ernest. *For Whom the Bell Tolls.* New York: Scribner, 1995.

Hemingway, Ernest. *The Sun Also Rises.* New York: Scribner, 1995.

Marías, Javier. *A Heart So White.* London: Harvill/New Directions Books, 2002.

Marsé, Juan. *The Fallen.* New York: Little Brown and Company, 1979.

Michener, James. *The Drifters.* New York: Random House, 1986.

Ruiz Zafón, Carlos. *The Shadow of the Wind.* New York: Penguin, 2005.

Simon, Greg and Steven F. White, translators. *Federico García Lorca: Poet in New York.* New York: The Noonday Press, 1988.

Vázquez Montalban, Manuel. *Southern Seas.* London: Pluto Press, 2000.

Vega, Lope de. *Three Major Plays: Fuente Ovejuna/the Knight from Olmedo/Punishment Without Revenge.* Oxford: Oxford Press, 1999.

NONFICTION

Brenan, Gerald. *South to Granada.* Kodansha Globe Series, 1998.

Brenan, Gerald. *The Spanish Labyrinth.* Cambridge: Cambridge University Press, 1990.

Buñeul, Luis. *My Last Sigh,* translated by Abigail Israel. Minneapolis: University of Minnesota Press, 2003.

Casas, Penelope. *Discovering Spain: An Uncommon Guide.* New York: Alfred A. Knopf, Inc., 1996.

Fraser, Ronald. *Blood of Spain: An Oral History of the Spanish Civil War.* New York: Pantheon, 1986.

Goodwin, Godfrey. *Islamic Spain.* New York: Viking, 1990.

Graves, William. *Wild Olives: Life in Majorca with Robert Graves.* London: Pimlico, 2001.

Hooper, John. *The New Spaniards.* New York: Penguin USA, 1995.

Irving, Washington. *Tales of the Alhambra.* Granada: Miguel Sanchez, 1932.

Menocal, María Rosa. *The Ornament of the World.* Boston: Little Brown, 2003.

Michener, James. *Iberia.* New York: Ballantine Books, 1982.

Orwell, George. *Homage to Catalonia.* New York: Harvest Books, 1969.

Pritchett, V.S. *The Spanish Temper.* New York: Ecco Press, 1989.

RESOURCES

Radford, John. *The New Spain*. London: Mitchell Beazley, 1998.

Schoenfeld, Bruce *The Last Serious Thing: A Season at the Bullfights*. New York: Simon & Schuster, Inc., 1992.

Schweid, Richard. *Barcelona: Jews, Transvestites, and an Olympic Season*. Berkeley, California: Ten Speed Press, 1994.

Tremlett, Giles. *Ghosts of Spain: Travels through a Country's Hidden Past*. London: Faber and Faber, 2006

Index

www.moon.com

DESTINATIONS | ACTIVITIES | BLOGS | MAPS | BOOKS

MOON.COM is all new, and ready to help plan your next trip! Filled with fresh trip ideas and strategies, author interviews, informative blogs, a detailed map library, and descriptions of all the Moon guidebooks, Moon.com is all you need to get out and explore the world—or even places in your own backyard. As always, when you travel with Moon, expect an experience that is uncommon and truly unique.

MAP SYMBOLS

▦▦▦ Expressway	○ City/Town	✕ Airfield	▰ Archaeological Site
▦▦▦ Primary Road	⊛ State Capital	✕ Airport	🛆 Church
▦▦▦ Secondary Road	⊛ National Capital	▲ Mountain	⛽ Gas Station
▪ ▪ ▪ Unpaved Road	⊛ National Capital	▲ Mountain	Mangrove
···· Ferry	★ Point of Interest	🌲 Park	Reef
┅━┅ Railroad	▪ Other Location	🎿 Skiing Area	Swamp

CONVERSION TABLES

°C = (°F - 32) / 1.8
°F = (°C x 1.8) + 32
1 inch = 2.54 centimeters (cm)
1 foot = 0.304 meters (m)
1 yard = 0.914 meters
1 mile = 1.6093 kilometers (km)
1 km = 0.6214 miles
1 fathom = 1.8288 m
1 chain = 20.1168 m
1 furlong = 201.168 m
1 acre = 0.4047 hectares
1 sq km = 100 hectares
1 sq mile = 2.59 square km
1 ounce = 28.35 grams
1 pound = 0.4536 kilograms
1 short ton = 0.90718 metric ton
1 short ton = 2,000 pounds
1 long ton = 1.016 metric tons
1 long ton = 2,240 pounds
1 metric ton = 1,000 kilograms
1 quart = 0.94635 liters
1 US gallon = 3.7854 liters
1 Imperial gallon = 4.5459 liters
1 nautical mile = 1.852 km

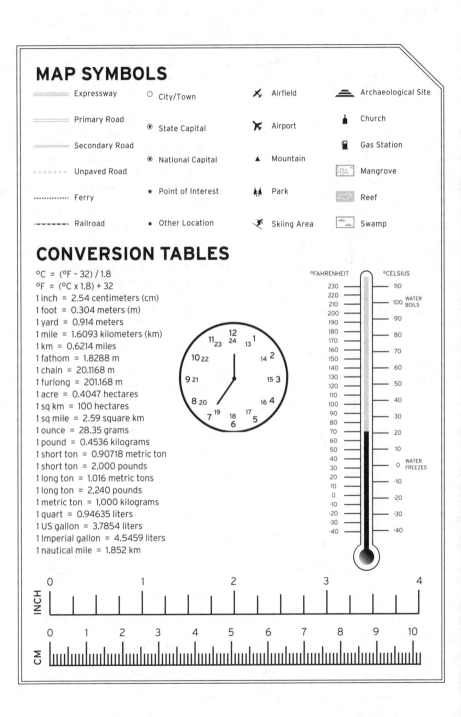

MOON LIVING ABROAD IN SPAIN

Avalon Travel
a member of the Perseus Books Group
1700 Fourth Street
Berkeley, CA 94710, USA
www.moon.com

Editor: Shaharazade Husain
Series Manager: Elizabeth Hansen
Copy Editor: Emily Lunceford
Graphics Coordinator: Lucie Ericksen
Production Coordinator: Lucie Ericksen
Cover Designer: Elizabeth Jang
Map Editor: Brice Ticen
Cartographer: Kat Bennett
Indexer: Judy Hunt

ISBN: 1-59880-090-6

Printing History
1st Edition – 2004
2nd Edition – October 2009
5 4 3 2 1

Text © 2009 by Candy Lee LaBalle.
Maps © 2009 by Avalon Travel.
All rights reserved.

Some photos and illustrations are used by permission and are the property of the original copyright owners.

Front cover photo: Spain, Cadiz, nightime market © Ralph A. Clevenger/CORBIS
Title page photo: a corner bar in Barcelona © Candy Lee LaBalle
Interior photos: page 4 © Bea Mora; pages 5-left, 6, 7-top left, 7-bottom right, 8-left © Cellar Tours; pages 5-right, 7-top right, 7-bottom left © Candy Lee LaBalle; page 8-right © Seve Ponce de Leon
Back cover photo: Albaicín, Granada © Candy Lee LaBalle

Printed in Canada by Friesens

KEEPING CURRENT

Although we strive to produce the most up-to-date guidebook that we possibly can, change is unavoidable. Between the time this book goes to print and the time you read it, the cost of goods and services may have increased, and a handful of the businesses noted in these pages will undoubtedly move, alter their prices, or close their doors forever. Exchange rates fluctuate – sometimes dramatically – on a daily basis. Federal and local legal requirements and restrictions are also subject to change, so be sure to check with the appropriate authorities before making the move. If you see anything in this book that needs updating, clarification, or correction, please drop us a line. Send your comments via email to feedback@moon.com, or use the address above.